THE HEART OF COUNSELING

D1710369

More than any other text on the market, *The Heart of Counseling* is effective in helping students to understand the importance of therapeutic relationships and to develop the qualities that make the therapeutic relationships they build with clients the foundation of healing. In these pages, students come to see how all skills arise from, and are directly related to, the counselor's development and to building therapeutic relationships. Student learning ranges from therapeutic listening and empathy to structuring sessions, from explaining counseling to clients and caregivers to providing wrap-around services, and ultimately to experiencing therapeutic relationships as the foundation of professional and personal growth.

The Heart of Counseling includes:

- case studies and discussions applying skills in school and agency settings;
- specific guidance on how to translate the abstract concepts of therapeutic relationships into concrete skill sets;
- exploration of counseling theories and tasks within, and extending from, core counseling skills;
- videos that bring each chapter to life;
- test banks, instructor's manuals, syllabi, and guidance for learning-outcomes assessments for professors.

Jeff L. Cochran is a professor in the department of educational psychology and counseling at the University of Tennessee.

Nancy H. Cochran is an adjunct faculty member in the department of educational psychology and counseling at the University of Tennessee and the treatment coordinator of the UT REACH Project.

THE HEART OF COUNSELING

Counseling Skills Through Therapeutic Relationships

2nd edition

Jeff L. Cochran and
Nancy H. Cochran

Routledge
Taylor & Francis Group

NEW YORK AND LONDON

Second edition published 2015
by Routledge
711 Third Avenue, New York, NY 10017

and by Routledge
27 Church Road, Hove, East Sussex BN3 2FA

Routledge is an imprint of the Taylor & Francis Group, an informa business

© 2015 Jeff L. Cochran and Nancy H. Cochran

First edition published by Cengage Learning 2005

Library of Congress Cataloging in Publication Data
Cochran, Jeff L.
    The heart of counseling: counseling skills through therapeutic relationships/by Jeff L. Cochran & Nancy H. Cochran.—
    Second edition.
    pages cm
    Includes bibliographical references and index.
    1. Counseling. I. Cochran, Nancy H. II. Title.
    BF636.6.C63 2015
    158.3—dc23
    2014027790

ISBN: 978-0-415-71242-2 (hbk)
ISBN: 978-0-415-71243-9 (pbk)
ISBN: 978-1-315-88406-6 (ebk)

Typeset in Sabon and Myriad Pro
by Florence Production Ltd, Stoodleigh, Devon, UK

The first edition of *The Heart of Counseling* was dedicated to "the many students that we have come to know through deep sharing of feelings and ideas." That dedication remains for this 2nd edition, with the addition of the many counseling students that we continue to learn with, plus the clients who continue to teach and inspire us to share our learning of healing and growth through therapeutic relationships.

CONTENTS

    Staying True   280

14 Heart and Mind: Major Counseling Theories and Therapeutic
    Relationships   301

15 Bringing Heart to All You Do   316

    Concluding Thoughts: Growing Your Therapeutic Relationship
    Skills to Become Who You Are   341

    Index   345

PREFACE

As counselor educators and supervisors, as well as counselors ourselves, we have written and now revise *The Heart of Counseling* to solve a series of related problems that we see as hurtful to the effectiveness of the helping professions for persons in need. We know from the literature of counselor development (Falender & Shafranske, 2004; Ronnestad & Skovolt, 2003; Stoltenberg, McNeill, & Delworth, 1998), as well as our experience, that it is natural for beginning counselors to yearn for quick fixes for client problems. It makes sense that many of us came into the helping profession to be active helpers, and therefore are eager to apply various counseling techniques. Confounding the situation is the contrast between beginning counselors' need for concrete skills versus the fact that counseling concepts, especially those of therapeutic relationships, are highly abstract. One result is that beginning counselors are often tempted to dive straight into counseling techniques aimed at forcing immediate behavior change without developing a therapeutic relationship to ensure that clients own the changes they make.

We know from experience and the growing body of supportive literature (Hubble, Duncan, & Miller, 1999; Norcross, 2002, 2011) that the therapeutic relationship a counselor forms with each client can be the most powerful tool for helping clients change. So one of our goals is to help readers see that "slow is fast"—to see the value of the therapeutic relationships they can develop. We frame all counseling skills through therapeutic relationships: from active listening and reflection to treatment planning, and explaining counseling to clients, parents, teachers and administrators; from deep empathy to structuring sessions such that change will happen; from unconditional positive regard for clients to helping clients manage crises; from genuineness with clients to reaching across cultures and beyond. We provide readers with extensive setting-based examples of counseling skills through therapeutic relationships in action. We help readers to be active learners, to see themselves in therapeutic relationships in their settings, and to develop themselves for the therapeutic relationships they will form. We help readers see how counseling skills through therapeutic relationships form a foundation for all that counselors do, including: integrating techniques from theories of psychotherapy aimed at immediate client change, skill-teaching and guidance; assessment and diagnosis; hallway moments with clients in schools and other interactions beyond individual sessions; career-focused counseling, group and family work; and all the wrap-around services and skills of a professional counselor.

We aim for the practical goal of making the hard-to-define concepts of therapeutic relationships into concrete skill sets, which we find to be especially important to meet early-stage learners where they naturally are in their development. We write from a conceptual approach for learners that benefit most from "getting a feel" for effective work. And we break elusive concepts down into highly specific guidance for learners that benefit more from step-by-step specificity.

We encourage readers to be active learners with primary skill objectives stated on the first page of each chapter, field- and learner-based focus activities to open each chapter, extensive setting-based examples to help readers see themselves in each skill, common problems in application sections to conclude chapters, and activities and resources for further learning within each chapter. But along with active learning, we focus on counselor development to be the best tool possible for each client served. We see a part of the urge in beginning counselors for quick fixes as stemming from a lack of therapeutic confidence in self. Carl Rogers (1980) wrote that even late in his career, before beginning with a new client, he often had to remind himself that he, as a person, could be enough in a facilitative relationship. But how can a beginning counselor know this when she has not experienced it yet? We see this understandable lack of confidence as part of what drives beginning counselors to hurry for the quick fix technique. We often see the errant thought as, "Surely a relationship with *me* could not be facilitative." So, we strive to help students see therapeutic relationships in action, to visualize themselves as effective counselors, and most importantly, to engage in the self-reflection and self-development necessary to become the best tool possible for therapeutic relationships with clients.

References

Falender, C.A., & Shafranske, E.P. (2004). *Clinical supervision: A competency-based approach*. Washington, DC: American Psychological Association.

Hubble, M.A., Duncan, B.L., & Miller, S.D. (1999). *The heart and soul of change: What works in therapy*. Washington, DC: American Psychological Association.

Norcross, J.C. (2002). *Psychotherapy relationships that work: Therapist contributions and responsiveness to patients*. New York: Oxford University Press.

Norcross, J.C. (2011). *Psychotherapy relationships that work: Evidence-based responsiveness* (2nd ed.). New York: Oxford University Press.

Rogers, C.R. (1980). *A way of being*. Boston, MA: Houghton Mifflin.

Ronnestad, M.H., & Skovolt, T.M. (2003). The journey of the counselor and therapist: Research findings and perspectives on professional development. *Journal of Career Development, 30*, 5–44.

Stoltenberg, C.D., McNeill, B., & Delworth, U. (1998). *IDM supervision: An integrated developmental model for supervising counselors and therapists*. San Francisco, CA: Jossey-Bass.

ACKNOWLEDGMENTS

We would like to thank our editor, Anna Moore, and Routledge for their diligence in inviting and taking on this project. We are glad that Anna was so very able to see the value of *The Heart of Counseling* (*Heart*) and its potential to help make the world a better place for persons in need.

We would like to thank Rose Gamble, who assisted especially in the final months of revisions in identifying new and interesting literature related to key aspects of *Heart* and for her conversations of the role of therapeutic relationships in her practice and issues from her experience teaching counseling skills course sections. We would like to thank Bre Banks, Dareen Basma and Emma Burgin for their input, including syllabus revisions for our revised Counseling Skills class and other input. And we would like to acknowledge Tiffany Brooks for her support and input, and for co-authoring the Chapter 15 section, "Career Counseling and Therapeutic Relationships—Balancing the Personal and the Informational."

We thank our many students and readers in close contact at all levels in their education and development, who have guided us with their thinking in reaction to *Heart*. We very much appreciate their part in making our work better. And we thank family friends Margaret Cubine and Luther Mundy, elders who dedicated their lives to mental health and human development, and who read the 1st edition, offering their input and support.

As always, we acknowledge our parents, who have worked so hard to give us the very best chance possible to learn and love, and who encouraged us to take risks in order to contribute our part as teachers and helpers. We state our great appreciation to Louis and Joyce Cochran, and Richard and Janice Haldeman, who sacrificed so much for us; and especially to Richard Haldeman for his thorough reading, input and support of the 1st edition.

And we acknowledge and thank our son, Erzhan Cochran (age 11 at the time of writing), for his contributions to our "family business" in teaching, research, and service in the counseling field. Especially lately he has joined us for numerous conferences and meetings that were appropriate for him to attend. He gives us the time to push the work forward, when one of us must be away for that. And most of all, he continues to build a strong and positive attitude, helping us daily to find joy in the present moment and in the work of helping others.

INTRODUCTION

It is only with the heart that we can see,
what is essential is invisible to the eye.

Antoine De Saint-Exupery

There is an organ in the body that, if it is righteous,
ensures that the whole system will be righteous . . .
This organ is the heart.

Muhammad

Why the "Heart" of Counseling?

The word *heart* in the title of this book is used to convey two main meanings: core and emotion. The word *heart* implies a central core, as in the saying, "Get right to the heart of the matter." Think, for a moment, of the implications of this saying for the counseling profession. We counselors are often trying to figure out how to be more efficient—to "get to the heart of the matter"—while also maintaining respect and caring for each client's individuality. The client's own pace and path to the "heart of the matter" can be easily overlooked in difficult moments for counselor and client. Thus, the skills we guide you through in this text are presented as the core, or "the heart," of what counselors do: a home base to return to when adrift, or as the strong foundation on which to build your career and all that you do as a counselor. These are the counseling skills that build courage and confidence. All other counselor tasks spring from and revolve around them.

The word *heart* also implies an active investment of emotional energy, as when referring to an athlete who competes with great passion one might say, "She plays the game with heart." Counseling can never lack investment of the counselor's emotion and energy. While you, as counselor, may become relaxed and more at ease in the work, you must continue to feel and respond to your clients' emotion with active compassion. The best and most efficient counseling is "heartfelt." Responding fully to emotion, both your client's and your own, is a theme woven throughout this text. Experiencing your clients' emotions with them, while remaining aware of your own as counselor, is the golden road to developing deep caring and making healing connections. Such connections are challenging and profoundly powerful in our development as counselors.

A Few Notes about Us

Jeff is primarily a counselor educator, a professor at this time. He has worked as a counselor for students at an elementary school, a middle school and at universities. He has provided counseling and related mental health services at outdoor camps, at residential treatment facilities and at high schools. Jeff has completed these works in several areas of the United States and overseas. He currently has the honor of supervising and consulting with counselors and mental health service providers across a great many settings. He continues to learn from these counselors and students.

Nancy has education, expertise and experience with a wide range of ages and persons as a school psychologist, as well as a counselor. Her primary work at this time is as the Clinical Director of the UT REACH Project, through which she and Jeff serve at-risk children and families with child-centered play therapy (CCPT; Cochran, Nordling, & Cochran, 2010), as well as supervising and training post-masters clinicians in CCPT. She has served as a counselor in private practice, as well as school and agency settings. She is certified through the National Institute for Relationship Enhancement in CCPT and CCPT-Supervision.

We have been married for 24 years. In that time we have had the opportunity to write, research, present, teach, work, play and parent together. Themes of our combined written works have focused on the importance and power of therapeutic relationships. We have enjoyed working together with children in schools and agencies, as foster parents, and as camp counselors. We have also enjoyed working together with graduate students in the classroom, and on various projects and research. In this work, we have experienced the power of building effective, fulfilling human relationships with students, serving as their teachers, advisers and supporters. The joy we find together in this work has helped to maintain and improve our own multifaceted relationship. We share our ideas and philosophical musings about life, and the challenges of counseling and the other helping professions quite a bit. Our ideas and beliefs are often complementary, or so similar that we don't know whose idea was whose, or if indeed the beliefs and ideas we have are spontaneously created between us!

By far our most important work together is in loving and parenting our wonderful son, Erzhan. Our family came together through his adoption during the writing of the first edition of *Heart*. This is challenging and joyous work indeed!

Theoretical Base and Background

The counseling theories that have been most influential in our education and our work have been the person-centered approach (Casemore, 2006; Cornelius-White, Motschnig-Pitric, & Lux, 2013; Rogers, 1961) and the cognitive approaches to counseling (Beck & Beck, 2011; Ellis & Dryden, 2007). Some of the influence that this background has on our text will be evident. We often emphasize persons' self-talk in examples and present counseling as an experience through which persons learn and grow, and through which self-talk and self-perception changes. We emphasize that the therapeutic relationship is the key factor in promoting meaningful change and growth for the individual client. These foci do not exclude any counseling theory, but are the result of our experience and study as counselors. Regarding theory, we strongly agree with the following quote from Carl Rogers: "There is one *best* school of therapy. It is the school of therapy you develop for yourself based on a continuing critical examination of the effect of your way of being in the relationship" (1987, p. 185).

Important Notes on Case Examples

We provide a great many case examples to illustrate the skills and concepts of counseling. Some case examples were based on clients of ours, some were based on clients of our students, and some examples are hypothetical or composite examples based on combinations of experiences with clients in similar situations. When case examples are based on persons served by one of us, we sometimes tell the example using "I" to refer to the counselor, which allows us to convey more personally how we were affected in interchanges. When the case examples are based on persons served by one of our students, or when they are hypothetical, composite examples, we present the example and refer to the helper as "the counselor" or create a name for the counselor. All case examples are presented without identifying information or with the information altered to protect privacy. Still, we would like to convey that each of these case examples may contain elements of stories from people who continue to remain special to us. We remember them well, and continue to care about them, respect them, and wish the best for them. Many of the stories, while changed from any specific person's situation, would not be possible without the deep sharing that happened between counselor and client.

Additionally, we occasionally use examples of children to help explain something important. Sometimes a child example is simplest and best. However, this book is mostly about counseling adults and adolescents. The same concepts are true in counseling children, but applications are different. Children's primary mode of communication, especially communication of the depth for counseling, is play, not talk.

Note of References to Clients and Gender

When referring to clients throughout *Heart*, we often refer to the client as an individual, because each client is a special person to us, as opposed to the generic "the client" or "clients." We often refer to the individual client as "your client" because we want you to see yourself in the role of the counselor when reading and because we know that each client will be special to you. And because of referring to the client as an individual, we usually assign the person being referred to a gender, so that we can refer to the person as she or he, rather than excessive use of he/she, him/her.

How to Use This Book

We challenge you to spend time *contemplating* the concepts presented. In most chapters, we suggest a few modes of contemplation, social and introspective. Idea exchange with others is often very helpful to learning. Thus we give you suggestions for how to implement social contemplation of the concepts and skills we present. Because such group learning is not always possible and because introspective contemplation brings its own values, we also suggest methods of introspective contemplation, sometimes borrowing from mindful meditation and creative arts. We hope you will try many and expand into the further contemplation methods that occur to you for your unique ways of learning.

We encourage you to actively study. Focus yourself on the subject at hand in each chapter with the Primary Skill Objectives and especially the Focus Activity for each chapter. Stop and contemplate each section, rather than just letting your eyes rush over words. Take time to contemplate the big ideas of each chapter, especially those that have struck you most from that chapter. Complete as many of the Activities for Further Study at the end of each chapter as possible, carefully choosing the ones you most need to focus on in your development.

References

Beck, J.S., & Beck, A.T. (2011). *Cognitive behavior therapy: Basics and beyond* (2nd ed.). New York: Guilford.

Casemore, R. (2006). *Person-centered counseling: In a nutshell*. London: Sage.

Cochran, N.H., Nordling, W.J., Cochran, J.L. (2010). *Child-centered play therapy: A practical guide to developing therapeutic relationships with children*. Hoboken, NJ: Wiley.

Cornelius-White, J.H.D., Motschnig-Pitric, R., & Lux, M. (2013). *Interdisciplinary handbook of the person-centered approach: Research and theory*. New York: Springer.

Ellis, A., & Dryden, W. (2007). *The practice of rational emotive therapy* (2nd ed.). New York: Springer.

Rogers, C.R. (1961). *On becoming a person*. Boston, MA: Houghton Mifflin.

Rogers, C.R. (1987). Rogers, Kohut, and Erickson: A personal perspective on some similarities and differences. In J.K. Zeig (Ed.), *The evolution of psychotherapy* (pp. 179–187). New York: Brunner/Mazel.

Pre-Chapter Quotes

Saint-Exupery, A. (1943). *The little prince*. Translated by Richard Howard. San Diego, CA: Harcourt, 2000 (p. 63).

Muhammad. As quoted in J. Fadiman & R. Frager (1998). *Essential Sufism*. Edison, NJ: Castle Books (p. 89).

1 TWELVE CONCEPTS
Roots that Ground and Grow with the Heart of Counseling

All wisdom is already within us; all love is already within us, all joy.
Yet, they are hidden within us until the heart opens.

Fadiman and Frager

Primary Skill Objectives

- Begin to understand and be able to explain foundational concepts for counseling skills through therapeutic relationships in your own words.
- Explain how these concepts fit with your core beliefs and how your core beliefs may develop as you develop as a counselor.

Focus Activity 1

Take time to consider, journal and/or discuss your beliefs about human nature as it relates to counseling. Consider the following questions: What generates behavior, shapes personalities, or creates well-being and mental health? What motivates change? What prevents it? Based on these beliefs, what do you imagine that you may do as a counselor to facilitate positive change and growth in others?

Focus Activity 2

Consider, journal and discuss ways that you are not the same as you were earlier in life. Think beyond aging and external context changes to core changes within you, such as outlook, predominant feelings, and values. Speculate what helped you change. Keep an open mind to the range of possibilities.

Introduction

Counseling is evidenced as highly beneficial. Lambert (2013) provided a seminal review of scores of studies—with most of the studies being meta-analyses (statistical analyses of separate studies combined)—concluding far-reaching effects in life-functioning, with clients achieving healthy adjustment for long-lasting periods. In discussing why counseling and psychotherapy work, Lambert, following from a long line of analyses (Bergin & Lambert, 1978; Luborsky, Singer, & Luborsky, 1975; Wampold, 2001; Wampold et al., 1997) pointed out that there is "little or no substantial difference between therapies with regard to client outcome" (Lambert, 2013, p. 194). Rather than particular techniques, the far greater predictors of positives outcome are therapeutic relationships, or counselor qualities in therapeutic relationships that capitalize on clients' internal strengths.

But the lure of a technique outside of ourselves is strong. Before having experienced the power of therapeutic relationships, it is difficult to see how a therapeutic relationship—with another human, no matter professional status—can heal. Duncan, Miller and Sparks (2004) explained that "the mental health field remains dangerously enamored of flashy techniques and miracle cures" (p. 38).

The Heart of Counseling is a skills text focused on helping you value and form powerful therapeutic relationships. We discuss how counseling techniques, skill-teaching in sessions, counseling modalities and theories—all that you do as counselor—integrate into your therapeutic relationships. But first we need to explain how therapeutic relationships *alone* are powerful in generating positive change for persons in need.

The following concepts underlie the work of therapeutic relationships. They are understandings that bind together all the works of counselors. They guide the skills we employ in our works. Contemplating and understanding these concepts helps sustain us through difficult moments in our works. We speak personally about these concepts and from our own experience. Before you read, consider the following guidelines, as it is likely that you will react personally and from your own experience to what you read.

Important Guidance for Your Study of these Concepts

Avoid Intellectual Overload

We encourage you to read slowly and to contemplate. While these concepts are interrelated, you may not want to read them all at once. Stop to consider each concept and your own views and reactions as you read. Perhaps stop to write your reactions after each concept (e.g., excited agreement with some parts, troubled disagreement with others, questions you would like answered to help you understand, questions you would like to discuss).

Remember that Experience is the Best Teacher

There are examples to aid understanding throughout this chapter, but many more throughout the skills portions of this book. Additionally, as you practice the skills of *The Heart of Counseling*, the underlying concepts will become clearer.

Learning and coming to know what you know, and believing what you believe through your practice and work is part of your development as a scholar and counselor. We only introduce these important underlying concepts in this chapter. Your deep understanding, your *knowing*, will develop from experience of the skills that are the focus of this book. Fully understanding these concepts may be the ongoing work of a lifetime for you, as it is for us.

Twelve Key Concepts

Becoming

Throughout the counseling field and all approaches to counseling, there is the notion that we are constantly changing, or *becoming*. Who we are today is not who we were in the past. The notion of becoming is that we are not permanently established at any point in our development. Rather, we are always becoming who we are. Becoming includes growth and age, of course, but also change through new experiences and meaning made from new experiences. Becoming assumes changes in context and resources, of course, but also internal change.

Internal change is physical, as well as psychological. McHenry, Sikorski and McHenry (2014) explained a key concept from neurobiology for counselors related to becoming: "Neuroplasticity theory clearly suggests that as each individual grows, develops, and incorporates new learnings, his or her brain is constantly modified and restructured. Consequently, the brain you had yesterday is not the same brain you have today" (p. 8). From their review of neuroplasticity and psychosocial genomics, Garland and Howard (2009) concluded that not only do new neuro-pathways and new brain tissue develop throughout our lives, but gene expression, the genetic code guiding the construction proteins from amino acids may also be affected by interactive experiences. Garland and Howard concluded: "Although our genes provide a basic outline for development, environmental influences such as social experiences shape gene expression and ultimately make us unique individuals" (p. 195).

Self-Actualization

With the concept of becoming stated, it also seems well established in the counseling field that there is a formative or actualizing tendency (Bohart & Tallman, 1999; Ellingham, 2002; Morowitz, 2004; Sheldon & Houser-

Marko, 2001). As with most chapters, we will limit extensive literature review in favor of readability as we explain self-actualization and the fellow concepts that stem from it in nurturing the growth of persons in need.

Every person is on a unique path to optimal existence. Each path is unique because each person's set of experiences, and especially each person's interpretation of experiences, is unique. This essence—this unique and crucial self—is at the root of a person's ability to develop and grow in positive, prosocial directions. This essence is "meant to be" from the beginning and so will continue to strive—even through adverse and troublesome times—to fully develop. The concept of self-actualization maintains that there is a unique, positive and mature ideal for each living person.

We are amazed with the unique beauty of each tomato in our garden. If you slice one near where its stem was, there is a green star-shape in the red tomato background. Each star shape is beautiful. Each is unique. Yet each can be recognized as the familiar star-shape inside a tomato. While each whole tomato is unique, we can recognize when each has reached its version of a ripe, mature tomato. Nature provides many opportunities to reflect on how living things tend to strive for growth and maturation of "what was meant to be" from the beginning. In fact, it is almost impossible not to recognize the drive, determination and resilience of many plants to survive and continue to exist. Dandelions, for instance—impossible to destroy—are constantly seeking out the conditions to fully develop into dandelions. Those irresistible fluffy round tops are constantly luring children (and some adults) to pick and blow—sending their multitudes of seedlings throughout the world. Just for the chance to get a wish! Those bright yellow flowers pop up everywhere, and actually duck when the lawnmower passes over them. How resilient and clever.

The concept of self-actualization maintains that each individual person's unique self—or essence—is likewise resilient, clever and *impossible to destroy*. In multitudes of humans—despite the pressure to conform and live up to cultural, societal, parental and other expectations—there is only one real you. And, like the star in the tomato, your essence is beautiful and unique. You will continue to develop into a human being, for that is what you are. However, you are not merely the expression of a class of living things, nor are you simply the end result of your past experiences and genetic makeup. The concept of self-actualization maintains that within each of us is our own crucial and unique self—sometimes waiting or hiding or resting—but ever resilient and clever, and wanting to grow in a positive, productive and prosocial direction.

At one time we wondered, and it is sometimes asked in classes, if each person is on a unique path to self-actualization, why wouldn't one, if given the opportunity, actualize into pure evil? Why is actualization positive? How can we be assured that actualization for some beings does not mean the allowance for the most perfectly developed evil beings? Are some human beings "rotten to the core" or "bad seeds" from the beginning? When a human being has committed acts of horrific violence and destruction, is this not an example of "the essence of evil?" Our answer to why we strongly believe this *is not* the case lies in our understanding of human nature and the power of therapeutic relationships. It is an answer we *continue to develop* in our experiences providing the optimum conditions and opportunities for our clients to self-actualize.

It may be most helpful to explain our confidence in self-actualization by focusing on the apparent mechanisms that explain how this is. None of us live in isolation. Each person, each living thing, interacts with the surrounding environment. Our environment seems to want us to reach our full potential and seems to prefer behaviors that in turn benefit the other members of our environment. For example, a human infant, without human touch and interaction, will fail to thrive. This is true even if the infant is fed enough for physical growth. Not to provide care and nurturing for infants is unnatural to humans, so unnatural that, thankfully, infants are *in most cases* interacted with, nuzzled, held, fed, cooed at and protected by parents and adult caretakers who find this activity pleasing and mutually beneficial. Perhaps what is most pleasing is the very basic feeling of warmth involved in a caring human-to-human interaction. This caring behavior toward human infants is in turn beneficial to all members of the environment. Especially because we both work as counselors, we are aware that human interactions, when warm and caring, are almost always mutually beneficial. If either of us tended to be surly, harshly controlling, grouchy, poor listeners and uncaring most of the time, people would understandably avoid us and we would find ourselves alone, with growing unhappiness. Thankfully, these are not our usual characteristics and we find that others are often warm and caring toward us. The more we are warm toward others, the more others are warm toward us, the more we want to be warm toward others, and the more this exchange of warmth grows through our communities.

Mutually beneficial and supportive systems of interaction seem to be the way of nature. Picture a very green, open, meadow hill. As it is so green, it seems to be fertile and get plenty of rain and sun. One fall day an acorn is dropped onto this hill, perhaps by a small animal. Through the winter and early spring, this acorn absorbs the moisture it needs, begins to germinate and sinks in as the ground begins to soften. Given its core conditions for growth (e.g., water, light, nutrients in the soil), that acorn will grow into a sapling.

If that sapling were truly alone on the hill, it might not develop to its full potential. Without the grass, its soil might erode, taking needed nutrients with it. But as it grows and its roots grow mighty, it can then hold the soil for a greater diversity of plant life. Just as the bacteria and critters developed the soil that this sapling needs, its fallen leaves, the smaller plants its roots make room for, and eventually its decaying limbs and trunk will provide fodder for more bacteria and soil critters to thrive.

This sapling may one day develop into a mighty oak, with branches almost as far across as it is tall. Such trees are visions of wonder and beauty. In maturity, they can take a rounded shape, in each season a different look and a different beauty. They keep the ground beneath them cool and moist through summer. They provide shelter from a storm. They provide homes for squirrels and launching pads for baby birds. Woodpeckers come to feed and keep the bugs that live on them to a healthy amount. They provide a pleasant respite for a nap on a hot summer day. They provide a peaceful silhouette at sunset.

For us, such trees have become a symbol of self-actualization. They remind us that we all have the potential to reach our ideal. They remind us of the value of providing conditions for the full, strong growth of self in others. They remind us that allowing for expression, individuality and the full self is good, and is beneficial and supportive to positive growth in others and the environment.

When Blocks Come into One's Path toward Self-Actualization and Ideal Maturity

Keeping this vision of a full and mighty oak tree in mind, imagine that lightning strikes the oak when it is a young adult. That lightning may split off and deaden branches on one side. Those branches may never recover. The tree may grow lopsided, instead of beautifully round in full strength. In a soaking rain and windstorm, it may fall over from this imbalance. It may die an early death, never reaching the ideal for its kind and not providing the full benefit it might to its environment.

For humans too, our paths to developing our potential may be interrupted. Sometimes these blocks to full development come from great tragedy, from trauma or abuse. Sometimes these blocks come from a lack of the conditions and nutrients we need to grow and thrive (e.g., food, water, love, safety). Oftentimes these blocks come from a combination of trauma or abuse, a lack of conditions for growth and our individual, human interpretation of these situations. A person's path to maturity can be interrupted, and thus that person's path to self-actualization may become much less than it would have been. But there are differences between human beings and the oak tree. These differences give us a much greater opportunity to recover, to readjust our path to self-actualization and to restart our striving for our ideal maturity. These differences empower counseling. We illustrate key differences in the sections that follow.

The Capacity for Awareness, to Reason, Question and Choose

A major difference between the oak in our example and humans is that we have a capacity for awareness, and abilities to reason, question and choose. While it is true that our genetic makeup, our upbringing and our life experiences shape us, and in turn seem to force each one of us to choose a certain path, it is also true that we have the ongoing ability to choose alternate paths. These capacities and abilities allow us to recover and restart our path to our ideal maturity. We are able to feel fear and choose to avoid dangerous situations. We are able to feel warmth from others and seek greater closeness with them. We are able to feel dissatisfaction or angst, then to question and change our life's direction. We are able to discern how our actions may leave us feeling and make decisions based on this understanding. We are able to feel with others, to have empathy. From there, we are able to discern how our actions may affect others, to choose the effect we would like to have and act accordingly.

We wish to note that these capacities and abilities may not be what we often think of as intelligence. While insight can be important, we do not mean to imply that it is all-important. From one of our studies (Demanchick, Cochran, & Cochran, 2003), we are reminded that even persons who have been consistently measured as having low intelligence (low enough to preclude insight, at least in the way that persons of normal or above intelligence tend to think of it) may benefit and change through therapeutic relationships and, through these relationships, restart their path to their full maturity.

Providing therapeutic relationships based on the skills of *The Heart of Counseling* is a way to prompt and help persons recover and restart their paths to ideal maturity. Such therapeutic relationships focus persons on their awareness, reasoning, questioning, and choosing. Such therapeutic relationships provide a safe, sheltered environment for persons to restart and reshape their growth processes toward their full potential, toward the ideal person that their environment would like them to be.

Interpretation of Experience and Development of Self-Concept

We humans interpret our experiences and develop these interpretations into a self-concept that defines who we are and how we relate to our world. Then this self-concept becomes self-perpetuating as persons interpret new experiences in ways to fit their initial interpretations. Consider the following example that illustrates, albeit without some of the real subtleties of life, how this can happen.

Imagine there are two babies of different parents. Call them Baby A and Baby B. Consider that Baby A is born to loving parents. They are reasonably together people, they love each other, and they really wanted to have a baby and to be parents. So, when their baby is hungry, uncomfortable, or cries for other reasons, they work to meet his needs. He finds that his whole world is this consistent care of primary caregivers, that these caregivers/his world will provide for him, and that he is safe, nourished and comfortable. We don't mean to imply that babies think in words and sentences, like adults, but instead that expectations of the world and the care from others begin to form even in infancy.

Then imagine that Baby B is born of parents under great strife. Their lives are very distressed. They have their own problems that draw their attention away from their child. They have great difficulty loving and seem unable to consistently care for her. So, their baby learns to expect that her world does not provide for her needs, and that her world is not a safe, nourishing and comfortable place.

From the very beginning, Baby A and Baby B are forming into beings with expectations of the world and others. Baby A grows into childhood being consistently well cared for and loved. Again, while not in words and sentences like an adult thinks, Baby A expects this. Baby B, on the other hand, grows into childhood without consistent care and love. She learns not to expect love, but to expect dislike, strife and danger.

Babies and young children are egocentric—they believe that their world revolves around them. Truly, if they are to thrive, it is best for their world to revolve around them. Babies and young children tend to believe that the events in their life simply happen for or because of them. So, Baby A, now Young Child A, begins to think (again, we are using adult-like words to represent child thoughts), "Hey, the world [his world is the whole world to him] is a pretty cool place. When I need something, it appears. These people that I really like, they really like me back! I'm lovable and wonderful . . . I must be a pretty cool kid!" But Baby B, now Young Child B, thinks, "This world [her world] is a dangerous place. I never know what's going to happen. People [her primary caregivers] don't seem to love or like me, and even seem bothered and upset by me. This must be my fault. I'm a terrible, unlovable kid!"

As Young Child A and Young Child B grow up they begin to act on their beliefs. Young Child A greets his parents warmly and reaches to hug them. They hug him back and all are happy. He reasons, "See, it's true, I'm a very cool kid!" Young Child B does not reach to hug others. Why would she? According to her expectations, it might not be reciprocated or might be met with strong negative reactions, having been just one more demand for over-stressed primary caregivers. Her belief system remains intact and is reinforced with her many lonely moments.

Now Child A and Child B go to school. Child A expects his peers and teachers to like him—after all, that's the way his world works. Of course, most of his peers and teachers do like Child A. Interactions with Child A are enjoyable and mutually beneficial. Most of those he meets are happy to return his warmth, to see his smiling face and his confident, pro-social behaviors. When there are a few who seem not to like him, he ignores their reactions as anomalies. Their reactions make no sense with what he *knows* is true of *his* world.

Child B, on the other hand, does not expect others to like her. She tends to scowl more than smile. She does not readily cooperate or follow instructions from her teacher. Why should she? She only relies on herself as she knows the world of others is unpredictable. So, with that attitude, her expectations are fulfilled. She is disliked and is isolated among her peers. When some teachers and peers do try to befriend her, she must ignore this or react with suspicion, as it makes no sense in the world she knows and expects.

When the school counselor becomes concerned for little Child B and invites her into a therapeutic relationship, the first thing she may do is work very hard to drive away this outreach by the counselor. Rejection is what Child B knows and expects, and it is familiar to her. She has come to believe that she can't be understood, and won't be loved and liked. But in time, a consistent therapeutic relationship with her counselor begins to place useful seeds of confusion in her belief system. As the counselor comes to know her and feel with her, and to prize the core essence beneath her misbehaviors, she begins to think, "Nobody understands me, loves or likes me . . . except . . . well, maybe my counselor. I've shown her everything. All my worst scowls and growls, and yet, she keeps consistently showing her caring for me." This new thought chain is way too long for an automatic thought (a repeating self-statement underneath fully conscious thought—Beck & Beck, 2011). Now Child B has a useful confusion that prompts her to reconsider what she believed of herself and her world, to reconsider the attributions and interpretations she has made of it. Her school counselor provided her with a consistently safe place to stop, feel and think, and to become aware of who she really is and what her relationship with the world can be. She provided her the opportunity to restart and renew her path to ideal maturity and her full potential.

Awareness of Existence, Choice and Questions of Self-Worth

We humans have the capacity to be aware of our existence and the opportunity to define ourselves. Toddlers go through a phase of asserting their existence, autonomy and choice through saying "No!" to their parents, often asserting "No!" over activities that they are not actually opposed to. Young children continue defining their selves by defining their likes and dislikes, picking favorite colors, animals and foods. Teenagers define their selves by which groups of friends they identify with. Young adults continue to assert their definitions of their selves through choices in clothes, hair care and activities of interest. Throughout our adult lives, we continue to define ourselves through our lives and occupational choices.

We see these and the multitude of human choices as a result of our awareness of our existence and as ongoing efforts to answer the core questions of "Who am I?" "Who do I want to be?" and "How do I relate to my world?" We as humans also tend to continually value or devalue ourselves, by asking questions like, "Am I OK, likable, lovable, worthy?" We attempt to answer these questions by considering how we relate to our world, asking questions like, "Do others like, love, or respect me?" "How do I compare to others? Am I better, stronger, faster, smarter?"

These questions are sometimes asked in full awareness, but are more often buried deep in our minds, under layers of other thoughts. We hear our answers to these questions in our minds over and over, and they affect how we feel and act, especially when we do not fully realize them. A metaphor for how this can be is the phenomenon of people working out in gyms. During most workouts, our minds are occupied with counting repetitions, miles and minutes, or with other surface-level thoughts. Many persons who work out in gyms like to have music playing that is energizing, motivating or calming. If the music was suddenly stopped and patrons were asked what song was playing, most would not know. Yet, most would agree that the gym's music has an effect on how they feel and what they do. Our self-talk answers to the questions of our identity and worth are much the same in that we often don't consciously hear them, but they are there, playing over and over, affecting our surface thoughts, our feelings and our actions.

As you invite clients into therapeutic relationships, you provide an atmosphere, a safe place and set of interactions that bring thoughts of self and self-worth to the surface for conscious consideration. In their therapeutic relationships with you, your clients will tend to shift from evaluating their worth in comparison to others to valuing their worth based on who and how they want to be. This work helps your clients reevaluate their answers to core questions of existence and helps them take responsibility for how they choose to define their selves.

Self-Responsibility is Anxiety-Provoking

With awareness of self, comes awareness of choice. With awareness of choice, comes awareness of responsibility. A young child learns, "I like," "I don't like." An older child learns, "I can choose what I like/don't like." And a yet older child learns that choices have consequences, from the kind of dessert received to how others respond to your actions. So choices come to be about results and responsibility is realized.

Responsibility can seem like an awesome power and persons may feel inspired. It can also seem like a heavy burden and persons can feel great discouragement and fear. In realizing that we own the ultimate responsibility for ourselves, which is made up of our choices, we humans often feel great anxiety. We will often give away our responsibility for our choices to others in order to avoid the anxiety that often comes with responsibility for ourselves and our actions. In the United States, the majority of citizens do not even vote, much less take an active role in our society's governance. Yet, those same persons who give over this responsibility will also often complain about our society's governance. The game there seems to be, "If I take no action, resulting effects are not my responsibility. Therefore, I am off the hook and can avoid the anxiety of responsibility and choice." Unfortunately, not choosing is a choice. If citizens do not choose, others will choose for them, and therefore we are each still responsible for the outcomes in society.

In spite of the discomfort of anxiety, when fully faced, experienced and owned, the anxiety of responsibility and choice is very useful in helping us humans to reach ideal maturity. When fully faced, experienced and owned, it sharpens our faculties and opens our hearts to make our very best, most satisfying decisions. The therapeutic relationships that you provide will help guide your clients to a safe place where they can face, experience and own this anxiety. This then allows them to begin to make fully responsible and optimally satisfying choices. At the same time, through your acceptance and empathy in these relationships, your clients can come to be motivated by, as well as at peace with, the reality of responsibility and choice. Certainly, a desired outcome of therapeutic relationships is not to make this anxiety go away, but to harness it. A desired outcome is not to make decisions for clients, but to enhance and empower each client's own process of anxiety leading to choice and responsibility.

Awareness of Aloneness

Along with awareness of our responsibility and its accompanying anxiety, at some level, we humans also sense that we are alone in our choices. We are alone in that while many can help, no one can live our lives for us or take the responsibility of our choices from us. This experience of aloneness drives us to relationships with others. This experience of aloneness is one of the elements that give great power to the deep connections of therapeutic relationships.

Emotions are Useful and Necessary for Growth

While we may fear, avoid or at least wish for painful emotions to go away, each is a useful, purposeful opportunity. Although it is an oversimplification, please consider our analogy between the usefulness of emotional pain and physical pain. If a momentarily unattended young child touches a hot burner, that child learns to be more careful around the stove. If that child didn't feel the pain of touching a hot burner, that child might not know to pull its hand back before serious injury. If a baseball pitcher develops a pain while throwing, that pain can be an early warning to make postural changes when pitching, in order to avoid a lasting injury.

We see emotional pain similarly. When it occurs, it has reason. When a person feels emotional pain after the break-up of a romance, there is opportunity through that pain, if fully experienced and contemplated, to decide and be motivated to make changes in one's self or actions for future relationships. When a person fully experiences the pain of a loved one dying, numerous lessons of how to live, how to care for one's self and others, can grow from that pain.

We have known clients who have come to counseling feeling emotional pain, anxiety or depression that they did not understand and that could not be easily explained. The natural inclination of persons in such situations is to try to make the pain go away. But to do so may be to lose the life lessons that the pain offers and to risk greater pain later. Jeff remembers one client in particular who was brought to face unexpected decisions and responsibility through unexplained pain.

This young client was living what he thought was a perfect life. He did well in school. He had good job prospects. His family loved his fiancée. But after learning of a friend of a friend's sudden death in an unexpected accident, he couldn't shake his feeling of anxiety and developed ongoing difficulty finding motivation for tasks he'd enjoyed so much before.

He asked me to help him make the pain go away. I offered him skills for managing or coping through painful emotions, but also offered him the opportunity to fully experience, explore and learn what there may be to learn from his feelings. While it sounded odd to him, he did accept and engage in a therapeutic relationship with me. Through the process of our therapeutic relationship, he decided that he had been trying to live the choices that he thought others wanted him to make and that his pain might be telling him that it was his life to live and that *he* was responsible for his choices. (These are not words he actually said, but how I remember his discoveries.) He didn't end up deciding to break off his engagement, as he decided his love for his fiancée was true, or immediately change his career path. He decided, at his time of crossroads and life changes, to end his unexamined life and begin a life that was full with his consideration for others and his consideration for himself.

You may note that this notion that all emotions have meaning and purpose also matches with a belief that all life has meaning and purpose. For example, suffering may have many purposes, including teaching strength and appreciation of joy. If there is such a thing as evil, it may have purpose in defining good. As the adage from Philosophy 101 goes, "You can't make an omelet without breaking a few eggs." We hope our use of that expression doesn't sound trite or flip. Rather, we have a great respect for and place a great value on the suffering that is part of life. In accepting that suffering is *a part of life*, we also understand our responsibility not to *take this part from the client*. It is not ours to take away, avoid or "talk the client out of." Because we want as helpers to care, to soothe and to take away pain, this allowance for our clients to fully experience anxiety and suffering is challenging, and is often where we counselors fail to trust in the power of the therapeutic relationship. Providing a therapeutic relationship will always involve deep caring, respect and empathy for the anxiety and suffering of another human being.

Every Action is a Choice of Destiny

As we write, we choose to be writers. In this moment we choose to work to communicate concepts that are very important to us and to our works in the hopes that they will be important to you and in your works.

Whenever we think of this concept—that every action is a choice of destiny—we are reminded of the many "choice moments" we have shared with children in child-centered play therapy (Axline, 1947; Cochran, Nordling, & Cochran, 2010; Guerney, 2001; Landreth, 2012). Years ago, during a training session with other play therapists, we viewed on video one of our favorite examples of this concept (Nordling, 1998). A little boy in a play therapy session is exuberantly aiming and shooting around the room with a dart gun. He turns toward his counselor and he shoots a toy dart at her. Without missing a beat, or showing shock or disapproval, the counselor quickly and calmly acknowledges the little boy's wanting to shoot the dart at her, but then sets a limit (with empathy) to his behavior of shooting her. With just a moment's hesitation, the little boy seems to contemplate, but then with a little grin on his face, points the toy gun at her again. After reflecting his choice to do this, the counselor informs him calmly but matter-of-factly that if he shoots the dart at her again, his play session will end for the day. The little boy then deliberates for a very *long* moment. During this moment, the choice belongs completely to him, and he vacillates between pointing the toy gun at her, or at the ceiling light. He is making a choice for that moment, shoot counselor/end session, shoot at the ceiling light/continue session, express emotion by hurting/defying another, express emotion without hurting/defying another. Yet, he is also making a choice to define himself. Using adult-like thought sentences to depict his thought process, he seems to consider, "Will I be hurtful and defiant of one who holds me in positive regard and understands me, or will I be a person who would not do that?" "Do I choose to end my special time with this person . . . *I can choose!*" After his long moment of deliberation, it is clear, as he chooses to shoot up at the ceiling light instead of at the counselor, that *his seemingly small choice of that moment* is also a choice of his destiny, a choice defining who he is and who he will be.

While it is not always so simple or clear, our every moment and our every choice is a choice of our destiny. We define and redefine ourselves with the choices of each moment. The therapeutic relationships that you provide, based on the skills of *The Heart of Counseling*, focus your clients on their choices of destiny and the personal meanings that each choice brings.

The Internal World

The skills of *The Heart of Counseling* are focused on clients gaining mastery of their internal worlds. It is a pitfall for caring counselors to focus on tragic or unfortunate circumstances of clients' lives, over which clients have little control, versus the choices, feelings and thoughts in response to those circumstances, over which clients have much greater control. The boy in the previous example may have had a very chaotic or abusive home life, and his counselor may have done what she could to bring about changes in his home life through consultation with the significant adults in his life. However, in his sessions, for him to make optimal progress, the focus should be on who he is, what he feels and thinks, and the choices he makes in the moments he is making them. Further, if his counselor focuses her thoughts, even after his sessions, on the troubles and deficits of his life, she will likely become discouraged. Instead, through providing a strong therapeutic relationship, she can tap into his resiliency and return him to his home environment having become stronger and more solid in his choices of who he is and who he wishes to be, regardless of how his environment changes with him. By dwelling more on her works to strengthen his resilience and choices, while also influencing his environment when possible, his counselor can both feel more encouraged and be more effective.

Locus of Control and Evaluation, and Being

It is desirable to shift our human locus of control and evaluation from others to ourselves. Because we have the capacity for empathy and because it is natural to desire relationships with others, if we live our lives based on our wants, we will satisfy ourselves *and* be considerate of others, rather than hedonistic. If we focus on valuing ourselves by our being, rather than valuing ourselves by how we compare to others or how we think others value us, we can make the clearest decisions of who and how we want to be, and how we want to treat others.

On the other hand, if we strive to shape ourselves based on how we think we compare to others or based on the person we think others want us to be, we will develop a misshapen external self that does not fit our internal self. Then, attempting to maintain that mismatch and hide that assumed unacceptable internal self requires a constant tension, a great expense and waste of energy, often leading to premature stress-related illness and limiting the potential possible in a congruent, self-actualized life.

The last underlying concept that we introduce is the belief that our human value is in being. We will never be able to count our value through our accomplishments or attributes. They are too tough to measure. There is always someone better. If we are unloved or disliked, even by those who we love, we are the same person. Our worth is always the same. This fits well with many spiritual beliefs (i.e., we are all part of the same creator or creation). It is a helpful view of fellow humans for a counselor to see her clients through.

However, such an internal locus of control and valuing based on being are very difficult to teach. Fortunately, they don't have to be taught. Rather, therapeutic relationships provide an environment and experience in which they are naturally learned or rediscovered. In such relationships there is nothing for clients to do but face their selves. If there are unsatisfactory behaviors, they will be realized and changed. If there are unrealistic expectations, they will be realized and adjusted. In therapeutic relationships, there is no one to defer evaluation to. In such relationships, there is no one to compare to, as the focus is empathically and acceptingly on one's self, alone.

Activities and Resources for Further Study

- Remember to continue to consider and refer back to these concepts as you study and implement the skills of *The Heart of Counseling*.

- Discern our explanation and rephrase in your own words why, if each person's path to self-actualization is unique, some would not naturally develop to pure evil. Then, given this explanation, explain why some persons do develop into bad behavior at times in their lives. From what you know so far, explain in terms of self-actualization and other key concepts from this chapter how therapeutic relationships help.
- Review Seeman (2002) and Barrett-Lennard (2005) for their perspectives on persons as parts of larger interpersonal systems, especially in regard to the notion of self-actualization.
- With a whole class or smaller group, take turns and allow each person to state what parts of these concepts make particular sense to you, what parts make no sense at all, what emotions you felt in reading them, and what related thoughts you had. Be sure to listen and accept each view expressed. After a view or feeling from one person is heard and accepted, another person's view or feeling may be added, whether or not it connects, differs or matches the view or feeling previously expressed.
- Follow a similar procedure over a meal or other refreshments shared with one or more interested peers.
- Take yourself to a place where you can feel comfortable and calm, perhaps under a tree, on a comfortable day. With a clock in your field of vision, contemplate each concept for a few minutes. Begin by reading or remembering each concept, then let your mind flow from the concept to whatever memories, related thoughts, or feelings occur to you. Don't censure your thoughts or feelings; none can be wrong. When you realize your thoughts have drifted quite far, return your thoughts to the basic concept and let your thoughts begin to wander again. After spending a few minutes associating thoughts with a concept, move on to the next concept. Note that we ask you to focus on both those concepts that appeal to you and those that *don't*. The point of this contemplation is not for you to convince yourself to agree, but if the disagreement between your views and the views we shared has struck something in you (i.e., irritation, boredom or strong judgments like "That's stupid"), then there is even more reason to contemplate. This could be a very fertile moment for your learning. Perhaps in this contemplation, you'll come to an unexpected new thought that is particularly meaningful to you. Perhaps you will learn something new and useful of yourself and your views.
- Think of, draw and/or build a symbolic depiction of each concept that will remind you of it and its meaning to you.
- Reread our tree metaphor and then contemplate a beautiful, full tree in your life. Contemplate its perfection just as it is, and describe how it contributes to its environment and how its environment contributes to it.

- Revisit the Focus Activities of this chapter. Consider what you might change of your answers now that you have considered our views.
- Review the Primary Skill Objectives of this chapter, checking that you have mastered each to your satisfaction at this time. Reread, contemplate, question, discuss and repeat further study activities until you have mastered each to your satisfaction at this time.

References

Axline, V.M. (1947). *Play therapy: The inner dynamics of childhood*. Cambridge, MA: The Riverside Press.

Barrett-Lennard, G.T. (2005). *Relationship at the centre*. Philadelphia, PA: Wurr.

Beck, J.S., & Beck, A.T. (2011). *Cognitive behavior therapy: Basics and beyond* (2nd ed.). New York: Guilford.

Bergin, A.E., & Lambert, M.J. (1978). The effectiveness of psychotherapy. In S.L. Garfield & A.E. Bergin (Eds.), *Handbook of psychotherapy and behavior change* (2nd ed.). New York: Wiley.

Bohart, A., & Tallman, K. (1999). *How clients make therapy work: The process of active self-healing*. Washington, DC: American Psychological Association.

Cochran, N.H., Nordling, W.J., & Cochran, J.L. (2010) *Child-centered play therapy: A practical guide to developing therapeutic relationships with children*. Hoboken, NJ: Wiley.

Demanchick, S.P., Cochran, N.H., & Cochran, J.L. (2003). Person-centered play therapy for adults with developmental disabilities. *International Journal of Play Therapy, 12*, 47–66.

Duncan, B.L., Miller, S.D., & Sparks, J.A. (2004). *The heroic client: A revolutionary way to improve effectiveness through client-directed, outcome-informed therapy* (revised ed.). San Francisco, CA: Jossey-Bass.

Ellingham, I. (2002). Foundation for a person-centered, humanistic psychology and beyond: The nature and logic of Carl Rogers' "formative tendency." In J.C. Watson, R.N. Goldman, & M.S. Warner (Eds.), *Client-centered and experiential psychotherapy in the 21st century: Advances in theory, research, and practice* (pp. 16–35). Ross-on-Wye: PCCS Books.

Garland, E.L., & Howard, M.O. (2009). Neuroplasticity, psychosocial genomics, and the biopsychosocial paradigm in the 21st century. *Health and Social Work, 34*, 191–199.

Guerney, L.F. (2001). Child-centered play therapy. *International Journal of Play Therapy, 10*, 13–31.

Lambert, M.J. (2013). The efficacy and effectiveness of psychotherapy. In M.J. Lambert (Ed.), *Bergin and Garfield's handbook of psychotherapy and behavior change* (6th ed.) (pp. 258–297) Hoboken, NJ: Wiley.

Landreth, G.L. (2012). *Play therapy: The art of the relationship*. New York: Routledge.

Luborsky, L., Singer, J., & Luborsky, L. (1975). Comparative studies of psychotherapy. *Archives of General Psychiatry, 32*, 995–1008.

McHenry, B., Sikorski, A.M., & McHenry, J. (2014). *A counselor's introduction to neuroscience*. New York: Routledge.

Morowitz, H.J. (2004). *The emergence of everything*. New York: Oxford University Press.

Nordling, W. (1998, April). *Child-centered play therapy*. Workshop series sponsored by the National Institute for Relationship Enhancement (NIRE), Baltimore, MD.

Seeman, J. (2002). Looking back, looking ahead: A synthesis. In D.J. Cain & J. Seeman (Eds.), *Humanistic psychotherapies: Handbook of research and practice* (pp. 617–636). Washington, DC: American Psychological Association.

Sheldon, K.M., & Houser-Marko, L. (2001). Self-concordance, goal attainment, and the pursuit of happiness: Can there be an upward spiral? *Journal of Personality and Social Psychology, 80,* 152–165.

Wampold, B.E. (2001). *The great psychotherapy debate: Models, methods, and findings*. Mahwah, NJ: Erlbaum.

Wampold, B.E., Mondin, G.W., Moody, M., Stich, F., Benson, K., & Ahn, H. (1997). A meta-analysis of outcome studies comparing bona fide psychotherapies: Empirically, "all must have prizes." *Psychological Bulletin, 122,* 203–215.

Pre-Chapter Quote

Fadiman, J., & Frager, R. (1998). *Essential Sufism*. Edison, NJ: Castle Books (p. 101).

2 THE RICH AND SUBTLE SKILLS OF THERAPEUTIC LISTENING

We get into and out of difficulties with each other to a large extent by the way we listen and by what we hear, mishear, and fail to hear.

G.T. Barrett-Lennard

Talk low, talk slow, and don't say too much.

John Wayne—advice on acting

Man, if you gotta ask you'll never know.

Louis Armstrong—reply when asked what jazz is

Primary Skill Objectives

- Understand the complexities and difficulties of therapeutic listening for beginning counselors, for all counselors, and especially for you individually.
- Be able to listen to another person speak on a topic that has at least a low level of personal, emotional content for at least several minutes with nearly full concentration and focus on what the speaker is telling you.
- Be able to correctly summarize the core content of what the speaker has said within a couple of minutes, without missing core content and without adding your judgments or opinions, even if meant to be helpful.
- Tune out the thoughts in your head so that you can tune in more fully to the speaker.
- Identify your listening body language and several words that describe how it feels to *be* yourself physically and emotionally while listening.
- Be able to consistently identify when you and the listeners you observe are missing important parts of a speaker's communication and adding things that were not communicated, especially concerning the listener's thoughts and judgments.
- Be able to consistently perform or avoid nearly all the items on the dos and don'ts list for therapeutic listening while applying the skills in real-time practice sessions.

- Be able to explain the broadness of reflecting and create varied, realistic examples.
- Be able to explain the connection and how taking the broad view of client communication can help you understand and implement a broad view of reflecting.
- Be able to explain what we mean by saying you are not, as counselor, a "paraphrasing machine."
- Understand how listening therapeutically is quite different from listening in everyday life, and experience some of the power inherent in listening this way.
- Explore common difficulties in beginning to listen therapeutically and anticipate of the difficulties you will face.

Focus Activity

In a group of three (better to work with classmates than friends or others with whom you have an emotional connection and vested interest), have one person take the role of speaker and talk to you for three minutes on a topic that has at least a low level of personal, emotional meaning. Strive to commit your full attention to what the speaker is telling you. Try not to think of what you may summarize in response.

At the end of the speaker's three minutes, summarize what you happen to remember. Summarize only what the speaker said to you. Do not add your thoughts or judgments, even if you mean them to be helpful. Strive to summarize all of what you heard from the speaker, without leaving out any significant parts.

The third partner, the observer, is also to listen to the speaker as well as to the listener's summary in order to help the listener know what errors he has made in summarizing the speaker's communication. While the speaker and listener are having their interchange, sit a few feet back to minimize any distraction you may present. Also, keep your eyes down or in the direction of the listener. This is to keep from encouraging the speaker from trying to communicate to the listener and to you at the same time, which is a natural inclination when two are listening. While hearing the listener's summary, prepare yourself to give feedback to the listener, including what he summarized well, missed, seems to have heard wrong and added, especially any of his own thoughts or judgments, no matter how well-meaning. We do not encourage the speaker to give feedback immediately following this first practice, as it is so very tempting to add to or change what was said. As observer, you may keep time for the speaker and listener. The observer's role can be filled by either one person or a small group of persons.

Rotate through speaker, listener and observer roles until everyone has had a turn. After each interchange of the speaker talking for three minutes, the listener summarizing for two, and the observer giving feedback to the listener, take a few minutes to discuss what seemed easy and difficult in the listeners' roles. Don't divert into the content of something a speaker said at this time or use this discussion to offer the advice or related thoughts that you may have wished to say. Dismissing such thoughts when listening is one of the difficulties of therapeutic listening; expecting to say them later will divert you from listening, when it is time to listen.

After each has had a turn at all three roles, discuss the things you have learned that may be informative about what counseling is like, both for counselors and clients.

Tuning In and Listening

We assume the focus activity was difficult. As Schuster (1979) wrote of the difficulty of listening well, "Although this requirement appears be extraordinarily easy to accomplish, in reality it continually slips through our [trained counselors'] fingers" (p. 71). While many of us think we listen well in our lives outside of counseling, good therapeutic listening is extremely rare. To illustrate this, we sometimes ask how long family, friends or acquaintances usually listen, before asking a question (which usually suggests a solution), directly suggesting a solution, or shifting the conversation with a "me, too" statement (such statements usually start something like, "I had a situation just about like that . . ." or "When I was your age, I . . ."). When we ask this of students and others, the answer we usually get is lightly stunned looks suggesting such listening time is quite rare in their daily lives. We often guess 10 minutes, and are told the time is not near that long, but more like zero to a few minutes.

Listening is a huge percentage of what counselors do. Therapeutic listening, described throughout this chapter, is profoundly different from listening in normal social interactions, and it is not easy. It is the first skill set of a developing counselor. In this chapter, we focus on the skills of listening and reflecting what you understand of each client's communication, situation, and person. These skills demonstrate to each client that you want to know her, that you are striving to understand her, and that you are beginning to understand and know her depth and complexities. In coming chapters, we focus more on expressing empathy, which communicates your deep understanding, feeling with, and personal connection to each client. Therapeutic listening is preliminary to the higher goal of an empathic and deeply personal connection.

The Many Levels and Nuances of Reflecting

The Broad Skill of Reflection: From Paraphrasing to Themes, to Confrontation, Challenge, Summary and Beyond

As you continue your study of this chapter, you should come to see that reflecting sounds simple but is complex and broadly encompassing. Briefly defined, *reflecting is counselors' attempts to communicate to clients that they are striving to understand, and perhaps do understand.* The simplest form is to paraphrase back what you heard your client say. Another simple form is when, without even trying to, your facial expression matches the tone or emotions of your client's communication.

Paraphrasing

Note that while paraphrasing and short summaries are the simplest and most common forms of reflection, they are only a place to begin. They are the simplest way to communicate your striving to understand, when you don't understand much yet. Since they are tools to communicate your striving more than your understanding, we encourage you not to worry over perfect wording, but to strive to understand the person of each client and his communication, and to say what comes to mind as you strive to understand. If you think too much of how to paraphrase your clients' communication, that thought process will take you away from a focus on a personal, emotional connection that is the greater key to the heart of counseling. As you know your client more, move to higher and more complex forms of reflection, rather than focusing on longer summaries. Descriptions of more complex forms of reflection follow.

Themes

One higher-level form of reflection is to reflect patterns or themes in your clients' communications. For example, a client has been telling her counselor about her romantic relationship. Clearly it has been on her mind, but she has assured her counselor that she is happy with it. So, the counselor has made simple reflections like, "So, it sounds like you are really quite pleased with your relationship." As the client continues to discuss the relationship frequently, her counselor may reflect the pattern, "Seems like your relationship has been on your mind frequently in our time together." (The counselor's tone is interested and neutral; she is not indicating that it should not be on her client's mind or that there is any implication given to the fact that it is.) If the client then adds, "Yeah, I think I think about it all the time. I guess I really have some worries . . ." her counselor might then respond, "Oh, so you see your relationship in a positive light, but now you've begun to have some concerns." (The counselor's tone would again be neutral, rather than perhaps excited that now we have a problem to talk about.)

If another client tells with disdain how another student acted toward him in class, then similar disdain for how his girlfriend acted toward him, and later tells a similar story suggesting his disdain at how his mother acted toward him, you might consider that he is communicating a theme. You might reflect, "I notice you noting a number of people who you see as disrespecting you. It's like your feelings in each instance are of complete disdain, as if you are thinking, 'How could *she* treat me that way!?'"

Confronting and Challenging

Reflections can cover complexities of communication and contradictions. One example of this can be, "So while you are happy with your relationship, it seems that was a little hard for you to say, and I thought you looked a little unsure when you said it." Another possible example is, "I get the idea that there is *so much* you like about him, and you are very glad to be with him, *and* you also seem to experience some doubts and worries." Another example could be, "A part of you wants very much to be with him, *and* a part of you wants something different."

Some counselors think of this level of reflection as confronting or challenging. Our thought is that such reflections are only confrontations if you have stopped striving to understand your client and mean to make a point. For example, a counselor who is confronting may be pointing out that there is a contradiction within his client and there should not be. That counselor may be implying that the contradiction he has discovered is particularly important for his client to consider—that he knows best what his client should communicate next. Or a counselor may imply, at least in tone, support for one contradictory inclination of a client over another. Such errors mean that the counselor has stopped listening and started telling, and tend to undermine harnessing each client's drive to self-actualize and the development of self-responsibility.

We guide you to keep your focus on listening and respecting each person's self-actualization process versus making a point about a contradiction that you notice. Your reflections will include contradictions that you see, but your purpose should remain saying what you see/understand of the person. This may include reflecting it when you see that your client's:

- statements contradict each other;
- words contradict actions;
- words contradict body language.

Discrepancies within persons are part of being human. So reflecting discrepancies when you see them need not be confrontational. Regarding challenge, however, we find that reflecting contradictions tends to be naturally challenging, as we humans tend to want to resolve internal conflicts in order to feel better and to be understood. But then reflecting in any form is often challenging—as your client hears of his experience through your eyes, as you strive to understand him, he learns more about himself. At least parts of what he learns about himself will be hard to hear, thus challenging, but also needed and helpful.

Summarizing

We urge you to let your summaries occur naturally as you come to understand the person of your client beyond the small understandings of her communication. As you come to know her more, say the larger understanding you have of her as a person in her context. Deep understanding of her as a person in her context is more important than summarizing content. Your focus on understanding the person of your client allows your summaries to be of the person rather than of the information she has given you; such summaries are naturally flowing rather than contrived. If you work to force a summary into your reflections, it will shift you to thinking what she has said and away from her as a person and the emotional connection that is more central to *The Heart of Counseling*.

To sensitively let your client see how you see her is a broad and advanced level of reflection. In an exasperated moment your client might say to you, "It's just that I'm so selfish!" Then, if it is true to your perception of her, and you have begun a strong therapeutic relationship, the following interchange might occur:

COUNSELOR: You see yourself as selfish and you *do not* like that about yourself.
CLIENT: Yes, it's *so* true. Isn't it terrible?
COUNSELOR: I hear that it's terrible to you. I hadn't seen you as selfish. I see you as being very careful not to hurt others.

The Broad View of Client Communication

While realizing the broad nature of reflections, it is also helpful to see the broadness of client communication. Everything your clients do or say to you is a part of their expressing who they are to you. This includes words, tone, facial expression and body language, pauses in speech, and even what is not said. From the previous example, if the client has discussed her relationship in each session, then one week says nothing about it, you might reflect, "I notice the subject of your relationship does not seem to be on your mind today." (Neutral tone—the counselor is interested, but not suggesting the client should talk about her relationship.)

A teenager was telling Jeff about difficult family situations regarding her mother's illness: It became very clear that she was talking about or all around her fear of her mother's death. I reflected something like, "I'm not sure, but I get the idea that you mean that this is so important to you, because you fear your mother may [slight hesitation] die." She paused, seeming stunned and acknowledged that this was very true before continuing her story with added awareness. When I made that reflection, I was very tentative because I realized as I said it that this was not something that she had quite said yet. I hesitated before saying the word *die* because I feared it would be hard for her to hear, and because it was a hard thing for me to say. This serves as a reminder that we are not listening machines. Therapeutic listening goes on between two people, not between one person and one "paraphrasing machine."

In another example of the broad view of communication from clients, you can see that questions from clients are also statements about themselves. In the brief vignette at the end of the previous section, the client asked her counselor, "Isn't it terrible?" Rather than answering, "Yes, it is terrible" or "No, it isn't terrible," the counselor took the question as a statement and reflected, "I hear that it's terrible to you."

In another example, a client told of a violent fight among her family with a very sweet smile. Her counselor reflected, "I gather this was *very* upsetting to you. I notice you smile while telling me about it." She responded, "Yes, that's what I do. I try to just keep smiling. If not, it would be too overwhelming."

For another example, if a client consistently describes wanting a particular change, but consistently hesitates from actions toward change, you might reflect (i.e., challenge/confront), "You've made it clear to me that you want to make this change, but something seems to be preventing you from the move you want." You do not need to wait for your client to say, "Something is preventing me from . . ." This has already been communicated from the fact of his wanting to change, but not taking action for change.

The Dos and Don'ts of Listening Therapeutically

You are Communicating with Your Actions

With the behaviors in the "do" list, you are communicating, "I understand what you are telling me." Even more basically, you are communicating, "I am listening," "I am striving to understand."

Do:

- use your personal version of listening body language;
- reflect your perception of what your client communicates;
- make your reflections declarative statements, when sure that you understand;
- make your reflections tentative declarations, when you are unsure if you understand;
- keep your reflections short, whenever possible;
- focus your reflections on your client's main point, or the things communicated that seemed most important, most emotionally laden to her/him;

- be prepared for and accept corrections;
- interrupt your client carefully to make reflections (considerations here are: (1) Will an interruption to reflect help your client clarify communication, thoughts, feelings? and (2) How much communication can you reasonably reflect in a short paraphrase, before becoming overwhelmed?);
- balance reflecting enough to encourage continued communication, to be engaged and for your client to sense your engagement, without inhibiting her communication with too frequent interruptions;
- allow your client to own most silences.

Don't:

- allow interruptions for reflections to set up a hierarchy where your communications would seem more important than your client's;
- ask questions, except in rare circumstances, or state reflections in a questioning tone.

Explanations of the Behaviors of the Dos and Don'ts List

While we use the Dos and Don'ts list to simplify counselor behaviors, such lists oversimplify the complex and subtle processes of counseling. For example, the list given here focuses only on therapeutic listening. While this alone can be powerfully helpful, the much more powerful skill that we are building up to in our explanations is combining therapeutic listening with expressions from a deep empathic connection.

Your Listening Body Language

We emphasize *your* in this item because listening body language is unique to each counselor. Listening therapeutically is a way of being, rather than a set of fixed behaviors. This is also true for the body language of the listener. When you are listening, tuned in, and experiencing empathy, it will show in your body language. A story from Jeff's early work illustrates how your listening body language can be quite individual, yet still effective if you are focused in your groove of listening:

> Especially when I was younger, my listening body language may have been peculiar. I tended to shift and move in my chair a lot. This caught my attention when watching a session tape in fast-forward motion. While my client was doing most of the talking, I was much less still than her. When I stopped to watch the session at regular speed, I realized that my mind and heart were absorbed in her communication. As I saw that her communication continually deepened, I could see that she knew that I was

listening, fully focused on her communication. The fact that I did not sit still was not a distraction to her.

Our recommendation for developing *your* listening body language is to be aware of yourself in conversations. Notice when you are fully focused on the speaker's communication and when you are not (i.e., perhaps bored or preoccupied with thoughts of your own). Watch your body language at these different times and how it shifts in subtle or blatant ways. Then videotape yourself in both role-play and real sessions. Again, watch for the changes in your body language when you are fully tuned in and when you are not. Use this knowledge of your listening and non-listening body language to prompt yourself to listen well, and catch yourself when you are off-track.

Consider these hints toward generic listening body language. Listening body language usually includes looking at the speaker, and frequently means looking into his eyes, but without staring. It is usually not a closed posture (e.g., arms crossed). Often you may see shifts in your posture that fit with what your client is expressing. For example, when your client is telling you something over which he is excited and wants you to fully understand, you will likely sit up or lean forward. When your client tells you, or indicates, that what he is saying is difficult and will take time, you may sit back, showing that you are settled in and ready to listen patiently.

Reflect Your *Perception* of What Your Client Communicates

No counselor or person can truly know what a client or speaker has communicated. Yet, it is the counselor's job to understand what is communicated. In striving, we may come very close. A key reason for never truly knowing what another person is communicating is a basic flaw of using language to communicate. Language is always culturally laden. Words and phrases have meanings defined in dictionaries and implied meanings defined by culture, tone, context, and more. On the island of Guam, the Chamorro phrase for thank you is "Si yu'os ma'ase." This translates something like, "Thanks be to God." This illustrates a cultural difference in language use. In America, the predominant culture seems more highly focused on the individual. We say, "thank *you*." It may be that the Chamorro culture is more focused on the collective, so the phrase used for thank you is quite different. For another example, in English we say, "You're welcome." In Spanish, the phrase commonly used in the same place is "De nada," which translates something like, "It's nothing." Again, there seems to be a cultural meaning implied. "You're welcome," may imply "Yes, I have done something for you and *you* are welcome to it, deserving of it." The Spanish phrase commonly used in the same conversational place seems to say, "I would like you to think nothing of what I have done." Of course, the tone and context of all these phrases adds still *much more* to the implied meanings.

We very intentionally label this behavior "your perception." Your reflections will always be your perception, rather than *the* truth. Everything a speaker says must first pass through her own mental filter (i.e., how one sees the world and one's self), and then through the imperfect medium of language (i.e., often there are no perfect words to say exactly what one means—poets often work hours to years to select just the right words). Then what the speaker has said must pass through your (as listener's) mental filter as your mind automatically puts what you hear into your worldview. Then, this whole process must be repeated as you reflect your understanding of what has been communicated to the speaker. Whew! It's quite a cycle, and one of the reasons Nancy enjoys counseling work with young children who aren't so reliant on words to communicate in counseling. So, the cycle of each reflection *begins* with the speaker's meaning, but then must proceed through a process that looks like this: Speaker's meaning > speaker's mental filter > language > listener's mental filter > listener's perception of meaning > listener's mental filter > language > speaker's mental filter > speaker's perception of what the listener said.

Therefore, we use such phrasings for reflections as, "I hear you saying . . ." and "It sounds like what you are saying is . . .". Beginning counselors tend to use these phrasings more. As counselors become more experienced and confident that they are close to understanding their clients' communications, they tend to use such phrases less. We encourage you not to overuse these phrases. Doing so can be stilted and unnatural, compared to simply saying what you see/hear—and risking being wrong.

Along with the development of your listening body language, you will also develop your idiosyncratic body language that expresses your level of understanding. For example, your furrowed brow might show your strain to understand. Your relaxed face and firm tone in speaking might convey your certainty. Your tentative tone in speaking might convey your lack of confidence in your understanding so far. However, don't let your tentative tone have you drift into a questioning tone. We suggest you preface your reflection by stating that you are unsure rather than shaping your clients' communication with inadvertent questions. For example, you might reduce your tentative tone by prefacing your reflection such as the following, "I'm not sure I understand yet, but I think you're telling me that what is so hurtful about it to you is the disrespect you heard in his tone."

Reflections as Declarative Statements

When the speaker's meaning is quite clear to you, your reflection should be a clearly declarative statement. For example, a client was telling how he had given directions to a coworker. He explained that he had spoken slowly, given the instructions a couple of different ways, and that it was really a simple task. He concluded emphatically, "So, I have told him and told him and told him, but still he doesn't get it!" A declarative reflection, over which the counselor could likely be sure, is, "You see that you definitely explained it well." A tentative declarative addition, over which the counselor might not be quite sure, would be, "And it seems to make no sense to you that he still does not understand." If this speaker then continued in the same vein, with emotions rising, and a look of irritation and disgust on his face, you might make an even more tentative reflection by saying, "I get the idea that you are *irritated* with his not understanding, maybe even disgusted."

The previous example begins to get into the realm of emotions. This is a most important topic and will be the focus of the next chapters. For now, the point is, when your client's meaning is obvious, drop phrases such as, "I hear you saying . . ." An example of this is, "What hurt you was his tone of disrespect." When your client's communication is not obvious to you, make your reflection a more tentative declaration, "You seem to have been most bothered by his tone of disrespect." When your client's communication is not clear to you, but seems quite important or emotionally laden to your client, make your reflection an even more tentative declaration, with a phrase such as, "I get the idea that . . ." An example of this is, "I'm not sure, but I get the idea that you heard his tone as disrespect and that is what hurt."

The Question of Questions or Questioning Tone

Skipping ahead to the second "don't" on the list (don't ask questions, except in rare circumstances, or state reflections in a questioning tone), it is important that you not let your tentative reflections end with a questioning tone. In fact, we recommend that you use questions only in rare circumstances (e.g., helping a client who has trouble getting communication started; clarifying when you have no idea of your client's meaning; or in managing situations of potential imminent danger, which are addressed later in this book). Questions or a questioning tone are usually focused on the counselor's rather than the client's need—for example, to satisfy a need to have perfect reflections, not to be seen as misunderstanding, or to apologize in advance for a possible failed understanding. In fact, *as long as the counselor's intent is to understand the client, there is no penalty for being wrong with a reflection.*

However, there can be numerous time and relationship penalties (at the very least time inefficiency) to questions or a questioning tone. Many clients will try to answer your question, whether it is what they need to communicate or not. A questioning tone usually implies a yes or no question (i.e., "Is this what you mean to say, ___?"), which tends to stop the flow of clients' communication. Further, questions often imply that you are investigating a perceived problem in order to prescribe a solution. The alternative of directing a client to "tell me more" carries with it the same problems as asking questions. It suggests to the client that *now you are onto an important topic, perhaps one that will be useful to me in prescribing a solution.* In reality, such solution-based prescriptions are rarely possible or helpful in increasing the emotional well-being or self-efficacy of clients. By many accounts we are excellent counselors, yet we cannot expect to successfully prescribe solutions for the ongoing struggles of our fellow human beings. If we could do this, we would. Then, we would be very rich, which so far we are not. Additionally, such problem-solving questions communicate to your clients that you, as the counselor, do not trust their judgment or care enough to have the patience to allow them to discern their own solutions, or even to define their own problems. We will continue to show you a non-questioning approach to counseling that avoids the problems of questions and maximizes time efficiency.

A vignette that illustrates some of the problems with using questions follows. We pick up the dialog midsession:

CLIENT: My boyfriend is so mean to me that I don't know what to do.

COUNSELOR: How long have you been together? [Counselor may have only wanted context to better understand what the speaker was saying or may have been attempting to judge whether her client was in a long- or short-term relationship and therefore whether it would be easy or hard, or even right or wrong, to end it.]

CLIENT: We, uh, we've been together for two months and we, uh, I, I, uh, I love him so much that we started you know [pause] being intimate last weekend.

COUNSELOR: You've been together two months and you decided last week-end that you loved him so much that you would be sexually intimate with him? [Questioning tone is denoted with question mark at end of statement.]

CLIENT: [Although it may or may not be true, at this time the client believes counselor is judging her critically. She looks down and pauses before she speaks.] Well, he's really a great guy . . .

COUNSELOR: [Interrupts to ask.] But you said he was mean to you? [This can be the worst kind of question. It seems like an argument from a lawyer on TV to a witness who has changed her story on the stand. The "counselor" who asks this believes she already knows the answer. Thus the question is rhetorical, pointing out that the witness is changing her story and now may be lying.]

CLIENT: Well, he really is; he has a great future, he's captain of the football team, all the girls love him, and he loves me.

At this point the client seems to be shifted to the opposite of what she came to say. She believes she must defend herself and her boyfriend from the counselor, whom she sees as disapproving. Their therapeutic relationship is in serious jeopardy. This client will not let her counselor know who she is while she fears critical judgment. As she cannot let her counselor know her real self, she cannot do much work on her real self.

However, let's assume a miracle happens and this client does get back to what she seems to have come to say:

CLIENT: What I mean by his being mean is that, well, he's scary sometimes.
COUNSELOR: Tell me more. [This is a directive that functions like a question.]
CLIENT: It's just that before we did it [pauses before going on to say something that is difficult to say] had sex I mean, he could be sooo rough, and even when we did . . .
COUNSELOR: Are you saying he is abusive?
CLIENT: Oh, no. [Confused, afraid, perhaps defensive again.] I, I told you he loved me.
COUNSELOR: But this is important. Is he hurting you?
CLIENT: I, I don't know . . . No, he would never do that. He's from such a good family and his parents love me too.

Now, while this counselor meant to have her client's best interest at heart and obviously cares about how weaker partners are treated in relationships, her questions and way of being with this client have produced a defensiveness in the client that may preclude, or at least greatly lengthen the time, it will take to help her. Also, if this client is sometimes easily manipulated, perhaps due to self-talk that tells her she is weak or undeserving or must/should depend on others, and can't make her own good decisions, this counselor's questions have reconfirmed this self-doubt. If this client is in an abusive relationship, even if the counselor were able to later talk the client into leaving the relationship after judging that it was abusive, the counselor would effectively be asserting herself in the place of the controlling boyfriend. One cannot control other humans in order to have them come to control themselves.

If, on the other hand, this counselor had focused her energies on therapeutic listening, especially with expressions of accurate empathy, this client may have soon come to develop and trust her own judgments of what she deserves, her understanding of how she is being treated, and how she wants to be treated. Consider the following small piece of how that work might go:

CLIENT: I just don't know . . . He's a great guy, everybody says so . . . But he scares me, sometimes.
COUNSELOR: [Tenderly, similar to the tone with which the client spoke.] You seem to feel confused. You've told me you love him, you know that others see him as a great guy, but you also feel scared by him, sometimes.
CLIENT: Well, yeah . . . [tearing a little] he's the best guy I ever had [long pause]. But when we fool around or even do it, he hurts me. [Quickly adding.] It's just little things, though.
COUNSELOR: I got the idea you wanted to make it clear to me that it's just little things. It also seems you're saying they *are* things that bother you.
CLIENT: [Very tentatively.] Yeah, I guess . . . a little. You know, the other night when he was drinking with friends and I didn't get the joke, he, well

he . . . he laughed at me [the pauses in this last statement were long and she was beginning to tear again].

COUNSELOR: [Again tentatively, close to her client's tone.] I gather from how hard that seemed for you to say, that that really hurt you.

Now, through therapeutic listening, this client is coming to express more of her relationship concerns to her counselor and importantly what *she* thinks and feels about her relationship. She is starting with what is easier to say first, but is moving toward what she finds is most important to say— which may well be the abuse that the heavily questioning counselor suspected. Through this therapeutic listening, she is coming to discover, perhaps admit to herself for the first time, what she feels. She seems to be beginning to trust what she feels and value what she feels as input to what she should do. Very importantly, she is coming to value herself, as her counselor values her enough to listen.

Also, if there is an imminent danger issue, it will most efficiently be uncovered through this process. In Chapter 10 we will illustrate how counselors assess for danger while maintaining therapeutic listening and respect for clients and their thoughts and feelings.

Keep Your Reflections Short, Whenever Possible

Therapeutic listening can be one of those times when "less is more." Because you are less involved in your client's situation, you will often be able to reflect your client's communication much more concisely than your client was able to communicate to you. A rule of thumb for the percentage of talking that you do versus the talking your client does would be a quarter of the communication by you and three-quarters by your client. This rule-of-thumb proportion is not something that you should concern yourself with during sessions, as it would take your focus off your client and your client's communications. Rather, you should consider it when reviewing your work after sessions. The shorter your reflections can be, while still capturing the truth and not being hurried, the more they will enhance versus pull your client away from expressing his experience to you.

The Special Issue of Verbatim Reflections

Verbatim reflections of client wording often make for the most concise, direct reflections. However, verbatim reflections are sometimes not ideal, as they could seem oddly echoing to clients. They are OK to being with, especially when they are said with empathy (focusing on the emotional meaning of the statement, rather than the words). Additionally, verbatim reflections are often just the right thing to do—for example, when your client has said something that is strongly emotional. When our clients state an absolute thought with strong emotions, such as "It's just impossible! He can't be worked with!" (stated with high frustration and exasperation) it often helps them to hear their words back. To this client statement, we would likely respond, "That's how bad it seems to you. You see that it's *impossible* to work with him." In many situations like this, our clients have responded something like, "Well it may not be impossible, but I've had enough of trying" (then decided to quit the relationship). Others have responded something like, "Well, it's not impossible. I have been thinking of a way to change his mind" (then proceeded to explore other possibilities). The point in making such a near-verbatim reflection was not to question the client's absolute thought (it should not be made with a questioning tone) but to let the client hear her own words and tone to fully realize her experience. Whether the situation is workable or not should remain your client's decision. Her best decision will come about through the counseling process of providing therapeutic listening (especially with empathy and unconditional positive regard). It is your role to focus on your client and her communications, without second-guessing, and to trust the process of therapeutic listening.

The following very useful application of verbatim reflection comes to mind from Jeff's work: I was working with a client whose daughter was getting married about a six-hour drive away. His mother had health concerns that made it difficult for her to travel and apparently seemed to manipulate and impose herself on her son (my client). He had made arrangements for his mother's travel and for her physical and personal care during the wedding. However, his mother refused those arrangements and insisted on traveling with her son to the wedding. My client very much wanted not to have to take care of his mother during the wedding. He wanted to enjoy the event and be focused on his daughter. At one point he was so exasperated that he shouted, "God, I hate her!" So I reflected almost as strongly, "You just hate her!" My client then quickly changed his communication and explained to me that he could never hate his mother. I accepted this by saying, "Oh, I misunderstood. You would never really hate your mother." The next session, my client explained that he had thought a lot about whether he did feel hate for his mother and that he certainly didn't want to hate her. These thoughts prompted him to set a firm limit with his mother; he told his mother that she could either accept the travel arrangements made for her or miss the wedding. My client explained that he had discovered he loved his mother, himself and his daughter. While he wanted his mother to attend the wedding, he was most concerned that he be there to help his daughter if needed and to enjoy the time, especially since he was confident that his mother did not actually need to depend on him that weekend. He continued to find situations in which he had thought others absolutely needed him, but he came increasingly to find that they could also be OK without him when he needed time or energy for himself.

Focus Reflections on Your Client's Main Point or the Things Most Emotionally Laden for Your Client

A common troubling issue for beginning counselors in approaching the 25/75 ratio is which communications to reflect. Your clients will often say a string of things in order to make one point. You cannot reflect everything. You must choose from a client's many communications, and you need to choose very quickly, in a way that will come to be automatic and natural with practice. Your choices will influence the next communications from your client. Clients tend to say more about the parts of their communications that you have reflected. So, reflect the heart of your client's communication, meaning: Reflect the part of the client's communication that seemed most meaningful to the client, most emotionally laden.

Don't let thinking about these choices take you off your focus on your clients and their experience. If your heart and mind are in the right place but you make a wrong decision, it will be inefficient, but there will be no harm to your therapeutic relationship. So you may wish to remember a quote that has often been helpful to our students and us: *As long as your* intent *is to understand your clients and their communication, there is no penalty for being wrong* (Eric J. Hatch, personal communication).

Be Prepared for and Accept Corrections

In the previous case example of the client traveling to his daughter's wedding, Jeff was corrected for stating a reflection that was almost verbatim. When corrected, it did not matter whether Jeff's statement had been actually correct or not. Whether you have actually misunderstood your client or your client thinks you have the respectful and efficient thing to do is to simply accept the correction. The correction becomes the client's communication. In the "going to the wedding" example, once Jeff's client told him that he could never hate his mother, that statement became the important piece of communication. Not to accept this would have been disrespectful and would have meant that Jeff had stopped listening to his client.

The Issue of Interruptions

You will need to interrupt clients in order to reflect. Many clients speak rapidly, moving from one topic to another without pause for you to reflect. Sometimes this is because they are nervous and talk or ramble in a fast pace when they are nervous. Sometimes clients seem to do this because they are afraid that if they give their counselor time to think and respond, the response will be critical. Most clients don't pause for you to reflect because they don't have any way to know that that is what you intend to do.

Interrupting is sometimes difficult. We, and many of our students, were taught as children that interrupting is disrespectful. Yet, in counseling, if you don't reflect, it will be difficult for your clients to know that you understand or respect them. One of your primary functions in therapeutic listening is to help your clients more fully understand themselves and their communications, thoughts, and feelings. To do this, you must reflect.

Further, especially for beginning counselors, if you let your client communicate a great deal to you before reflecting, it may overwhelm your ability to listen, comprehend, and remember. If your intent is to briefly reflect your understanding of the heart of what your client has told you, your interruption will enhance, rather than stunt, your client's communication to you. If you interrupt with an intention other than reflecting the heart of your client's communication, it may signify that you see your responses as more important than your client's communication. This would stunt your client's continued communication.

Assuming your client does not naturally leave you a space to reflect, interrupt to reflect once a point is made that seems to have felt significant to your client. However, there are exceptions to almost every rule. One of Jeff's adult clients came and told him that she had remembered sexual abuse from her childhood. She made it clear, first with her body language, then with a direct statement, that she felt she needed to get the whole story out without stopping. He respected her decision for her use of the time and made very few reflections in her session.

A more common situation is the client who continues to talk rapidly, with few pauses. In such situations, ready yourself to gear up to this client's pace as much as possible, to make your reflections very short, and to make them while your client is still talking. For example, if your client is rapidly explaining multiple sides to a decision and seems to be describing himself as feeling torn or pulled in many directions, you may reflect as he continues to speak, reflecting single words or phrases with empathy and in his tone, like "torn," "so pulled," "you know you want that," "that is what you fear." Such sessions come to be as if you and your client are improvising music together. Your client provides the main melody, while you provide short phrases that repeat and underscore parts of that melody. When watching or listening to a recording of a session that you think is like this, you can check to see that your work is effective by noticing that your client does hear you, even though he does not stop talking, and that your underscoring parts of the melody help develop the song that you both are making, which is really his song, with you playing backup. One way or another, usually in easier ways than those described here, each client and you will develop a rhythm of communication and reflection that is natural and unique to the two of you together.

Balance

From the issue of interruptions, we need to consider questions of balance. Remember, what you are communicating through listening therapeutically is: "I understand," or "I am listening/striving to understand," all with warmth that also communicates "I care." This way of being will encourage your client's continued and deepening communication. So, your goal is to communicate your understanding or listening, without having the amount that you interrupt to reflect inhibit your client's communication. Often we find this means less frequent reflections than most beginning counselors expect. Often beginning counselors set out to work too hard, while working easy and giving your client time to communicate can be more efficient than working hard.

Allow Your Clients to Own Most Silences

There are quite a few good reasons why a client may fall silent after you reflect. She may be thinking of the next thing to say or to say it. She may be girding her strength to tell you something very emotional or that is difficult for her. She may have been taken aback, surprised by the reflection she heard from you. She may be taking a valuable moment to sit with a feeling or thought, to experience it fully. She may simply, naturally communicate at a pace slower than natural to you. In these cases, it may have seemed to her that there was not a silent moment at all.

Counselors sometimes feel awkward with silent moments and either believe that their clients are much more uncomfortable with silent moments than they actually are and/or believe that they, as counselors, should be doing something to fill the silences. Remember that if clients fall silent after you have reflected, then it is not your turn to communicate again until they have. An easy, if overly simple, quote to remember for this is, *the client owns the silence.*

It is also important to realize that the talk is only part of the communication in a counseling session. So, if in a silent moment after you reflected, your client looks at you with enlarged eyes and raised eyebrows, then shrugs his shoulders and turns his palms up to you, this is *not* silence. Your client has probably communicated something like, "You are not saying anything. I don't know what to do next, yet I think I should do something and I feel uncomfortable." To those highly communicative gestures, you could reflect something like, "We've fallen silent and something seems to feel uncomfortable to you about that."

In later chapters, we discuss providing questions or other help to clients who seem slow to start and are very uncomfortable with the slowness. But for now, we ask you to work to see how far you can go in facilitating communication through allowing most silences.

Consider another example from Jeff's work: I remember a time when I was too quick with such an assumption. I was counseling a young man who was struggling with an important decision, over which he felt very anxious. He had put it off for a long time and was now under pressure to decide soon. We were developing into a rhythm in which he would tell me a part of his decision process or an aspect of his situation, I would reflect, then he would fall silent for 2–5 minutes. I misunderstood his facial expression and body language in an early one of these silences. My mistake was because of my awkwardness with silence and the thought that I should end it. It was also because I hadn't realized the emotional impact the decision had for him. So, I interrupted a silent moment to say, "We've fallen silent and I gather you are uncomfortable with that." The look on his face then turned to surprise and mild irritation. He explained, "No, I wasn't uncomfortable with *that*, I'm uncomfortable *with the decision*." That was a clear sign for me to learn to wait my turn. I came to understand the function of counseling for him around this decision as follows. Because he felt anxious around the decision, when he was away from counseling he avoided the anxiety by avoiding thinking it through. He came to counseling to discuss and contemplate the decision. In the silences, he was thinking and feeling about the decision fully. So, those silent moments were very much what he needed from counseling. We continued in our rhythm for several sessions while he made his decision.

Therapeutic Listening Differs from Listening Outside of Counseling

It is important at this juncture to revisit the fact that therapeutic listening is very rare outside of counseling. Loved ones, friends and family usually listen to emotional communications only for fleeting moments, if at all, before attempting solutions, reassurance, or shifting the conversation with "me, too" statements. When loved ones, friends, and family discuss emotionally laden situations, there is often a fairly equal give and take, a sharing of experiences related to the topic. This can be very helpful. We often learn from the sharing of experiences and the guidance of significant others in our lives, but that is not counseling.

How and Why Listening Therapeutically Works

It is partly the vast differences from conversing with loved ones, family and friends that makes therapeutic listening therapeutic. The very fact that your clients have met with you, a counselor and person who responds differently, helps them to begin to shift away from troubling habits, patterns, and ways of being.

Therapeutic listening prompts clients to focus on their situation, and their experience of it, rather than others' thoughts and feelings about their experience or others' stories of their similar, but different experiences. Especially when experiencing anxiety, we humans often avoid thinking through the anxiety-provoking situations. Anxiety can be quite uncomfortable, so we avoid it. This sometimes takes the form of thinking a lot about the situation, but unproductively thinking the same thoughts over and over. When addressing the issue of silences previously, Jeff gave the example of a young man who used therapeutic listening in counseling to keep himself focused on a decision that made him anxious—one that, outside of counseling, he worried over but did not think through or make progress toward.

Your therapeutic listening will let your clients know you are right there with them, even when they communicate and experience emotions that are very scary to them. As you listen, your clients can and will take opportunities to face thoughts and feelings about themselves that they have avoided and kept hidden from themselves. As you listen, your clients face these thoughts and feelings with true responsibility for themselves, yet with you. You are there with them, experiencing with them, yet not protecting them from their emotions and full experience, even if they fear their emotions, and even when the emotions hurt.

As in the example that Jeff gave under verbatim reflections, clients increase their self-awareness and insight through therapeutic listening. In that example, Jeff's client became aware of his strong irritation and of feeling trapped by his mother's behavior. His insight was that he was not satisfied with his relationship with his mother, it was hurting other relationships, and it was possible to make changes. He made changes in his relationship with his mother especially, but also in relationships with others.

It is important to add here that while insight is often a by-product of therapeutic listening, it is not the goal and may be overrated. This is especially true if insight is misconstrued as analysis. An example of analysis as a mistaken goal of counseling came to us as a counselor strove to help her client understand that he was angry and that he lashed out at others because he was humiliated by his father. Although the analysis sounded highly plausible to us, the client did not accept it. He didn't agree that he was angry and lashing out at others. Further, he seemed to feel humiliated to have such an analysis suggested. Finally, after his counselor pushed the possibility, he accepted the analysis, but he still felt humiliated and still acted angrily.

A research project underscored to us the fact that insight (especially if referring to analysis) may be overrated. In this research, one of our former students provided person-centered play therapy to adults with developmental disabilities. Based on these clients' IQs, there was no possibility of intellectual insight, at least as many of us may think of it. The clients had minimal verbal abilities. Yet, through their counselor being tuned in to them, listening therapeutically to their communications through their actions and play, and through their emotional connection with him, they made behavioral and emotional progress that was important to them and to their caregivers (Demanchick, Cochran, & Cochran, 2003).

Therapeutic listening works because it is empowering. Through listening therapeutically, your behavior tells your clients that you value them and their experience, that you have faith in them and their movement toward self-actualization.

What's Difficult about Listening—Common Problems in Listening for Beginning Counselors

Common Interfering Thoughts

One of the basic difficulties is tuning in to the speaker. We must strive to quiet our minds during sessions. Often the voices in the minds of beginning counselors say things like, "What should I reflect? Is my client OK? Does my client like and respect me as counselor?" Such thoughts may be inevitable in the beginning. In most cases when they occur, your job is to refocus your attention on your client and on listening to your client's experience. The following may help you with these commonly interfering thoughts.

What should I reflect?

We gave our answer to what to reflect through our list of dos and don'ts (item: focus your reflections on your client's main point, or the things communicated that seemed most important, most emotionally laden to your client). When you are listening, this main point will automatically occur to you. So state what occurs to you and remember that *as long as your* intent *is to understand your client and her communication, there is no penalty for being wrong* (Eric J. Hatch, personal communication).

And you may be able to make your decision of what and when to reflect on an emotional level. As the most emotionally laden communication is important to reflect, study empathy through the coming chapters. When you feel strong emotion hit you from your client, let that be your prompt to reflect.

Is my client OK?

We will address the challenge of assessing for imminent danger and managing crises within your therapeutic relationship in Chapter 10. However, brief guidance on this question follows, as it often interferes with listening: Remember that your clients are letting you know if they are OK or not OK in their communication to you. Listen and you will know. Then, when a client has given you reason to be concerned over imminent danger, let that client know your concern and that you are working to assess her safety while listening.

Does my client like and respect me as counselor?

This is not something counselors need to wonder about. As you listen to your clients, your clients will let you know their experience of counseling with you. For example, if your client seems eager to tell you more, then your client likely feels encouraged by your therapeutic listening. If after you reflect, your client gives you a disgruntled look, you may next reflect, "Something seemed to bother you about my last statement."

In reviewing recordings of your sessions, you may learn that your clients seem to be making progress in moving toward the heart of what they have to say. For example, a client's communication may progress from speculations about the future to who he is now, how he is in relationships now, what he is not satisfied with, and how he wishes to be different in relationships. Another client's communication may progress from missing a deceased parent to feeling guilt when thinking he does not live up to what he knew his parent's expectations were and feeling proud when he does live up to them.

Ultimately, it does not matter much whether your clients like and respect you. If counseling is particularly difficult for a client or a client does not yet see the value of counseling for himself, you may help him to hang in and work through the difficulty by explaining how his use of counseling can help him and therefore why you do what you do as his counselor (we address this skill in Chapter 8). While most of your clients will come to like and respect you, this is not a primary determinant of their progress. It's nice, but not necessary. The thing that's important is that your clients experience your genuine caring and concern (Cohen, 1994). Then, as you are consistently caring and concerned, your clients will come to know you that way.

Therapeutic Listening is Not Normal

Because therapeutic listening is very different from usual conversations, it can feel odd to beginning counselors. Some of our beginning students tell us they feel awkward and out-of-control with the skills. This out-of-control feeling makes perfect sense. When listening therapeutically, each counselor is in self-control but is exerting little control of the content of the session. That control is given in trust to clients and in trust that the process of counseling will go where each client needs to go. This is a leap of faith on the part of the counselor. You have to do it and have it work in order to *know* it works. With effort, skill, and the right intentions, you will experience success and your role in counseling will come to feel familiar, comfortable, and natural.

The Urge to Fix Immediately

Many counselors choose the counseling vocation out of a desire to help others. Many gravitate to it because they realize that others have frequently come to them with their problems and for advice. Thus, when faced with a client who is struggling or suffering, many beginning counselors are sorely tempted to give advice or take action to lead their client to a quick solution. However, to give advice or attempt a quick solution is equivalent to admitting to yourself and your client that you have given up faith in the counseling process and in your client. Such directing is disempowering to your client and inhibiting to the therapeutic relationship that the two of you need to form. We encourage you to take the leap of faith of therapeutic listening, then to keep the faith and see it through.

Sometimes Clients Want a Quick Fix

Sometimes clients want what they expect will be a quick fix (e.g., advice or some other magical problem-solving technique). A first step in such a situation is to acknowledge (or reflect) your understanding of your client's desire. For example, "That's how difficult this is for you. You want a solution *now!*" or "That's what you expected from counseling, that you could give me a description of the difficulties in your relationship, then I could give you advice on how to handle it." Very often in hearing their experience reflected, clients withdraw their request for guidance. When such a request continues to be what your client wants, you may then need to explain or re-explain how she may best use counseling (example explanations of therapeutic relationships can be found in Chapter 7). And in some cases, it is quite reasonable or wise and necessary to provide skills or informational guidance within your therapeutic relationship (see Chapters 13 and 14), but that is not a quick fix.

The Desire to Ask Informational Questions that are of Interest to You

Beginning counselors often feel a temptation to ask questions of interest to them—for example: "Where is your mom now?" "How old were you when your father died?" or "What were the circumstances then?" Sometimes such questions help to convey your interest. More often they imply that you are gathering the information that you know to be pertinent in order to produce the best solution or course of action. We think of clients' experiences as compelling novels. While we may want to know the end of the novel at the beginning or may want to know certain details of characters' lives, we may not know until the author presents the information. In the case of counseling, the controlling author is both the client and the counseling process, but not the counselor. With that said, if asking a question or two will help you maintain focus and engagement, at least until your patience grows through confidence in the counseling process, please do—as long as your goals and focus are therapeutic listening and understanding.

Stories

In wanting their clients to make progress quickly through therapeutic listening, our students often worry that their clients are telling stories of others, rather than telling what their own experience is. We often tell students that everyone's stories are ultimately about themselves. As we tell you little stories of our interactions with students or clients, we are inadvertently telling you that we see ourselves as good teachers and counselors. As we strive to address all critical aspects of counseling skills, we convey investment in your success with efficient counseling skills. Jeff had an uncle whose stories usually included someone having wronged him. Thus, his stories conveyed that the world seemed unfair to him. We had another relative who often told disgustedly of others who are lazy. It seems she did not approve of laziness.

From our interests and expertise in counseling children, we know that highly significant parts of a child's counseling may be a battle in a sand tray between opposing forces or may be a dollhouse play with robbers and rescuers. In these situations, the counselor may never know just what the play says about the child. It usually does not matter. What matters is experiencing the story with your client and responding to the emotion of your client's experience. We will address this empathic connection through stories and other communications in later chapters.

Returning to Important Communications

Sometimes clients say things that seem very emotionally important to them only to move on to other communications before their counselor has the opportunity to reflect. Our students sometimes want to help their clients focus on the communication that seemed most important by asking/directing them to go back to the topic that seemed more important and to tell them more. While the direction may be useful, the way of doing it can be disempowering to clients. It is as if the client is communicating freely, following her impulses and intuition, coming to trust herself and this process, then her counselor breaks in to say through his question/directive, "I know better than you what is important for you to talk about. So talk about ___."

A more empowering way to help a client go back to what seemed important to her would be a reflection like, "A moment ago when you spoke of your loss, it seemed important to you—you seemed to have strong feelings, then you changed the subject." From a reflection like this, the client may see that she does want to go back to the topic that was emotional, she may come to see that she routinely changes the subject from emotional topics, or she may correct her counselor in explaining something like, "Yeah, when I think about the loss it hurts, but the most important thing for me is to focus on what I'm going to do now." Whichever the client's choice and experience, it is the counselor's job to listen to that next communication.

Multitasking with Therapeutic Listening

Every other task in counseling is in addition to therapeutic listening, never instead of. In upcoming chapters you will add the skills of experiencing and expressing empathy; establishing and striving to maintain unconditional positive regard; working to ensure that your listening, empathy and positive regard are genuine; helping clients get started; structuring and explaining counseling; assessing for progress; managing crises; and more. We hope this list does not sound daunting, but rather inspires you to practice therapeutic listening more often, both before and while adding more and more skills.

Activities and Resources for Further Study

- Now that you have read about and contemplated complexities of listening therapeutically, try the Focus Activity for this chapter again. Notice how the qualities of your listening have changed. Repeat the exercise until you are satisfied with your proficiency for the time being.
- Advancing from the previous activity, practice real-time therapeutic listening. Have a speaker (a classmate, peer) talk to you about a topic that has at least some emotional content. Follow the dos and don'ts list and the guidance that you have read for in this chapter. You may have one or more observers as well; they can give you feedback on your effectiveness and suggestions for improving. Begin with short practice sessions, 10–20 minutes, and expand to full-length practice sessions of 50 minutes.
- Journal or essay about difficulties in your development that you anticipate through practice, from readings and from experiences with initial clients with therapeutic listening practices. Be specific and give examples of these difficulties, whether hypothetical or actual. Address what it is about you that may prompt these difficulties. Explain what you are doing and will do to work through these difficulties.
- Do the same for your anticipated and experienced strengths with therapeutic listening.
- Look back at the primary skill objectives and review or practice until you see that you have mastered each to your satisfaction. Perfection is not necessary and perhaps not possible, as you may always be working to perfect these core skills.

References

Cohen, J. (1994). Empathy toward client perception of therapist intent: Evaluating one's person-centeredness. *Person-Centered Journal, 1*, 4–10.

Demanchick, S.P., Cochran, N.H., & Cochran, J.L. (2003). Person-centered play therapy for adults with developmental disabilities. *International Journal of Play Therapy, 12*, 47–65.

Schuster, R. (1979). Empathy and mindfulness. *Journal of Humanistic Psychology, 19*, 71–77.

Pre-Chapter Quotes

Barrett-Lennard, G.T. Listening. (1988). *Person-Centered Review, 3*, 410–425 (p. 410).

John Wayne and Louis Armstrong quoted in E.M. Beck (Ed.), J. Bartlett (compiler) (1980). *Familiar quotations* (15th ed.). Boston, MA: Little, Brown & Company (p. 870; p. 847).

3 STRIVING FOR EMPATHY

Emotion is the chief source of all becoming-conscious. There can be no transforming of darkness into light and of apathy into movement without emotion.

Carl Jung

When the eyes of the heart open, we can see the inner realities hidden behind the outer forms of this world. When the ears of the heart are open, we can hear what is hidden behind words; we can hear truth.

Fadiman and Frager

I learn by feeling . . . what is there to know?

Theodore Roethke

Primary Skill Objectives

- Develop a beginning understanding of what empathy is and what it is not. (A full understanding can come only through experiencing, receiving, and providing empathy.)
- Develop a beginning understanding of how and why empathy gives power to counseling and is a healing force.
- Be able to explain the purposes and functions of empathy in counseling.
- Make significant progress in your ability to empathize. (Complete progress in this ability is a lifelong endeavor.)
- Identify what does, or might in the future, prevent your full empathy.
- Begin working to overcome the factors that prevent your full empathy.

Focus Activity

You must experience empathy before you can express it. Attempts to use words to express empathy sometimes get in the way of beginning counselors' ability to experience empathy. So, odd as this activity for experiencing empathy may seem, we urge you to work through it.

Videotape and/or have a third partner observe this focus activity. Have a partner communicate to you on a topic that has at least some emotional content for him/her. You are to listen and strive for empathy. The speaker may use words to communicate to you. You may not speak in response. We urge you not to try to convey your empathy but also to make no attempt to hide it. Your task is to simply be with the person who is communicating to you and strive to feel what that person feels. We use the word "simply" to imply that this is your *only* task, not that it is an *easy* task. It may help you to be aware that empathy is not restricted to big, dramatic emotions. It is also used for the normal flow of emotions through all of us humans and can be seen in all of our communication and being.

If you catch yourself thinking of a solution to your partner's problem while he/she communicates to you, you have strayed from empathy and listening. If you catch yourself thinking of similar situations in your life, you have strayed from empathy and listening. If you catch yourself thinking of the word for what your partner feels, you have strayed from empathy and listening. When you catch yourself straying in these ways, know that it is normal and inevitable, and then refocus yourself to feel what your partner feels. Seeking pure empathy in this exercise may frustrate you just like a meditation that focuses your mind on a single thought or mental behavior. Yet, in this case, rather than a single mental behavior, your task is to focus on a single emotional behavior. An irony is that once you realize you are on track with empathy, you are no longer on track. Pure empathy is purely feeling with the person communicating to you.

We estimate that you will need about 10 minutes of listening to your partner while you strive for empathy to learn well from this activity. More than 10 minutes would ask too much of the speaker. Less than 10 minutes will not give you enough practice time to contemplate. As usual, we suggest your partner be a classmate or other student of counseling and related fields.

After the session, journal and discuss what was difficult for you as you strove for empathy. Journal and discuss at what points your empathy felt pure and at what points you strayed. Ask your partner if he or she can remember the points in communication in which he/she felt/thought your empathy was pure and when you had strayed. Ask the same of your observing partner. It may be helpful to review video of the practice session together. When you review your video, check for moments when it seemed your empathy was pure and when you strayed. Then consider what you looked or felt like or what other indicators there might have been when your empathy was pure and when it strayed.

After the activity, journal and discuss what you have learned. Address what seems to get in the way of empathy for you. This could be certain subjects or emotions; it could be your urge to solve the other person's problem or tell about yourself; it could be unrelated thoughts that pop into your mind. After addressing what gets in the way for you, describe the signs (i.e., thoughts, feelings, physical sensations, facial expressions, posture, gestures) that you may be able to use to indicate to yourself when you have strayed from empathy. Describe the signs that let you know you are experiencing empathy.

Introduction

For something that occurs naturally, empathy can be very hard. We do not expect your work in the focus activity to have come easily. We see empathy as both so often difficult to provide, yet so crucial to counseling that we have separated this chapter, "Striving for Empathy," from the next, "Expressing Empathy." We want you to spend more time in the study of this crucial skill. We do not want you to confuse the behaviors of expressing empathy with the skill of experiencing empathy and letting it be felt within you.

Additionally, in our skill objectives we have indicated that you are beginning what may be your ongoing path to providing strong empathy. For us and for many we know, developing empathy and our ability to express it is a lifelong and continually rewarding path. From this chapter, we expect you to begin to understand the power of empathy, while fuller understanding will come in the experience of providing empathy in counseling relationships. We expect you to make significant progress in your ability to have and express empathy. We expect you to identify and begin overcoming factors that prevent you from experiencing fuller empathy. Once it is well begun, your growing empathy can be a steady-flowing, ever-unfolding and joyful endeavor.

What Empathy Is and Isn't

Understanding What Empathy Is by Considering What It Is Not

Empathy is not a thought process. If you try to think of what another person is feeling, you have taken yourself away from empathy, away from connection with the other person, and into the separate world of your thoughts. Babies know what others feel and react to it. If parents are upset, their baby will know and react, even if the parents keep themselves from crying, yelling, or otherwise showing their stress. In times like this, many babies will cry or react with emotion. For those who don't cry, if you watch closely, you can see them tense up and become watchful and wary. Symphonies evoke strong feelings in listeners without using words. Music scholars can often tell you what tools were used to convey these emotions. Yet listeners feel the emotions even without the intellectual skills to figure out what the composer may have meant to convey and how.

Jeff remembers a moment from childhood that helps him remember that empathy is not a thought process: My grandparents had a horse named Tony. I hadn't been around horses much, so I was a little afraid of him. Tony was gentle, but *so* big. We were going to saddle Tony up when my grandfather told me not to be afraid around Tony because he would know it and then get skittish and jumpy. I did my best to talk myself out of my fear, reminding myself how gentle Tony was. I replaced some of my fear with remembering how much I loved Tony. Still, I was a little scared and after what my grandfather had told me, I watched Tony. I saw that he was a little skittish around me. I remember wondering, how could Tony know I was afraid? It was especially confusing since I thought I was pretty good at hiding fear and couldn't see how my interactions with him were that different from my cousins, who were more used to horses.

If horses and babies feel with others and experience empathy, then empathy must be a natural occurrence and one that requires only basic preverbal awareness. Indeed, thought may be what dilutes the clarity of empathy. Our students sometimes ask us early in their work what they can do to develop their empathy and tell us that it does not seem natural to them. We see that their task is less one of developing their empathy skills and more one of dropping the things they do that get in the way of empathy. Empathy is natural to babies. As people grow up, their ability to reason develops. We get so enamored with our ability to think that we try to use reasoning for all of life's tasks. It is as if we have discovered what a versatile and powerful tool a hammer is and we try to use it to replace a window—it can work for getting the old glass out but not for putting the new glass in. Thus, we stop developing our natural skills for empathy, and even hold back furthering developing these skills. However, once persons begin to attend to their skills in empathy, these skills begin to grow again rapidly.

Empathy also is not sympathy. Sympathy is what we feel *for* others, rather than *with* them. When we know a friend has had a loved one die, we feel great sorrow and sadness for that friend. This is because we assume, often from similar personal losses, how badly our friend probably feels. Such sympathy can feel supportive, but it is not empathy. Persons experiencing such a loss feel sets of emotions unique to themselves and their situation, which might include sorrow, relief, anger, guilt and other emotions. Both sympathy and empathy convey caring, but they convey different messages of understanding. In this case, sympathy conveys, "I understand how badly it hurts to have a loved one die," while empathy conveys, "I understand you through sensitively being with what you feel right now."

There is growing neuroscience research to support the understanding of empathy as an automatic, non-calculated knowing of what the other is experiencing (Watson & Greenberg, 2009), including the notions of mirror neurons in humans and primates (Decety & Lamm, 2009) and automatic, beneath-conscious processing deep in the brain's amygdalae (Ohman, 2002). Yet Siegel (2012) makes it clear that while we can know that there is much that we do not know about the brain, clearly we are hard-wired for relationships and knowing what each other feel. In this chapter and others to follow, we encourage you to work to understand and value empathy in practice, to grow your capacity for empathy—or readiness, as your capacity may already be strong, when accessed. And we encourage you to explore your thought and feeling patterns that may get in the way of your capacity for empathy.

Intricacies of Empathy

From our thoughts on what empathy is not, we see that it is deeply feeling what another person feels in a given moment in that person's unique life experience. Rogers (1980) described empathy as meaning that "the therapist senses accurately the feelings and personal meanings that the client is experiencing, and communicates this understanding to the client" (p. 116). Further, empathy means "to sense the client's private world as if it were your own but without ever losing the 'as if' quality" (Rogers, 1957, p. 99). We take the phrases "personal meaning" and "private world" to clarify that while empathy is deeply feeling with another person, it also indicates a totality of experiencing with the other person. So more broadly, empathy means fully experiencing another's world. The other person's emotions are key, but empathy also includes thoughts, beliefs and perceptions; actions; and the interplay between emotions, thoughts and actions. Empathy is experiencing the inner world of another, the other person's full and unique personal experience.

The phrase "without ever losing the 'as if' quality" is also important, as empathy does not mean to lose your self in being only a mirror to others. Rather, empathy takes place between two separate persons while one is striving to experience with the other. Consider this longer quote from Rogers (1980) on empathy, which helps explain the delicate balance of remaining yourself in your counseling sessions while fully experiencing with your client:

> An empathic way of being with another person means entering the private perceptual world of the other and becoming thoroughly at home in it. It involves being sensitive, moment by moment, to the changing felt meanings that flow in this other person, from the fear or rage or tenderness or confusion or whatever he or she is experiencing. It means temporarily living in the other's life, moving about in it delicately without making judgments—it means sensing meanings of which he or she is scarcely aware, but not trying to uncover totally unconscious feelings, since this would be too threatening. It includes communicating your sensing of the person's world as you look with fresh and unfrightened eyes at elements of which he or she is fearful—You are a confident companion to the person in his or her inner world.

(p. 142)

Bernard Guerney (2002) refers to the level of empathy that we wish for you in your counseling as *deep empathy*, explaining that this shared experience is so strong that your empathic responses may sometimes include "the next emotion that the speaker might have said . . . the next wish or desire, or the conflict underlying what the person has told you, but did not verbalize" (p. 3). He explains that it is better to strive for deep empathy and risk being wrong than to maintain accurate but pedantic active listening (paraphrasing what your clients have said), with no risk of being wrong but also with no empathic connection.

Empathy is what makes therapeutic listening powerful. Empathy is what takes therapeutic listening beyond just words, beyond mere paraphrasing. Reflective listening without empathy is a parody of counseling. It might be the outward behaviors of counseling but is still not counseling.

A Sample of the Preponderance of Literature Clarifying the Power of Empathy

Carl Rogers was the first to introduce the helping professions to empathy in a big way, introducing it as a key factor in the core conditions of counseling (including empathy, unconditional positive regard and genuineness) (Rogers, 1957). We owe a great debt to Rogers and other thinkers, writers and practitioners in the person-centered approach for this contribution and its ongoing development.

Research and professional literature in the helping professions has repeatedly confirmed the importance of the core conditions for therapeutic relationships. In their research review, Orlinsky and Howard (1978) concluded that there is substantial evidence in support of the relationship between clients' perception of the core conditions and outcome in counseling. Other authors reviewing research seem to concur (Bergin & Lambert, 1978; Cooper, Watson, & Holldampf, 2010; Elliott, 2002). Meta-analyses (careful designs for the study of results from large numbers of existing studies) suggest that therapists' qualities, such as the core conditions and especially empathy, are crucial to and predominate explanations of counseling successes (e.g., Bohart, Elliott, Greenberg, & Watson, 2002; Elliott, Bohart, Watson, & Greenberg, 2011; Lambert & Okiishi, 1997; Luborsky et al., 1986; Wampold, 2001, 2006). Patterson (1984) concluded in his review that "the evidence for the necessity . . . of the [core conditions] is incontrovertible" (p. 437). Recent studies continue to suggest the importance of empathy in a variety of ways, across client–counselor populations and settings (e.g., Cochran, Cochran, Fuss, & Nordling, 2010; Cochran, Cochran, Nordling, McAdam, & Miller, 2010; Cochran, Cochran, & Sherer, 2012; Cochran, Fauth, Cochran, Spurgeon, & Pierce, 2010; Kwon & Jo, 2012; Moyers & Miller, 2013; Vanaerschot & Lietaer, 2007).

While the core conditions, especially empathy, can be seen as effective in and of themselves, they are valued across widely differing theories of counseling. From their review of empirical studies, Keijsers, Schaap and Hoogduin (2000) concluded that the core conditions are clearly associated with successful outcome in CBT. From meta-analysis, Bohart et al. (2002) concurred that empathy may be particularly important to outcome in CBT. Further, Haaga, Rabois and Brody (1999) concurred that CBT works best for therapists who convey empathy clearly to their clients. Linehan (1997) described empathy as a key element in dialectical behavior therapy; Kohut (1984) as a centerpiece in self-psychology; Scharf (1996), its importance in Adlerian therapy; and May (1989) and Havens (1986) from an existential perspective. Duan, Rose and Kraatz (2002) summarized that because empathy is the basis for understanding, one can conclude that no effective intervention can take place without empathy, and all effective interventions must be empathic.

From recent analysis of dozens of individual studies and multiple existing meta-analysis, Elliott et al. (2011) concluded that "The most robust evidence is that clients' perceptions of feeling understood . . . relate to outcome;" and that "An empathic stance . . . [is essential] regardless of theoretical orientation, treatment format, and severity" (p.47). Further, "because research has shown empathy to be inseparable from other relational conditions, . . . [empathy should be offered] in the context of positive regard and genuineness;" yet Elliott et al. assert in conclusion that empathy is both "an 'ingredient' of a healthy therapeutic relationship, as well as a specific, effective response that promotes strengthening of the self and deeper exploration" (p.48).

There is also a renewed and growing interest in the importance of empathy in non-counseling relationships. This further evidences the power of empathy and also seems particularly relevant as counselors weave their skills through relationships at differing levels, foci and purposes in today's school and clinic settings (e.g., individual counseling; process-oriented or psycho-educational group counseling; parent, teacher, administrator, stakeholder or community consultation; classroom guidance or community-based mental health skill-teaching). Examples include the following. Blake and Garner (2000) noted the importance of empathy in teachers of students with behavior disorders; Sweeney and Whitworth (2000) for the success of beginning teachers; Clifford (1999) in the connection between mentor empathy and protégé teacher self-efficacy; Kountz (1998) for composition teachers assisting students in overcoming writing anxiety. The importance of empathy has been discussed in pastoral counseling, and within and between diverse faith communities (Augsburger, 1986; Everding & Huffaker, 1998; Kinast, 1984; McCarthy, 1992). Davis (2009) asserted the role of empathy for provider-patient relationships in health care; Neumann, Bensing, Mercer, Ernstmann, Ommen and Pfaff (2009) in outcomes of medical care. Lenaghan (2000) asserted the importance of teaching students empathy for understanding cultural differences; Lickona (2000) for preventing peer cruelty among children; Stanbury, Bruce, Jain and Stellern (2009) in reducing middle-school bullying. Cochran, Cochran and Hatch (2002) introduced an approach to empathic communication for conflict resolution among children. Kilpatrick, Bissonnette and Rusbult (2002) evidenced the connection of empathy to accommodating behaviors, including commitment level, in early married couples. Gillespie and Hunter (2008) asserted the role of empathy for parents in helping babies manage strong emotion; Brooks and Goldstein (2001) in developing children's resiliency; Laible, Carlo and Roesch (2004) in developing adolescent self-esteem.

The empathy-based approaches of filial therapy (Guerney, 2013) and relationship enhancement (Guerney, 1977) go far in clarifying the power of empathy in family relationships. Through filial therapy, parents learn to engage empathy in approximation of child-centered play therapy skills in special playtime with their own children. In relationship enhancement, couples gain closeness through learning to respond empathically to each other. The wide-ranging positive effects of filial therapy have been evidenced in meta-analysis by Bratton, Ray, Rhine and Jones (2005) and continues to be well researched (Baggerly, Ray, & Bratton, 2010; Cornett, 2013; Hetrich, 2013; Lim & Ogawa, 2014). The relationship enhancement model has been effectively applied in couples counseling (Ginsberg, 1997; Scuka, 2005) and in marriage/couples education (Ortwein & Guerney, 2008).

Why Empathy Is Powerful

Connecting at the Core and Shifting Self-Perception

Our emotions connect to our core selves. As empathy is an emotional, true and honest understanding of one person from another, it allows clients to explore deepest, darkest fears. At times in our lives, many of us seem to believe that if others really knew us, they would not like us. Fritz Perls (1970) described personalities as layered with a phony outer layer that hides the true self, then a phobic layer of catastrophic fears that if others saw our true selves, they surely would reject us. In other writing, we have illustrated how children with conduct-disordered behaviors (CD) often seem to believe that at their core they are unlovable and unlikable, so they act out to drive others away from understanding this core (Cochran & Cochran, 1999). In the classic film series in which Gloria served as client for three different therapists, demonstrating their theoretical approaches, she seemed to tell Rogers that if he really knew her, he would find her unlovable (Shostrom, 1965). So by providing empathy, we help our clients show us their true selves. Then, in expressing empathy, we help them recognize what it is that we see and experience. In the case of our conceptualization of children with CD, your clients may come to see that you really came to know them yet were not repulsed by what you saw and experienced.

When experiencing your empathic understanding of their core, some clients then decide they truly do not approve of what they see and hear from their counselor's expression of empathy and so make changes in themselves. Other clients decide that the rotten core they feared is really not so bad, that they are lovable as they are. When it happens this way, we think of sailors from before the time people knew much of what is within the dark ocean. When humans didn't know what was in the water, many imagined great monsters and felt great fear. Now that we know more, we know that there are things to fear, but there probably are no great sea serpents or other monsters. Another metaphor that comes to mind is a child who sees scary shadows in his dark room at night and imagines unseen dangers. Then, when a trusted adult helps him turn the light on, he discovers that it is only a coat thrown over a chair, or when searching under the bed with a flashlight, he learns there was no creature ready to grab him, just old dust and lint. Your empathy can be like turning on the light for your clients to see all there is to discover and to learn from their personal "dark shadows."

Joining on a Scary Journey

It is a scary thing to explore our hidden emotions and the deep recesses of our selves. Many of us heavily defend the secrecy of these parts of ourselves. Like sailing with our modern knowledge of oceans or spending first nights as a child in dark rooms with shifting shadows and imagined creatures under the bed, once it's been done a few times, we know we are all right and our fear diminishes. But part of what is so hard about these first few times is going into the scary unknown alone. Your empathy communicates to your clients, "I'm right here with you," while they search into their scary places and their deepest fears. We have had experience in accompanying children on outdoor adventures. In those experiences, the children's autonomy and self-responsibility grew, but it helped the children to meet their challenges for us to first communicate with our actions and even in our words, "I'm right here with you." As Rogers (1980) wrote, "You are a confident companion to the person in his or her inner world" (p. 142). Your empathic presence is your message, "I'm right here with you," that gives your clients the strength to look into the shadows. You, with your empathy, become your clients' opportunity to examine those parts of themselves that they might never explore alone.

It is important to add here that while you may share these explanations of the power of empathy with your clients, usually you won't. Most clients do this work without ever completely articulating what they and you are actually doing in their counseling. We add this note because explanations and examples of counseling are sometimes like highlight films of ball games. The highlights can make it seem like the whole game was ecstatically dramatic. Yet, viewing the whole game would show a lot of action that both appears mundane and was really hard work as players struggled to maintain their concentration. We want you not to feel discouraged when your and your clients' experience is long, hard work together, rather than just highlight film.

Self-Awareness

As you join your clients through empathy, they come to know themselves further, how they work, and why. Rogers (1980) explained, "As persons are empathically heard, it becomes possible for them to listen more accurately to the flow of their inner experiencing" (p. 116). We also think there is a modeling effect. As you, their counselor, attend to their inner experiencing through empathy, your clients will attend their inner experiences.

Self-Experience

Through your empathy, clients come to experience their emotions more fully and deeply. This fuller experience is quite durable once started. During or after sessions, it is often the level of emotion that clients feel that leads to action. Often, a person's level of experienced discomfort with a current situation needs to become greater than her fear of change in order to produce change. At other times, this fuller self-experience helps persons realize that the answers to dilemmas they have been unsuccessfully trying to solve through a logical analysis rest in their emotional response. For example, decisions for how to respond to others in relationships, whether to continue or begin a romance, often cannot be reasoned from the mind but can be decided based on understanding of what is in the heart.

A Profoundly Different Relationship—Challenging Self-Perceptions

Another power of deep and full empathy is that it is so rare. It is often the profound uniqueness and depth of an empathic counseling relationship that makes it powerful. As a child with conduct-disordered behaviors goes through life, he experiences the relationships that he expects. That child may expect to be disliked and so drives others away to avoid the pain of that rejection. In response to these behaviors, others do recoil from him. Yet, in an empathic counseling relationship you respond very differently. You respond to his feelings much more than to his actions. Thus, you see him not as a set of repulsive behaviors but as a person with feelings. Such a child will then experience a useful confusion. While his old self-statement sounded something like, "No one can love me. Everyone will reject me," your relationship begins to change that statement to one that sounds something like, "Well, I thought everyone would reject me, but my counselor didn't, and she really knew me." Such clauses in negative self-statements are the beginnings of great change in the emotions and behaviors driven by such statements.

Some clients enter counseling expecting to be told what to do, how to act, and how to be. Often, this is because such telling, whether subtle or blatant, permeates and defines relationships they have with others. If you don't offer them this same direction, it may present them with an anxiety-producing experience. If, in their other relationships, they are rescued from responsibility with direction, they will expect and want this from you. If you meet them with an empathic acceptance of the anxiety they experience, experiencing it fully with them rather than working to make it go away, they also experience a useful confusion and must face the challenge of reconciling your reaction to them and their anxiety with the very different experience they have had with others. Here, many clients seem to shift from a belief that says, "I am not capable and need others to decide for me," to one that says, "But my counselor, who seemed to really know me, didn't seem to believe I needed her to decide for me; she experienced my anxiety and didn't think we must work to make it go away." So many of the clients we have served have found this experience greatly empowering, although awkward at first. In a side note, some adolescents and adults may also need you to help them understand what the two of you can do in counseling and why they need to tolerate and experience this anxiety in order to work through it. We illustrate such situations and useful explanations in Chapter 8.

Joy in Connecting

We would like you to know that the power of empathy isn't just about pain. Many clients experience great joy in their counselor's empathy, as they realize their counselor "gets them." We have experienced a great many clients who took to empathy from their counselor like a thirsty person takes to water on a hot day.

Jeff recalls one such client: A young man that I served had great difficulty fitting in socially. His interests were certainly not with the mainstream. He often seemed to say and do the wrong thing socially. He very slowly came to explain that he knew he didn't fit in, that he hurt with loneliness, and that he feared he was missing out. He was only direct with such communications in furtive, brief moments. Most of his time in counseling was spent telling me of the things that interested him very much but that most people would not take the time to listen to. As I experienced excitement with the things that excited him, not necessarily because they excited me but because I felt his excitement, he seemed to come to experience joy and pride that someone "gets him," not always his interests, but him. His self-talk seemed to change from, "No one will understand me," to "Others may not understand my interest, but they may come to understand me." From this change, he moved on to a successful group counseling experience (a process group, in which persons come to interact and share themselves vs. a psycho-educational skill training group) and a general change in reaching out and risking letting others know him.

In Nancy's work with parents and children, she sometimes trains parents in filial therapy (Guerney, 2013), which includes teaching parents to play with their children with a strong quality of empathy and acceptance. As children involve their parents in their play, they are given a chance to express the inner workings of their worlds, minds, and hearts freely and without fear of correction or punishment. The joy in experiencing this connectedness with their parents becomes powerfully clear and can be a beautiful process to watch unfold. The look of the parents when the deep connection is working is sometimes described as "the filial glow." This "glow" is always evident when relationships are enhanced through deep connectedness. Seeing the parent–child connection during filial therapy helps us see that all relationships are opportunities to experience this "glow"—this connection of caring.

Furthering Communication and Connection

Providing empathy has the effect of clients wanting to tell you more and share more of themselves with you. As we think of ourselves receiving empathy, we know that we have felt warmly toward and satisfied with others who have come to understand us with empathy. We've felt motivated then to let them know more of our story, kind of like a storyteller who checks the audience's eyes for interest before deciding to let a story grow into the next, bigger, more revealing story. Empathy gives momentum to counseling. Still, getting your client to tell you more is only a side effect. The real point is for your clients to experience a connection with you in which they would like you to know more and more about them. The connection is worth more than the telling.

What Gets in the Way of Empathy

To experience empathy, you need to open yourself to others' feelings *and* to your own. As you come to feel more fully and be OK with that, you will become more ready to feel the emotions of others and to let what you feel with them be apparent in you. Your tolerance for emotions and their ambiguities and intensities will increase. Additionally, experiencing emotions with others will elicit emotions in you that will include both the emotions of your clients and those unique to you. You may remember similar experiences in your life and feel your own hurt that is unique to you and not of your clients. You may fear for the further pain that your clients seem destined to experience, and you may worry for their safety. Experiences like that are not empathy but are part of the closeness that empathy brings.

Considering the need for you to develop your ability to feel your emotions and those of others more and more deeply, search the following barriers that can get in the way of empathy for what gets in the way of *your* empathy and how so. We find that many of these barriers still affect us, and since we are pleased with ourselves by this point in life, we certainly see no shame in identifying with these barriers. We challenge you to discover any other barriers to your empathy.

Habit

First, painful feelings tend to hurt, so we avoid them. It seems that in much of modern society we have developed many ways to avoid feelings. We have TV and Internet uses that take our minds off upsetting personal situations, drugs and alcohol used in attempts to obliterate painful emotions, posters of cute puppies that tell us to cheer up, and the option of keeping ourselves too busy to feel anything except the constant urge to hurry on to the next thing.

People get out of the habit of empathy and experiencing feelings just from becoming enamored with our ability to reason. For many of us, the ability to reason comes to seem a skill for all occasions. However, just as in life there are times when experiencing strong emotions may be problematic and limiting, overuse of the ability to reason is problematic and limiting in counseling. Reason is a useful tool, but like any tool, it is useful in some jobs and not in others. For a metaphor, money can fix many problems in life. If I need a car to get to work, money can help, but if I were lonely and wanted to find someone to love and be loved by, money could only help in peripheral ways, if at all.

Fear of Feelings

Beyond the basic avoidance of what hurts, many of us seem to become afraid to feel as we grow up. Some of this fear appears to be social programming from hearing such statements when emotional as "Big boys don't cry," "Don't be such a cry-baby," or in some harsher instances, "Dry it up or I'll give you something to cry about." Here, the fear of feeling seems to be a self-statement that sounds something like, "If I show strong emotions, I will actually show weakness and if others see this, I will feel ashamed, embarrassed, and that will be awful." Jeff relates a part of his experience with this:

> I have learned that for a time in life I felt anger instead of other emotions. I didn't cry. When others did, it was upsetting to me. When others cried, it seemed like an internal panic started in which sirens sounded, lights flashed, and a voice from a loudspeaker extorted me, "Do something! Can't you see they're crying?!" With much work, conscious effort, and help from loved ones and counselors, I have come to know that I can cry, even in front of others, and it's OK now; when others cry in my presence, I sometimes see just one flash of red light in my mind. I know it is the old alarm starting. I remind myself that the important thing is to be fully present with this person, which includes feeling what she or he feels. I sometimes also remind myself that this person, whether a loved one or client, can be OK feeling the feelings that produce her or his tears, and so will I.

We have known some persons to fear strong emotions and to recognize that their fear is based in a thought that once they begin feeling painful emotions, it will be like opening a floodgate; they will be overwhelmed and swept away. Many clients have told us thoughts similar to this, then used counseling as a safe place, a place where they are accepted but autonomous, on their own but not alone; a place to try letting themselves feel strong painful emotions and see what happens. For some of these clients, it was their diligent defense against painful emotions that kept them from connecting with others, kept them from feeling joyful emotions, kept them overly stressed and not well.

For many counselors, just like for some of the clients mentioned in our earlier section, "Why Empathy is Powerful," the fear is that our core is rotten and if we and others could see it, it would be known, and that would be a terrible thing. With a mindset like that, a counselor can be prohibited from feeling strong emotions with clients. Such a counselor can get a sense that emotions lead to our core, may even *be* our core. So, the empathy-prohibiting belief of this counselor could be that "Certainly, I must not feel." And the application of that belief would be, "So, instead of working to feel with clients, I must work to prevent or squelch strong emotions."

Misattributed Responsibility

Sometimes counselors mistakenly see themselves as responsible for a client's pain or at least responsible for making it go away. Since empathy leads to more and deeper emotions, it can seem like it causes them, but *cause* is the wrong word for it. A more fitting description is that empathy *allows* more and deeper emotions; it provides a safe place and time, with a listening ear.

Additionally, some counselors worry about errors in their empathy. Because empathy is assisted by but does not rely on emotions being described in words, there is the risk of being wrong, of perhaps going off on a tangent of feeling that is misshaped by your personal feelings separate from your client's. Some counselors worry that this would produce new feelings in their client. We encourage you to strive for accurate empathy, but to avoid letting concern over error inhibit your empathy. You may consider that meta-analytic research has suggested that empathic accuracy is, of course, important to counseling outcome, but less so than client perception of empathy (Elliott et al., 2011). Client perception of empathy comes much more from your *intent* and your *feeling with* your client than from your spoken description of your client's experience. Your empathy, even if wrongly expressed, will not cause significant emotions in your clients that were not already present beneath the surface, as long as your intent is empathy. Our guidance in Chapter 2 on therapeutic listening and in Chapter 4 on expressing empathy will help you avoid errors that take your client off-track from their needed emotional experience.

Rather than something to worry over, when a new feeling does develop in your client from your response, the new feeling simply becomes your client's next communication to you. For example, if you shed a tear of empathy with your client, your client may react by stopping her crying, feeling concern and guilt at thinking her situation has hurt you. When we have seen counselors respond with empathy to their client's concern and guilt, their new empathic response has proved a valuable learning experience to the client. In one such situation, the client learned just how much she tried to protect others, even her counselor, from feeling for her. She then experienced a strengthened motivation to be and feel who she is and to allow the same for others while being right there with them in their pain.

It is not the responsibility or even the purpose of the counselor to make feelings go away. Ironically, while persons often come to counseling to make painful feelings go away, and while that normally happens, suppressing feelings cannot be the purpose of counseling or it will greatly limit the potential of counseling. Emotions are useful to experience (i.e., discovering that you are lovable, not rotten; learning who you really are and what you want; making fully self-informed decisions) and can be destructive to suppress (i.e., remaining partially blind to your behaviors, their meanings, and relation to self; experiencing somatic pain from working so hard not to feel or show feelings). If you as counselor want too much to make your clients' painful feelings go away and are unable to be OK with what they feel, your empathy will be inhibited and your clients' suffering prolonged.

This is not to say that we would not also teach our clients skills for coping with painful emotions. But before doing so it is best to help your client understand what it is she is asking for, what alternative uses she can make of counseling, and the ramifications of taking such an approach in counseling. Chapter 8, in which we provide examples of explaining the use of counseling, will help with such situations. Then Chapters 13–15 can help you see how other counselor skills and tasks integrate into your core skills.

Letting Go of Control

Empathy requires partially letting go of control over what you feel. This can be scary, as it can threaten your believed/perceived need to be in control and stimulate fears of feeling. As your feelings follow your client's, you can reassert control at any moment by pulling back a little and becoming thoughtful. To be most efficient, your ideal should be to pull back in this way as little as possible. Rogers (1980) addressed this challenge to counselors:

> To be with another in this way [with empathy] means that for the time being, you lay aside your own views and values in order to enter another's world without prejudice. In some sense it means that you lay aside yourself; this can only be done by persons who are secure enough in

themselves that they know they will not get lost in what may turn out to be the strange or bizarre world of another, and that they can comfortably return to their own world when they wish.

(p. 143)

We wish for you to work steady at this crucial skill in order to be maximally helpful to a great many others. Our hopes are with you on this worthy path.

Activities and Resources for Further Study

- We have provided a great many activities, resources for further study and citations for this chapter. Understanding and expanding your capacity for empathy is crucially important to the success of your work and your ongoing development. Make time for as many of these activities as possible.
- Repeat the focus activity at the beginning of the chapter now that you have come to a greater understanding of empathy and potential barriers to empathy for you. We encourage you to repeat the activity as often as possible until you are satisfied with your consistency and learning. We especially urge you to take time after each practice to contemplate the barriers to empathy you experienced.
- This same exercise and others like it in this book present an opportunity in the role of speaker to develop your strength in feeling what you feel, learning what feelings come when you strive to express your feelings, or exploring through your communication your barriers to feeling your feelings and to empathy.
- We have known beginning counselors to benefit from watching their tapes while stopping themselves from evaluating their work and working solely to feel each client's emotions. This has helped them be ready both for the emotions that are thematic for that client and, in developing their empathy skills, to be more ready for all clients. Consider following this procedure with your tapes of practice sessions with peers/classmates.
- A variation is to review session tapes with the sound off with the sole purpose of feeling with the client in order to become less dependent on words.
- Another variation is to watch a well-acted movie segment, with or without sound, with the sole purpose of practicing empathy, feeling what the characters feel.
- The same could be done while listening to music, especially music without words and music that evokes a range of emotions, like many forms of classical music.
- To remember that you need not name the emotions (a cognitive, rather than empathic activity), you may want to practice or read about a form of meditation called *contemplation*, or "one-pointing"

(LeShan, 1974, p. 73). This approach is not the same thing as empathy, but it can help you master the skills required for empathy. In this approach, you are to contemplate an object without using words. It is difficult, as we humans are often so enamored of words and the naming of things, and it can be eye opening.

- We urge you to carefully read works by Carl Rogers and other writers and thinkers in the person-centered approach; and we encourage you to take a look at the *Person-Centered Journal* and the *Journal of Person-Centered and Experiential Psychotherapy*, as they often include articles discussing topics involving and related to empathy.
- While the focus on empathy may be strongest in the person-centered approach, the importance of empathy is relevant across theory and setting foci, so we also urge you to seek out the many discussions of empathy and its importance in various conferences and journals in the helping professions.
- We encourage you to review works by the National Institute for Relationship Enhancement (nire.org), as persons involved with that institute have done great work in operationalizing empathy in counseling, family, and other relationships.
- Review the Primary Skill Objectives of this chapter and see that you have mastered each to your satisfaction, for the moment. If you have not yet mastered them to your satisfaction, spend more time rereading and contemplating, and more time in practice, then carefully note areas in which you are dissatisfied to keep in mind for continued improvement through upcoming chapters.
- And last but not least in our values, seek a strongly empathic counselor for yourself, especially to give yourself the time to work through barriers to empathy and feeling fully.

References

Augsburger, D.W. (1986). *Pastoral counseling across cultures*. Philadelphia, PA: Westminster Press.

Baggerly, J.N., Ray, D.C., & Bratton, S.C. (2010). *Child-centered play therapy research: The evidence base for effective practice*. Hoboken, NJ: Wiley.

Bergin, A.E., & Lambert, M.J. (1978). The evaluation of therapeutic outcomes. In S.L. Garfield & A.E. Bergin (Eds.), *Handbook of psychotherapy and behavior change* (2nd ed.) (pp. 139–189). New York: John Wiley.

Blake, C.R.L., & Garner, P. (2000). "We may give advice but we can never prompt behavior": Lessons from Britain in teaching students whose behaviour causes concern. ERIC Document Reproduction Service No. 442209.

Bohart, A.C., Elliott, R., Greenberg, L.S., & Watson, J.C. (2002). Empathy. In J. Norcross (Ed.), *Psychotherapy relationships that work* (pp. 89–108). New York: Oxford University Press.

Bratton, S., Ray, D., Rhine, T., & Jones, L. (2005). The efficacy of play therapy with children: A meta-analytic review of the outcome research. *Professional Psychology: Research and Practice, 36*, 375–390.

Brooks, R., & Goldstein, S. (2001). Raising resilient children: Fostering strength, hope, and optimism in your child ERIC Document Reproduction Service No. ED 449921.

Clifford, E.F. (1999). A descriptive study of mentor–protégé relationships, mentors' emotional empathic tendency, and protégés' teacher self-efficacy belief. *Early Childhood Development and Care*, 156, 143–154.

Cochran, J.L., & Cochran, N.H. (1999). Using the counseling relationship to facilitate change in students with conduct disorder. *Professional School Counseling*, 2, 395–403.

Cochran, J.L., Cochran, N.H., Fuss, A., & Nordling, W. (2010). Outcomes and process through stages of child-centered play therapy for a boy with highly disruptive behavior driven by self-concept issues. *Journal of Humanistic Counseling, Education & Development*, 49, 231–246.

Cochran, J.L., Cochran, N.H., & Hatch, E. (2002). Empathic communication for conflict resolution among children. *The Person-Centered Journal*, 9, 101–112.

Cochran, J.L., Cochran, N.H., Nordling, W., McAdam, A., & Miller, D. (2010). Monitoring two boy's processes through the stages of child-centered play therapy. *International Journal of Play Therapy*, 19, 106–116.

Cochran, J.L., Cochran, N.H., & Sherer, L.C. (2012). Unconditional positive regard and limits: A case study in child-centered play therapy and therapist development. *The Person-Centered Journal*, 19, 3–28.

Cochran, J.L., Fauth, D., Cochran, N.H., Spurgeon, S., & Pierce, L.M. (2010). Reaching the "unreachable:" Case descriptions of a person-centered experiential for highly aggressive youth. *Person-Centered and Experiential Psychotherapies*, 9, 302–320.

Cochran, N.H., Nordling, W., & Cochran, J.L. (2010). *Child-centered play therapy: A practical guide to developing therapeutic relationships with children*. Hoboken, NJ: Wiley.

Cooper, M., Watson, J.C., & Holldampf, D. (Eds.) (2010). *Person-centered and experiential therapies work: A review of the research on counseling, psychotherapy, and related practices*. Ross-on-Wye: PCCS Books.

Cornett, N.A. (2013). Filial therapy and the family: Examining the impact of child parent relationship therapy (CPRT) on family functioning. *Dissertation Abstracts International: Section B: The Sciences and Engineering*, 74, 4-B(E).

Davis, M.A. (2009). A perspective on cultivating clinical empathy. *Complimentary Therapies in Clinical Practice*, 15(2), 76–79.

Decety, J., & Lamm, C. (2009). Empathy versus personal distress: Recent evidence from neuroscience. In J. Decety & W. Ickes (Eds.), *The social neuroscience of empathy* (pp. 199–213). Cambridge, MA: MIT Press.

Duan, C., Rose, T.B., & Kraatz, R.A. (2002). Empathy. In G.S. Tryon (Ed.), *Counseling based on process research: Applying what we know* (pp. 197–231). Boston, MA: Allyn & Bacon.

Elliott, R. (2002). The effectiveness of humanistic therapies: A meta-analysis. In D.J. Cain & J. Seeman (Eds.), *Humanistic psychotherapies: Handbook of research and practice* (pp. 57–81). Washington, DC: American Psychological Association.

Elliott, R., Bohart, A.C., Watson, J.C., & Greenberg, L.S. (2011). Empathy. *Psychotherapy*, 48, 43–49.

Everding, H.E., & Huffaker, L.A. (1998). Educating adults for empathy: Implications of cognitive role-taking and identity formation. *Religious Education*, 93, 413–430.

Gillespie, L., & Hunter, A. (2008). Emotional flooding: Using empathy to help babies manage strong emotions. *Young Children, 63(5)*, 46–47.

Ginsberg, B.G. (1997). *Relationship enhancement family therapy*. Hoboken, NJ: Wiley.

Guerney, B.G., Jr. (1977). *Relationship enhancement: Skill-training programs for therapy, problem prevention, and enrichment*. Hoboken, NJ: Jossey-Bass.

Guerney, B.G., Jr. (2002, September 30). Deep empathy, part II. *Relationship Enhancement Newsletter, 4*, 2–3.

Guerney, L. (2013). *Group filial therapy: The complete guide to teaching parents to play therapeutically with their children*. London: Jessica Kingsley Publishers.

Haaga, D.A.F., Rabois, D., & Brody, C. (1999). *Cognitive behavior therapy*. Hoboken, NJ: John Wiley.

Havens, L.L. (1986). *Making contact: Uses of language in psychotherapy*. Cambridge, MA: Harvard University Press.

Hetrick, N.J. (2013). Filial therapy with adoptive families: An exploration of professionals opinions. *Dissertation Abstracts International: Section B: The Sciences and Engineering, 74*, 6-B(E).

Keijsers, G.P.J., Schaap, C.P.D.R., & Hoogduin, C.A.L. (2000). The impact of interpersonal patient and therapist behavior on outcome in cognitive-behavioral therapy: A review of empirical studies. *Behavior Modification, 24*, 264–297.

Kilpatrick, S.D., Bissonnette, V.L., & Rusbult, C.E. (2002). Empathic accuracy and accommodative behavior among newly married couples. *Personal Relationships, 9*, 369–393.

Kinast, R.L. (1984). The dialogue decalogue: A pastoral commentary. *Journal of Ecumenical Studies, 21*, 311–318.

Kohut, H. (1984). *How does analysis cure?* Chicago: University of Chicago Press.

Kountz, C. (1998, April). The anxiety of influence and the influence of anxiety. Paper presented at the Annual Meeting of the Conference on College Composition and Communication, Chicago, IL ERIC Document Reproduction Service No. ED 448461.

Kwon, K.I., & Jo, S.Y. (2012). The relationship among counselor experience level, empathic accuracy, and counseling outcome in the early phase of counseling. *Asia Pacific Education Review, 13*, 771–777.

Laible, D.J., Carlo, G., & Roesch, S.C. (2004). Pathways to self-esteem in late adolescence: The role of parent and peer attachment, empathy, and social behaviours. *Journal of Adolescence, 27*, 703–716.

Lambert, M.J., & Okiishi, J.C. (1997). The effects of the individual psychotherapist and implications for future research. *Clinical Psychology: Science and Practice, 4*, 66–75.

Lenaghan, A. (2000). Reflections on multicultural curriculum. *Multicultural Education, 7*, 33–36.

LeShan, L. (1974). *How to meditate: A guide to self-discovery*. Boston, MA: Little, Brown & Company.

Lickona, T. (2000). Sticks and stones may break my bones AND names WILL hurt me: Thirteen ways to prevent peer cruelty. *Our Children, 26*, 12–14.

Lim, S., & Ogawa, Y. (2014). "Once I had kids, now I am raising kids": Child–parent relationship therapy (CPRT) with a Sudanese refugee family—a case study. *International Journal of Play Therapy, 23*, 70–89.

Linehan, M.M. (1997). Validation and psychotherapy. In A. Bohart & L. Greenberg (Eds.), *Empathy reconsidered: New directions in psychotherapy*. Washington, DC: American Psychological Association, 353–392.

Luborsky L., Crits-Christoph, P., McLellan, T., Woody, G., Piper, W., Liberman, B., Imber, S., & Pilkonis, P. (1986). Do therapists vary much in their success? Findings from four outcome studies. *American Journal of Orthopsychiatry, 51,* 501–512.

McCarthy, M. (1992). Empathy: A bridge between. *Journal of Pastoral Care, 46,* 119–128.

May, R. (1989). *The art of counseling*. New York: Gardner.

Moyers, T.B., & Miller, W.R. (2013). Is low therapist empathy toxic? *Psychology of Addictive Behaviors, 27,* 878–884.

Neumann, M., Bensing, J., Mercer, S., Ernstmann, N., Ommen, O., & Pfaff, H. (2009). Analyzing the "nature" and "specific effectiveness" of clinical empathy: A theoretical overview and contribution towards a theory-based research agenda. *Patient Education and Counseling, 74(3),* 339–346.

Ohman, A. (2002). Automaticity and the amygdala: Nonconscious responses to emotional faces. *Current Directions in Psychological Science, 11,* 62–66.

Orlinsky, D.E., & Howard, K.I. (1978). The relation of process to outcome in psychotherapy. In S.L. Garfield & A.E. Bergin (Eds.), *Handbook of psychotherapy and behavior change* (2nd ed.) (pp. 283–330). New York: Wiley.

Ortwein, M., & Guerney, Jr. B.G. (2008). *Mastering the mysteries of love*. Cedar Park, TX: Relationship Press.

Patterson, C.H. (1984). Empathy, warmth and genuineness: A review of reviews. *Psychotherapy, 21,* 431–438.

Perls, F.S. (1970). Four lectures. In J. Fagan & I.L. Shepherd (Eds.), *Gestalt therapy now* (pp. 14–38). Palo Alto, CA: Science and Behavior Books.

Rogers, C.R. (1957). The necessary and sufficient conditions of therapeutic personality change. *Journal of Consulting Psychology, 21,* 95–103.

Rogers, C.R. (1980). *A way of being*. Boston, MA: Houghton Mifflin.

Scharf, R.S. (1996). *Theories of psychotherapy and counseling: Concepts and cases*. Pacific Grove, CA: Brooks/Cole.

Scuka, R.F. (2005). *Relationship enhancement therapy: Healing through deep empathy and intimate dialog*. New York: Routledge.

Shostrom, E.L. (Producer/Director) (1965). *Three approaches to psychotherapy*. Corona del Mar, CA: Psychological and Educational Films.

Siegel, D.J. (2012). *The developing mind: How relationships and the brain interact to shape who we are* (2nd ed.). New York: Guilford.

Stanbury, S., Bruce, M., Jain, S., & Stellern, J. (2009). The effects of an empathy building program on bullying behavior. *Journal of School Counseling, 71–27.*

Sweeney, J., & Whitworth, J. (2000). Addressing teacher supply and demand by increasing the success of first-year teachers ERIC Document Reproduction Service No. ED 440944.

Vanaerschot, G., & Lietaer, G. (2007). Therapeutic ingredients in helping session episodes with observer-rated low and high empathic attunement: A content analysis of client and therapist post-session perceptions in three cases. *Psychotherapy Research, 17,* 329–342.

Wampold, B.E. (2001). *The great psychotherapy debate: Models, methods, and findings*. Mahwah, NJ: Erlbaum.

Wampold, B.E. (2006). Not a scintilla of evidence to support empirically supported treatments as more effective than other treatments. In J.C. Norcross, L.E. Beutler, & R.F. Levant (Eds.), *Evidence-based practices in mental health: Debate and dialogue on the fundamental questions* (pp. 299–307). Washington, DC: American Psychological Association.

Watson, J.C., & Greenberg, L.S. (2009). Empathic resonance: A neuroscience perspective. In J. Decety & W. Ickes (Eds.), *The social neuroscience of empathy* (pp. 125–138). Cambridge, MA: MIT Press.

Pre-Chapter Quotes

Carl Jung quoted in E.M. Beck (Ed.), J. Bartlett (compiler) (1980). *Familiar quotations* (15th ed.). Boston, MA: Little, Brown & Company (p. 754).

Fadiman, J., & Frager, R. (1998). *Essenial Sufism*. Edison, NJ: Castle Books (p. 101).

Roethke, T. (1969). The waking. In *The contemporary American poets*. New York: The New American Library (p. 234).

4   EXPRESSING EMPATHY

Every vital development in language is a development of feeling as well.
                                                                    T.S. Eliot

Primary Skill Objectives

- Understand and begin to effectively express empathy.
- Be able to explain the dos and don'ts, and nuances of expressing empathy.
- Anticipate the effects on your work from the common difficulties, pitfalls and dead ends in expressing empathy.
- Evaluate your strengths and difficulties in expressing empathy at this time, and how you may overcome your difficulties and develop your strengths.
- Be able to explain what expressing empathy looks, sounds and feels like to you when you are working effectively.

Focus Activity

Now it's time to let yourself express the empathy you feel. Have a partner communicate to you about a topic that has emotional content for her or him. Strive to feel what your speaker feels and to express what it is you feel with her/him. Your expression may take a variety of forms. Try not to worry about the form your expression takes. This worry would distract you from empathy. For this exercise, you are adding one intention beyond experiencing empathy, which is expressing the empathy that you feel. An irony to work through will be that while you aim to express empathy, you can't think too much about how to express your empathy because that will take your focus away from empathy. So, a useful way to think of it is to think of removing the restraints that we asked of you in the focus activity of the previous chapter; freeing yourself to express what you feel with your partner.

You should also practice therapeutic listening with this activity. It would be hard not to, as much empathy will be expressed in the tone of your reflections. However, don't let yourself worry right now about things like reflecting. Rather, focus on freeing yourself to experience and express empathy.

A reasonable length of time for this practice can be 10–30 minutes. Have a third partner observe and/or video. Use feedback from the speaker, observer, and video review to discern when your empathy was clearly expressed and when it was not, when you were connected best to your speaker and not.

Note that when you are in the role of speaker, you may be able to give your listener helpful feedback regarding her or his expression of empathy. However, you really can't focus on watching for your listener's skills while speaking. Rather, it will be best if you purely focus on expressing whatever comes to your heart and mind. Then later, if you remember something of your listener's skills it will be nice to tell her/him, but the most help you can be to your listener is to maintain your focus on you and what you wish to say.

Discuss with your partners, small group or class, and/or journal what you have learned from this exercise. Describe the ways of expressing empathy that seemed to work for you and the ways of expressing empathy that you hear or see in others' work that may work for you. Remember that empathy is not sympathy or thinking of what others feel. Notice and describe when sympathy and thinking may have gotten in the way of empathy. Also describe any other challenges encountered in expressing empathy.

One final reminder with this exercise: Do not be discouraged if this work is difficult at first. If it is difficult for you, you are in good company.

Various Ways to Express Empathy

Probably the purest way to express empathy is through the emotion that is returned to your clients from you as you feel with them—the emotion they can feel from you as you feel with them. As you may have found in the practice activities for this and the previous chapter, overt expressions of empathy do occur when striving only to feel, without even an attempt to express it. Your work will be best, you will be most focused, and the process will be most natural when you are focused on feeling and allowing yourself to express empathy versus being focused on your expression.

Ways of expressing of empathy cross an array of modes, from involuntarily emitting the emotions, which your clients simply feel from you as you feel with them, to saying the words for what you feel with your clients. We don't see any one method as necessarily better than others. Which is best may be determined by which comes naturally to you in each situation and can be determined by doing what feels natural to you in each moment, then observing if your clients seem to perceive your empathy. Next, we introduce a few ways of expressing empathy.

Matching the Client's Tone

As you feel empathy, your tone of expression will match your client's. Your voice will tend to rise and fall following your client's. Your pace of speech will tend to quicken and slow following your client's. In watching tapes of your sessions, you will be able to hear the quality of your client's emotion in your spoken responses.

Facial Expression and Body Language

We discovered some time ago that neither of us has a "poker face." Not having a poker face is an asset to counselors. What we are feeling can be obvious to our clients or to anyone watching. So, as we strive for empathy and succeed in feeling with clients, our empathy is expressed through our faces mirroring the emotions of our clients.

Empathy is at times expressed through hand gestures and other body language. For example, one client was explaining how her father would sound and move when he was about to come angrily after her and her siblings. When she made the sound and threatening move, both she and her counselor made a body gesture that suggested ducking one shoulder and head while starting to run. That gesture symbolized the fear-filled response that she and her siblings had. The counselor was not mimicking her client. It was a gesture she made while absorbed in listening and empathy, without thought of expressing empathy. Her client did not comment on the gesture but knew in that moment that her counselor was with her.

In other moments, we have watched counselors clasp their hands to express empathy when a client expressed a feeling of connectedness, or shift back and move their hands wide apart when their clients excitedly expressed that what they are saying is *really* big for them. We have seen counselors push their fists together and grimace when their client expressed dread over an impending conflict. We have seen counselors brush their hands against each other as if dusting off sand or fling them out lightly as if flinging the last drops of water off their hands into the sink when their clients expressed that they were done with a troubling situation. Importantly, each of these gestures was natural, not contrived; not thought of, but born of feeling with clients and allowing expression of empathy to flow.

The Most Overt Means—Words

Sometimes the gestures, facial expressions and tones that served to express empathy were also accompanied by words that named the feeling. Naming the feeling in words is what most people think of when thinking of expressing empathy. Using words to name feelings can make your empathy most overt. It can make what you feel in empathy least subject to interpretation, at least for persons of similar linguistic and cultural backgrounds. However, expressing empathy through feeling words also brings its problems. When you work at thinking of the word for the emotions, the thoughts take you away from empathy and listening.

Additionally, if you work hard at thinking of the word, your response often comes out sounding like an assessment, or the answer on a quiz show. When this happens, your client will tend to stop expressing and stop feeling. In these moments, it feels to clients as if that was somehow the end of the conversation or that you have made your diagnosis, so they wait for your prescription. It will help you avoid this to remember that your task is not to identify feelings so much as it is to help your clients feel more fully and to be right there with them through it all. But saying the word for the feeling helps your clients know that you are right there with them, that you are OK with what they feel, not afraid to feel what they feel and go with them to their emotional places, that you are "a confident companion . . . in his or her inner world" (Rogers, 1980, p. 142).

Dos and Don'ts of Expressing Empathy

Empathy can be an esoteric concept. It is abstract, complex and subtle. Yet, we want to make it as concrete and observable as possible. So, with our previous explanations of the purpose of empathy and some varied ways in mind of expressing it, consider the following "dos" and "don'ts," which allow us further discussion and which you may use to check your work in expressing empathy.

This Dos and Don'ts list is an extension of the dos and don'ts list for therapeutic listening. Experiencing and expressing empathy are listening at an even deeper level. Experiencing and expressing empathy in your meetings with clients are in addition to therapeutic listening. The balance of therapeutic listening with expressing empathy differs with each situation. You will learn to thoughtlessly balance responding to content in therapeutic listening and responding to experience by expressing empathy.

With these behaviors, you are communicating truths like "I understand what you feel and experience it with you," "I understand your situation," "I sense what is important to you," "I'm striving to feel as much as I can with you, to feel as if I were you," and, ultimately, "Through experiencing with you, I'm coming to understand you."

Do:

- focus your attention primarily on your client's emotions, but also on thoughts, actions, and the connections of your client's thoughts, emotions and actions;
- strive to feel what your client feels vs. attempting to think of what your client feels;

- feel what your client feels such that your expression of your client's experience is expressed naturally through your words, tone, facial expressions and body language;
- reflect your client's feelings with words for the emotions you feel with them, when natural, and with openness to a variety of ways of expressing empathy;
- state your empathy in declarative statements, when reasonably sure;
- when unsure, state your empathy as tentative, with more tentative declarations from your struggle to understand your client's feelings and underlying thoughts;
- use reflections to restate client feelings and underlying thoughts more clearly and directly, precisely and concisely;
- reflect themes of personal meanings implied in client communication;
- reflect emerging communication, feelings and underlying thoughts that seem implied;
- reflect themes of personal meaning that seem to be implied in client communication;
- reflect your client's experience that may be hard to hear (don't be afraid to confront)—allow your client to be confronted by her/his experience;
- be prepared for and accept corrections of your empathy.

Don't:

- let your words for what you feel with your client come out sounding like assessments;
- respond with a hidden agenda of what you believe your client should realize;
- do most of the talking;
- make "me too" or "must feel" statements;
- be afraid to reflect implied or emerging communication—that which is communicated in action, inaction, tone, facial expressions, body language, how or when things are said, and what is not said;
- be afraid to confront or be afraid to allow your clients to be confronted by contradictions in his/her experience, feelings, thoughts, words, and actions.

Explanations and Discussion from the Dos and Don'ts of Expressing Empathy

Much as we may try, the complex and subtle skill of expressing empathy can't be truly captured in a dos and don'ts list. So, carefully consider the following explanations.

Focus Your Attention Primarily on Client Emotions, but also on Thoughts, Actions and the Connections of Thoughts, Emotions and Actions

Full empathy is a total connection with a person, in which you understand the person in ways that go beyond the information he tells you about himself to experiencing his world through his communication to you. Sometimes your expressions of empathy may reflect thoughts and actions. For example (with tone capturing your client's anger, agitation), "You decided he'd crossed a line and you yelled at him for it!" Expressions of empathy can address both emotion and action, "You're so mad about this you can hardly sit still." At other times, we have seen naturally occurring expressions of empathy focus on a client's implied thoughts. A client was expressing exasperation and amazement with peer errors and his critical judgment of this. His counselor responded with the same exasperation and amazement in her tone, "So, you're thinking like, 'What are they thinking?! They must not be thinking!'" Still, while we hope for you to free yourself enough to respond with empathy to clients' thoughts and actions, keep this secondary to your focus on and expression of empathy to emotions. *Emotions lead most efficiently to a connection with each client's core and experiencing each client's world as that person does.*

The work of cognitive behavior therapy and rational-emotive therapy (Beck & Beck, 2011; Ellis & Dryden, 2007) brings to our awareness the connections between a person's thoughts, feelings and emotions. This awareness influences how we see clients and comes out in our reflections. A complex reflection may sound like "You felt *hurt* that your teacher said that; you saw it as wrong, *unfair*; when you saw it as unfair, you got *mad* and yelled back." We encourage you to risk such complex reflections. However, we also want you to know that *more complex does not = better*. While the complex reflection above might present your client with an opportunity to learn about his pattern; if it feels like teaching, it might get in the way of connecting. Connecting is most important and should always be your primary goal. Communicating shared emotional experience is the most powerful way to connect. So, primarily your attention is to emotion. To that same upset youth in the complex reflection example above, depending on the context in time of your work together, the best reflection might simply be, "You were mad! And you felt hurt by that."

Strive to Feel with Your Client

Remember that this is almost always your primary purpose and function. Aim not to get wrapped up in things like analytic thoughts, thoughts of what you'll say next, or concern for your client's satisfaction with your work. These things will be part of your work (we address them later), but the main part is feeling with your client. This is the core of your work.

Express Empathy Naturally through Your Words, Tone, Facial Expression and Body Language

Remember that these modes of expressing empathy can be as powerful and clear as using words to express your empathy. Sometimes these ways of expressing empathy catch more of clients' subtle communication. In one session, a client was expressing her dread and frustration at her mom taking a former boyfriend, who had been abusive, back into her life. The client wanted to be OK with it and supportive of her mom but already saw her mother changing to allow him back, even changing house rules to fit his needs in ways that she would not have changed them for her daughter. When the client said this, her counselor uttered a sound that was somewhere between a groan and a growl. His client heard this, and while she didn't stop to acknowledge it, she glanced at his eyes, grinned, and picked up her pace and the emotional intensity of her expression. She knew that her counselor felt her feelings that went along with both her dread of what she expected to follow from the situation and her wish to drive the ex-boyfriend off and protect her mom, her territory, and herself. Such unplanned expressions of empathy happen naturally, when you are feeling with your client and allowing your expression to flow.

Reflect Client Feelings with Words for the Emotions

Use words to express the emotions you feel with your clients. These can be feeling words, "You feel so mad about this!," "Now you are really hurting." Or your words can convey feelings in tone without naming emotions, such as when addressing client thoughts and actions from sections above, as long as your tone contains the emotions you feel with your client:

- (Stated with tone capturing your client's anger, agitation.) "You decided he'd crossed a line and you yelled at him for it!"
- "So, you're thinking like, 'What are they thinking?! They must not be thinking!'"

And words can convey what you feel with your client in metaphor. For example, "It's like you're slogging hard, through cold rain and snow, just to get through your day."

State Your Empathy in Declarative Statements, and When Unsure, State with More Tentative Declarations

When your client's emotion is strong and you are sure of what you feel with her, state it strongly. For example, "You're tired of hurting with this. Now you're mad and deciding not to take it anymore!" If you are less sure, you may make a more tentative statement: "Sounds like you feel confused and unsure of what to do next."

If you are greatly unsure and think you may be too far out ahead of your client but still think it's important to say, you can express your experience in an even more tentative phrasing, "I'm not sure, I know you're exasperated with him, but as you talk, I get the feeling you are also hurt." Each of these statements attempts to say what the counselor feels with her client. They also say, through behavior, that the counselor is striving to understand her client, and that while the counselor would like to be accurate in empathy, she is willing to risk being wrong in order to understand.

Note that no matter how tentative, these expressions of empathy remain declarative statements. They do not include a questioning tone. We find that asking a client what he feels elicits a thought response (i.e., an explanation of feeling or what the client thinks he is supposed to feel), rather than helping him feel more of his true feelings with you.

Use Reflections to Restate Client Feelings and Underlying Thoughts More Clearly and Directly

As your clients strive to express themselves to you and you strive for empathy, it will often be clear to you just what they feel or think when it is not yet clear to them. Because you are separate from their feelings, you may experience the feelings with less inhibition, less fear of feelings, and confusion. For example, a client who has been hurt by a loved one might have a hard time expressing herself. She may try to communicate to you but struggle to get words out: (Pausing between phrases, speaking in spurts) "I just can't believe he did that . . . It makes no sense . . . I'm so mad . . ., but how could he? Didn't he think of me at all?" Hearing your client's tone, knowing the context of what she is saying, you may not only reason that she is feeling shocked and hurt, but even more decisively through emotional connection, you may clearly *feel* the shock and hurt as she speaks. Thus, you may respond tenderly: "As you see what he's done, and tell me about it now, you feel shocked and hurt." It will be easier for you, as you strive to feel with clients but remain separate, to experience and state feelings more clearly, directly, precisely, and concisely. Through feeling with them, you will be able to get to the heart of your clients' communication more quickly and easily than they can. This is one of the benefits you offer your clients.

Reflect Emerging Communication that You Perceive Your Client to Imply

Remember that just as your reflections are more than just your words, your client's communication and experience is expressed in more than just her words. Experience is communicated in tone, facial expression, body language, how a thing is said or its context, and what is not said. If your client drops her voice to speak very softly and her speaking takes on a halting quality, you may reflect, "Something about this is very hard for you to say, hard to get out." If a client is telling you she is not worried about the upcoming exam, but her face and body seem held so tight, anguished, you might reflect: "I think that a part of you really doesn't care, but it stays on your mind a lot, as if maybe a part of you really does care." Or if a client who you know to be very close with family, highly affected by their reactions to her, does not mention family at all related to some big decision (e.g., new job, college, committing to a relationship from newly sparked romance), you might reflect: "I notice that while you sometimes care very much about what [husband, mother, children] think[s], you have not mentioned thoughts of that at all with this decision."

Our choice of the words "that you perceive" is important. We don't want you to be so concerned with accuracy in your empathy that it becomes inhibiting and only allows you to respond to experience that your client has already named. You will sometimes reflect experience that your client has stated, and you often will reflect the ones that you sense in your client. Just as with therapeutic listening to the content of what your client communicates, *there is no penalty for being wrong in expressing empathy.* If you have misunderstood, your client can correct you and in correcting you, reach a greater self-understanding and fuller experience.

Reflect Themes of Personal Meaning

Especially at the level of empathy—deep understanding of the person—you will learn to see the themes of your client's communication. For example, you may see how much a particular client prides himself in setting and reaching goals (perhaps priding himself in consistently setting and meeting new athletic and educational goals). You may reflect: "You like when you reach your goals. You like that you continue to set and meet goals. You are proud of that way of being and feel good about yourself when you meet each goal." We would note to you that such a way of being can be very effective, but can also leave the person open to traps of perfectionism, conditional self-acceptance, and blind spots in development. But *if* that is true of him, that learning will come from his own experience as you connect, accept him as he is, and respond with empathy. Usually, it is counterproductive to jump ahead with cautionary thoughts for the personal meaning that your client is forming.

For another example, you may have a client with opposing themes apparent to you. She may see herself on one hand as non-judgmental and strive to be a person who loves and accepts everyone, but who also frequently expresses irritation with others who don't live up to her expectations. So, you might reflect: "I notice competing themes for you. On one hand, you work hard at loving and accepting everyone as they are, but at least lately you've been able to tell me of a number of times when you felt quite irritated with others not living up to your expectations."

Don't Be Afraid to Confront

At times you will reflect experience that is hard to hear. When a client realizes his full experience, this often serves to confront. You have to let your empathic responses allow your client to be confronted by his/her experience. For example, with the client above who prides himself in consistently setting and meeting new athletic and educational goals, but may also seem completely stuck in moving forward in interpersonal relationships with teachers, parents, and maybe a special friendship, you might reflect: "James, I know how much you pride yourself in setting and meeting your goals; and I know how successful you have been with that, but I also see how stuck you seem in personal relationships. I get the idea that you are held back by not letting others close to you." Or to a client who repeatedly allows herself to be abused in a relationship, knows that if she answers the text message and meets the guy again, she will be abused again and continue the cycle of feeling bad for what she has allowed . . . but feels drawn to him, you might reflect: "So, you are thinking, 'maybe you will answer—maybe you will give him one more chance.' This seems very different from how bad you were hurt last time and how sure you were that you would allow no more chances for him—but some part of you has you feeling really drawn to restart the pattern again; at this time once again thinking, 'maybe?'"

Be Prepared for and Accept Corrections

Being wrong in your struggle to express empathy, to understand and connect, is not a problem and can even be beneficial, as long as you are striving to feel with your client. When a client corrects us after making an error in empathic understanding, we usually respond something like, "Oh, I misunderstood there. You are very angry but not hurt. It is important to you that something like this cannot hurt you."

Sometimes corrections are not quite overt and only come in a feeling or facial expression. For example, after reflecting anger with a strong tone, if my client crinkles his face and lowers his head, and I get a feeling like the wind went out of his sails, I may reflect: "Something happened when I responded to what I thought was the strength of your anger; seems like you suddenly lost your momentum." In both these examples, the client's response to the counselor's error and the counselor's acceptance of this response helped the client further realize his experience and reiterated the importance that his counselor placed on understanding and experiencing with him. It is the same as being corrected in therapeutic listening to content. There is no point in going back and explaining why you thought your expression of empathy was true. By the time the correction or client response to our statement has occurred, your client has moved on to a new expression.

An exception to not going back and explaining might be when it seems clear that a pattern of misunderstanding persists. For example, if you believe your client has repeatedly expressed emotions that are similar to anger, and you expressed your empathy with these angry emotions in your tone and words, but your client continually rejects your expressions of empathy, it may be important to comment on the process of interactions between you. This comment may be something like, "I'm trying, but I seem to keep misunderstanding you on this. Several times I've felt sure you were really mad about this situation, but you've let me know that I misunderstand you." Such responses can open the door for your client to express what he experiences in relationship with you or to further clarify for you and himself what it is that he is experiencing.

Don't Let Your Words Sound like Assessments

Remember that using feeling words can be a useful shorthand. Feeling words can make your empathy most overt. However, using them also brings difficulties. Remember when using feeling words that your point is expressing what you are feeling with your client, rather than finding the correct word for what your client feels. Finding the correct word is a cognitive function. Work to minimize such assessment functions in your counseling relationships. Such assessment functions have the effect of inhibiting useful client experience and expression, and tend to be disempowering.

Don't Respond from a Hidden Agenda

While we encourage you to risk being wrong in expressing empathy and to know that even errors in empathy can be beneficial, it is important to check that you are not wrong because you have an agenda other than understanding your client. For example, some beginning counselors may see clients' lives or dilemmas as simple, when they are not. This mistake seems to come from a cognitive error like the following: The counselor cares for his client in such a way that he almost believes that he can't stand to see his client suffering more. Thus, the counselor convinces himself that one emotional realization or another will bring swift relief of suffering for his client. However, this is seldom true as life in and out of counseling is rarely that simple. This is an important error to avoid, as a counselor following that path has strayed far from empathy.

Don't Do Most of the Talking

As your expressions of empathy will be more precise and concise than your clients' communication, you should only need to do a small percentage of the talking. Further, when you focus your responses on emotions, there is less to say than when listening for content. Emotions need not be explained, justified, or proved, and once understood, take few words to express.

Don't Make "Me Too" or "Must Feel" Statements

Sometimes counselors, including us, are tempted to "me too" our clients. By this we mean that we mistakenly attempt to tell them what we have felt in similar situations or think we would feel in their situation. A sneaky way of making this error is to phrase an expression of empathy as, "That must really hurt." This places an assumption on what the client feels that may or may not be true and is suggestive, thus taking the client away from expressing what she actually does feel. The assumption in this error seems usually to be based on what the counselor thinks *she* would feel in her client's situation or what the counselor thinks anyone would feel in her client's situation. The assumption may be that we humans would all feel the same things in the same situation. This conclusion is unlikely, and the line of thought strays far from empathy.

It is possible as a last resort when you are very unsure what your client feels, to use a very tentative phrasing like, "I imagine that you feel hurt." In this phrasing, the focus is kept on your striving to understand. You may be making an assumption, but your assumption is your attempt to understand the unique person that is your client and his unique reaction to his situation.

Nuances of Expressing Empathy

Remaining Animated, Natural and Spontaneous

We encourage you to allow yourself to be animated in your counseling sessions. What we mean is that we wouldn't want you to think so hard and try so hard to do the right thing and respond the right way that striving to have and express empathy gets in the way of your having and expressing empathy. You will need to make a great many judgments about how to respond to your clients that will be unique to given situations, persons and moments.

Variation of Tone

Generally, you want the level of emotion in your tone to match the level of emotion in your client's tone. Usually, if you are striving to have and express empathy, this will happen without you actually paying any attention to your tone. However, there are always exceptions. For example, you may have a client who denies his emotions when he hears the strength of it in your tone. When this is your hunch, you may try expressing a little less intensity of emotion in your tone, since you already know he does not accept the stronger tone and in order to allow him to feel less threatened by what he hears back from you and accept more of his emotion.

On the other hand, you may have a client who seems to assume that she should not express strong emotions, even in her sessions with you, repeatedly understating her feelings. In this case, you could let her know that it is OK to express strong emotions with you by responding to her restrained expression with a tone that is slightly stronger and more intense than her own.

Such decisions will become automatic. At this time in our work, such decisions are more felt than thought. Our point is for you to use our Dos and Don'ts list to help you, but not to let it make you rigid. Remember, the most powerful thing you can offer your clients is an empathic relationship with *you*. While we hope following our model helps you become more empathic, we want you to continue to be you, to remain focused on empathy and to trust your intuition.

The Range of Response Options from Content to Feeling to Emerging Communication

Just as in responding to implied content with therapeutic listening, you will often respond to implied emotions with expression of empathy. Most people, in or out of counseling, do not name their emotions when expressing feelings. An example of responding to implied emotions follows.

A teenage client had a behavior pattern of fighting with other boys, especially when drinking. He related the story of a fight that he had been in the weekend before to his counselor. In that fight, the other boy was hurt badly. The police had been called, but the client left before they came. As he told of the fight, he explained to his counselor that the other boy must feel terrible, that the way his face had looked, he just could not go back to school and be seen. A reflection of content to his communication would be: "You know how bad this must be for him. You know that he just couldn't be seen with his face beat up." This would be a good and powerful reflection. The client might then respond with more direct expression of the emotion he feels. An alternative response, expressing empathy for the emotion that he already strongly implied could be: "You seem to feel so sorry for him. You seem to feel guilty for your part in his humiliation."

A less clearly implied emotion from this same example is that as this client told of the fight, he sometimes spoke loudly, quickly, and with bright eyes. The undercurrent emotion his counselor felt with him during this part of his story was elation. Empathy could be expressed to this implication by saying, "As you tell me of the fight, you get excited. You seem to feel elated."

Either way of responding to implied emotions—with content reflection, as in the first part of this example, or with stated empathy—could be effective. The most helpful thing was for his counselor to respond fully and honestly to his emotion, whether it is first through tone in a content reflection, giving him the opportunity to express emotion more fully and directly, or through a more immediate expression of empathy. Responding to his emotion helped him realize his emotional experience. It may have been this experience that was most powerful in helping him change. It may have been very helpful for him to realize his guilt and remorse fully in order to avoid repeating such fights. It may also have been helpful for him to realize the elation he had when telling of the fight in order to honestly know what drew him to fights. Most likely it was not just that he saw himself as justified in fighting (the other boy did hit first, etc.), but that it was also a thrill, a sense of power and mastery to beat up another boy.

Responding to Unpleasant Emotions

It is important also to see from the previous example that counselors need to be ready to respond to unpleasant emotions. Just as these emotions can be hurtful for clients to realize, they can also be hurtful for counselors to respond to. Counselors sometimes avoid them simply because they hurt and humans are naturally repulsed by pain. It may also be that counselors sometimes fear losing themselves in the strong currents of clients' unpleasant emotions. For us and the other counselors who knew of the boy in the previous case example, the emotions around elation in telling of the fight ran counter to our "shoulds," our beliefs about behaviors toward others (our use of the word *shoulds* as a noun in this or other sections comes from writings by Albert Ellis; e.g., Ellis & Dryden, 2007). In our worldview, it is wrong and unaccept-able to derive pleasure from hurting others. Sometimes experiencing the dark side of clients' emotions scares us as it reminds us of our own dark sides, the parts of our selves that are difficult for us to accept (our use of the term *dark side* owes a debt to the Jungian concept of the *personal shadow.* See works by Jung or about analytical psychotherapy, such as Jung, [1935]/1956; or Douglas, 2005).

We encourage you to work to make this boundary unnecessary in your work. Steady yourself to experience hurtful, repulsive emotions with your clients in order to be the best tool possible for your clients' self-actualization. Do your own personal growth work so that you are able and confident to experience your clients' strong emotional currents without losing yourself. Work to be aware of your shoulds, so that you can temporarily suspend them in order to experience with your clients. Take on the long-term task of knowing your own dark sides to help you be able to temporarily set aside your convictions of right and wrong in order to experience fully with clients in crucial moments. Remember that *empathy does not equal agreement*, but requires coming as close as possible to shared experience while remaining separate. We offer additional guidance to you for this work in Activities for Further Study at the end of this chapter.

Discerning When to Respond More to Emotions and When More to Content

There is no prescription of how often you should respond with therapeutic listening to the content of your clients' communication and how often you should express empathy to the emotions of their communication. As a rule of thumb, you should respond to emotion as much as possible, but how much is possible will vary with each moment and client. The best way to discern how much you may respond to a client's emotions in a given moment is to watch for her response when you do. If it was right to respond more heavily to emotion, your client will likely respond with intensified emotion. If it would have been better to respond more to content, your client may respond to your expression of empathy something like this: (After a mildly confused pause) "Well, yeah, but what was happening was . . ." Such a response can indicate that your client sees getting the story out as more important in that moment. But, as with most basic skills, this is not a decision we knowingly make in our work any more. The decision has become more felt than thought, and so is virtually instantaneous. Such decisions for you will also become automatic over time in practice. Use the activities of this and other chapters, the feedback you get from the practices, and the feedback you get in supervision to help you grow this decision process into a natural, felt way of interacting.

Issue Areas: Addressing Behavioral, Cognitive, Affective and Interpersonal Issues

Some counselors think in terms of different counseling approaches to address each of the major areas of a person's functioning. In some counseling theories that can be true. Reality therapy (Wubbolding, 2010) is heavily focused on behaviors—what the client is doing, but also focuses on wants, motivations and feelings. Cognitive-behavioral therapy is mostly focused on helping clients to change thinking in order to accomplish change in feelings, behaviors and interactions. Regarding your core counseling skills—your therapeutic relationships, we would like you to see that your empathic way of being, once well developed, will naturally address all areas of your client's life, fitting with a range of approach theories, as needed. A client who is most troubled with feelings, behaviors or relationships will tell you that directly or by implication through the process of empathic listening. If a client has patterns in thinking that are important for you to respond to, this will become evident, if you are open to it in empathy.

You might review the early tapes of your work with areas of functioning in mind. You can then judge if you have a tendency to over- or under-attend to certain areas that might be inhibiting or distorting your responses to clients' communication.

Some agency settings may ask you to report on each of the major issue areas; and in some school settings it could help you in your role in consulting on behalf of clients to think in that way. We encourage you to restrict that kind of thinking to after sessions, as much as possible, rather than during sessions. During sessions, we encourage you to maintain your focus on connecting to and understanding the person of your client; then review after or late in sessions to see if your client has not naturally informed you of all his major areas of functioning. See Chapter 8 for more on conceptualizing client difficulties.

The Question of Probing

While it sounds rather medical to us, some think of the counselor's role as "probing" or searching out hidden areas of concern. We do not think of our role as probing. We wouldn't want you to feel restricted from it, so probing is not on our Don'ts list. But we would like you to see that as you develop your skills in empathic listening, you would rarely, if ever, need to probe. If something of your client seems oddly unsaid, that would be something you would reflect.

The empathic listening process is dramatically powerful in leading clients to communicate what they need, including from hidden areas of their life and mind. We are constantly amazed at the hidden areas found with clients that we would not have thought to probe for. If you probe, you risk disempowering your client and the empathic listening process, and risk missing areas of your client's experience that your client would have completely missed if instead of the empathic listening process you were following the chain of your ideas of what to probe for.

Common Difficulties

Thinking of the Word, Rather Than Feeling with Your Client

In the section "Various Ways to Express Empathy" above, we explained that naming clients' feelings sometimes stops their communication. When counselors work hard to think of the name of a feeling, it takes counselors into a cognitive realm, away from empathy. When counselors name the feelings that they have thought of, it comes across sounding like a conclusion or the final answer on a quiz show. So instead of fostering clients' further expression, it stops it. Some beginning counselors think too much of expressing empathy as naming the feeling. Remember that language is almost always inexact for what we humans really mean to say. If words come to you that seem very close to expressing what you feel with your client, it can be helpful to say it. If not, remember that you have a variety of means to express what you feel with your clients.

Trying Too Hard to Get It Right

A closely related difficulty is worrying about being wrong. We remind you that as you strive for empathy, errors are not harmful and are sometimes accidentally helpful. Beyond the usual limitations of language, especially for feelings which are abstract, there rarely is a right word because feelings seldom exist in isolation. Usually feelings are mixed like flavors in a dish that is not finished cooking. Feelings are ever changing, in constant motion. It is right to try to understand exactly what your client feels, to try to experience right with her. You may accomplish this at times. It is right to try to find just the right way to express what you feel with her, but remember that there will seldom be opportunities to find just the right words to express it.

A metaphor for thinking too much might help. If we learned to ride a bike as an adult (as children, we were more talented at thinking less and simply being), we may need to think of where to sit, how to hold on, how to pedal without having our feet slip off the pedals, how to steer, how to break, and so on. At first it may feel quite unnatural, but soon it would be time to forget all the skill pieces and just ride, letting the forward momentum of our base skills pull us along. Yet, as soon as we think, "Hey, I'm really getting it. Look at me," our break in concentration of purely being and doing the complex set of behaviors of riding, we just might wobble, lose our balance, and fall. However, if we continue to think too much of each complexity in base skills, we may keep ourselves from the joy of riding and from the other layers of skills available to us, like jumping ramps, riding on trails, riding through traffic and through different terrain, landscapes, and weather. So like riding a bike, you may practice your base skills until they come naturally and do them almost without thinking. Also, you may find your way of being that feels right for you in counseling, that feeling when you know you are doing your base skills well even though you are not having to think about them much; that way of being where you know you are concentrating on what you are doing, but you are much more doing it than consciously thinking about it.

Limited Vocabulary for Feelings

Related to the difficulty of finding just the right word for a feeling can be lacking an extensive vocabulary for feelings. Occasionally, our students study lists of feeling words to increase their vocabulary of words for feelings. Some find this helpful. We imagine that if we had tried to develop our vocabularies for feeling words in this way, our focus in sessions might have veered to the list and away from our client. For us, extensive vocabularies of words for feelings have come from being open to and focused on feelings, from desiring to express feelings, and finally from gaining more and more experience in expressing empathy as counselors and expressing our feelings to our counselors, friends and family, while remembering that words are only one medium of expression.

The Problem with Claiming Understanding

Again, just as with therapeutic listening to communication content, it is almost never helpful to say "I understand" or "I feel what you feel." When you think you understand something or believe you are experiencing with them, then say what you understand or experience. If you are right, your client will then know you understood. If you are wrong, your client can know you are trying. In life outside of counseling, acquaintances, friends and family often tell each other that they understand or know what each other feels. In many cases, the person who hears this does not believe it. Such statements from errant counselors often leave us thinking of young teenagers whose parents tell them "I know just what you're going through." When we were teenagers, we rarely believed such statements, even from very caring adults. It seems that what persons often mean when making such claims of understanding is really something like "I'm pretty sure I know what I felt in situations that seemed similar to me." Now this might actually be a useful sharing of experience among friends, acquaintances or family, but it is not the empathy that you can express much more powerfully in counseling.

Personal Confidence and Trust in the Counseling Process

Beginning counselors are sometimes tempted to stray from expressing empathy due to a belief that goes something like "Surely my expression of empathy cannot be enough." This is sometimes a lack of trust in expressing empathy and related counseling skills. When that is the problem, experience in giving these skills a solid try and assessing progress will go far toward curing doubt.

In a sense, empathy is not enough, as it is a core of what counselors do, but not all that counselors do. However, more often we find that doubting the power of empathy in counseling is more about ourselves as counselors than about empathy. It seems to tap more into a core of self-doubt that says, "Surely *I* cannot be enough. This skill is too dependent on *me*. Surely a technique invented by someone else would be better."

Particularly because we know how difficult such self-doubts can be, we would like to offer some helpful thoughts and suggestions. First, you are not alone. We still sometimes face such doubts, even though we have quite a lot of evidence of our effectiveness. Also, the more success we have had, while trusting the power of empathy, related skills and ourselves, the less self-doubts we have had. We expect a similar progression for you. We have also found it helpful not to let ourselves get isolated. We have known ourselves and our friends to work too much so that the work becomes consuming. We find it helpful to back off from that myopic consumption to meet regularly with like-minded counselors, to share our experiences, our successes and our self-doubts. This book is no doubt only a part of your study. For us, an ongoing scholarship with the core conditions of counseling is continually uplifting. Finally, we have found it very helpful to seek counselors who honor empathy and the core conditions for ourselves. As we are confident in the self-actualizing process, we know that we have continuing work to do in our ongoing self-discovery and acceptance.

Lack of Unconditional Positive Regard

Another difficulty in expressing empathy can be a lack of unconditional positive regard. A counselor may be so overwhelmed with critical reactions to a client who has done or said something that runs against one of the counselor's shoulds, that the counselor may have difficulty finding and expressing empathy. In a seemingly opposite scenario, a counselor may feel so fond of a client that his positive regard becomes possessive, accepting the client only if and when she makes expected, desired progress. This too would inhibit experiencing and expressing empathy. Our next chapter, "Striving for and Communicating Unconditional Positive Regard," will provide you with ways that you may work through difficulties in experiencing unconditional positive regard that limit your expression of empathy. We hope you will see that empathy and unconditional positive regard work in tandem to support each other and all counselor actions.

Activities and Resources for Further Study

- Review the instructions from the focus activity. Now that you have read and contemplated this chapter, practice expressing empathy following the guidance given in this chapter. When giving and receiving feedback from partners and video, check for adherence to the items of the dos and don'ts list. Also check for the various ways of expressing empathy that seemed to work for the listener in each practice round. Repeat practice rounds until each partner is reasonably satisfied with her or his adherence to the dos and don'ts, percentage of accuracy, tone and way of being in expressing empathy.

- Our dos and don'ts list is our best attempt to boil down the behaviors of expressing empathy to the bare skeleton of what happens. We add narration to explain the behaviors. Still, the behaviors will come naturally to you sooner if you create understandings that are most meaningful to you. So, through class or small-group discussion and private contemplation, first check that you understand the dos and don'ts list items, then explain them in your own words. Once you have your own explanations, you may choose to rename some of the dos and don'ts based on how you phrase what they mean to you. You will then have your personalized dos and don'ts list for expressing empathy that may become most automatic in counseling sessions. After working out your personalized list, you may then return to class or small-group discussion to explain the adjustments you have made, hear from others and benefit from the shared perspectives.

- Discuss possible hidden agendas (or overt agendas) that might tempt or motivate you away from expressing empathy as counselor and how these agendas may affect your work. Don't be shy about admitting such temptations. They would not be so much wrong as normal. Being with persons in pain is not easy, and sometimes much of our background prompts us away from expressing empathy. Here are a couple of examples to get you started: (1) Seeing a client suffer with painful emotions and inadvertently holding yourself back form expressing empathy in the hope that she will not have to feel her pain so fully; (2) feeling compelled to give a solution that you think is simple for a client who is in pain (especially a client who you see as experiencing a difficulty you have faced) and believing that this advice might help your client avoid pain.

- Hold a discussion of the various difficulties that you know or imagine will affect you in expressing empathy.
- Give special consideration to the difficulties counselors face in experiencing and expressing empathy with unpleasant emotions. Speculate on the difficulties you may face. What emotions of others do you know or imagine you will be most comfortable and most uncomfortable with? Why? Plan ways to overcome your limitations in that work.
- Notice your reactions to unpleasant emotions in life, and real and practice sessions. Contemplate the meanings of what you notice in your reactions for yourself and in your work. Design practice sessions to challenge the weak points that you identify.
- Use counseling and other contemplation opportunities to discern your shoulds, so that you can knowingly set them aside.
- Use counseling and other opportunities for deeply honest human interactions in which you can risk expressing and coming to know yourself, in order to come to know and accept your dark sides, so that you need not fear them and need not limit your experiencing with clients.
- Journal your thoughts, feelings and understandings of self and the subject of expressing empathy, especially as they result from these practices and discussions of uncomfortable emotions for you.
- Review the Primary Skills Objectives and your satisfaction of your mastery of each at this point in your development. Use your review to guide you in the additional reading and practice you seem to need.

References

Beck, J.S., & Beck, A.T. (2011). *Cognitive behavior therapy: Basics and beyond* (2nd ed.). New York: Guilford.

Douglas, C. (2005). Analytical psychotherapy. In R.J. Corsini & D. Wedding (Eds.), *Current psychotherapies* (7th ed.). Belmont, CA: Brooks/Cole.

Ellis, A., & Dryden, W. (2007). *The practice of rational emotive therapy* (2nd ed.). New York: Springer.

Jung, C.G. (1935/1956). Two essays of analytical psychology. In C.G. Jung, *The collected works of C. G. Jung*, vol. 17. Princeton, NJ: Princeton University Press.

Rogers, C.R. (1980). *A way of being*. Boston, MA: Houghton Mifflin.

Wubbolding, R.E. (2010). *Reality therapy*. Washington, DC: American Psychological Association.

Pre-Chapter Quote

T.S. Eliot quoted in E.M. Beck (Ed.), J. Bartlett (compiler) (1980). *Bartlett's familiar quotations* (15th ed.). Boston, MA: Little, Brown & Company (p. 809).

5   STRIVING FOR AND COMMUNICATING UNCONDITIONAL POSITIVE REGARD

All sentient beings should be looked on as equal. On that basis, you can gradually develop genuine compassion for all of them.

Dalai Lama

Nothing we do, however virtuous, can be accomplished alone; therefore, we are saved by love.

Reinhold Niebuhr

Primary Skill Objectives

- Explain how unconditional positive regard is and is not expressed, and how it is and is not perceived, and why.
- Explain the applications of unconditional positive regard in life in general, but also in your life, as well as in your present and/or future counseling sessions.
- Understand and be able to explain the inhibiting factors for unconditional positive regard discussed in this chapter; be able to explain the factors that may inhibit your unconditional positive regard.
- Be able to explain the likely relationship between counselor burnout, difficulty expressing unconditional positive regard and the potential effects of this counselor difficulty on clients.
- Outline your plan for avoiding the burnout that may inhibit your unconditional positive regard and negatively affect your clients.
- Discern how you may maximize your strengths and improve your weaknesses in providing unconditional positive regard.

Focus Activity 1

There is a quote from Carl Rogers (1961) that we find quite true and profound, but at first it seems not to make sense. It is an important paradox to resolve for understanding therapeutic relationships and unconditional positive regard. The quote, in two parts, is "When I accept myself as I am, then I change," and "We cannot move away from what we are, until we thoroughly accept what we are. Then change seems to come about almost unnoticed" (p. 17). The paradox to us is that it seems logical that if people accepted themselves, they would stagnate, lose motivation to change. Yet, we do not find this to be true in others and in ourselves. Contemplate, journal or discuss how Rogers's observations could be true, despite seeming not to make sense. Work at it until you have a tentative explanation that seems meaningful to you. Apply your speculative answers to yourself and to clients whom you know or imagine.

Focus Activity 2

Journal and discuss your thoughts on the following sets of questions with peers. Answer as many of the questions as possible. Don't allow yourself to quit easily on these difficult questions. Build your answers in discussion. Take time to contemplate, rather than answering quickly. Ponder and look for themes in your answers and those of your discussion group.

Additionally, in case they begin to, try not to let your answers prompt self-criticism. There are no wrong answers, and consistent positive regard may be more rare than some might think. Whatever your answers are is simply a part of who and how you are at this time. Our sets of questions to ponder are not meant as a means of right/wrong, good/bad evaluation. Also, for this focus activity we refer to consistent or frequent positive regard, instead of using the term *unconditional positive regard*, which we define in the chapter.

1. Describe the persons or things that you almost always have positive regard for: What or who are they? How did they come to be in your life? How has it happened that you hold them in such frequent positive regard? What sets them apart from the persons or things that you have less consistent positive regard for or that you have negative regard for? How do you feel, think, and act when you hold them in positive regard? When you do not? How do you feel, think, and act toward persons for whom you have much less frequent positive regard?

2. Describe your relationships with persons, if any, who almost always hold you in positive regard: Who are they? How did they come to be and remain in your life? How has it happened that they hold you in such frequent positive regard? What sets you apart from the persons or things that they seem to hold in less consistent positive regard or hold in negative regard? How do you feel, think, and act in response to receiving nearly consistent positive regard? How do you feel, think, and act differently when this positive regard is not there, or when negative regard is?

3. Now think of positive regard in relation to yourself: How consistently do you hold yourself in positive regard? On what does the positive

regard in which you hold yourself seem to be based (e.g., number of and closeness with loved ones; just being; a spiritual conceptualization of yourself as part of a higher, more perfect being; level of accomplishments; some combination of these and other factors)? What does the negative regard you sometimes have for yourself seem to be based on? How do you feel, think, and act in response to the times you hold yourself in positive regard? In negative regard? Does your reaction seem to vary when the positive or negative regard seems to be based on different motivations? How so?

From your considerations: (1) What do you conclude? (2) Is there a connection between giving and receiving positive regard? If so, what? (3) Is there a connection between positive regard to or from others and with yourself? If so, what? (4) Is it difficult to give and receive consistent or frequent positive regard? Why do you think this is or isn't? (5) What do you think your difficulties will be in holding clients in positive regard and how might you improve?

Introduction

Paths to Holding Others in Reasonably Consistent Positive Regard

Having taken ourselves through the focus activity, we are reminded that consistent positive regard can be quite difficult. We find that outside of counseling it can be difficult for us to give and to receive positive regard consistently. We have found it easier to hold clients in positive regard than some persons outside of counseling, and sometimes ourselves. Part of what has led us to most frequently hold our clients in positive regard is connected to our having devoted a large portion of our work to counseling children. We tend to see children as innocent, more pure, perhaps closer to the unity of life or for us the higher power that we believe we are a part of, which is more perfect than individuals. We also clearly see that children are constantly, instinctually learning, self-improving; and, except for massive interruption, rapidly self-actualizing. Counseling persons of various ages, we have broadened the breadth of persons that we see encompassed by the innocence of a child. Our definition of whom we hold in this same positive regard as children continues to widen.

To see that our clients are each instinctually striving to learn, self-improve, and self-actualize has helped us hold consistent (for the most part) positive regard for our clients. This is easily seen in cases where clients come to counseling saying, "I want to use counseling with you to better myself." But we also find this is true in the much more common cases where the client was referred by a concerned person (e.g., teacher, parent or spouse) or, as is often the case in schools, was invited to counseling by you, even in the cases where he/she is reluctant to use counseling. In all these cases, we have found that if we look for it, we can see that each person is striving to self-actualize. We also find that engaging our clients with the core conditions of counseling tends to help us see their striving to self-actualize and also seems to strengthen this striving. So with counseling, a self-perpetuating cycle begins that the more we meet clients with the core conditions, the more they strive to become their best and the more we can see this striving and the easier it is to hold them in positive regard. Then, the more easily we can hold them in positive regard, the more their natural striving is strengthened.

As we have already implied, we sometimes find our way back to positive regard for others and for ourselves, after having strayed, through our spiritual beliefs. We prefer to keep our comments on this few and as open to your views as possible. We do not mean to imply that a spiritual connection with positive regard for clients is necessary or within every counselor's path. Still, other authors have also noted a connection of unconditional positive regard to well-being and growth in the tenets of major religions. For example, Purton (1996) equates the Buddhist concept of counteracting *lobha* or greed, with the development of unconditional positive regard, and Wilkins (2000) with the forgiveness and compassion at the heart of Christian (and other) beliefs.

The Tandem: Empathy and Unconditional Positive Regard

We think of unconditional positive regard and empathy as a tandem—as in a two-wheeled carriage pulled by two horses or a tandem bicycle (Oxford Dictionaries, 2014). They are linked and can work more powerfully together for the goals at hand than the two working separately. In our work, empathy has been a key to finding unconditional positive regard possible in difficult moments. For some supervisees, refocusing in unconditional positive regard helps them renew their strength in empathy (e.g., Cochran, Cochran, & Sherer, 2012). Rogers (1951) described "deep understanding and acceptance of attitudes consciously held in the moment [i.e., unconditional positive regard]" as possible through "struggle to achieve the client's internal frame of reference [i.e., striving for empathy]" (pp. 30–31).

As with empathy, Carl Rogers introduced the helping professions to the importance of unconditional positive regard (Rogers, 1942, 1957). The assertions of empathy, unconditional positive regard, and genuineness—counselor qualities—asserted in Rogers's 1957 article, "The Necessary and Sufficient Conditions of Therapeutic Personality Change," seemed to open the eyes of the helping professions that counselor qualities matter, quite possibly much more than technical expertise (Farber & Doolin, 2011). By now the importance of counselor qualities or therapeutic relationship seems well accepted (Duncan, Miller, Wampold, & Hubble, 2010; Hubble, Duncan, & Miller, 1999; Norcross, 2002, 2011) and by some meta-analyses, perhaps at least twice as important to successful outcome as technique (Asay & Lambert, 1999; Wampold, 2005).

Like empathy, the concept of unconditional positive regard can seem esoteric, and it can be difficult to grasp just how to provide it. We can't promise to tell you just how to provide unconditional positive regard because that process can be unique to each person. As Farber, Brink and Raskin (1996) pointed out, it is difficult to tease out particular words or actions representing unconditional positive regard, even in transcripts of Rogers's work. Our goals for this chapter and your study are to make the concepts as tangible as possible, for you to grow your capacity for unconditional positive regard, and for you to find the ways of communicating unconditional positive regard that come most naturally to you.

What Unconditional Positive Regard Is and Isn't

Beginning Thoughts on What Unconditional Positive Regard Is

Rogers associated the terms *warmth, acceptance* and *prizing* with unconditional positive regard (UPR) (Wilkins, 2000). Rogers (1961) explained that UPR is "a warm caring for the client—a caring which demands no personal gratification. It is an atmosphere which simply demonstrates care'; not care for you *if* you have behaved thus and so'" (p. 283). Mearns and Thorne (1988) explained: "The counselor who holds this attitude deeply values the humanity of her client and is not deflected in valuing any particular client behaviours" (p. 59).

Of acceptance, Rogers (1980) wrote: "The therapist is willing for the client to be whatever immediate feeling is going on—confusion, resentment, fear, anger, courage, love, or pride" (p. 115). So the acceptance is just as true for emotions that the counselor might see as negative or positive in situations outside of counseling. For example, if a counselor outside of sessions finds others' expressions of anger distasteful, in sessions this counselor will need to work past distaste in order to accept all of the emotions her clients express. If we believe persons should feel guilt for their actions that hurt others but a client in a session expresses elation rather than guilt over such behavior, in order to be helpful, we must accept and respond with empathy to this elation. We have known clients to begin to reevaluate their reactions and change their hurtful behaviors with counselor acceptance of feeling elation. We have known clients to hear their own elation for the first time when it is met with warm acceptance and empathy, then to find it distasteful and begin a process of realizing how they have been motivated into hurtful behaviors. However, an important paradox to realize is that when faced with such a situation, you cannot meet this elation with warm acceptance and empathy in order to have your client change. If you did so, this would be your agenda for your client and not true acceptance. Such a reaction would thwart the change or bring a superficial change at best—a change that is meant just to please you and may last no longer than your presence. Such an agenda-laden response might also prompt guilt without further self-discovery, and thus enhance a cycle that drives hurtful behaviors in your client.

We like the use of the word *prizing*. It suggests to us that clients are treasures, that it is a joy and pleasure to discover them. We think of the way parents may prize their new baby: "Oh, look—another poop! He's so healthy!," "Feel how she clasps. So strong!," "Uh-oh, he's tired. It must be time to go lay down." Such prizing is often infectious to clients and helps them find the strength to renew and enhance their drive to self-actualize.

We want to emphasize but not overstate this quality of prizing. Prizing isn't infatuation, but it is sensitively caring for and appreciating the uniqueness of each client, including enjoying with your clients as they discover themselves. It can be appreciating the big dramatic parts of their discovery, which are really quite rare, as well as the mundane details and little nuances, which occupy most of the "discovery time" in counseling.

We also like the reference to UPR as prizing because it is an action verb. UPR has been an active and ongoing process for us within the relationships we have had with the clients we have served. Our clients have allowed us to see the more abrasive or harder-to-like parts of themselves at that time in their life. We hope that each new client will allow us to see these aspects of himself, as these are likely important parts of himself and aspects that may not easily meet with acceptance in other relationships.

Note that UPR does not mean agreement. We have counseled persons whose behavior we would not have approved of outside of counseling. Oftentimes, through counseling, those clients chose to change those outside behaviors that we would not have approved of. We have counseled persons when we strongly disagreed with some of the things they were saying. Our work in child-centered play therapy (CCPT—Cochran, Nordling, & Cochran, 2010; Landreth, 2012; Ray, 2011) has been helpful here. In CCPT, play is the child's primary language, not words. Often children play out characters that are not at all like they are outside of counseling, but are characters that represent at least a part of their experience of self and must be realized in order to make decisions related to such characteristics. From this, we have been reminded that when adults in counseling use words that are upsetting to hear, those words are a means of expressing only a part of who they are and how they feel in that moment, and that the words are less important than the person saying the words. The words may not represent the person's core experience.

An example from Jeff's work: I had an adult client who frequently made racist statements and harsh-sounding statements about what he considered liberal ideas or persons. I sometimes wanted to argue with these statements or at least tell him that I disagreed. He seemed to be beginning to show me his abrasive side, and I guessed that this part of him had been formidable in driving others away. Rather than focusing on the content of those words, I continued to hold his person in positive regard, even when I disagreed with his words. His words were more important in counseling as a manifestation of how hurt and bitter he felt than for the content they conveyed.

We also like the use of the word *acceptance* to understand the meaning of UPR. Acceptance seems less positive than prizing, but sometimes it is the most we can muster. Acceptance suggests the existential notion that persons, things and situations simply are what they are. Knowing that they are what they are, that they are the best they can be in that moment doesn't mean that we might not wish for change or that they will not change. Change is inevitable. For example, if the day is cold and gray and I wish it were sunny with a dry breeze, I will only frustrate myself wishing it were different. My wishing will not change the moment. If I accept the current weather conditions, I have the best opportunity to experience what that day has to offer and to be better for it. Accepting the day can then bring me closer to prizing the day.

To us, the use of the word *acceptance* also suggests part of our belief that we are all part of a greater whole, a whole that is more perfect than any of us are separately. For example, in some geographic areas cold, gray days in winter are required to prepare for spring. Spring must come before summer, and the heat of summer helps us appreciate fall. Our point is that acceptance partly means to us seeing each person as a part of a whole. If that part is hard for us to accept in that moment, we can help ourselves by remembering that they are a necessary part of the whole, as are all things.

Like empathy, we believe that UPR is natural to all humans. So, learning to provide reasonably consistent UPR for your clients will not be a task of learning a new skill but of discovering an old way of being that may have gotten squelched by personal inhibitions, social pressure, or other factors. When award-winning kindergarten teacher Vivian Paley used the words *kindness* and *interest in others*, she described what sounds to us like a universal UPR that is a strong and natural force among children (Wingert, 1999). This inspires and reminds us that UPR is natural to all people.

What Unconditional Positive Regard Is Not

Wilkins's (2000) way of considering what UPR is not may help you better understand what it is. *Conditional positive regard* would mean "offering warmth, respect, acceptance, etc. only when the other fulfils some particular expectation, desire or requirement" (Wilkins, 2000, p. 25). We have known a great many persons in and out of counseling whose parents raised them with conditional positive regard as a primary motivator. For such persons, the result often seems to be a sense of self-worth that is based on continually compiling accomplishments, manifested in behaviors that we consider maladjusted, such as taking hurtful advantage of others or becoming so discouraged that self-development is greatly thwarted.

In counseling, holding conditional positive regard for a client would mean that the counselor has a particular agenda for her (Wilkins, 2000). Thus, the counselor's behavior communicates, "I will accept you *when* you make progress in a particular direction." As with a parent using conditional positive regard as a primary motivator, such counselor behavior would only produce temporary, elusive progress at best. Any progress that occurred would then be based on conditional self-acceptance and risk a high level of dependency on the counselor, a crash to a greater low for the client, and inhibited client decision-making.

Unconditional negative regard would communicate to the other person, "Whatever you say or do, however you are, I will hate and despise you" (Wilkins, 2000, p. 26). In its extreme forms, it is the root of racism, homophobia, sexism, and the like. While the counselor's way of being may never include hate, we have seen counselors display unconditional lack of acceptance of clients from populations that counselors have become badly burnt out with (e.g., clients who are addicted, parents who are neglectful, youth with rule-breaking behavior). See our notes on burnout later in this chapter.

Unconditional positive disregard would mean that one person refuses or neglects a relationship with another. "In an extreme form, it is the complete negation of the existence of one person by another. This can be so powerful that receivers of it come to doubt their right to life" (Wilkins, 2000, p. 26). We have theorized that children with conduct disorder have perceived something like this from their parents at a key stage in development (often the parents were preoccupied with their own difficulties, illness, depression, dissolving marriage, substance abuse, etc.). The children then developed a set of self-statements that include such thoughts as "No one will like or love me. Therefore I am unlovable." In the magical thinking of childhood, this sometimes manifests in a fear that "I may cease to exist. I may have so little impact on my world that I will disappear." Such children then act out in mistaken attempt to reprove their existence, reestablish a personal power, and drive others away before experiencing a rejection that they believe will be inevitable and intolerable (Cochran & Cochran, 1999). "A distressed, bored or unengaged therapist is in danger of offering unconditional positive disregard" (Wilkins, 2000, p. 26). And, as with our theory of conduct-disordered behaviors, unengaged interaction can be interpreted by persons in vulnerable positions as a major and painful rejection.

In summary, UPR is not an agenda (whether known or unknown) to accept only parts of the person, her emotions, or the content of her expressions. UPR is not dislike. It is not a judgment of right, wrong, good, or bad. It is not agreement or approval. It is not disapproval or disengagement. It is not going through the motions of liking or merely acting as if you want to be with the other person. It is a warm, caring, non-possessive acceptance of the person, her emotions and the content of her expressions. It is a sensitive caring for and prizing of that person.

A Sample of the Literature Clarifying the Power of Unconditional Positive Regard

There is, of course, strong evidence supporting the power of the core conditions of counseling as a set (e.g., Bergin & Lambert, 1978; Cooper, Watson, & Holldampf, 2010; Elliott, 2002; Orlinsky & Howard, 1978; Patterson, 1984) and also regarding UPR as a singly important factor (e.g., Farber & Doolin, 2011; Farber & Lane, 2002; Orlinsky, Grawe, Parks, Bergin, & Garfield, 1994; Orlinsky, Howard, Garfield, & Bergin, 1986; Truax & Carhuff, 1967). Wilkins (2000) explained that "the communication of UPR is a major curative factor in any approach to therapy" (p. 23), and it is *the* curative factor in the context of congruence and empathy. Orlinsky and Howard concluded that patients' perception of therapists' manner as affirming the value of their person is significantly associated with good therapeutic outcome. Chiu (1998) concurred, explaining that UPR is the context to his holistic biopsychosocial approach. Jacobs (1988) recorded that psychodynamic counselors would expect "unconditional regard" to encourage positive transference (p. 13). Bozarth (1998) described it as the curative factor for client-centered therapy. From their meta-analysis, Farber and Lane stated that "positive regard seems to be significantly associated with therapeutic success," especially when judging by clients' perspectives on positive therapeutic outcome (p. 191). Farber and Doolin (2011) explained that, at a minimum, unconditional positive regard "sets the stage" for other interventions and, in some cases, "may be sufficient by itself to effect positive change" (p. 191).

Farber and Doolin (2011), regarding the value of positive regard across approaches to counseling and psychotherapy, concluded:

> From a psychodynamic perspective, positive regard serves to strengthen the client's ego (sense of self or agency) and belief in his or her capacity to be engaged in an effective relationship; from a behavioral perspective . . . positive regard functions as a positive reinforcer for clients' engagement in the therapeutic process, including difficult self-disclosures; and from a more purely humanistic perspective, the therapist's stance of caring and positive regard facilitates the client's natural tendency to grow and fulfill his or her capacity as a human being . . . nearly all schools of therapy now either explicitly or implicitly promote the value of this basic attitude.
>
> (p. 62)

To consider applications of UPR in counselor services that go well beyond individual sessions in schools and agencies, consider examples of the power of UPR across a range of helping relationships: Peacock (1999) included UPR as a primary quality needed in custodial interactions in therapeutic communities; Sweeney and Fry (2012) asserted UPR as an alternative term for the altruistic love valued in spiritual leadership, encouraging individuals and communities to realize full talents; Muravchick (2012) asserted that Protestant ministers have drawn heavily on Rogers's work, especially amplifying the importance of pastoral UPR. van Ryn and Heaney (1997) saw UPR as an essential component in health education practice; Davies, Shen-Miller and Isacco (2010) in Men's Center programing focused on men's health and mental health issues at universities. Cramer (1994) evidenced that self-esteem is determined by the degree to which one has a close friend seen as providing the core conditions, especially UPR; Scheffler and Naus (1999) that a perception of UPR from fathers predicts self-esteem and a lack of fear of intimacy in daughters. Huntsinger and Jose (2009) evidenced the cross-cultural importance of acceptance as an element (i.e., acceptance balanced with control) in parents across cultures exerting a positive influence on their children's adjustment; and Hayes, Jones, Silverstein and Auerbach (2010) as an important program element for the "stickin to" for fathers in a low-income, Early Head Start fathering program. Watts (2009) suggested the importance of UPR for a successful radio show in which persons call in for advice, guidance or psychological perspective.

Why Unconditional Positive Regard Is Powerful

We hope that the focus activity of this chapter was helpful to you in beginning to discover some of how and why UPR is important and powerful. One way to understand why it is powerful is to know some of the ways people respond to experiencing warm, heartfelt positive regard from others. We humans often have a variety of responses to experiencing this positive regard, including coming to see ourselves in a more positive way; coming to accept ourselves; feeling empowered; reducing defenses, feeling encouraged to learn more about ourselves; and feeling empowered to risk going into scary places of self-discovery.

Jeff offers a hopefully instructive example of his reaction to UPR: Though it sounds a little odd to me, I sometimes have a twinge of guilt when I realize that others hold me in near unconditional positive regard. This seems to be connected to my thinking that I don't deserve it, mostly because I don't hold others, even those who frequently hold me in warm positive regard, as consistently in the warm positive regard that I think I should.

Even when a client has a reaction like this to UPR and his counselor meets this reaction with deep, heartfelt empathy, this can be very useful to the client. This can be the opening of the door for that client to reconsider his self-statements, to review who he really is, his standards for himself, and what he wants those standards to be. Such a client reaction can be quite painful but a moment of opportunity to begin great progress through the process of counseling focused in genuine empathy and UPR.

Self-Acceptance = Change

Rogers (1961) wrote of a paradox of UPR, "When I accept myself as I am, then I change," and "We cannot move away from what we are, until we thoroughly accept what we are. Then change seems to come about almost unnoticed" (p. 17). From our contemplations of this paradox, we have a few thoughts we would like to offer. Accepting one's self requires knowing one's self. If we do not know ourselves, we cannot know who or what it is we are or would like to change. Yet, if we humans do not accept ourselves, we will not allow ourselves to know who we are. Each of us humans will keep the parts that we might imagine are flawed, embarrassing, or shameful hidden from ourselves in the darker recesses of our inner selves, and not let them out into the light of conscious examination. But once we do let all of our true selves into the light of conscious examination, we will then either reduce the self-expectations that we find unreasonable or change the ways of being that we find unacceptable.

At this stage of acceptance, the force of change is incredibly strong and the counselors' work is so easy it is almost obsolete. If a client asked us to guide her behavior through life in a stage of counseling before such self-acceptance, we would not usually give this guidance (see later chapters for exceptions). Doing so would likely prevent her from further self-discovery and self-acceptance, and may help her defer impetus to true, deep and lasting change.

On the other hand, once reaching a stage of more realistic self-perception and self-acceptance, our clients normally find the personal skills they need and have come to readily want, without our moving into a teaching mode. If in that stage our clients did ask for help with learning skills for the changes they want, we could freely teach without change-inhibiting influence.

UPR = Full Expression of Emotions

You may remember a story from the last chapter of a boy who told his counselor of a fight he had been in (page 81). A part of his full and honest telling included his expression of elation regarding the fight. Had his counselor not provided him with a relationship based in a large part on her UPR, he would have censored that part of his story, if he told the story at all. Fortunately, she did hold UPR for him. His full realization of his elation seemed a significant part of his discovering who he was at that time, what parts of his self he was dissatisfied with, and how he really wanted to be.

As We Accept Our Clients, Our Clients Accept Themselves

Modeling is a strong force within therapeutic relationships. It takes great effort from a client not to accept herself in the face of a counselor who knows her well through deep empathy and provides her with nearly consistent UPR.

A related example from Jeff's education illustrates this: Years ago I was counseling and learning under the influence of a group of counselors who were focused in cognitive-behavioral approaches to counseling. My supervisor and I were glad to see my clients making progress in changing the self-statements that drove their misbehaviors and negative emotions. She asked me, "So, what do you think it is about your work that is most helpful to your clients in changing these critical self-statements?" At first I wasn't sure, so I pondered and observed my work with my clients further in search of an answer that satisfied me enough to present to my supervisor who I greatly admired. I was expecting to credit something from cognitive-behavioral techniques. But what I concluded seemed too simple to be profound. I discovered that they seemed most helped in changing their self-statements by the fact that I didn't try to force them to change these self-statements, but I also simply did not agree with their globally critical self-statements. I created a safe and empathic environment for each client to let me know who she really was. And as I knew the person that each client really was, I accepted and prized that person. I decided it was my UPR that most helped my clients change their critical self-statements.

A Safe Environment

Both empathy and UPR are essential ingredients for producing a safe environment for self-exploration and self-revelation. If we were clients to counselors whom we feared were judging or diagnosing, as diagnosis can often be taken for or used for judging a person as flawed, we would not feel safe and would be guarded from sharing parts of ourselves that we might see as shameful or embarrassing (see later chapters for thoughts on integrating assessment and diagnosis with therapeutic relationship skills).

However, UPR and this safe environment are more than just not making major errors in judging clients. When people have opportunities to bask in the glow of those who care for us and hold us in very frequent positive regard, we *want* to tell them more and more of ourselves. We want to have those caregivers really *know* us.

Others' Evaluations: A Poor Guide for Self

Experience is the best teacher. Yet, it often takes UPR to build that place of safety to stop denying the experience of our emotions, to risk experiencing emotions fully, to discover who we are, what we really want, and how we want to be. Then with UPR, deep empathy enhances, clarifies, and brings clients' emotional experience into full consciousness. We have known clients in this context to make decisions that they felt great confidence in, and looking back, we agree that these decisions were mature. We have counseled persons who were acting out with misbehavior, or experiencing great somatic pain, or feeling greatly depressed, discouraged, and unmotivated for their life's tasks but did not know why. In the atmosphere of UPR and deep empathy, they discovered that they had internalized life paths that they had believed others wanted them to take and that they were deeply dissatisfied with these paths. Yet, until motivated to counseling by troubling symptoms, and until finding themselves through UPR and deep empathy, they had not realized their level of dissatisfaction with their current paths.

Having now made comments on the importance of UPR, we want to insert a reminder that valuable work in counseling is not simple. We don't want to imply that it is simple by telling only the beginning and end, as in the examples just described. Such self-discoveries of our clients through UPR and deep empathy sometimes occur quickly, but are almost always the product of patient acceptance.

Rewards for the Counselor and the Client

Rogers (1980) wrote: "I have found it to be highly rewarding when I can accept another person" (p. 20). He explained that each of us are islands unto ourselves, in a very real sense. We take this to mean that, while it is right and helpful to strive for it, we humans cannot reach true and complete understanding of each other. The best that persons can do is understand what we see of each other through our worldview, formed of our unique set of experiences and meanings made of those experiences. This understanding, and especially our communication of it, must then pass through some medium (e.g., language, play, art), which brings limitations to the connection. But when we feel safe enough to, and are permitted through UPR and shared emotion, to express who we really are, we begin to experience moments of connection. When we counselors accept the feelings, attitudes, and beliefs that are vital to who our clients are in that moment, we help them build their connections, initially to their counselor but also to all life beyond their self. Rogers explained that this work, this connecting, is highly rewarding to him. It has also been highly rewarding for us.

We have often thought that our clients and our students bring out the best in us. We find that when they strive to be who they are with us, and through UPR come to be the best of their potential, this brings us a warm joy and contentment with them and with ourselves. So, from that feeling grows a desire and capacity to provide more and deeper warm acceptance, and prizing of these persons and others. This process has greatly improved who and how we are.

How Unconditional Positive Regard Is and Is Not Communicated

It would be difficult to tell a client that you feel unconditional positive regard for her, or that you like, love, or warmly accept her. In life, such things are sometimes said but not meant, or are misinterpreted or disregarded. Sometimes a part of what brought persons to counseling is that they have difficulty hearing and believing such statements. In counseling, the need to explain such statements might steal any power that such statements could have. For example, if one of us had a client that we struggled to like, whose statements or expressed emotions were distasteful, but we were successfully working through the distaste to achieve a level of warm acceptance for this client, to state the acceptance would also seem to require explaining what it is based on, which would sound conditional, or at least impersonal.

Additionally, if it became your habit to state your UPR in moments when you realize it, your clients could come to assume that if you don't state your positive regard, you don't feel it. Further, if you would state your moments of positive regard, would you be willing to also state your moments of negative regard for your clients? We would not normally be willing to do. Doing so would take our focus far from empathy, therapeutic listening, and helping our clients self-discover and self-evaluate.

Fortunately, when you feel UPR for your clients, it will usually be clear to them without stating it. In the less common situations in which your clients do not perceive the UPR that you feel for them, their misperception of how you feel toward them, how they think you see them, will come to light through therapeutic listening and empathy. Then, their perception of how you see them will be important for them to learn about. This same sort of misperception may be problematic for them in life.

An analogy from romantic relationships may be helpful. When people are attracted to others, the person they are attracted to usually know this at some level, especially if the two persons have frequent contact. To express this attraction, the people who are attracted need only be at a level where they can be themselves and accept how they feel toward others, versus being greatly inhibited. The people receiving the attraction could probably figure it out by interpreting their admirer's actions, but this is a highly fallible process. Instead, when we humans are open to it, we know without thinking when we are liked. If we are inhibited from knowing this, that would be something worth working on in counseling, and this work would occur through experiencing UPR, empathy, and a therapeutic listener who can respond to the little clues that her client is having difficulty perceiving acceptance or liking from others. One such little clue to a therapeutic listener might be a statement like, "Well, you'd be bored if I tried to tell you about that." To such a statement, we would express awareness and acceptance of her inhibition by reflecting with genuine warmth and mild surprise, "Oh, so you thought to tell me about that but decided to discard it on the assumption that I would be bored." Then, depending on whether this was a pattern and on how she reacted, we might add, "I'd like you to tell me the things that seem important to you, and I will be interested, as I am interested in you." Another little clue might be a client who seems so concerned with saying the right thing that he has difficulty getting started saying anything at all. To him, we might tenderly reflect, "You seem to worry over finding something good or profound to say." Then a useful discussion of the topics he is discarding will ensue. Accepting, prizing, and attending to clients' experiences and communications (or lack of verbal communication) communicates your UPR and, when needed, opens the door to clients discussing with you their perception of your perception of them (in

Chapter 8, "Structuring Therapeutic Relationships," we discuss helping clients understand how they can most effectively decide what to discuss in counseling, when necessary).

A clear way to know that you are expressing UPR for your clients is to review your work to check that you attend to all client expressions equally, based on the level at which they are expressed to you. The only factor influencing which expressions to respond more to should be your perception of which expressions seem most important to your clients.

One manifestation of UPR is contained in how you accept corrections from clients. As discussed in Chapter 4, under the section "Be Prepared for and Accept Corrections" (page 78), clients will sometimes correct your reflections in therapeutic listening or expression of empathy. In such a moment, it is not important to convince them that they misunderstood you. To hear their correction and strive to understand that new communication demonstrates both your primary intention to understand as well as your acceptance.

In case it is still difficult to discern whether or not you are expressing UPR for your clients, we would like to offer thoughts regarding how you may know if your clients are perceiving UPR from you. UPR tends to bring about a sense of calm, a feeling of being at peace with oneself. This shift is most obvious with children and less obvious with adolescents and adults who may have more greatly solidified and inhibiting self-statements that say things like, "Others will not like me," or "I am unlikable, unacceptable," and who tend to be more guarded against close connections. So with children and sometimes with adolescents and adults, you will see their breathing become more abdominal, see their shoulders relax, see tensions fall off their body. When you see this, what you are seeing is your client experiencing the physiological sensation that all is safe and OK with you. This would not mean that your client does not have many more strong emotions to express. When experiencing this safety, child clients go most efficiently to the places they need to go in that moment or the ways they need to be. They may become wildly silly or aggressive in play. This is your client letting his guard down, letting defenses drop. This is your client letting self-imposed and societal restrictions drop because at a level close to his core, he feels freedom from judgment and warm acceptance from you.

What Gets in the Way of Unconditional Positive Regard

While we can know the value and some of the roles of UPR, Rogers (1951) acknowledged that in some moments with some clients, counselors will have only "conditional positive regard—and maybe negative regard" and that "unconditional positive regard exists as a matter of degree in any relationship" (p. 101). It is understandable that ruptures will occur in therapeutic connections (Safran, Muran, & Eubanks-Carter, 2011) and Farber and Doolin (2011) explained that ruptures will often be the result of "occasional inability to demonstrate minimally facilitative levels of positive regard" (p. 63).

So, knowing that errors in UPR will occur, but should be avoided as much as possible, we discuss the issues that we have found in our teaching and practice to most often get in the way of UPR. Consider which issues relate to your experience and begin your process in overcoming issues in you that may inhibit your UPR.

Having an Agenda for Your Client

Any agenda you may have for a client amounts to placing a condition on your positive regard for your client. Wanting too strongly for clients to change, to improve, is an agenda and inhibits change and improvement. Believing or hoping that just maybe the process of counseling and your client's self-actualization through counseling can be hurried lengthens the process. Ironically, the less you try to hurry the process, the more efficient you become. Yet, not hurrying for the sake of efficiency is also an agenda. Strive for UPR, deep empathy, and therapeutic listening because they work and because it is the right, most respectful thing you can do. Efficiency will follow.

We do not mean to say that your client may not have an agenda or goal for his own development. This is different from your having an agenda for your client. We discuss helping clients understand how the process of counseling may or may not help them reach their goals in Chapter 8.

We believe that having no agenda for clients, even for them to improve as we or you may see it, may be impossible. Yet, we know that to be most effective, we need to strive to have no agenda and to be totally non-possessive in our way of accepting clients. The closer we come to this way of accepting, the more efficient we can be.

Counselors Believing They Know Better Than Their Clients

Some counselors approach their clients as if they (the counselors) can see and fully comprehend the complexities of each client. They approach them as if they have analyzed their clients' internal thoughts, beliefs, fears, and motivations, as if they have assessed the realities of clients' outer worlds, which would include the inner worlds of the people that their clients' lives contact. From this vantage point, these counselors seem to assume that they are able to know which behaviors their clients should employ in order to have the greatest success and happiness. This approach also assumes the counselor knows what success and happiness would be for each client and that the counselor's conception of success and happiness is the same as that which would satisfy each client. Such counselor beliefs then lead to conditional acceptance at best, communicating, "I will accept you when you make the changes I prescribe."

Pardon our slight hyperbole and mild sarcasm in working to make this error clear in the previous paragraph. Probably counselors who take a well-meaning, heavy skill-teaching approach, without acceptance, do not knowingly intend the assumptions we characterized. More likely, in hopes of being quickly helpful, they come to see life and people as much simpler than we do. To us, people and their problems rarely boil down to a need for a discreet set of new skills. In our interactions with counselors who work this way, we find that given time in this way of working, they become discouraged, frustrated, and burnt-out, and come to fill more and more of their work time with non-counseling tasks.

Rogers (1961) explained that he found himself wishing to rush in to "fix things" (p. 21). However, the more he listened to and learned of himself, and the more he tried to extend that same listening to others, the more respect he came to have for "the complex process of life" (p. 21). So, through listening, he became less and less inclined to hurry in to fix things, to mold people, to manipulate and push others to be the way he might have liked them to be.

Burnout

What Burnout Is

Burnout can be seen as a widespread threat to counselor effectiveness (Bilot, 2013; Campbell, 2014; Lambie, 2006). When counselors experience burnout, they often feel discouraged, frustrated, and bored with their work, and they have great difficulty connecting with clients. We believe burnout usually comes from caring greatly but finding one's self or one's work ineffective. Gunduz (2012) evidenced a causal relationship from self-efficacy to burnout, especially in depersonalization and personal accomplishment dimensions, in school counselors. Such ineffectiveness or self-perception of ineffectiveness could come from poor training or it could come from the ways of being described in the previous section that interfere with UPR. This sense of ineffectiveness could also come from serving very difficult client populations. In such cases, the counselor's work may be excellent, but still client progress is small.

What Burnout Does

Whatever the cause, we find that burnout creates what Wilkins (2000) terms *unconditional positive disregard*. Wilkins writes: "A distressed, bored or unengaged therapist is in danger of offering unconditional positive disregard" (p. 26). Sometimes counselors in this predicament, though usually unaware, have decided that they just can't hear any more and certainly can't feel pain with clients any further. Yet, counselors in such predicaments sometimes do not stop work and continue to hold "counseling sessions." Unfortunately, entering sessions in such a state makes engaging clients through UPR nearly impossible.

Avoiding Burnout

We may not have great answers for avoiding burnout and hope you will seek other authors who can offer more than the few suggestions we describe here. First, although it is not simple, work to drop your agendas for and assumptions about your clients. Strive to meet each client with UPR, deep empathy, and therapeutic listening.

Second, especially when serving clients with very difficult situations, research the effectiveness of your work. Early in his career, Jeff agreed to serve a population of students of whom more than half could be expected to drop out of or fail school. Not all of them could be served in counseling due to time limitations. This situation set up an opportunity for a comparison of the progress of students served in counseling and those unserved in counseling (the two groups were similar in key variables and received alternate services). Those unserved continued to drop out or fail at about the same rate, but those receiving counseling came to succeed at a significantly higher rate. These findings were very encouraging within otherwise very discouraging work.

Researching the effectiveness of your work does not have to be complicated. Experimental designs are not necessary. Qualitative/quantitative studies that indicate how small numbers of clients have progressed, or how they perceive themselves to have progressed, can also be very encouraging. Our point is that sometimes in the face of clients who experience very difficult lives and who may not make the level of progress that we wish for them, it can come to seem like they made no progress at all. Yet, careful but not necessarily complex research can show that they are making significant progress. Results can serve to keep counselors heartened, to keep them open to feeling with clients and ready to accept each client for who she or he is, and to help them accept the rate of progress that seems possible at the time.

Third, we encourage you to remember to care for yourself as well as your clients. Strive to base your self-care on being, rather than doing. A void in self-acceptance to be filled only by compiling accomplishments will never be filled. There is always the next accomplishment before acceptance.

We recommend you to seek and accept help from others. Gunduz (2012) "found that counselors who take social support have a positive attitude toward their profession" (p. 1761). We find ourselves fortunate in that when we stop to notice, there are others in our lives willing to offer support. The question in our self-care is if we will take this support or not.

We encourage you to rest and recreate, to do some of the things in life that bring you pleasure, happiness, and joy. Stop and smell the roses! And as it is supportive of the UPR that we hold for others, consider reinvigorating your spiritual faith or contemplating your own individual role in the world as being a necessary part of something much bigger than you alone. In our view there is a positive life force, a collective self-actualization process. It is helpful for us to see ourselves as a part of a greater whole—a part of the collective self-actualization process that is life.

Lack of Self-Acceptance

It is difficult to accept others when persons do not accept themselves. It seems that we humans often criticize or refuse to accept aspects of others that we find unacceptable in ourselves. As we strive to accept ourselves without conditions, to accept ourselves for being rather than doing, and for being just how we are—mistakes and human flaws included—this striving seems to encourage and increase our capacity to accept others unconditionally.

Counselors Inadvertently Seeking to Fill Their Own Needs through Clients

If we, or you, wanted too much for clients to show like or appreciation of their counseling, it would lead to conditional positive regard—accepting clients only as they express that appreciation. Often clients do express appreciation, but counseling can be thankless. We believe it is best for our and your self-care, as well as most efficient in counseling, to have no expectation of being liked or appreciated by clients. Though many times appreciation of the counselor comes naturally as part of being in a therapeutic relationship, it is best to get needs for being liked and appreciated met elsewhere.

Another need that a counselor might mistakenly try to have met by clients is a need to be needed. This may set up the conditional positive regard that shapes clients to continue to be dependent on their counselor. The inadvertent message from the counselor's behaviors, ways of being and responding, would be, "I'll accept, value, and prize the parts of you that need me (as opposed to all parts of you equally)."

Still another such need is to see one's self as helpful and effective. The message of the counselor's behaviors, ways of being, and responding here would be, "I'll accept and prize you when you change." This would set up the condition of accepting clients only when they obviously change and improve. This condition would inhibit client self-acceptance and produce temporary, artificial change at best.

The Analytic Mind

Some in the counseling field have brilliantly analytic minds. When this is the case, beginning counselors may feel frustrated or ineffective when their client is not doing or saying something clearly symbolic or deeply meaningful. If such counselors are not careful, this can set up a dynamic of conditional acceptance, communicating: "I'll accept you when your work is clearly symbolic or deeply meaningful." This is a difficult demand to meet and the pressure would inhibit self-expression.

Hard-to-Like Clients

Often the abrasive (perhaps surly, manipulative or condescending) parts of clients come forward in counseling. This is a good thing. As these aspects of your clients meet with your UPR, deep empathy, and therapeutic listening, this initiates your clients' process of deciding just who and how they want to be.

An illustrative example from Jeff's work: I once made the mistake of smiling or grinning warmly when a client hit into me angrily for not helping her the way she wanted. The content of her attack seemed to be that if I were a really good counselor, I would surely be at some more prestigious school than the one that accepted her. She misinterpreted my mistaken smile as amusement with her. So, I had to explain.

What was going on in my mind was that I had known that she was hurting very much and acting in self-hurtful ways. Yet, she had struggled to start the counseling process that I believed would help her. She very much wanted an immediate solution, one that would not require her to engage in a process of self-discovery, one that would not require her to begin showing me more of who she really was. So, when she finally got mad, I saw it as the start of being real.

I did explain my mistake and she did continue. I can't say she came to live happily ever after; perhaps no one does, and her life had been especially difficult. However, she did let me know who she really was, both her surly, sharp parts and her child-like vulnerable parts. And she achieved a much greater level of self-acceptance, happiness, and success.

I say that my smile was a mistake not just because it was misinterpreted but also because I slipped from empathy with the anger she was expressing to my own happiness at seeing what I took to be progress. My smile also signaled a mistake because it marked my pleasure at her taking the path that was my hope, my agenda for her. I quickly noted my mistake and got back on track.

Clients vs. Moral Constructs

Conflicts between client behavior and counselors' values are inevitable. For example, we have strong moral constructs around the care of children. We believe that good, conscientious, loving care of children is right, and is what all persons raising children should do. Yet, we have had clients who got pregnant, not because they wanted to love and care for children but because they hoped the pregnancy would make a permanent romantic relationship. We have also had clients who attempted to justify in sessions their continuing in abusive relationships with spouses despite the effect on their children or their failure to pay child support. It was a great challenge to work through our moral constructs to maintain warm acceptance for such clients. It took work and effort for us to maintain our faith that our acceptance would be part of healing for the clients, and so also for their children. With that said, we don't mean to say that we would never express our views of a client's behavior in counseling. We address that possibility in following chapters.

We have often noticed in our own work, and in the work of our counselor interns that we all tend to "get the clients we need." What we mean is that we find that counselors tend to meet the clients that fit right into their weak spots and force them to grow. This is a blessing, we guess. Certainly, we have grown from clients that hit our weak spots. Those persons have brought us opportunities to expand our capacity to accept.

Initial Judging Thoughts

Rogers (1961) explained that it is necessary to *"permit oneself to understand another"* (p. 18). He explained that for himself and many people, our first reactions to others' statements are almost always evaluations. When someone expresses some feeling, attitude, or belief, our base response is usually to think "That's right" or "That's stupid," "That's normal" or "That's not very nice" (p. 18). Rogers explained that we rarely permit ourselves to understand precisely the meaning of the statement to the other person. He explained that such understanding is risky. If we human individuals understand this other person, it might change us—it might challenge and contradict our beliefs about ourselves and our world in unknown ways. And we humans tend to fear the unknown. So, counselors must overcome the fear of such understanding and change. Outside of awareness, this fear would certainly inhibit UPR and empathy.

Unconditional Positive Regard in Counseling and Outside Counseling

We have noticed that we continue to experience less consistent UPR outside counseling sessions than in counseling sessions. However, we are pleased that working to maintain UPR in sessions increased our UPR outside sessions. Sometimes the strategic thinking parts of our minds almost believe that UPR might not always be best outside counseling. Yet, we find that the more we maintain UPR in life, the greater the strategic effect (i.e., the more easily we are able to influence situations, the more others want to support us, the less persons with opposing views want to oppose us). Ironically, if we worked to maintain UPR in order to achieve strategic purposes, that UPR would not be real. UPR is not a means to an end. It is a worthy end, in and of itself.

Activities and Resources for Further Study

- Revisit the focus activities of this chapter now that you have considered the meaning, purpose, importance, and inhibiting factors of UPR. How might you now explain the paradox from Focus Activity 1 differently?

- Regarding Focus Activity 2, journal or discuss your new considerations. How have your answers and related thoughts of UPR changed? How have they been strengthened by what you read? How might you want the impact and fullness of UPR in your relationships to change? How can you work toward this change?
- Journal or discuss the factors that you anticipate may inhibit your expression of UPR in sessions. For example, what are your moral constructs that may make it hard for you to accept certain client behaviors and communications?
- Also journal and discuss how you perceive UPR from others. What makes it easy for you to realize UPR from others? What makes it difficult?
- Journal or discuss what the presence and absence of UPR has meant in your life, and what it may mean and what it may effect as UPR becomes a more consistent presence in your life.
- Now that you have a fuller understanding of UPR, hold practice sessions with partners. Continue your skill practice with therapeutic listening and expressing empathy, but now focus your attention on the levels of UPR that you genuinely maintain. In reviewing your work, consider Wilkins's (2000) clarification of UPR made by reversing each of its elements. Are there evidences of UPR's reversed elements in your work (e.g., conditional positive regard)? Again, we suggest that the person in the role of the client discuss a topic with some emotional content. Also, we suggest that you have an observer and/or video tape your session so that you can collect feedback from these sources as well as from the speaker and from recollection. How well do you think you maintained UPR? How did you express it? What did your ways of being that may have expressed UPR look like? How well and how was your UPR for the speaker perceived? What are some of your strengths and inhibiting factors for holding your client in UPR?
- Think of alternate ways of defining and explaining what UPR is and why it promotes persons' progress in self-actualization. Journal and discuss the meanings of these alternate ways of defining and explaining UPR in order to develop understandings that fit personally for you.
- Read the sources we have used to develop our explanations of UPR in this chapter, especially works by Carl Rogers and Paul Wilkins's article, "Unconditional Positive Regard Reconsidered." UPR is certainly an abstract concept, although it need not be esoteric. Our hope is that you will continue to study it in order to broaden and deepen your understanding of it.
- Another source for further reading and thought on UPR is Jerold Bozarth and Paul Wilkins's (2001) book of edited essays that help to further clarify UPR's meaning and importance.
- Revisit the Primary Skill Objectives of this chapter and verify that you have mastered them to your satisfaction at this time. If not, seek

additional practice, reading, and discussion to achieve the level of accomplishment that satisfies you.

- Take time to read and contemplate the following poem, written by our friend, Armin Klein, who wrote from a wealth of rich experience as a psychotherapist and reflected on aspects of that experience in creating this poem.

Unconditional Positive Regard

Deep Openness

When people come to me asking for help
    With their confusion about themselves, about their lives,
I offer to try to facilitate their own growth process,
    Their own self explorations.

I try to open myself, empty myself of any thinking about them
    Before I meet them. That is very difficult for me.
My background, my early training, has always been to think,
        to problem-solve.
    What knowledge, what identities will provide understanding?
At first, my openness—when I can reach it—feels small and guarded,
    Scared as I am about new interactions and scared as I am, especially,
About facing the unknown—without structures.
    As I try to open, I cannot fool myself that there is any place
To which I am going other than to the unknown and to the
        unpredictable.
    So I am fearful, though I have grown very comfortable with my fears,
    Excited about the growth they promise me.

When we meet, I begin to relax as I begin to sense, to experience,
    Something more of the person, the individual being.
Some of this comes from our talk.
    More sensing of their being comes from our non-verbal communication,
The moments and the ways in which we each smile, we cry, we laugh, and
        we frown.
    We touch each other powerfully in those moments— without words.
We facilitate each other—and my openness grows.
    My mind empties itself of my conditioning—and all of its structures.
        My understanding becomes less "problem-solving."
            I experience it, and myself, as more deeply empathic.
        My empathy comes more from my inner self, what I like to call
            my heart.
            I experience myself as more deeply genuine.
    When I become very open, or very "empty"—to the extent that I can—
        My interest simply, and apparently naturally, deepens and changes.

My interest becomes very loving—without any apparent motivation.
I experience my positive regard as unconditional.
I feel myself moving much further into that way of being.

* * *

I love the process of opening, emptying, that has developed for me in my
work.
It has enriched and changed my work, which I love.
This process, however, has also changed my life.
It has become a wishful model for all my relationships and my self
exploration,
Although the framework of non-therapy relationships is markedly different.

In psychotherapy, I am devoted to the explorations of the other person.
I am always surprised at the unexpected gifts I receive from their
explorations.
In my friendships, the structure jumps over all the possibilities.
The responsibilities are more in the background, and they are more
shared.
I am still, however, always trying to be more open and more empty of
culture.
When I succeed, I feel, here also, very loving.
I experience my positive regard as unconditional.

This model has become my vision of how, with many ups and downs,
I am trying to live. The ups are joyful.
I sense the deepening of my openness and my emptiness as
Being at the core of the successes and joy
That I have both in my work, and in my friendships.
When I am less open, closing a little or closing a lot,
I diminish my genuineness,
The people who work with me in psychotherapy are very forgiving.
My friends are also very forgiving.
I am very grateful and encouraged that both groups of people
Recognize and treasure my struggle to be deeply open with them and
myself.

Reaching for the place of deeper, loving openness brings me
To Unconditional Positive Regard.

Armin Klein
January 2001

Note

References

Asay, T.P., & Lambert, M.J. (1999). The empirical case for the common factors in therapy: Quantitative findings. In M.A. Hubble, B.L. Duncan, & S.D. Miller (Eds.), *The heart and soul of change: What works in therapy* (pp. 23–55). Washington, DC: American Psychological Association.

Bergin, A.E., & Lambert, M.J. (1978). The evaluation of therapeutic outcomes. In S.L. Garfield & A.E. Bergin (Eds.), *Handbook of psychotherapy and behavior change* (2nd ed.) (pp. 139–189). New York: John Wiley.

Bilot, J. (2013). The relationship between wellness and burnout among novice counselors. *Dissertation abstracts international section A: Humanities and social sciences*, 74(2). Available through ProQuest (2013–99150–140).

Bozarth, J.D. (1998). *Person-centered therapy: A revolutionary paradigm*. Ross-on-Wye: PCCS Books.

Bozarth, J.D., & Wilkins, P. (2001). *Unconditional positive regard*. Ross-on-Wye: PCCS Books.

Campbell, J. (2014). Prevalence of compassion fatigue and compassion satisfaction in mental health care professionals. *Dissertation abstracts international: Section B: The sciences and engineering*, 74(7). Available through ProQuest (2014–99020–225).

Chiu, E. (1998). A patient who changed my practice. *International Journal of Psychiatry in Clinical Practice*, 2, 231–232.

Cochran, J.L., & Cochran, N.H. (1999). Using the counseling relationship to facilitate change in elementary school students with conduct disorder. *Professional School Counseling*, 2, 395–403.

Cochran, J.L., Cochran, N.H., & Sherer, L.C. (2012). Unconditional positive regard and limits: A case study in child-centered play therapy and therapist development. *The Person-Centered Journal*, 19, 3–28.

Cochran, N.H., Nordling, W., & Cochran, J.L. (2010). *Child-centered play therapy: A practical guide to developing therapeutic relationships with children*. Hoboken, NJ: Wiley.

Cooper, M., Watson, J.C., & Holldampf, D. (Eds.) (2010). *Person-centered and experiential therapies work: A review of the research on counseling, psychotherapy and related practices*. Ross-on-Wye: PCCS Books.

Cramer, D. (1994). Self-esteem and Rogers' core conditions in close friends: A latent variable path analysis of panel data. *Counselling Psychology Quarterly*, 7, 327–337.

Davies, J.A., Shen-Miller, D.S., & Isacco, A. (2010). The men's center approach to addressing the health crisis of college men. *Professional Psychology: Research and Practice*, 41, 347–354.

Duncan, B.L., Miller, S.D., Wampold, B.E., & Hubble, M.A. (2010). *The heart and soul of change* (2nd ed.) Washington, DC: American Psychological Association.

Elliott, R. (2002). The effectiveness of humanistic therapies: A meta-analysis. In D. Cain & J. Seeman (Eds.), *Humanistic psychotherapies: Handbook of research and practice* (pp. 257–281). Washington, DC: American Psychological Association.

Farber, B.A., Brink, D.C., & Raskin, P.M. (1996). *The psychotherapy of Carl Rogers: Cases and commentary*. New York: Guilford.

Farber, B.A., & Doolin, E.M. (2011). Positive regard. *Psychotherapy*, 48, 58–64.

Farber, B.A., & Lane, J.S. (2002). Positive regard. In J.C. Norcross (Ed.), *Psychotherapy relationships that work* (pp. 175–194). New York: Oxford University Press.

Gunduz, B. (2012). Self-efficacy and burnout in professional school counselors. *Educational Sciences: Theory and Practice*, *12*, 1761–1767.

Hayes, D., Jones, D.A., Silverstein, L.B., & Auerbach, C.F. (2010). In their own words: Early Heat Start fathers. *Psychology of Men and Masculinity*, *11*, 241–250.

Hubble, M.A., Duncan, B.L., & Miller, S.D. (1999). *The heart and soul of change: What works in therapy*. Washington, DC: American Psychological Association.

Huntsinger, C.S., & Jose, P.E. (2009). Relations among parental acceptance and control and children's social adjustment in Chinese American and European American families. *Journal of Family Psychology*, *23*, 321–330.

Jacobs, M. (1988). *Psychodynamic counselling in action*. London: Sage.

Lambie, G.W. (2006). Burnout prevention: A humanistic perspective and structured group supervision activity. *Journal of Humanistic Counseling, Education and Development*, *45*, 13–26.

Landreth, G.L. (2012). *Play therapy: The art of the relationship*. New York: Routledge.

Mearns, D., & Thorne, B. (1988). *Person-centred counselling in action*. London: Sage.

Muravchick, S. (2012). "Be the love of God rather than talk about it": Ministers study psychology. *History of Psychology*, *15*, 145–160.

Norcross, J.C. (2002). *Psychotherapy relationships that work: Therapist contributions and responsiveness to patients*. New York: Oxford University Press.

Norcross, J.C. (2011). *Psychotherapy relationships that work: Evidence based responsiveness*. New York: Oxford University Press.

Orlinsky, D.E., Grawe, K., Parks, B.K., Bergin, A.E., & Garfield, S.L. (1994). *Handbook of psychotherapy and behavior change*. New York: Wiley.

Orlinsky, D.E., & Howard, K.I. (1978). The relation of process to outcome in psychotherapy. In S.L. Garfield & A.E. Bergin (Eds.), *Handbook of psychotherapy and behavior change* (2nd ed.) (pp. 283–330). New York: John Wiley.

Orlinsky, D.E., Howard, K., Garfield, S.L., & Bergin, A.E. (1986). *Handbook of psychological behavior and change*. New York: Wiley.

Oxford Dictionaries (2014). *Oxford dictionaries: Language matters*. New York: Oxford University Press. Retrieved from: www.oxforddictionaries.com/us/definition/american_english/tandem

Patterson, C.H. (1984). Empathy, warmth and genuineness: A review of reviews. *Psychotherapy*, *21*, 431–438.

Peacock, S. (1999). Internal mental space. *Therapeutic Communities: International Journal for Therapeutic and Supportive Organizations*, *20*, 301–314.

Purton, C. (1996). The deep structure of the core conditions: A Buddhist perspective. In R. Hutterer, G. Pawlowsky, P.F. Schmid, & R. Stipsits (Eds.), *Client-centered and experiential psychotherapy: A paradigm in motion* (pp. 455–467), Frankfurt-am-Main: Peter Lang.

Ray, D. (2011). *Advanced play therapy: Essential conditions, knowledge, and skills for child practice*. New York: Routledge.

Rogers, C.R. (1942). *Counseling and psychotherapy*. Boston, MA: Houghton Mifflin.

Rogers, C.R. (1951). *Client-centered therapy*. Boston, MA: Houghton Mifflin.

Rogers, C.R. (1957). The necessary and sufficient conditions of therapeutic personality change. *Journal of Consulting Psychology*, *21*, 95–103.

Rogers, C.R. (1961). *On becoming a person*. Boston, MA: Houghton Mifflin.

Rogers, C.R. (1980). *A way of being.* Boston, MA: Houghton Mifflin.

Safran, J.D., Muran, J.C., & Eubanks-Carter, C. (2011). *Repairing alliance ruptures. Psychotherapy, 48,* 80–87.

Schefler, T.S., & Naus, P.J. (1999). The relationship between fatherly affirmation and a woman's self-esteem, fear of intimacy, comfort with womanhood and comfort with sexuality. *Canadian Journal of Human Sexuality, 8,* 39–45.

Sweeney, P.J., & Fry, L.W. (2012). Character development through spiritual leadership. *Consulting Psychology Journal: Practice and Research, 64,* 89–107.

Truax, C.B., & Carfhuff, R.R. (1967). *Toward effective counseling and psychotherapy: Training and practice.* Chicago: Aldine.

van Ryn, M., & Heaney, C.A. (1997). Developing effective helping relationships in health education practice. *Health Education and Behavior, 24,* 683–702.

Wampold, B.E. (2005). The psychotherapist. In J.C. Norcross, L.E. Beutler, & R.F. Levant (Eds.), *Evidence-based practices in mental health: Debate and dialogue on the fundamental questions* (pp. 200–207). Washington, DC: American Psychological Association.

Watts, G. (2009). "Seeds for success" radio program. *The Psychologist-Manager Journal, 12,* 72–77.

Wilkins, P. (2000). Unconditional positive regard reconsidered. *British Journal of Guidance and Counselling, 28,* 23–36.

Wingert, P. (1999, March 22). The edge of kindness: A veteran kindergarten teacher on what she's learned. *Newsweek,* p. 78.

Pre-Chapter Quotes

Dalai Lama. (2002). *The Dalai Lama's little book of wisdom.* New York: Barnes & Noble Books (p. 103).

Niebuhr, Reinhold quoted in E.M. Beck (Ed.), J. Bartlett (compiler) (1980). *Familiar quotations* (15th ed.). Boston, MA: Little, Brown & Company (p. 823).

6 THE DELICATE BALANCE OF PROVIDING EMPATHY AND UPR IN A GENUINE MANNER

The most exhausting thing in life . . . is being insincere.
Anne Morrow Lindbergh

Truth can never be told so as to be understood, and not be believed.
William Blake

The essence of therapy is embodied in the therapist.
Bruce E. Wampold

Primary Skill Objectives

- Be able to explain the meaning of the term *genuineness and congruence in counseling.*
- Understand and be able to explain difficulties that beginning counselors often face in providing empathy and UPR in a genuine manner.
- Discern and be able to discuss the difficulties that you experience or anticipate experiencing in providing empathy and UPR in a genuine manner.
- Be able to explain why your genuineness is important to the positive outcomes of your counseling sessions.
- Understand and be able to explain when and how you would express your thoughts and emotional reactions to clients, as well as how your decision process would play out.

Focus Activity

Observe communications and/or discuss ways that persons (you, acquaintances, friends, and family) are and are not genuine in everyday communication. For example, do you notice that persons in your life sometimes express understanding, agreement, or concern with statements like "I understand," "I know what you are going through," "I feel for you," when they do not understand, know, or appear to feel with you? In what other ways and situations do you notice persons saying or expressing one thing when it seems that they really mean something different? What seem to be the functions of these mismatches between persons' internal reactions and external expressions? How might these mismatches at times be helpful and at times be hurtful?

We suggest that you keep these questions in mind over the course of a week. Establish a couple times a day that you stop and reflect on your communications that day and contemplate your and others' genuineness in communication.

Note that we do not want this exercise to set up criticism of communication that is not genuine. Such communication may serve necessary expedience or cordiality, or may be evidence of persons coming as close to being genuine as is reasonable in the context. Communication outside counseling is very different from communication in counseling. For that matter, completely genuine communication would not even be reasonable in counseling, although it is much more of an expected ideal in counseling than outside. Use your discussions or observations to consider how persons' genuineness is the same in counseling and out of counseling, how different, and why.

Introduction

By now, our experience has taught us that the more open we are to letting others know who we really are and what our experience really is, the better for everyone, the closer we are to others, and the more joy-filled our lives have become. Beyond seeming like the right way to be, this way of being has also proven effective in getting good works accomplished. When we are genuine and respectful with others, we find that others more often respond in kind. Thus, we are more able to find common ground when we disagree and are more able to give and receive support.

Yet genuineness in counseling, like most counseling concepts, is more complex than it sounds. For an overly simple thought to spur your contemplations, consider the following: As difficult as it is to have one person fully understand another, if a counselor tried to have a client fully understand his experience of her (i.e., the counselor's thoughts and feelings in reaction to her), the explanation would take so long that the roles would switch. The counselor would become the client or primary speaker explaining his experience, and the client would become the listener. Therefore, counselors must carefully choose what limited parts of their experience of clients to communicate. Further, we titled this chapter "The Delicate Balance of Providing Empathy and UPR in a Genuine Manner" because we want you to focus much more on a genuine expression of your empathy and UPR than on a genuine expression of your whole self and your full set of reactions to clients. We want you to realize the delicate balance in decision-making between remaining focused on your client and sharing your experience of your client.

What Genuineness Means and Does Not Mean

As with each of the core conditions of counseling, Rogers (1957) is credited with bringing the importance of counselor genuineness to the consideration of the helping professions. Rogers (1980) explained that this core condition or element of the counselor's way of being could be called "genuineness, realness, or congruence" (p. 115). He explained: "The more the therapist is himself or herself in the relationship, putting up no professional front or personal façade, the greater is the likelihood that the client will change and grow in a constructive manner" (p. 115). So to us this means that the counselor cannot hide behind the façade of being the assessor (i.e., taking on a role of assessing or analyzing her client, rather than meeting her client fully and experiencing with him). It means that the counselor cannot hide behind a professional persona of being all-knowing and omnipotent, of probing and prescribing what her clients should communicate and experience in their counseling sessions.

Rogers further explained that the counselor attitude of genuineness means that the counselor "is openly being the feelings and attitudes that are flowing within at the moment" (1980, p. 115). He explained that for the counselor, "what he or she is experiencing is available to awareness, can be lived in the relationship, and can be communicated, if appropriate" (p. 115). In our section, "How Counselor Genuineness Is and Is Not Communicated," we lead you through an exploration of when it may and may not be appropriate to communicate your experiences of your client that occur outside of empathy and UPR. For this beginning section, know that by genuineness, we do not mean communicating any or all of your experiences. Think of genuineness as you making your strivings for empathy with and UPR for your clients every bit as much of who you are as possible. It would not be very helpful for you to respond like an "empathy and UPR machine" simply saying the right things. While in some moments it may be the best a counselor can do, it would not be effective for you to go through the motions of conveying empathy and UPR that you do not really feel.

Rogers explained that the core condition of genuineness means "the therapist makes himself or herself transparent to the client; the client can see right through what the therapist *is* in the relationship; the client experiences no holding back on the part of the therapist" (1980, p. 115). This notion lof your clients experiencing no holding back on your part underscores the importance of your working through the things that get in the way of your experiencing empathy and UPR. For example, we believe that all people are at least somewhat inhibited from full experience of emotions. However, if your inhibitions of full emotional experience significantly inhibit you from experiencing your clients' emotions, this may cause you to go through the motions or say words as if you are fully experiencing with your client, when you are holding yourself back. Your work might then look like counseling on the surface but not actually be therapeutic. At some level, clients know when their counselor is holding back in this way, when their counselor is merely putting up a façade of empathy. Such a façade will limit client progress.

An additional quote from Rogers (1980) may clarify: "To be with another in this way [deep empathy and UPR] means that for the time being, you lay aside your own views and values in order to enter another's world without prejudice" (p. 143). Laying aside views and values can be difficult. It may be an impossible goal to reach in perfection, but it is essential to your clients' progress that you come close to it most of the time, and that you continually work to expand your capacity for empathy and UPR so that you continually come ever closer to perfecting this goal.

A Sample of Literature Clarifying the Importance of Genuineness

We suspect that it is even more difficult to research the outcome effects of genuineness or congruence than empathy and UPR because, as we see it, genuineness is a way of being that underlies providing empathy and UPR, rather than a separate quality or set of behaviors. However, in this section we suggest a sample of sources clarifying the importance of genuineness.

Understandably, most outcome research into genuineness or congruence has focused on congruence as part of the set of core conditions of therapeutic interactions. Patterson (1984) explained that such studies provide "a body of research that is among the largest for any topic of similar size in the field of psychology" (p. 431).

Meta-analytic reviews help us sort out the research across the decades. Kolden, Klein, Wang and Austin (2011) summarized the research, explaining, "Congruence or genuineness is a relational quality that has been highly prized throughout the history of psychotherapy, but of diminished research in recent years" (p. 65). Kolden et al. pointed out that prior to their meta-analysis, there had been at least 10 previous similar meta-analyses of the role of genuineness to counseling outcome. From their earlier meta-analysis, Orlinsky and Howard (1978) reported that two-thirds of the studies they reviewed on genuineness (20 in all) showed a significant positive relationship of genuineness to outcome. In their later review, Orlinsky and Howard (1986) reported that 20 of 53 studies showed the same positive relationship and noted that this positive relationship was strongest in studies that used client perception as part of the assessment of counselor genuineness. Grafanaki's (2001) findings demonstrated the possibility that counselor congruence without empathy and UPR may not have a positive impact. Truax and Mitchell (1971) concluded that empathy and warmth can only be facilitative when they are at least minimally real in the counselor. Kolden et al. confirmed, finding genuineness important to outcome in itself, and perhaps more importantly asserting that neither empathy of UPR can "even be conveyed unless the therapist is perceived as genuine" (p. 65).

Numerous studies have addressed the effects of the match or mismatch between counselors' expressed and implied messages (implied through the way things are said or through nonverbal behavior). Findings by Haase and Tepper (1972) suggested that congruence is an essential underpinning of the communication of empathy and that inconsistency between verbal and nonverbal counselor messages may undermine even highly empathic messages. Findings by Graves and Robinson (1976) suggested that inconsistent counselor verbal and nonverbal messages may prompt clients to see them as less genuine and prompt clients to maintain greater interpersonal distances from their counselor, especially when nonverbal messages are negative and verbal messages positive. Further, from this study it was suggested that when verbal and nonverbal messages have equal intensity, the credibility of the counselor's message is enhanced. Recent research into the similar construct termed "the real relationship" (Gelso, 2011), evidenced that the greater the real relationship, the lower the tendency of clients to hide true feelings and avoid attachments (Fuertes et al., 2007; Marmarosh et al., 2009; Moore & Gelso, 2011). Findings by Sherer and Rogers (1980) suggested that counselor nonverbal behavior has an impact on perceptions of counselor warmth, empathy, and genuineness, and that because ratings of warmth, empathy and genuineness were highly interrelated, the concepts are probably quite similar at a nonverbal level. Findings by Tyson and Wall (1983) seem to concur, suggesting that congruent verbal and nonverbal behavior enhances the impact of the counselor's message.

Kolden et al. (2011) explained that "Although most fully developed in the client-centered tradition, therapist congruence is highly valued in many theoretical orientations" (p. 65) and across settings including school counseling centers, inpatient, mixed and outpatient settings; with the strongest relationship of genuineness to outcomes occurring at school counseling centers. Kolden et al. suggested that counselor genuineness is especially important with adolescents and young adults (their analysis did not include studies of counseling services to children), explaining that "The congruent therapist communicates acceptance and the possibility of engaging in an authentic relationship, something needed, but not easily expected from the often formal and authoritarian adults in the lives of [youth]" (p. 70).

The Role of Genuineness in Counseling

Keeping Therapeutic Listening, Empathy and Unconditional Positive Regard Real

Making the therapeutic listening, empathy and UPR that you provide your clients an integrated part of who you are means that your skills and your way of being is not a façade that covers you, but instead it is authentic and who you truly are. In Chapter 3, we explained part of the importance of empathy through our conceptualization of what drives conduct-disordered (CD) behaviors in troubled children (Cochran & Cochran, 1999). As we continue our work providing child-centered play therapy (CCPT—Cochran, Nordling, & Cochran, 2010) to children in the UT REACH Project (providing and researching CCPT and related services in high-poverty schools), we find "relationship-resistant" a useful term in describing the behaviors of these children. We see that therapeutic relationships focused in deep empathy and UPR break down the troubling belief systems that drive relationship-resistant behaviors, such as believing "I am unlovable and no one can understand me . . . I can't bear the possibility of abandonment I have previously experienced in relationships . . . so, to protect myself from further hurt, I must act out to drive others away." For such children, though it can be challenging, we have found that it is UPR and the opportunity of being in and experiencing a genuine, deeply empathic therapeutic relationship that is curative. It is what provides *evidence in experience that this troubling belief system is not true.* We are finding that it is what allows these children to change and accept, and to be in healthy, pro-social relationships. If, instead of being offered a therapeutic relationship, a child client who is determined to resist being in a relationship is simply taught skills or repeatedly redirected, this opportunity for change is lost. While mentoring and other outreach might have some therapeutic value, this would be vastly less than experiencing a therapeutic relationship with a counselor who has integrated therapeutic listening, empathy, and UPR into her genuine way of being.

Genuineness in the Set of Core Conditions

Genuineness and Empathy

Bozarth (1998) describes a "conditions loop" (p. 80) in which the three core conditions are ultimately one. Bozarth explains a loop of genuineness with empathy, in that the more a therapist is able to be aware of her own experience, the more that therapist will be able to be aware of her client's experience. Then, the more that therapist is able to be aware of her client's experience, the more she is able to be aware of her own experience. Thus, Bozarth defines genuineness as "a natural awareness of the therapist to her own experience" (p. 80).

We take Bozarth's explanation of a conditions loop and definition of genuineness to mean that ideally you would be primarily aware of your client's experience in sessions and secondarily aware of your own experience in sessions. To us, the importance of your self-awareness in sessions is not so that this experience can be expressed to clients but so that you can manage it, so that it enhances rather than detracts from your therapeutic listening, empathy, and UPR. Virginia Satir (1987) wrote of her work:

When I am in touch with myself, my feelings, my thoughts, with what I see and hear, I am growing toward becoming a more integrated self. I am more congruent, I am more "whole," and I am able to make greater contact with the other person.

(p. 24)

Genuineness and Unconditional Positive Regard

Lietaer (1984) views congruence or genuineness and UPR as parts of a more basic attitude: openness. Lietaer asserts that openness with self creates a greater openness with clients.

The more I accept myself and am able to be present in a comfortable way with everything that bubbles up in me, without fear or defense, the more I can be receptive to everything that lives in my client.

(p. 44)

Connection and Collaboration

Other authors have suggested the importance of therapeutic alliance (Horvath, Del Re, Flückiger, & Symonds, 2011) or goal consensus (Tryon & Winograd, 2011). Kolden et al. (2011) pointed out the role of genuineness in attachment or bonding, explaining that genuineness can include carefully considered self-disclosure, feedback or explanation of thoughts, opinions and feelings in response to client communication. This open, two-way communication regarding your client and her context supports deep, personal connection, as well as a sense of alliance and goal consensus—the sense that we are two people engaged in working on this together.

Modeling

Counseling is a process of helping clients become congruent (Purton, 2013; Rogers, 1957). Therapeutic listening, empathy, UPR, and genuineness play roles in this process. Therapeutic listening and empathy help clients realize who they are and who they want to be. UPR provides a safe and nurturing environment in which clients allow their counselor and themselves to know who they really are and who they want to be. Genuineness makes empathy and UPR real, rather than techniques, but also provides clients with a model of a congruent helper and person.

While we often refer to the three core conditions, Rogers (1957) actually introduced six conditions for therapeutic personality change. One is that the persons should be in psychological contact. Two more are that the therapist experiences UPR and empathic understanding. Another is that this empathy and UPR are at least minimally communicated. The other two include the client being in a state of incongruence and the therapist being in a state of congruence.

We believe that the therapist's state of congruence, with empathy and UPR integrated into her being during her time with clients, has a powerful modeling effect. The conditions for modeling are present. The two persons have a close, personal relationship. The first person tends to be vulnerable through incongruence, through the nature of seeking or needing help, and through the fact of entering a world that is new to him but familiar to his counselor. So clients tend to look up to and respect their counselors. Thus, the counselor's modeling of genuine empathy and UPR helps clients come to have self-empathy (Hatch, 2000), to fully realize what they feel, and to develop self-UPR, to fully accept who they are even while they are motivated to improve.

Jeff has had a number of his adult clients illustrate this process for him in a way that may help you understand: Some of my particularly articulate adult clients have told me at the end of our work together that early in our counseling, when faced with a painful dilemma, they would hear my voice in their head fully accepting and understanding what they were going through. They told me that they used this voice to make decisions full with care for themselves and others. Later, this voice became their voice, and they came to realize that they were coming to need time with me much less.

When I first heard this from a client during our therapeutic process, I was alarmed that I was being overly influential, perhaps inadvertently shaping my clients to be like me. However, I have come to see this as a process of clients modeling their treatment of self and others after the empathy and UPR they experienced from me. While I have been honored to have this role, I have come to know that I was not influencing my clients to be like me, especially when I realized that they made decisions, with self-empathy and UPR, that were best for them but that were not always the decisions that I believe I would have made in their place or that I would have suggested for them, had suggestions been a part of my role.

Creating a Safe Place for Emotional Honesty

Congruence allows counselors to be perceived as safe and solid to clients. If a counselor goes through the motions of empathy and UPR but these motions are not genuine, clients can sense this incongruence at some level. Then, having a vague awareness that something is untrue in their counselor, the clients understandably become suspicious of their counselor and come to see their counselor's actions as only tricks or techniques.

A metaphor may be helpful in understanding this effect. We, and many people we know, have experienced romantic or other relationships where one person wants it to work out so badly that he tries to make himself into just the person that he believes his partner wants. That person is then in a state of incongruence. When this happens, the partners do not share a relationship between two solid persons but a relationship between one person who may be solid and one person who is not. Such relationships usually dissolve into mistrust. Such relationships often leave the solid partner wondering, "Just who are you?" and thinking in frustration, "How can I find out how I fit with you, when I can't tell who you really are?"

Another example of incongruence may help further understanding. We have noticed that some adults will ask children to fully disclose on a topic, even when the adult is withholding key information. Jeff observed a blatant example of this in an elementary school.

A school adult pulled a child into a meeting to discuss a bus incident. The adult had already decided that she knew what this child had done and who was at fault. Yet, she opened the discussion of bus behavior with a feigned willingness to listen to the child's side of the story. Sensing her insincerity, the child clammed up and became unwilling to talk. After the child left, the adult complained, "How can I help him, if he won't be honest with me?" Jeff imagined this interchange as a card game in which the dealer insists that the other player show all his cards and tell his strategy, while this dealer continues to cover her cards and hide her strategy, then complains that the other player is unwilling to play by the rules.

How Counselor Genuineness Is and Is Not Communicated

Declarations of Genuineness Are Rarely Helpful

Your genuineness is not something you can express in a statement. Rather, it is a way of being to strive for. When your empathy and UPR are genuine, they will come close to being consistent in you. Just as the child in the bus incident knew not to trust the terms of the discussion, your clients will usually know when you are being genuine with them and when not. If your client continues to doubt your genuineness, it will be helpful to see and respond to this doubt through empathy so that your client can realize and learn from it.

Jeff often remembers the futility of claiming genuineness by remembering that when other teens that he grew up with were exaggerating a story, they would preface the exaggeration by declaring, "Ain't no lie, man." Such statements became a communications flag for Jeff, from which he would note, "The following is probably a distortion of truth, at best."

Sometimes Counselors' Experiences of Clients "Bubble Up"

Bozarth (1998) clarifies his definition of genuineness, explaining that genuineness may be purely internal awareness or may involve a statement to a client. Regarding when or how genuineness may be a statement, Bozarth relays Rogers's explanation that when he is empathically attuned to his clients and working with them within their frame of reference, sometimes statements of his experience of them seem to "bubble up" in him, and he makes the expression aloud. Consider Jeff's description from his work.

At times I have been surprised by a change in a client, perhaps upset at a setback or very happy that a client made progress she had long wanted. I don't have much of a poker face. So, when I have had these feelings in response to clients, my clients have easily known this. For example, when a client noticed that I seemed frustrated as he told me of slipping back into a pattern of depression and self-doubt after having made progress, I responded, "You seemed to see a reaction cross my face, and then a look of alarm crossed yours." He then half-heartedly disclaimed his reaction, saying, "Oh no, it was nothing," then looked down in silence. To which I caringly responded, "You say it was nothing, but now you seem intimidated, hurt by me." Then, he let more of what I thought was his true feeling show, blurting, "Well, you're probably all critical of me, thinking I just make my own problems." Realizing his concern, I was glad to reflect and explain my reaction, saying, "Oh, that is what you figured was going on with me. No, I am not thinking critically of you, but I do feel frustrated with this setback. I know how much you have wanted to feel better." So he told me, "Yeah, I'm frustrated, too." Then, I, of course, shifted myself back to therapeutic listening, empathy, and UPR. I responded: "So, you too. I also have the thought, that I'm not sure of but I got the impression a moment ago, that *you* are critical of you, and you have at least a little thought that you make your own problems." This seemed to open a door for him to come to realize that while it was true that he very much wanted to feel better, his depression was also a temptation serving a purpose of his avoiding responsibility. A representative thought pattern for this might be, "I can't help it, I am Depressed." Depression gets a capital D, as a defining label, rather than a description of feelings. My expression of frustration was an accident, but within the context of careful listening, empathy and UPR, it became useful to his self-discovery.

State Your Reaction When It Interferes with Empathy and Unconditional Positive Regard

Stating enough of your reaction for your client to understand what is going on with you is sometimes necessary to stay on track with a relationship focused in empathy and UPR. Consider the following examples from Jeff's work.

Example 1

I got the news of the unexpected death of a friend's child just before beginning a small group session. There was nothing I could do to help my friend immediately, so I kept my session appointment. As more than one client was telling the group and me how they felt overwhelmed by stresses of school and work, I had begun to listen poorly, but I didn't realize it. So, without realizing what I was doing, I phrased a reflection something like, "So, these little things are really starting to seem overwhelming to you." Fortunately, a group member awoke me from my lack of awareness by calling me on my error, saying, "These things aren't little to us." As I attempted to get back on track and reflect correctly, she added, "And you seem bored today, like you don't think these things are that important." To which I just told the truth, something like, "Yes, I am having difficulty focusing and listening right now." I added explanation because I wanted her and the others to understand that my error was due to factors outside of the group, saying, "I just got the news of the death of a friend's child before we met, and I'm having difficulty getting the pain that I imagine my friend feels out of my mind so that I can focus with you, here." Having said that, I became more able to focus on group members' communications, reactions to me, and to each other. The group members soon moved on and continued to share the stressors that were important to them and also seemed to come to see their stressors in the context of the news that I shared with them. Again, my lapse in empathy was an accident that forced an explanation of my incongruence. That explanation may have been mildly helpful for group members to scale the stressors they were experiencing. However, that small outcome was only an accident. I don't think the group members perceived their stressors in any particularly distorted way before my lapse in congruent empathy and following explanation.

Example 2

In another example, I was working with a client whom I had begun to think was trying to get me to dislike him by making racist and political statements that he seemed to assume I disagreed with. Through these statements over a few sessions, I worked to keep my focus on his experience, to lay aside my views and values in order to enter his world without prejudice. For example, he might have said as a side note to his worries over not getting hired by a top firm, "Well, you probably don't agree with this, but the blacks and women are using the courts to every advantage they can get." While I did feel an urge to argue with this side statement, I decided that the crux of what he was expressing was his fear that he might not get the job he had dreamed of. So this was what I focused my reflection on: "You have this anger toward blacks and women and courts, and your great worry is that you'll never get the job with ___."

However, when he later told me that he didn't pay his child support because his ex-wife manipulated the courts and other events against him, his views and actions had so affected me that I was listening poorly. So, I decided to tell him the truth of my reaction to him. I stopped him and explained: "I am having a hard time listening and understanding your experience, as I think I strongly disagree with some of your views." I then gave a couple of examples of my disagreement, that I thought child support was owed to the child, regardless of the other parent's behavior; and that I thought it unfair to blame blacks and women for whether or not he was able to get the job he dreamed of. I then managed to maintain warmth in a process reflection, saying, "Also, I have the idea that you've made these statements in shocking ways, assuming I would react critically." He explained that he had not intended to shock me and that these were ideas that he firmly held, and he did figure I strongly disagreed. Yet, he also seemed to consider my process reflection as at least possible. While we continued to work together for some time after that moment, we certainly never argued about his views. Additionally, in the time that we were together, he began sending his child support, and when he expressed views that he assumed I would disagree with, he stated them as his opinion, rather than fact. It seems to me that his views softened over the time we had together. He became much more open with his emotions, expressing them as his emotions more often than as political views. I attribute his change much less to that moment when I expressed my views in disagreement than to the many more moments when I successfully responded to him with empathy and UPR.

Please realize that it would be a problem for us or any counselor if the numbers of statements or persons to whom we have difficulty listening with empathy and UPR were significant. More important than expressing your disagreement in rare moments when your listening is greatly inhibited, is ever expanding your capacity for empathy and UPR with greater ranges of persons and topics. This is our ongoing path, as well.

Being Who You Are in the Phrasing of Your Reflections

Your reflections and expressions of empathy are meant to express your understanding or feeling with your clients. Yet, they also are expressions of who you are and how you see life. You may remember that in Chapter 2 we described each communication from a client as coming to you through the mental filter of your views and that any response from you must pass back through that mental filter. Your understanding of your client is never a true understanding but the best understanding you can muster, given the limitations of perception and language. So, while we would like your (and our) reflections to be true images of clients, they are not. They are a combination of your clients, your striving to understand them, and you. For example, we tend to think a lot of the existential notions of choice, personal power, and decision-making. This is part of the mental filter through which we hear our clients' communications and through which we express our understandings. So, the phrasings of our reflections often are peppered with words that suggest such notions: "You have decided that is not possible for you," or "You are choosing not to do that any more."

Additionally, significant influences on Jeff's development as a counselor and person come from rational emotive (Ellis & Dryden, 2007) and cognitive behavioral therapy (Beck & Beck, 2011). Belief systems from these theories have become a part of his worldview. Thus, he tends to hear the thought patterns behind his clients' feelings and actions and include these in his reflections. For a different example, a counselor with strong beliefs aligned with feminism might have a mental filter that prompts her to hear client communication in the context of power differentials in clients' lives and the effects of these differentials. So, each counselor's reflections become, at least inadvertently, a manifestation of that counselor's worldview. This seems to us yet another important reason for counselors to strive to know themselves, to improve themselves, to ever expand their capacities for understanding, empathizing with, and accepting others.

Make Judicious Self-Expressions, Beyond Your Ever-Present Empathy and Unconditional Positive Regard

Remember, whether through the phrasings of your reflections or outright expressions of reactions to clients, keep your influence limited, giving favor to helping your client find her own meanings for her experiences. There is a tremendous power differential between client and counselor. By virtue of presenting as clients, your clients are in a state of incongruence and hence are vulnerable. It is extremely unlikely that there might be an equal exchange of views between counselor and client.

What Makes Providing Empathy and Unconditional Positive Regard in a Genuine Way Difficult

The Errant Thought—I Am Who I Am

We have known some beginning counselors to misunderstand the concept of genuineness. Their misunderstanding was that it meant being their personality traits as they are in whatever current stage of development they have achieved. For example, more than one beginning counselor has expressed to us her resistance to empathy and client process, saying, "But I'm a take-charge person. So, when I guide my clients' lives, I'm just being genuine."

As you may guess, we see a number of errors in such beginner counselor's statements. For one thing, such statements seem to assume that the persons making the statements are static, that whatever qualities they have at the time of the statement are the predominant qualities they will *always* have. But as every person is constantly developing, we do not accept that any one stage in a person's development is permanent.

However, our key disagreement for this context is over the meaning of genuineness. We urge you to develop the core conditions and their resulting skills into the core of who you are, instead of trying to develop a way of working to fit who you are in your current stage of development.

The Challenge of Clients Who Are Hard to Like

Clients who are hard to like present a particular challenge and opportunity for counselors to expand their capacities for making therapeutic listening, empathy, and UPR a greater part of who they are in their therapeutic relationships. Whenever we find a client hard to like, it is because that client strikes against some cognitive construct of ours, probably regarding how people should be or act. In such situations, counselors are presented with opportunities to review and perhaps open such constructs in order to be able to accept and empathize with a broader range of client experiences. Supervision or the counselor's own use of therapy offer venues for this work.

The Need for a High Level of Self-Development

Counselor Maturity and Personal Development

In light of the previous section, it makes perfect sense that Lietaer (1993) points out that congruence requires therapists to be psychologically well developed and integrated. Lietaer goes a step further to assert that personal maturity can be considered a therapist's main instrument in therapy.

Self-Awareness

We see self-awareness, of course, as a key to counselor maturity and personal development. Especially, we see it as key to congruence. It would be difficult for a counselor to maintain reasonably consistent congruence if he is not reasonably aware of his internal experiences and external manifestations.

With insufficient self-awareness, counselors may express reactions of which they are unaware, and may even deny them when asked. Such a denial may prompt client self-doubt and be unknowingly dishonest, modeling just the opposite of the open communication that you would like to see from your clients. Consider the following explanation by Tudor and Worrall (1994):

> It is likely that if as therapists we consistently ignore or deny some of our feelings and experiences we will out of awareness, communicate such an unassimilated or partially accommodated material to our clients. Clients, for instance, who are particularly sensitive to anger, may sense in us an irritation, which may or may not have anything to do with them. If they question us about their sense that we are irritated, we need to be sufficiently aware of our selves that we can identify and acknowledge any grain of truth to their perception, if there is one.
>
> (p. 2)

Kolden et al. (2011) drew the comparison of genuineness or congruence to mindfulness, explaining, "we might say that the therapist is mindfully genuine in the therapy relationship, underscoring [the counselor's] present personal awareness [required for] genuineness or authenticity" and further that "Congruence . . . thus involves mindful self-awareness and self-acceptance" (p. 65).

Self-Acceptance and Self-Honesty

It seems to us that self-acceptance is prerequisite to the high level of self-awareness needed for genuineness. If we counselors are highly critical of our experiences, especially our experiences with clients, it will be difficult to see our actions clearly. Without the honest, clear sight of self-acceptance, our self-awareness and any communication of our experience is inhibited. However, while we emphasize this high standard for your development, it is also important to remind you that perfection is not human, not possible, and maybe not even desirable. We want you to work hard to move yourself toward this important goal but not to let that work become an inhibiting factor.

Knowing the Difference between Your Reactions to Clients, to Things Other than Clients and Your Shoulds

In discussing guidelines for counselors' expressions of their reactions to clients, Tudor and Worrall offered the following explanation: "We need to be able to tell what, of all that we are experiencing as we work, is a response to our client, and what is a response to a bad night's sleep or the morning's post or some similarity between our client and some other person we know" (1994, p. 4). We add that we counselors also need to be aware of enough of our shoulds (i.e., rules that we humans believe that we and others should, ought, or must live by, which can sometimes be beneath our awareness; Ellis & Dryden, 2007), that these shoulds do not greatly affect our experience of clients.

Consider the following example: If you have a should that says "People should be nice to others and if people are not nice to others, it is terrible, awful!" you may react to a client who is telling you about things he has done that were hurtful to others by communicating your hurt, irritation, or disappointment over his hurtful actions. Or you might simply tune out from listening and attending during the parts of his sessions in which he is trying to tell you of his hurtful actions. With either of these reactions, you stifle your client's opportunity to learn from experiencing his actions. Having his full experience enhanced by your empathic response can help this client come to realize his dissatisfaction with his actions, then decide to change and own that decision. Further, through your empathic response, he may even learn what the personal meaning of his hurtful actions have been and thus learn how else to find this same meaning. So, we encourage you to continue to work through your shoulds expand your capacity for consistent therapeutic listening, empathy, and UPR, as a part of who you are.

Expressing Positive and Negative Impressions of Clients

We have sometimes noticed that beginning counselors are excited to express reactions to clients that could be thought of as positive, such as their admiration of clients surviving adversity or their joy in client progress. We are not saying this is wrong. However, we believe it is important for beginning counselors to realize that to be consistent, the flip side of these positive expressions might be expressing annoyance with clients who seem to have it easy or frustration with a client's lack of clear progress. There would be an equal rationale for expressing these negative reactions. We think that as you choose to express your reactions, it is best to express them consistently, positive or negative—that way your clients will know that your intention is to help each fully process experience, and you are honest in doing so.

The Need for High-Level Attending Skills

Sometimes an initial tip that one of us is expressing subtle incongruence to our client is the client's reaction. For example, if a client tells of her actions, while moving in a way that suggests wincing, we could guess that she is assuming a criticism from her counselor. If such an assumption of criticism is true, then she might understandably not be fully disclosing. If she were correct in assuming her counselor's criticism, it would be better for the counselor, after reflecting, to either acknowledge the truth of the assumption (owning his personal reaction—see Scenario A) or honestly dispel the assumption. Either way, such situations require high-level observational skills, therapeutic listening, and empathy. The counselor cannot genuinely respond to this client's perception of the counselor if he does not sense it. Fortunately, such perception grows through developing empathy. A dialog illustration of how such a scenario might play out follows. We offer A and B scenarios, based on different counselor internal reactions.

Scenario A

COUNSELOR: [Picking up after the client had developed a pattern of making a motion that suggests wincing, while telling of her actions.] I notice you almost wince when telling me that. I'm guessing that you're worried I'm thinking critically of you.
CLIENT: [Shrugging.] Well, I guess anybody would be.
COUNSELOR: So, this is an assumption you'd have of anybody, and that includes me.
CLIENT: [Seeming to get irritated.] Well, come on, everybody knows it's wrong!
COUNSELOR: [Who does have critical thoughts in this instance.] Yes, I do find these actions that you are telling me of hard to listen to. I find myself distancing myself from you when I hear them.
CLIENT: [After stunned pause, looks at counselor and shrugs.]
COUNSELOR: While you expected it, you seemed stunned by what I said.
CLIENT: [After a pause.] Yes, I hurt very much over how my actions have affected others. Really, I want to be liked, too.

Scenario B

(Picking up at the point that it differs from Scenario A.)

COUNSELOR: [Who does *not* have critical thoughts in this instance.] I wasn't thinking in terms of right or wrong in that moment. I mostly was aware of how much you are struggling with this. And now you seem to tell me that part of that struggle is that you see that everybody knows it's wrong.

CLIENT: Yeah, everybody [thoughtful pause]. Oh, I'm so embarrassed.

COUNSELOR: You're embarrassed that so many might have seen your mistakes.

CLIENT: Yeah, I guess I'm embarrassed because I think it's wrong, too.

Clients Who Ask How You See Them

Some clients ask how you see them. In such situations with adult or adolescent clients, we are generally glad they ask and are willing to give an honest answer. Such answers can be very high-level reflections. Still, there are some tricky aspects to answering such questions. Because our focus is on helping the client fully experience his or her self and situation, we would first reflect what the client seems to have communicated with the question. For example, if a client asks one of us, "Am I normal?" depending on the intent of the question that we inferred from her tone and the context of her question, we would reflect something like, "That's something you'd like to figure out, and you're thinking it'd be helpful to know my opinion." However, after such reflections, we find that while we are ready to answer the question, our clients often withdraw the question, following instead the trail of their experience in other directions.

But this question "Am I normal?" brings up other important complications. If your client asks if you think she is normal, that is not really just a question about how you see her. It is also a question that requires knowing what normal is. We don't believe we know what normal is.

This issue of normalcy also reminds us that if you tell clients how you see them, you should stay away from judgments (i.e., good vs. bad, normal vs. abnormal). It is best to respond with how you feel in response to your client, rather than how you think. Consider the following answer scenarios.

Scenario A

Client withdraws the question:

CLIENT: I just can't believe how nervous I am about this. Is that normal?

COUNSELOR: In your shock over how nervous you feel, you wonder if it's even normal to feel so nervous.

CLIENT: Yeah. Of course, I guess I worry over what's normal a lot and that leaves me even more nervous [goes on to express frustration with worry].

Scenario B

Client does not withdraw the question (continuing from counselor reflection of the intent communicated in the question):

CLIENT: Yeah. I sure wish I could just know that. What do you think?

COUNSELOR: [Speaking slowly, thoughtfully.] I don't know. I don't think I can figure out what normal is. I try not to think of you in terms of normal and abnormal [seeing a frustrated look on client's face]. You were hoping for more of an answer from me.

CLIENT: Yeah. Can't you tell me anything?

COUNSELOR: [Saying what he thinks of client without judgments.] I see that what's normal and how others see you is very important to you. Also, that the effects of your decision on you and your family are very important to you. Then, placing value on both these things (how others see you and effects on your family) leaves you feeling very, very stressed and nervous.

CLIENT: I think maybe I worry too much about the future. I want to start doing what feels right, right now.

Scenario C

A feeling response is more fitting than thoughts from the counselor (after having gotten frustrated and yelling at her counselor that if he were really good he would not be working at this lousy school anyway):

CLIENT: [Looking both still mad and sheepish at the same time.] Oh God, I bet you hate me.

COUNSELOR: [Speaking with a tone of interest and acceptance that was invigorated by her strong emotion.] I would like you to know how I feel toward you, but first I want to note that you expressed strong anger to me that I assume had been building up for some time.

CLIENT: [Still frustrated but also calming down.] Oh, I'm just mad today [pause]. But, God, that was mean. You must hate me now.

COUNSELOR: You are troubled that I might hate you now. I don't hate you. I know that your situation now is *very* hard for you. I wish it could just be over and you could already be at the place where you've done the work you need and are feeling better. I long for this. But, as part of that work, I'm glad you will show me how you really feel, even if what you feel is anger at me.

CLIENT: [Tearful.] It's so hard [short pause]. God, this sucks.

A few more notes about these scenarios: If the normalcy question had been about use of counseling, we might have taken more of an opportunity to educate about counseling (see Chapter 8 for examples). Note from Scenario C that while the counselor expresses feelings in response to his client, feeling words are only part of expressing emotion. Feelings are often expressed in tone and wishes, as well as single words for emotions.

Balancing Freedom that Optimizes Personal Connections and Allows Experiences to Bubble Up, with Avoiding Influence that Limits Client Expression

In the classic film demonstration (Shostrom, 1965), Gloria finishes an honest humble statement to Rogers by saying: "All of a sudden while I was talking to you I thought, 'Gee, how nice I can talk to you and I want you to approve of me and I respect you, but I miss that my father couldn't talk to me like you are.' I mean, I'd like to say, 'Gee, I'd like you for my father.' I don't even know why that came to me." Rogers responded to her instantly and warmly: "You look like you'd make a pretty nice daughter. But you really do miss the fact that you couldn't be open with your own dad."

We assume this was one of those instances when Rogers's genuine response simply bubbled up in him and he stated it aloud. While his statement may not be what we would imagine one of us saying in the same situation, we can see the beauty of it. We see that he allowed himself the spontaneity to say what was in his heart, coupled with empathy for her experience. We can also see how the same statement, "You look like a pretty nice daughter," might have been meant to encourage, to try to convince her to see herself differently. Yet, we see that what makes this not the case is that Rogers's statement came from his being in touch with Gloria's inner world and being personally moved by it. If a counselor meant to convince Gloria to see herself differently by that same statement, that counselor would have erred in being more in touch with his own inner world and likely thinking how he *must* convince that client to suffer less (and hence, to experience less). This is a difference of intent that gives a statement from a counselor a deeply different meaning.

Ultimately, we want you to develop such confidence in your therapeutic listening, empathy, UPR, and judgment of when to express that you would allow important statements of your experience with your clients to bubble up from you, through your connection with your client's experience. The balance is to be free enough to make optimal personal connections, yet settled enough in your intentions that you don't use your significant influence to limit your clients' learning from their own experiences. It is important not to take such client-limiting influence. It is also important not to let your intention to avoid undue influence cause you to think too much, to be stiff and to lack the human connection that is key to therapeutic relationships.

Willingness to Engage

Kolden et al. (2011) used the term "willingness to engage" (p. 65) in describing what is required in order to be genuine with clients. We like that term. To us, it can mean willingness to share your reactions and thoughts; it means allowing yourself to be affected by clients; and it means doing—being—your imperfect best in a relationship.

Discipline, Practice and Effort

Genuineness is a quality that at first sounds simple—"just be real, just be myself." But as we hope you have seen thoughout this chapter, genuineness is both simple, subtle and complex. Kolden et al. (2011) concluded that "[Counselors] can mindfully develop the intrapersonal quality of congruence. As with all complex skills, this will require discipline, practice and effort" (p. 70). We encourage you to accept the challenge to your self-development as you continue your studies of counseling skills through therapeutic relationships.

A Closing Thought on Genuineness

In interviewing school counselors identified by peers as highly effective with students with conduct-disordered behavior, Jeff found one counselor's description of her work as representative of other outstanding counselors serving such youth. She described her work as "loving them, crying with them, laughing with them, and hurting with them" (Cochran, 1996, p. 97). In his time with her, Jeff learned that strong empathy and warm acceptance were quite consistent in her relationships with students in and out of their counseling sessions. This strong empathy and warm acceptance were clear expressions of who she was with them. When asked what advice she might give to other counselors beginning or expanding their work with such youth, she first answered, "Really listen and empathize. Don't try to tell them [students with CD] what they should and should not do. Through listening and empathy . . . lead them to find answers for themselves." She added a final thought: "Love them. If you can't love them, at least be honest enough not to fake it" (p. 106). Our desire is for you to find the strong empathy and UPR in you and to make these ways of being who you really are with your clients.

Activities and Resources for Further Study

- Revisit the focus activity for this chapter by making a new set of observations or reviewing your notes and answers to the questions of the activity. How have your observations, understandings and thoughts related to genuineness changed?
- Review your tapes of practice sessions, or real sessions if you are using this book while seeing clients, to search for moments that were particularly moving due to your and/or your client's genuineness. Also review for moments when you, your client or both seemed less than fully genuine. What were the effects of those moments in the process of interactions between you and your clients, and on your clients'

expressing and processing their experiences? Did your clients seem to know, at any level, when your empathy and UPR were not fully genuine? If yes, how so? Additionally, if you have the appropriate permissions, exchange tapes for review with other counselors in order to assist with these reviews of others' work and they of yours.

- Imagine moments in sessions in which you realize that your client does not perceive your empathy and UPR as genuine. Based on your learning from this and previous chapters, how do you imagine that this might happen and how might you respond once you realize it? What might you say and how? Be sure to consider reflections that go well beyond pedantic paraphrasing. What would likely be the advantages and disadvantages of ways you might respond in such moments? Discuss your scenarios and responses with peers.

- Working with a group of peers or on your own, devise a tentative set of rules, explanations and exceptions that you might use to guide when and how you would express your thoughts and emotive reactions to clients.

- Review works by Albert Ellis and others that help you understand the concept of your shoulds that may make it difficult for you to keep your empathy and UPR fully genuine with some clients. Identify your shoulds, especially those that affect how you see others. Speculate when and in what situations they may affect your work. Strive to overcome or reduce the influence of these shoulds.

- Review the literature on genuineness or congruence. We suggest you start with Tudor and Worrall (1994), Lietaer (1993), Wyatt (2001) and Cornelius-White (2007).

- Review the Primary Skill Objectives of this chapter. Consider if you have mastered them to your satisfaction at this time. If not, practice, discuss and seek further readings until you have mastered them to your satisfaction at this time.

- Continue to review your behavior, thoughts, feelings and communications in and out of counseling. Note when you are not as fully congruent as you would like and what seems to have inhibited your congruence in that moment. Especially in your sessions, continue to strive for fully genuine expressions of your empathy and UPR.

References

Beck, J.S., & Beck, A.T. (2011). *Cognitive behavior therapy: Basics and beyond* (2nd ed.). New York: Guilford.

Bozarth, J.D. (1998). *Person-centered therapy: A revolutionary paradigm*. Ross-on-Wye: PCCS Books.

Cochran, J.L. (1996). The status of services to students with conduct disorder by their elementary school counselors. *Dissertation Abstracts International*, 57, 03A (University Microfilms No. AAI96–24171).

Cochran, J.L., & Cochran, N.H. (1999). Using the counseling relationship to facilitate change in students with conduct disorder. *Professional School Counseling, 2*, 395–403.

Cochran, N.H., Nordling, W., & Cochran, J.L. (2010). *Child-centered play therapy: A practical guide to developing therapeutic relationships with children.* Hoboken, NJ: Wiley.

Cornelius-White, J. (2007). Congruence. In M. Cooper, M. O'Hara, P.F. Schmid, & G. Wyatt (Eds.), *The handbook of person-centred psychotherapy and counselling* (168–178). New York: Palgrave Macmillan.

Ellis, A., & Dryden, W. (2007). *The practice of rational emotive therapy* (2nd ed.). New York: Springer.

Fuertes, J.N., Mislocack, A., Brown, S., Gur-Arie, S., Wilkinson, S., & Gelso, C.J. (2007). Correlates of the real relationship in psychotherapy: A study of dyads. *Psychotherapy Research, 17*, 423–430.

Gelso, C.J. (2011). *The real relationship in psychotherapy: The hidden foundation of change.* Washington, DC: American Psychological Association.

Grafanaki, S. (2001). What research has taught us about congruence. In G. Wyatt (Ed.), *Rogers' therapeutic conditions: Evolution, theory and practice. Volume 1: Congruence* (pp. 18–35). Ross-on-Wye: PCCS Books.

Graves, J., & Robinson, J. (1976). Proxemic behavior as a function of inconsistent verbal and nonverbal messages. *Journal of Counseling Psychology, 23*, 333–338.

Haase, R., & Tepper, D. (1972). Nonverbal components of empathie communication. *Journal of Counseling Psychology, 19*, 417–424.

Hatch, E.J. (2000). Self-empathic dialogue as a therapeutic tool. *Psychology: A journal of human behavior, 37*, 5–8.

Horvath, A.O., Del Re, A.C., Flückiger, C., & Symonds, D. (2011). Alliance in individual psychotherapy. *Psychotherapy, 48*, 9–16.

Kolden, G.G., Klein, M.H., Wang, C., & Austin, S.B. (2011). Congruence/ Genuineness. *Psychotherapy, 48*, 65–71.

Lietaer, G. (1984). Unconditional positive regard: A controversial basic attitude in client-centered therapy. In R. Levant & J. Shlien (Eds.), *Client-centered therapy and the person-centered approach: New directions in theory research, and practice* (pp. 41–58). New York: Praeger.

Lietaer, G. (1993). Authenticity, congruence and transparency. In D. Brazier (Ed.), *Beyond Carl Rogers* (pp. 17–46). London: Constable.

Marmarosh, C.L., Gelso, C.J., Markind, R.D., Majors, R., Mallery, C., & Choi, J. (2009). The real relationship in psychotherapy: Relationships to adult attachment, working alliance, negative transference, and therapy outcome. *Journal of Counseling Psychology, 56*, 337–350.

Moore, S.R., & Gelso, C.J. (2011). Recollections of a secure base in psychotherapy: Considerations of the real relationship. *Psychotherapy, 48*, 368–373.

Orlinsky, D.E., & Howard, K.I. (1978). The relation of process to outcome in psychotherapy. In S.L. Garfield & A.E. Bergin (Eds.), *Handbook of psychotherapy and behavior change* (2nd ed.) (pp. 283–330). New York: John Wiley.

Orlinsky, D.E., & Howard, K.I. (1986). Process and outcome in psychotherapy. In S.L. Garfield & A.E. Bergin (Eds.), *Handbook of psychotherapy and behavior change* (3rd ed.) (pp. 331–381). New York: John Wiley.

Patterson, C.H. (1984). Empathy, warmth and genuineness: A review of reviews. *Psychotherapy, 21*, 431–438.

Purton, C. (2013). Incongruence and "inner experience." *Person-Centered and Experiential Psychotherapies, 12*, 187–199.

Rogers, C.R. (1957). The necessary and sufficient conditions of therapeutic personality change, *Journal of Consulting Psychology, 21*, 95–103.

Rogers, C.R. (1980). *A way of being*. Boston, MA: Houghton Mifflin.

Satir, V. (1987). The therapist story. In M. Baldwin & V. Satir (Eds.), *The use of self in therapy* (pp. 17–25). New York: Haworth Press.

Sherer, M., & Rogers, R. (1980). Effects of therapist's nonverbal communication of rated skill and effectiveness. *Journal of Clinical Psychology, 36*, 696–700.

Shostrom, E.L. (Producer/Director) (1965). *Three approaches to psychotherapy*. Corona del Mar, CA: Psychological and Educational Films.

Truax, C., & Mitchell, K. (1971). Research on certain therapist interpersonal skills in relation to process and outcome. In A. Bergin & S. Gardfield (Eds.), *Handbook of psychotherapy and behavior change* (pp. 299–344). New York: John Wiley & Sons.

Tryon, G.S., & Winograd, G. (2011). Goal consensus and collaboration. *Psychotherapy, 48*, 50–57.

Tudor, K., & Worrall, M. (1994). Congruence reconsidered. *British Journal of Guidance and Counselling, 22*, 197–206.

Tyson, J., & Wall, S. (1983). Effect of inconsistency between counselor verbal and non-verbal behavior on perception of counselor attributes. *Journal of Counseling Psychology, 30*, 433–437.

Wyatt, G. (2001). *Rogers' therapeutic conditions. Volume 1: Congruence*. Ross-on-Wye: PCCS Books.

Pre-Chapter Quotes

Anne Morrow Lindebergh and William Blake quoted in E.M. Beck (Ed.), J. Bartlett (compiler) (1980). *Familiar quotations* (15th ed.). Boston, MA: Little, Brown & Company (p. 867; p. 404).

Wampold, B.E. (2001). *The great psychotherapy debate: Models, methods, and findings*. Mahwah, NJ: Erlbaum (p. 202).

7 BEGINNING WITH NEW CLIENTS AND QUESTIONS OF CLIENT CONCEPTUALIZATION

Well begun is half done.

Aristotle

Primary Skill Objectives

- Understand and be able to explain the purposes of client conceptualization and what can be learned from initial session reports.
- Understand how to gather information for client conceptualization through therapeutic listening.
- Understand and be able to give examples of treatment plans for school and agency settings that feature the role of therapeutic relationships.
- Be able to explain how counseling-related assessment can be incorporated into therapeutic relationships and the difficulties that may arise in doing so.
- Understand and be able to make an initial explanation of counseling.
- Understand and be able to explain common counselor and client problems with goals and solutions for establishing well-reasoned goals.
- Be able to give examples of reasonable and unreasonable goals.

Focus Activity

What are your thoughts and emotions around getting started with a new client? What might your worries and considerations be in an outpatient setting in which your client asked for an appointment and you did not know until the session just what his or her concerns may be? What about for a school setting in which teachers, parents, or other concerned persons refer your clients to you, rather than your client self-referring? What kinds of decisions related to counseling and/or other aspects of service to this person do you anticipate making when getting started with new clients? Journal and/or discuss your thoughts and feelings in response to these questions.

Introduction

In this chapter, we focus the basics of getting started with new clients, including gaining an initial understanding of the person and her/his concerns—often referred to as "client conceptualization." We focus on structuring the therapeutic relationship in Chapter 8, which is also a part of beginning with new clients; then on helping clients who may need particular help getting started in Chapter 9. In this chapter, we want you to think through integrating skills of information gathering, assessment, establishing goals and making basic explanations of counseling with your skills of therapeutic listening, empathy, UPR and genuineness.

Conceptualizing Client Use of Counseling and Related Services

Consider this skill set through the "initial session reports" required in more formal counseling settings (i.e., community agencies, private practices, large counseling centers in schools). These reports are often called "intakes" or "assessments." We refer to them as "initial session reports" because this more accurately captures how we see the first meeting with each client. The word "intake" suggests a meeting for information gathering only, information on which decisions for ongoing counseling and other services will be made. However, it is not uncommon across settings for clients to complete only one session. Thus, we would not want you to miss an opportunity to implement a therapeutic relationship that is encouraging of ongoing work, while you are focused on gathering information in the only meeting you may have with a client.

In initial sessions we focus ourselves in therapeutic listening, with empathy and UPR provided in a genuine manner. We often ask only one question, something like, "What brings you in?" In other words, we just start counseling. Through this way of working, we find that our adult and adolescent clients almost always give the information we need for their initial session report. We find several important advantages to beginning this way versus beginning focused in information gathering. First, beginning counseling focused in relationship, where information gathering is a natural by-product, allows our clients to begin their healing process from our first moments together. Second, clients are most likely to continue counseling, because from the beginning they have been sensitively attended to within a therapeutic relationship. Third, if that initial meeting turns out to be the only meeting we have with a client, chances are that the client began to fulfill *her* need, rather than only giving information *we* needed. Fourth, if our work is to be ongoing, clients are not set up with a mistaken expectation of counseling—that is, that it will be mostly question–answer information gathering.

With that said, in almost every setting you have a responsibility to monitor for client safety, develop an understanding of client functioning, including initial understanding of what "the problem" is and why, and initial thoughts on what will help in counseling and related services. If a client does not naturally offer information needed through the therapeutic listening process, you should stop at some point in her initial session to check whether you are getting the information you need for key understandings while there is still time to shift to information gathering. When we stop to check, and certainly if we need to make a shift to information gathering, we tell our client what we are doing and why. For example (interrupting her thoughtful communication sensitively), "Let me stop you for a moment, June. What you are telling me now seems important, like you may have much more to say. I also have to watch our time today. I want to make sure I've asked for background to understand your situation before we stop today." In this chapter, we address areas of understanding that we normally want to have very early in our service responsibilities to each client.

Practical Reasons for Information Gathering in Initial Sessions

There are at least a few practical reasons for gathering information in initial sessions. A critical reason can be to assess for client safety. We will address incorporating that assessment into your work in Chapter 10. Two additional reasons include planning for ongoing counseling and planning for client service needs that you may be able to help with that fall outside counseling sessions.

Planning for Ongoing Counseling

With adolescent and adult clients, we usually get a sense in the first session whether they plan to continue or whether they expect and want only that one session (for children, we believe this is, at most times an adult/caretaker decision). We have found that while most come for ongoing counseling, a small but important minority of our adult and adolescent clients come expecting only one session, often because they expect to explain their problem and get a prescribed answer. Either way, if it isn't readily apparent while listening, we strive to get a sense of our clients' expectations for ongoing counseling.

If a client's expectation is for a single session, we may concur that that is a reasonable use of counseling. Jeff remembers a client who came to tell of the sexual abuse she had suffered in childhood. She didn't want to continue counseling after that. It seemed that session had been quite helpful to her in sorting through some of her confusion and hurt. While he would have liked her to continue, and offered her this option as well as expressing his interest in continuing, there was no reason to question her decision for her use of counseling. She was functioning well personally, socially and academically. Her judgment seemed reasonably sound and her intention was clear. She came to tell what had happened to her and leave it behind, at least for the time being.

For clients who we sense expect to have a single session in which they will explain their problem and receive a solution/advice, we first reflect our sense of their expectation. Then, if that expectation does not seem reasonable for the persons' concerns, we explain our view. We tell such clients that we very much wish we could help in that way, but since each person's situation is quite unique, we cannot prescribe a solution for them. We also help them understand, of course, that they can use counseling to come to understand their situation and their self better, and from that understanding reach their own more effective conclusions about how they want to handle their situation or make explanations of counseling that are less generic and more specific to the person and his concerns.

Through listening in initial sessions, we also try to get a sense of what each client's expectations for counseling are, just *what* it is that she wants and expects from counseling. This is an ongoing process, but if, in that first session, we can discern that a client, for example, clearly needs and wants to be listened to; has great difficulty accepting herself; is in great pain with grieving the loss of a loved one; has experienced abuse or trauma that seems so profound for her that it may take time to sort through thoughts, feelings, and resulting actions; is concerned with a specific problem such as academic or social anxiety, or a specific dilemma or decision; we would like to know in order to adjust our expectations and either make explanations then or think through and offer explanations later of how this person may use counseling to assist her particular life situation. We address such explanations further in the next chapter.

Planning for Service Needs that You Can Help With, Which Fall Outside Therapeutic Relationships

Through therapeutic listening in initial sessions (and throughout) you may think of services available outside the counseling sessions that may help address your clients' concerns and wishes. For example, if your client has a life situation for which you know there is a well-run counseling group, you may give him that information to consider. If you learn that your client is in need of career decision-making information and skills along with the more personal difficulties that brought him to counseling, you may offer to also help with that. If you offer to provide this service yourself, see if you can provide it in meetings that you specifically plan for that purpose, so that it is "in addition to" vs. "instead of" your counseling sessions focused primarily on therapeutic relationship and the client self-expression and self-learning that goes with a good therapeutic relationship.

In a related thought, we will sometimes offer information to our clients, if we believe we know information that will be helpful to them and if they have indicated that they would want to hear the information. For example, we have sometimes given clients who are becoming deeply depressed information that we have collected regarding physical self-care (i.e., sleep, nutrition, exercise) and personal self-care (e.g., restarting previously joyful activities when possible). It is very important not to let such information-giving veer into advice-giving, or to set up an expectation that counseling will mostly be about clients receiving information from their counselor. It is also very important to watch for clients' reactions to the information, and to respond to those reactions with careful empathy and UPR. For example, very depressed clients might understandably react with dread and discouragement to information on ways to manage their painful emotions through self-care. This is no cause for counselor frustration but an emotional expression for you to respond to with empathy and warmth, and an opportunity for the client to begin learning from such emotional expression and your response. We discuss the integration of such informational teaching services in depth in Chapters 13–15.

In concluding this section on gathering information and implementing your therapeutic relationship in your clients' initial session, we want you to know our firm conviction that if we only have one hour with any client, we would most want to spend it providing him with the core conditions. Even if circumstances beyond clients' control prohibit their continuing counseling, they will have already experienced a powerful and unique relationship, one that may be the spark that reawakens the flame of their drive to self-actualize. We have sometimes discovered that this new relationship is confusing to clients, and have known that to be a useful confusion. If clients believe they cannot be understood, accepted, liked, and loved but you meet them with the core conditions, even for an hour or less, that exception to their absolute belief system can be the sand that forms the pearl in their oyster. Your therapeutic relationship is a valuable gift; it is an offer of yourself in that time, and that is the best anyone can offer.

Incorporating Assessment with Your Skills in Therapeutic Relationship

In counseling, always strive to incorporate assessment and information gathering with your skills of therapeutic relationship, rather than shifting to assessment and neglecting your therapeutic relationship. When you realize that your task in assessing or information gathering interferes with your therapeutic relationship, be genuine and warmly say so (e.g., "Most important to me is to hear what you are telling me of how you are affected by this, but I am thinking while I listen to consider if there is anything else in particular that I should ask about to help in understanding"). It is important that you establish that you are working together, that your client's desires for counseling are important to you, and that you will keep your client fully informed of what you are doing and why. If your assessment or information-gathering tasks interfere with your tasks of therapeutic listening, and providing genuine empathy and UPR, it can appear to your clients that you are hiding something or taking some expert role that they are not entitled to know about. This can cause suspicion and inadvertently create a relationship where your client is unlikely to fully disclose.

Writing an Initial Session Report

In order to give a clearer picture of how information is gathered and may be conceptualized, we illustrate examples by commenting on the kinds of things that we would likely write and how the information might come about for the items of our initial session reports. These items may need to be modified for your settings. The items of your initial session report should fit the common concerns of most people as well as any concerns specific to the clients you serve, and the information your work setting would like recorded if it is in addition to those concerns. Additionally, the items included on our or other well-crafted initial session reports should be designed to build toward treatment planning—the last item on most initial session reports.

The clients for whom initial session report data are suggested in these examples are completely fictitious. Rather than being based on actual persons, they are based on composites of common clients and fictionalized. In the last subsection, "Treatment Plan," they are given fictitious names, as it became too impersonal to write about them without names.

Identifying Information

Parts of the identifying information could be collected from an intake questionnaire or other sources (e.g., school records, teacher input in team meetings). In this section, we usually include information that can be understood without much explanation, that doesn't take up much space or time, and that reminds us who the person of the report is (in situations where counselors see large numbers of clients, it can be difficult to remember each individual, especially if each person might not be seen every week). This would usually include age, grade, gender and ethnicity (if known). It could include fairly permanent physical attributes, such as very long blond hair, shaved head, slight frame or very tall. If there were some other easy reminder of the person, such as having been referred by a particular teacher, include that as well.

Presenting Problem/Concerns

This is simply a brief summary of why clients said they came to counseling. Examples might be: "upset over recent break-up with long-term boyfriend," "feelings of confusion and self-doubt related to parents' divorce," "surprised by sudden, unexplained lack of motivation for school/work, unusual tiredness, sadness, and irritability," "very strong anxiety and avoidant behavior related to public speaking," and "lack of career direction brought to her awareness through junior career decisions process."

History of the Problem/Previous Interventions

For this section, we note the history of the presenting concern that may help us understand this person and her concerns.

- For a client upset over a recent break-up, we would likely want to remember how long the two were together; if they have had other break-ups; how this one is different; the depth of meaning that this relationship seemed to have for (i.e., if either or both of them had pictured a permanent future together, if the client's self-esteem seemed to be tied up in the relationship's continuing), and perhaps if it seemed different from or similar to previous relationships that she mentioned.
- For a client whose parents divorced, we might want to remember how long ago the divorce took place, the client's age at that time, what the parents' relationship had been like before the divorce, what it has been like since the divorce, and how the client's reaction to the divorce has evolved.
- For a client with sudden lack of motivation, we would be curious to know how long she has had this feeling, what her motivation level was like before, and what she has tried so far to regain this motivation.
- For a client with anxiety and avoidant behavior around public speaking, we would likely want to remember the course of development of this anxiety (i.e., has it seemed to always be there and is just now becoming a problem, or does it seem quite new?), and what the client has tried toward overcoming the anxiety.
- For a client who has become aware of career indecision, we would like to remember such things as how his career aspirations have evolved and changed, and what he has done to ready himself to decide.

In conclusion, it is the very fact that the histories are logically connected to clients' present situations that causes most clients to give such histories, often without our having to ask.

Reason for Coming to Counseling Now

It often helps us conceptualize clients' situations if we consider why they seem to have come to counseling that week, as opposed to a few weeks or months earlier or later.

- For the client upset over the recent break-up, this may be obvious—the break-up just happened, but the less obvious part may be that she is worried that the break-up means that she will always be alone or is somehow a flawed person.
- For the client whose parents divorced, this may not be so obvious if the divorce was some time ago. Upon reflection, this client or we may

realize that he sees himself as currently faced with long-term life decisions and is questioning his own ability to make decisions.

- The client with sudden low motivation might be facing some deadline or may have watched someone she cares about and identifies with fail at some task that she sees as catastrophic.
- The client with anxiety related to public speaking may be facing a speech soon or may be hurting by having perceived others as laughing at him during a public speaking situation.
- The client who has become aware of career indecision may have come because of a decision deadline but may have been prompted by other events, such as a build-up of general frustration with herself and her indecision or perhaps awareness of a loved one's regret over a career decision thought to have been an error.

For a client who is facing some imminent deadline, we might expect and try a very tentative reflection of her intentions for counseling like, "I'm not sure, but I gather that since this is coming up soon, you hoped for or expected very quick work in counseling." On the other hand, for a client who seems to worry that she is flawed or is riddled with ongoing self-doubt, we might attempt a tentative reflection of her expectations for ongoing counseling with a statement like, "So far, I understand that you are really hurting with this, and that you take your situation and struggle very seriously. So, I gather you might expect our work together to be ongoing, beyond today." From these reflections, a more specific conversation related to ongoing work and expectations in counseling can ensue.

Alcohol/Drug Use and/or Medical Concerns

With this item, we prompt ourselves to look for potential physical complications or causes alerting us to be careful that the client may have some physical/medical situation that would indicate counseling may need to be augmented with inpatient treatment, medical consultation, chemical dependency assessment, etc. For example, if a client reports near overwhelming depression and heavy alcohol use, we would recognize that the heavy alcohol use may be perpetuating and intensifying the depression. Then, if that situation becomes clear and continues, we may see a need for a chemical dependency assessment.

Related Family History/Information

Family relationships are often important parts of clients' concerns, and we find that most adolescent and adult clients indicate the connections between their family history and current concerns without prompting. Also, because this connection is frequently important, we normally want to remember how each client describes this connection. Examples of the kinds of connections that might occur follow:

- The client upset over the recent break-up might explain that she sees a parent, role model, or other loved one as growing old alone and miserable, or may see a parent as character flawed or mentally ill and worry that this is inevitable for herself as well.
- The client whose parents divorced might also see one or both parents as flawed or mentally ill and assume this is his fate, or he might have little faith in permanent relationships and fear being alone.
- The client with sudden low motivation may see a parent or sibling as a failure and believe this will be her intolerable fate, or, on the other hand, she may have lived and worked hard to fill her perception of her parents' expectations, even though those expectations did not fit with her interests and abilities.
- The client with anxiety around public speaking may also believe that he can never live up to his parents' expectations or may perceive himself as already having failed in his parents' eyes.
- The client who became aware of career indecision may also have tried to live up to her parents' expectations and find it difficult to fit her interests and abilities to those expectations. She may have perceived herself as frequently criticized and unaccepted by her parents, and that may prompt her indecision.

Major Areas of Stress

In an initial conceptualization of a client we would want to consider the person's major areas of stress. This understanding often helps us put her concerns in perspective. The client who is upset over a recent break-up, for instance, may find she can hardly think of or focus on anything else. Yet, the client whose parents divorced may be nagged by related concerns, motivated to explore them, and perhaps make changes but be even more stressed over ongoing car trouble and financial concerns.

Academic/Work Functioning

For clients whose primary role is student, we would want to know how their concerns affect their schoolwork and how the demands of their school work may be affecting their concerns. For clients whose primary role is worker, we would be interested to know of the connection between their concerns and their studies or work. Because persons' school experiences or occupations are often strongly related to their identities and sense of self-worth, most clients offer some indication of these interactions and it is noticeable and worth reflecting on when they do not.

Social Resources

For this item, we are interested to see if each client seems to have a social support system and to what extent. We are interested to know how each client's friendships are affected by his concerns or how his concerns are affected by his friendships or perhaps lack of friendships. Possible examples follow:

- The client who is upset over the recent break-up may have let friendships dwindle during her heavy focus on her romantic relationship or may have seemed to be isolated by a controlling romantic partner. On the other hand, she may have many friends or acquaintances who now tell her that they never liked her romantic partner anyway, that they always knew he was bad, and this may be prompting her increasing self-doubt.

- The client whose parents divorced may have relied heavily on the support of friends during the time of the divorce. He may either have strongly supportive friendships or may be experiencing great anxiety and dependence due to ongoing doubts around friendships. He might either connect deeply with friendships or keep himself at a superficial distance with friends. This is not something we would expect him to describe himself, but something that we may watch for and notice as he describes his friendships.

- The client with sudden low motivation may seem to be using drinking and time with friends or acquaintances to avoid tasks over which she feels low motivation. As with the client above, this is not something we would expect her to say. Rather, it may occur as a possibility when we notice that she has lately been drinking and spending time with friends more than before. This is not a guessed observation that we would be likely to state in an initial session because it may be heard as a criticism, interfere with the accepting atmosphere we want to establish, and may well be a wrong early assumption on our part. Still, we may consider it as a possibility for understanding her.

- The client with anxiety around public speaking may also be generally shy or seem to seek out only those acquaintances who he is sure would never be critical of him. Or if we learned that public speaking seemed to be his only area of anxiety, this might help us understand his situation differently.

- The client with career indecision may, for example, enjoy time with many friends who have great interest in the arts, yet believe that her parents would only respect and help pay for more "practical" areas of study.

Initial Impressions or Understanding of the Person and Concerns

In order to show you how we use this item, we offer entries for each of the clients about whom we have been hypothesizing through the items of our initial session report.

Client Who is Upset Over Recent Break-up

Desirae is deeply hurt over a recent break-up with her boyfriend. While she is pushing herself to continue her work and other life tasks, the tasks seem difficult for her, and the break-up seems at times to be all she can think about. The break-up seems deeply wounding for her at this time for several reasons. They had been together for over a year and she had integrated him into the pictures she imagined of her future. Also she was so dedicated to making this relationship work that she has lost contact with friends. Now that the relationship has ended, she assumes that it is her fault and that his no longer wanting to be with her means there is something clearly wrong with her. In spite of the great pain she feels at this time, she is continuing to take reasonable care of herself (e.g., she is experiencing some loss of appetite and craving for junk foods, but continues to eat what seems a reasonable amount of healthy foods).

However, she also has year-end standardized testing coming up. She is having great difficulty concentrating. She alternates from being worried how her great pain and loss of concentration will affect her test performance to saying/thinking she doesn't even care about the tests any more.

(Because she is served in school, some of our input for understanding comes from teachers.) She has been a B student. Her teachers see potential for her in college, if she can hold herself together emotionally (they have noticed her upset and referred her). She had not seemed particularly emotionally fragile to her teachers before this point.

Client Whose Parents Divorced

James has been dating the same person for three months, which is much longer than he has dated others. He and his girlfriend had sex for the first time recently. Since then, he finds himself attracted to and thinking of other romantic partners frequently. He explained that his father "cheated" on his mother repeatedly with other women before their divorce and that his father even involved him (client) by taking him (client) with him to make it appear to his mom that he (father) was not meeting another woman. James now worries that he will hurt his girlfriend the same way his father hurt his mother. While he has not quite said so, he seems deeply worried that there is something inherently wrong with him that is beyond his control. He explained that he has a few close and supportive friends but that he has never told anyone what his father did. He seems to have a way of seeming "all together" on the outside, which seems to contrast the doubt he has begun to express.

Client Who is Experiencing Sudden Low Motivation

Gina is quite surprised and perplexed by her sudden low motivation, tiredness, sadness, and irritability. She acknowledges that, corresponding with these new feelings, she has been spending more time with friends and especially drinking alcohol in larger amounts and more frequently. The reason for this change is unclear. However, Gina described her life up to this point as rather perfect (i.e., excellent grades, strong career expectations, ideal boyfriend). Then, when I reflected that some sort of disgruntlement that seemed to cross her face as she stated these things, she became tearful in stating that she was unsure whether she had ever wanted these things. It could be that she has been working toward life goals that were not her own. In an oddly related event, Gina explained that a friend of a friend died in a freak accident and she finds that she thinks about it a lot. Though unstated, through this she may have been reminded of her own mortality, and this may be prompting her to reconsider her life decisions and directions. Additionally, while she is experiencing very low motivation compared to normal for her, she is continuing to function well and does not seem to be in any work place, academic, or other danger.

Gina has been a leader in extracurricular activities at school. Because her teachers are not aware of what she is going through or her use of counseling, I have not checked with them directly. However, she has not been discussed at all in team meetings, suggesting her teachers have not noticed any change in her actions.

Client with Anxiety Related to Public Speaking

John's anxiety around public speaking has come to greatly limit his academic progress and career plans. He is in college studying for a degree that will greatly advance his career and is paid for by his employer, but cannot pass due to anxiety related to public speaking. At first, he would try to miss classes in which he had to speak publicly and accept the lower grades. He has now dropped classes in which he must speak publicly. Yet, these are classes he must have for his major. He would consider a different major, but he already works in the business field and his employer is sending him to school to complete his degree. He explains that he is not otherwise shy, except that he will also not talk with his instructors (e.g., to explain his dilemma over public speaking or to ask for help with other matters) outside class either. However, he explains that he is not concerned with what his instructors or classmates might think of him. He reports very high functioning in all areas except his presenting problem. He explained that he had hoped I could provide him a waiver so he would not have to engage in public speaking. I explained that

I cannot, and invited him to continue counseling. He reluctantly agreed to continue counseling. John appears to either have low insight and awareness, despite his apparent intelligence, or is possibly reluctant to discuss his thoughts and feelings openly in counseling. Although he agreed to continue counseling, his reluctance and desire for some sort of permission to avoid public speaking is clear.

Client Who Became Aware of Career Indecision

Chondra seems to know that she loves art and areas of study that she sees as creative. She believes her teachers give her strong indications that she has significant creative abilities. Yet, she worries that these areas of study are impractical and, while she did not clearly say so, seems to worry that her parents would not respect or be willing to pay for such areas of study. It may be that her indecision is prompted by a conflict between what she sees as practical, what she thinks her parents will support, and where she thinks her true interests and abilities lie. Her reaction to her results from career interest testing over the first few weeks of her junior year is that she doesn't want to do "*any* of those things that the stupid test suggested."

Treatment Plans

In this section of our initial session report, we explain how works within therapeutic relationships are expected to help the client, how we expect to respond and why, and what actions outside counseling we have or may recommend.

Client Who is Upset over Recent Break-up

Desirae's counseling will allow her to discuss the loss and discern its meanings for her. As she seems to see herself as flawed, it will be particularly useful for Desirae to fully explore who she is, who she wants to be, and whether she is satisfied with herself and her expectations for herself, and to make new life decisions based on her conclusions. As she discerns her views in these areas and implements her resulting decisions, she can change parts of who she is and thus fit romantically with a very different type of person from her recent boyfriend. If she concludes that the energy she committed to her friendships and romantic relationship were unproductive, she can decide to readjust this balance in the future. Further, the support of counseling will help Desirae to continue to value herself and maintain her self-care, and academic and work-place progress during this difficult time.

Sorting through her current difficulties in empathy and UPR can help her learn from her current difficulties. While she is experiencing very strong emotions, she also seems to be working hard not to feel. Therefore, in our work together, therapeutic listening and empathy will increase her awareness and acceptance of feelings. She seems to be an emotional person who is trying to deny that part of herself. As a result, she is making decisions on impulse, closed off from any real consideration of what she feels and wants (e.g., "*He* will make everything OK [i.e., keep me from bad feelings]. Thus, I must have him").

It will be particularly important that I communicate my unconditional positive regard for her as Desirae seems to carry great shame and sees herself as significantly flawed. Viewing herself fully and clearly may be quite scary for her. She seems to expect criticisms from others and works to hide parts of herself that she believes others would criticize. I informed her of our Young Women's Support Group, which she is considering. While I see no evidence that she is at any risk of harming herself or others, this should be continually monitored, since she is in significant emotional pain.

In regard to the time pressure of upcoming year-end standardized tests, Desirae needs counseling and perhaps a support group as outlets for her emotions. At this time, she is trying not to feel, but having strong emotions pop to the surface as she tries to concentrate. Expressing and coming to accept her feelings in counseling, plus realizing that she can let them out in counseling and put them aside after counseling should help her increase her ability to concentrate. I will monitor her ability to concentrate. An alternative possibility would be to teach a thought-stopping or relaxation technique, but these would take more weeks to master than she has right now and the process of self-expression and self-discovery in counseling will take less time with more long-term benefit.

Client Whose Parents Divorced

I expect James to use his time in counseling to further explore how he feels about his girlfriend, their decision to have sex, his attractions to others, the effects of his father's actions on him, who he is, who he wants to be and aspects of himself that he sees as inherently wrong, as well as whether and which of these aspects are within his control.

It will be important for me to listen carefully, emphasizing empathy and unconditional positive regard, since James has begun to share personal information over which he is quite inhibited. Additionally, while James's emotions affect his actions, he seems largely unaware of them. Increasing this awareness will greatly inform his future decisions.

As he expressed his interest in taking actions that may help him succeed in his relationship, I recommended and he decided to pursue our Relationship Skills Group in addition to individual counseling. While I see no reason to suspect that he is at any risk of harming himself or others, I will continue to monitor for this, since he seems to have significant doubts about himself and his future.

Client Who is Experiencing Sudden Low Motivation

In Gina's counseling, her experience of therapeutic listening with empathy and UPR will help her clarify her vague thoughts of why she is experiencing this sudden, unexpected change. I will carefully monitor for any deteriorating effects of her increased use of alcohol.

As she is now questioning whether she still wants the life goals she has worked so hard for and experienced success in moving toward, empathic responding to and for her open self-expression in this process will be key for her in resolving her doubts regarding these goals and in regaining the motivation she would like. No need for additional resources is apparent at this time. Gina asked if I thought she should consult her physician to see if there is a medical reason for her sudden change. I supported this consultation, as she wants to pursue every possibility and reports a good relationship with her physician. While there is no reason to suspect imminent danger or deterioration, I will continue to monitor for this, since her current situation is unusual for her.

Client with Anxiety Related to Public Speaking

Therapeutic listening and empathy will be particularly important in counseling John because he seems unaware of other emotions besides the anxiety he reports around public speaking, plus being unaware of any thoughts related to this anxiety. He may benefit from evaluating the thought patterns that put pressure on him around public speaking, once he gains some awareness of those thoughts. I may suggest that he begin to journal thoughts and feelings of the times that he is aware of feeling even mild anxiety.

As he seemed to strongly deny thoughts and feelings that I had thought seemed true for him, unconditional positive regard—acceptance of him as he sees himself, will become particularly important in order for him to risk exploring his thoughts and feelings. Additionally, he may need to spend time discussing subjects other than his anxiety related to public speaking in order to begin his use of counseling with less threatening subjects.

While John agreed to continue counseling, his commitment is unclear. As he lets me know him more, I will be particularly careful to help him understand how his use of counseling can help him toward his goals. I will carefully monitor to reflect and discuss his reactions to the counseling process itself, including resistance, if resistance or reluctance becomes apparent.

Client Who Became Aware of Career Indecision

Chondra seems to need to explore her career interests and inhibitions toward decision-making. As she seems easily influenced by others and doubtful of her own inclinations, it will be particularly important to convey full acceptance of all aspects of her decisions, thoughts, and feelings. Further, she seems to be trying to make decisions from a solely thought/logic approach. Therefore, empathy will be particularly important so that she may come to realize the potential emotional aspects of her decision process. And if this first impression seems true in the next meetings, it may be important to share with her, especially as it may relate both to her career decisions as well as other life decisions, and to her use of counseling.

It seems that Chondra may also benefit from a greater wealth of information for making her decisions. She seems to dichotomize the world of work between "art/creative works" and "practical works." I offered to introduce and explain our resources for exploring the world of work and to sit with her while she begins this exploration. She accepted, and we set an additional meeting time for this work. I have not suggested further career interest inventories at this time, as her knowledge of herself and the world of work seem immature and will develop through personal counseling. Further, a career interest inventory that suggests occupations or occupation types might only be an additional judgment that she accepts more than her own judgment as she is underconfident and lacks both self-knowledge and knowledge of the world of work.

Concluding Notes on Initial Impressions of the Person and Treatment Plans

The Process is More Important than the Plan

Never let these somewhat analytic attempts at understanding and planning for your clients encourage the hubris in which you come to see yourself as "all-knowing" or think something like, "Because I know what my client must do in counseling, I must control this person in counseling." Even if you or we did know best for our clients, this would only be minimally helpful, since clients are the ones who need to know, decide, and take ownership of their actions in and out of counseling in order to maximize their path of self-actualization. Further, such thinking may lead you to place more faith in *your controlling* the process than you place in *the process* of providing therapeutic listening, empathy, and UPR. While we often offer adult and adolescent clients some explanation or justification for the work we propose (based on their concerns), we are always accepting that our initial impressions may have been wrong. We strive to remember not to be discouraged when our therapeutic relationship with a client takes us to an unexpected solution for a problem we initially misunderstood. Rather, the resulting value to both clients and us reconfirms our faith in the power of therapeutic relationships.

Explaining the Core Conditions in Your Plan

You may notice that with each treatment plan example, we emphasized providing a therapeutic relationship based in the core conditions. For any client we see in need of ongoing counseling, this will be the heart of our recommendation. We wish for you to feel free to add other aspects to the therapeutic relationships you provide, as we have included a few possibilities in the previous examples, when you see such additions as necessary and fitting to both who you are and who your client is. However, we hope for you never to add something to a treatment plan that takes away from or interferes with the therapeutic relationships that you provide. Always remember that this therapeutic relationship is the essential core.

Common Difficulties in Getting Started with New Clients

What's normal in getting started with new clients? Well, almost nothing. We find it best to review what information we have regarding a client before meeting in order to begin getting to know that person, and in case there is something we really should know first (e.g., a safety issue we should be concerned about monitoring for). However, we also strive to have no expectations of how each new client will be in counseling.

A Need to Know What to Expect

Having said that, we do think that most new clients need to know what to expect. Many clients come to counseling not knowing what opportunities await them in counseling or with mistaken assumptions. So, you may commonly offer explanations of counseling. When you offer such explanations, it is most helpful, most concrete, to begin with what your client and you will mostly do in your time together, and a very brief explanation of why. We offer examples in the next section and fuller discussions of the complexities of such explanations in the next chapter.

Anxiety

We also find it reasonable to expect anxiety in your clients. Such anxiety may be a part of why they have come. It is also understandable that many clients feel anxiety about getting started in counseling. Beginning clients face the unknown of a new relationship with an unknown person. Some beginning clients react with mild frustration or lack of understanding to your actions in reflecting. This can be because, while therapeutic relationships share qualities with other relationships, counseling responses are quite unlike those of other relationships. It may be that you are not yet artful at your tasks, that providing therapeutic responses do not yet come naturally to you. For you and for your client, remember that reflection and the other tasks of therapeutic relationships are *unusual* forms of communication, unlike talking to a friend or acquaintance. We have found that if counselors first accept and empathize with new clients' anxiety, frustration, or other emotional reactions, and can explain what they are doing and why, clients come to adjust and value the counseling process.

Additionally, the physical act of coming to counseling leaves many persons anxious. Some worry over whether they have been seen. Some assume use of counseling to imply that they are somehow needful, broken, or flawed. Certainly that is a self-perception that needs to be considered in the open communication facilitated through empathy and UPR. Whatever the reason, you may expect anxiety, but also know that it may not be there. If it is there, accept it and respond with empathy. If some other emotion or way of being is there instead of anxiety, accept this and respond with empathy.

An Explanation of Counseling that Helps Clients Begin

Our standard explanation of counseling goes something like, "You can think of our work together this way: Your role is to help me understand you. You may start anywhere, with whatever seems on your mind or in your heart. My role is to strive to understand you and to say what I think I understand, first probably in little understandings of what you tell me, then later with the bigger picture of how I see you. Through this process you come to understand yourself better and to use that enhanced understanding for new decisions. Even when I am wrong in how I understand you, if you help me understand you better, you still learn."

Some of our interns have let us know what they have found helpful to add, at times, to our very basic explanation. Perhaps based on setting or population, a number found it important to tell their client that they (the counselor) are not judging, diagnosing, or analyzing. The style of one of our interns was to add his warm direction for his client to "Tell me about yourself," or "Tell me your story." A number added a quality that sounds simple but isn't always easy, explaining that in order to help clients understand how to begin, they (the counselors) needed to be as relaxed as possible with themselves. We refer you also to Chapter 8, in which we discuss more customized explanations of counseling, and to Chapter 9, in which we focus on the dilemmas that occur and tools to use when clients seem to need special help getting started.

Finally, while we offer examples and further discussions in Chapters 8 and 9, it is important to note here that it is most helpful to customize your explanations of counseling to the unique person and situations of each client. Our examples of persons with various presenting problems offered above should give you some preliminary guidance as to how you can customize explanations for each client's use of counseling. The last two items of our initial session report, "Initial Impressions or Understanding of the Person and Concerns" or "Treatment Plans," include how we see each client and how we expect each individual may utilize the therapeutic relationship of counseling.

Information Clients Should Know When Getting Started

Confidentiality

Especially in settings where it is not already clearly conveyed to clients, you need to routinely explain confidentiality to your clients in their first session. It is best to make this explanation brief but clear, and early, before your client might communicate anything that falls outside the limits of confidentiality.

You may need to customize your explanation of confidentiality to your client's age or other unique aspects, as well as your setting. Your explanation must include what confidentiality is and what the limits of confidentiality are. A generic statement of confidentiality that we often give to adolescents and adults is: "Our work together is confidential, meaning I won't tell others things that you do or say here. Of course, you can talk to others about our work together if you wish. There are a few limits to confidentiality. If you tell me something that gives me reason to suspect child abuse or that you are in danger, I may need to contact others to try and get you further help or to stop the child abuse. And there are some circumstances that I could be court ordered to give information from your counseling. I would tell you if one of these were the case." Make such explanations flatly, meaning not mechanically or uncaringly, but without implying anything more than what is said. As with any statement made to a client, watch to see how your client reacts, especially whether he seems to understand or not, and respond to his reaction with acceptant empathy.

A customization that sometimes occurs is a need to let clients who were referred by others or seem particularly concerned with what others might know about their use of counseling that the confidentiality you provide includes the person who referred them or about whom they are concerned (assuming this is the case and you are not making an additional exception to confidentiality). For example, if a client was referred by or showed concern that a parent, teacher, employer or spouse might have access to information about his counseling, let him know that confidentiality and its limits apply even to this person. In care for the feelings of the referral sources, we are careful to inform this person the reasons why she/he would want to allow reasonable privacy of counseling use for the loved one or student that they are referring, plus that while we should not give information from the client's session, we may still (this depends on context) be able to communicate regarding understandings of the client and how she/he (person referring) can best help.

Who and/or Why Referred

Especially for adolescents and adults who were referred by others and seem to wonder why they have been invited to counseling, we think it best to tell them. We find that if we withhold such information when our client has indicated that she wants to know, it will interfere with developing a therapeutic relationship. Again, in consideration of the referral source, this explanation is usually something we have cleared with the referring person first. We usually keep such explanations at least a little vague. The purpose of this vagueness is not to hide any truth but to avoid giving our client the expectation that we expect them to talk about certain things. For example, "Your mother let me know that you attempted suicide and so she and I agreed that you may be hurting and may make use of counseling;" "Ms. Smith let me know that your grades have dropped quickly, and so we wondered if you are troubled and might wish to make use of counseling;" "Mr. Brown let me know that he is concerned for you. He told me that he sees you as acting out in class."

Such explanations are not always necessary. Especially, the last example seems like it might imply that this client is expected to talk about his behavior. So, we added clarification regarding this person's use of counseling. Even if a client makes an assumption about her use of counseling based on these explanations, we find that this assumption goes away in time and that it is better than beginning with a secret about our client when our client has indicated that she wants to know. Again, it is important to make such explanations with a tone that does not imply there is more meaning to the explanations than the facts stated. Of course, it is crucial to respond to your client's reaction to the statement with acceptant empathy. If the client from the last example responds by saying forcefully, "He's out to get me and I've done nothing!" then you reflect something like, "That's the first thing you want me to understand, and you're aggravated with the assumption that you've done wrong!" Even if this client had interrupted his counselor during the statement, we would have stopped to reflect, then finished the explanation.

Potentially Helpful Guidance Related to the Presenting Problem

If we think we have information that is critical, important and related to the difficulties an adult or adolescent client is having, we may offer this information in her initial session. For example, if we believe a client is becoming so deeply depressed that the progress of the depression might overwhelm her before she has been able to give counseling enough of a try, we may give information that we feel confident in regarding immediate steps she may take to begin to manage the depression through self-care. For another example, if we had thought carefully and felt sure that a particular client would benefit from assistance outside our therapeutic relationship in counseling (e.g., career information, a support group, assistance with study skills), we may go ahead and suggest this assistance in the first session.

Goals

A final and often important part of initiating therapeutic relationships is the question of goals. Some counselors are required by settings or by third-party payers to establish goals after the first session or soon thereafter. Beyond setting requirements, you may also want to keep reasonable goals to give yourself an opportunity to measure progress. This is the beginning of good and simple research. As you see clients' progress toward reasonable goals, it will help you remain encouraged in your work, which will surely be difficult at times.

The Problem with Asking Clients for Goals

Most clients don't come to counseling knowing what goals to work on. This would require a sophisticated knowledge of counseling and self. Most clients just come knowing that they are hurting. Or, worse still for establishing goals, they come at the urging or direction of others versus from a self-directed choice. If you ask a young adult who has just lost a romantic relationship that she expected to be lifelong what she would like to change as a result of counseling, she might well answer: "To get him back," or "To have him say, in a way that I'll believe, that I am desirable and that there is nothing wrong with me, that my future will work out and I will be happy." Another hurting client might simply quizzically answer, "I want to feel better." Rarely would a new client answer, "What I want from counseling is to reevaluate the meanings I've made of my experiences," or "I want to evaluate who I am and who I want to be, to evaluate whether the expectations that I've placed on myself are reasonable; to examine myself, my feelings, thoughts, and actions in the light of our communication and decide what I think of me, what I want to change and what I want to and can accept." Further, if you tried to take a client's spoken goal and move toward it in a straight line, you may find yourself giving her direction into how to get the lost partner back, or how to force that partner to answer questions that he/she can't answer, but that could be effectively answered from within herself through her use of counseling.

Background to Reasonable Goals

As you will remember from Chapter 1, it is well accepted that each person is on his/her path of self-actualization. Further, while each person's path is unique, each person's path includes achieving the normal skills of mentally healthy persons, such as the ability to love and to work, the subskills within these areas, such as the ability to enjoy positive social interactions and to reasonably master accomplishments within her/his given ability range.

Often the difficulty bringing a person to counseling is, at its core, a block to his/her path to self-actualization. This can include not having been provided the core conditions or not having had physical needs provided for, then having interpreted this lack of one's environment/caregivers as having meaning about ones' self, world, and relationship to the world. It can include a recent traumatic event or growing effects from a long-ago trauma.

Your role is to provide therapeutic relationships, which provide a fertile ground for each individual's self-actualization process to restart. Thus, the goals you set or measures of goals can be any area of success or well-functioning that would normally be expected for the person if not for the problem area that brought him to counseling (i.e., the issues that can be thought of as the block to his path to healthy self-actualization).

Examples of Reasonable Goals

Counselors may set any goals for clients who are within the normal range of behavioral possibilities for the persons based on such factors as their age and abilities. Then, through therapeutic relationship, progress toward these goals will almost always occur.

For your client who has lost the romantic partner she believed would be always with her, a reasonable goal could be to become comfortable enough in herself not to let the recent loss impede her ability to succeed at school/work and to reestablish friendships. Reasonable measures might then include improving failing grades to her previous average, receiving acceptable work reviews, reachieving a reasonable level of concentration during testing, and reporting positive relationships and enjoying time with friends.

You can use informal measures of progress, such as your notes of client self-report in areas listed above. We often also use more formal standardized measures in establishing goals and outcomes. For example, the Child Behavior Checklist (Achenbach & Rescorla, 2001) uses parent, teacher or self-ratings of youth to identify levels of problematic behaviors across areas of difficulties. Ratings of difficulty areas can be scored as Clinical or Normal. A very reasonable goal for a youth with areas of concern in the Clinical range could be for the concerns to reduce to the Normal range through the course of counseling and related services.

For another example, the widely used Beck Depression Inventory (Beck, Steer, & Brown, 1996) screens indicators of depression with scores falling into ranges of severity. A goal could include reducing from a high range of severity to a low range. Or if a client currently met the criteria for a diagnostic category such as "Major Depressive Disorder" (APA, 2013, pp. 160–168), the goal could be to no longer meet the criteria (e.g., major depressive episode) in the areas of diagnostic criteria most fitting of and hurtful for your client.

Grades are a less standardized, but independent measure that can serve in establishing goals. Goals could include, for example, for a student who seems able, to raise grade average to B or higher.

Unreasonable Goals

Perhaps this is obvious, but just in case, we reiterate that goals must be reasonably within a person's ability. For example, in behavior management plans for behaviorally troubled children, we have sometimes included the goal, "Follow directions the first time told." However, this is something for the child to work toward—it is not a goal over which perfection would even be reasonable. We certainly do not always follow directions the first time told, and think that only an unthinking person would always do this.

Grade-based measures may provide examples of unreasonable measures of goals. An A grade would not be a reasonable measure if the student had always been a hard-working B student, with good study habits and reasonable support resources, before a noticeable drop in grades. Also, it would be unreasonable to base a measure on previous grades (i.e., before a noticeable drop) if the student's previous approach to studies had seemed perfectionist, or if it seemed she had obsessed and resented the work all along.

For your client who experienced great pain at the loss of her romantic relationship, if she had seemed to enjoy her studies but had never been highly motivated for As, her work in counseling might or might not help her come to want As. However, the most reasonable goal/measure would be to return to her previous level of grade motivation and success.

Communicating Goals

Then there is the question of whether or not to state goals that you record. We never like to think we are keeping something from our clients that they may want to know and may find helpful. So, if we must record goals, we think it may be best to tell adult or adolescent clients our thoughts on goals for them and hear their reactions. What we don't like about this is that without careful empathy, there is great room for misinterpretation of the goal suggestions (e.g., I will accept you when your grades improve), although, as always with statements to clients, we would be ready to attend with empathy to all reactions. Another thing we don't like about communicating these goal suggestions to clients is that the goals may suggest a focus for client communication in sessions (e.g., you should spend your counseling time talking of the effort you are putting into friendships vs. free-flowing communication of who you are). In such situations of misunderstanding, you may need to explain (or reexplain) how you see her best using counseling to accomplish your/her goals.

We conclude that if goals are to be recorded for adult or adolescent clients, in most cases it seems only considerate to inform your clients what you are recording or will record, at least in general, thus giving each client the opportunity to assert changes. We like that communicating such goal suggestions may lead to valuable discussion of how counseling can work and how it can most effectively be used. We emphasize explanations of counseling in Chapter 8.

Activities and Resources for Further Study

- Revisit your answers and thoughts from the Focus Activity for this chapter now that you have considered our guidance through this chapter. How have your thoughts changed? Do you now see some of your worries as unnecessary? Have we inadvertently suggested new worries? If your answers, thoughts and feelings have changed, find opportunities to discuss this with peers.

- Think about times in your life that you used or can see that you might have used counseling. Complete an Initial Session Report on yourself at one or more of those times, working all the way through "Initial Impressions or Understanding of the Person and Their Concerns" and "Treatment Plans."
- Revisit the concept of self-actualization from Chapter 1 and from works by Carl Rogers and others (Bohart, 2007; Bozarth, 1998; Farber, Bohart, & Stiles, 2013; Rogers, 1961, 1980). Keep in mind your understanding of the drive to self-actualize whenever treatment planning, generating goals or explaining potential uses of counseling.
- In a practice initial session, practice explaining confidentiality for a scenario that encompasses complicating factors introduced in the section "Information Clients Should Know When Getting Started" (page 157).
- In a practice initial session, practice making an initial explanation of counseling, including client and counselor roles, to a client who is uncertain and anxious over how to begin.
- Practice writing Initial Session Reports after your practice initial sessions. Discuss what you have written and thought with the persons who were in the roles of your client and observer.
- Practice generating reasonable goals based on your practice initial sessions.
- Consider and discuss with peers any adaptations of Initial Session Reports that you may want or need in your expected work settings.
- Review the Primary Skill Objectives of this chapter to see that you have mastered each to your satisfaction. If you have not yet mastered them to your satisfaction at this time, reread, seek more practice and seek additional readings until you have mastered them to your satisfaction.

References

Achenbach, T.M., & Rescorla, L.A. (2001). *Manual for the ASEBA school-age forms and profiles*. Burlington, VT: University of Vermont, Research Center for Children, Youth, & Families.

APA (2013). *Diagnostic & statistical manual of mental disorders* (5th ed.). Arlington, VA: American Psychiatric Association.

Beck, A.T., Steer, R.A., & Brown, G.K. (1996). *Beck depression inventory-II*. San Antonio, TX: The Psychological Corporation.

Bohart, A.C. (2007). The actualizing person. In M. Cooper, M. O'Hara, P.F. Schmid, & G. Wyatt (Eds.), *Handbook of person-centred psychotherapy and counselling* (pp. 47–63). New York: Palgrave Macmillan.

Bozarth, J.D. (1998). *Person-centered therapy: A revolutionary paradigm*. Ross-on-Wye: PCCS Books.

Farber, B.A., Bohart, A.C., & Stiles, W.B. (2013). Corrective (emotional) experience in person-centered therapy: Carl Rogers and Gloria redux. In L.G. Castonguay & C.E. Hill (Eds.), *Transformation in psychotherapy: Corrective experiences across cognitive behavioral, humanistic, and psychodynamic approaches* (pp. 103–120). Washington, DC: American Psychological Association.

Rogers, C.R. (1961). *On becoming a person.* Boston, MA: Houghton Mifflin.

Rogers, C.R. (1980). *A way of being.* Boston, MA: Houghton Mifflin.

Pre-Chapter Quote

Aristotle (quoting a proverb) in Nicomachean Ethics, bk. V, ch. 4, quoted in E.M. Beck (Ed.), J. Bartlett (compiler) (1980). *Familiar quotations* (15th ed.). Boston, MA: Little, Brown & Company (p. 88).

8 STRUCTURING THERAPEUTIC RELATIONSHIPS

Every river has its banks, every ocean has its shores. Limitations should not always be seen as negative constraints. They are the geography of our situation, and it is only right to take advantage of this.

Taoist meditation

Primary Skill Objectives

- Understand and be ready to implement the structures of therapeutic relationships in counseling.
- Anticipate potential difficulties in structuring time in counseling.
- Be ready to give a general explanation of the normal structure of therapeutic interactions in counseling.
- Be ready and able to provide customized explanations of counseling use for a variety of persons and situations.
- Consider how helpful explanations of therapeutic interactions for clients may also be helpful to significant others in clients' lives.

Focus Activity

Imagine yourself going to see a counselor for your first time during a time when you are upset and hurting. Assume that you know very little about counseling and that some of what you know may be unrealistic. Discuss with others or describe in writing what would be helpful for you to know about counseling. Consider what anxieties you may feel over not knowing or perhaps initially not receiving what you expected from counseling. From what you know of counseling now, consider which of your anxieties it would be helpful for your counselor to attempt to assuage with structural information or explanations in order to guide your use of counseling and to help make your use of it tolerable to you, not overwhelming to the point where you quit. Imagine the information and explanations that would have been helpful to you. Also, consider which of your understandable anxieties would be best for you to work through without your counselor attempting to relieve them with information or explanation. Speculate why it might be best to work through some of your anxieties related to counseling. Then, discuss or describe several ways that you believe the experiences of others may vary from yours in regard to these questions.

Introduction

Because many clients either come to counseling not knowing what to expect or with mistaken expectations, one of your tasks as counselor is to structure or clarify clients' use of counseling. This includes the basic time structure, as well as explaining what the person's best use of counseling may be.

Time-Frame

Session Length and Ending Sessions

Some of the arrangements of counseling that we find important to explain to clients include the length and frequency of sessions, and issues related to scheduling and rescheduling. Regarding the length of sessions, we usually tell clients, "Our meetings will normally begin on the hour and end 10 minutes before the next hour. I will let you know when we have about 5 minutes left in our meeting." As with all statements we make to clients, we watch to see how our clients react and then respond with empathy. Normally after this statement, clients look at their counselor as if to say, "OK, that's fine." To such a look we respond, "That makes sense and is OK with you."

On hearing this advice for letting clients know the time structure of counseling, one of our beginning counseling students exclaimed amusedly, "Oh, I wondered why my counselor always ended before my hour was up. I thought he was cheating me out of 10 of my minutes."

Letting Clients Own Their Endings

Within this explanation of session length is the structural information that you will give a 5-minute time warning. These time warnings and generally ending your sessions on time allow your clients ultimate responsibility over use of their time in counseling. For example, if your client is working up to telling you something before the end of the time, it is helpful for her to know when his meeting with you is nearly ended for that day. Or, if your client has been quite emotional in the session, he may choose to take time to dry tears and pull himself away from the strong emotions before going out in public.

To maintain your client's right to choose how she uses her time with you, it is also important to end your sessions on time. We have sometimes found that clients want to tell their counselors about parts of their lives over which they may feel shame or embarrassment near the end of a session in order to say it with no time remaining to see their counselor's reaction. We think it is true for many of us humans that no matter how much we have come to trust others, we would sometimes rather not see their reactions when we tell them the things of which we feel shame.

An extreme example of this comes from early in Jeff's work: I had worked with a young man for 10–12 sessions. I am confident that he had perceived the core conditions from me. He had shared with me parts of his life that were important to him and difficult for him tell me. In the time that we worked together, he was recovering from cutting and other self-injurious behaviors. Just before we began working together, he had left his family's church, to which he had belonged all his life. He helped me understand that he had internalized many self-criticisms from the teachings of that church and from his perceptions of his parents' criticisms of him. His parents had broken off contact with him after he left the church, but he and they were working to reestablish a relationship over the weeks that he worked with me in counseling. His girlfriend, for whom he had very strong feelings and had hoped to marry, had broken up with him shortly before he left the church. His life had been in turmoil. During our time together, he had worked hard reviewing and reconsidering many of his former self-critical beliefs and self-doubts. When we began, he had seemed quite fragile. By the time we ended, he was strong and seemed to be getting stronger each day. Much of his process had been to tell me things from his past over which he felt shame or guilt. It seemed to me, as he told me of these actions and worked through his self-criticisms, doubts, and feelings of shame and guilt, that he had come to deeply trust my respect for him and for his judgment, and that he was taking clear responsibility for and ownership of his use of counseling. I thought he had finished this work, as his time of telling me such things had seemed to reach a crescendo, then subsided. He had also known well in advance when our ending would be.

Then, in the last 5 minutes of our last meeting (we had known that it was definitely our last session, as we would be unavailable to each other after that time), it seemed to me there was something more on his mind. I reflected this. He paused and hesitated. He told me again how much he appreciated our time, how much he had grown, and how much of a support our work had been. I knew that he meant these things and that there was something more he was ready to add. In our last moment, he told me that he had pressured his girlfriend to have an abortion a year before and that I was the first person he had told. He said this at the door and left immediately, leaving me no chance to respond. I took this to be a huge disclosure, as I knew that his former church would have considered it a great sin.

However, it became clear to me that this was his choice of how to end, that it was no accident. For myself, I wanted him to stay. I wanted him to have more time to discuss his reactions to the abortion. I wanted to hear more of his reactions to the abortion. Yet, my role had been to respect and accept him as he presented himself to me. This included his decisions of how to use his time in counseling. I thought quickly as to whether I should seek him out for safety concerns, but I knew that he was future oriented, strong and gaining in clear-headed strength, and had given me believable, solid reasons why he had stopped any self-injurious behavior and would certainly never suicide (we had discussed these things earlier in his work). If it had been possible for me to call him back, this may have conveyed to him how much I cared. Yet, I was already confident that he knew I cared deeply. So, if I had had an opportunity to call him back, it would have communicated that I did not trust him and his decision of how to end, from which he may have generalized that I hadn't trusted others of his decisions. Then, because he had made it clear to me that my views were very important to him, he may have concluded that his self-doubts and self-criticisms had been deserved after all.

That experience serves as a strong reminder to me to remember to allow clients to know how much time we have, then to stick to my commitment of that time. Endings of sessions and counseling relationships are important. They belong to your clients. As I was able to rule out imminent danger concerns, I needed to trust his decision of how to end, of what he wanted to tell me in our last moment and how. Such trust had been my role with him, and it would have been a violation to change in his final moment, even as I wanted to know more and do more for him. As you structure your counseling consistently, your clients are empowered to use their time, including endings, as they see best.

Exceptions to Ending on Time

As with any guidance, there are always exceptions. An example of an exception to ending on time comes from a client that Jeff first mentioned in Chapter 2. In an initial session, she had explained that she had something big to say and that she just had to get it out. She told a story of sexual abuse in her childhood and explained that she had never told anyone and it was hard for her to say. At 45 minutes into her session, instead of giving a 5-minute warning, I interjected something like the following, "We are nearing the end of our normal meeting time length. It seems that you are in the middle of telling me of a part of your life that is very important to you right now. I can extend our time a half-hour if you wish." (I was fortunate not to have another meeting scheduled immediately after hers. If I had, I would have had to schedule a time to continue.) She agreed and stated her appreciation. Near the end of our extended meeting, I gave time-structuring statements as usual.

Another exception to ending at 50 minutes, and the only obvious situation for which counselors should allow themselves to be made late for a following meeting, would be sessions in which risks of imminent danger are unable to be resolved by the normal ending time. When such situations occur, you have a legal and ethical obligation to resolve safety issues before your client leaves. While this is true, we still don't like the message this may give to the client for whom you are late—that the time of persons who are in crisis may be more important to you than those who are not. So, avoid this exception to ending on time whenever possible by addressing issues of imminent danger within the normal meeting time (managing situations of imminent danger is addressed in Chapter 10).

Guidance for Awkwardness of Giving Time Warnings

Some beginning counseling students tell us they feel awkward learning to give time warnings. They worry that the time warnings stop their clients' communication and perhaps make it appear that they (the counselors) are more interested in time than in their clients' communications. We offer a few thoughts for such situations:

- Pair 5-minute time warnings with reflection. An example is, "We have 5 minutes left today. You were telling me that while you feel uneasy, you are proud of the break you have made."
- Sometimes clients will change the subject following time warnings to discuss rescheduling or ongoing work. This does not necessarily mean your client thought you were disinterested. Perhaps she simply saw a need to take care of planning for ongoing work at that time.
- Once your clients are used to your routine, you can usually give time warnings quietly, without even stopping their communication to you.
- Endings have to come some time. Endings based on time are artificial. Yet, our culture and its institutions are based on coordinated time use. Thus, for you to make your time available to a number of persons, you must use the artificial endings based on time.

Varying the Time Warning Structure for Some Clients

Again, there are always exceptions. You may choose to give a client who has difficulty ending first a 10-minute and then a 5-minute warning, in order to give that person more time to prepare to end. Also, we often give a 1-minute time warning. In some situations, a 5-minute plus a 1-minute time warning can be overdoing it. But when we sense the ending is still going to feel abrupt after a 5-minute time warning, we will also note when there is one minute remaining: "We just have about 1 minute left today."

A Few More Suggestions on This Time Thing

Place your Clock Conveniently

Place a clock you can easily read in your field of vision so you can be aware of the time without having to be highly distracted or having to make a distracting motion to check the time.

Realize Your Keeping Time Maximizes Your Client's Freedom to Express

You are keeping track of time so your clients do not have to. Rather than being restrictive, your keeping track of time is freeing to your clients. Because you keep track of time and give time warnings, your clients are free to focus their attention on their self-expression and use of counseling.

Losing Track of Time

There will be those sessions where you simply lose track of time. This is usually due to having gotten so caught up in your client's experience that you simply forget about the time. In those cases, once you realize your mistake, simply do the best you can to approximate a compromise that allows for time warning and ending close to on time.

Helping Clients Understand the Structure of Interactions in Counseling or How Counseling May Work for Them

The primary and most frequent structure of interactions between counselor and client is this: A client tells the counselor about his self and life; the counselor reflects the part of that communication that she saw as most important to her client; the client reacts to reflection in deepening communication of his self and life. Some clients come expecting such interactions. In a great many cases, clients learn this structure of interactions and its value simply through participating in it, without explanation.

You may remember our base explanation of counseling that goes something like, "Your role is to help me understand you. You can start with any part of yourself and your life. My role is to strive to understand and to say back to you the parts that I think I understand, first little pieces, then a larger picture of who you are." We sometimes add to this explanation one of the purposes of this process: "You can then use my understanding of you to increase your self-understanding. When I am wrong, you may come to a more accurate understanding of yourself by correcting my misunderstanding. When I am right, it may spur deeper self-understanding on your part. You can then use these new understandings for improved decisions based on knowing who you are, and who and how you want to be."

This explanation is imperfect and not entirely accurate. We use the word *understanding*, when what we really mean is *empathy*. This is because "empathy" may be harder for clients to understand, without too much thinking. Yet, "understanding" is usually readily understood. Also, this explanation does not capture the essence of therapeutic relationships, which is each client's perception of genuine empathy and unconditional positive regard from his counselor. While these qualities are more important than the description of new insight in the explanation above, the explanation does reasonably describe counselor and client interactions (i.e., what each does), and gives clients a useful initial idea of what counseling can be like.

A very helpful way to improve such explanations, especially when clients continue to struggle with how to use counseling, is to customize your explanations to individual client situations. Examples of personalized explanations follow below.

A Client Who Asks for Guidance—Empathy to Expectations, then Response

We have served many clients who have become accustomed to being controlled by others yet, especially as an adolescent or young adult, resent this control. The following is an example from Jeff's work.

I was working with a young man who was referred by his physician for stress-related health concerns. He had described his father to me as very controlling and communicated that he felt great pressure to perform for his family. He was studying in a very difficult field, which he explained he did not have much interest in but knew that it was what his father wanted and his family expected.

Respond with Warm Empathy to his Expectations for Counseling

I felt his intense frustration with this dilemma. At first, when he asked in exasperation for my guidance regarding how to solve the dilemma, I reflected, "That's how *frustrating* it is for you, so much that you really like guidance from me." When, after further expressing his frustration, he confirmed that he really would like guidance from me, I responded by briefly reflecting, "That really is what you want," then continued explaining: "I'd like you to think of counseling working this way . . ." (I gave our explanation of roles in counseling, from the previous section.) When I saw a look of dissatisfaction cross his face, I reflected, "I get the idea that you were bothered by the suggestion for counseling that I just gave." He responded, appearing to make great efforts to maintain respect for me while expressing his dissatisfaction, "Yes, I need help. I don't know what to do."

A Rationale for Not Guiding (Guidance Available in Existing Relationships; Guidance May Impede rather than Support Development)

At that time I gave further explanation, customized to his situation and our therapeutic relationship. I explained with warmth and empathy, "I'd like you to consider . . ." (I paused, then continued speaking slowly and carefully because his perception of my words were very important to me.) First, I don't believe I can know what is best for you to do. I believe that each of our situations is quite unique. But even if I did, then I'd worry that you'd be trading taking direction from me for taking direction from your father, whose control you want to move beyond." A look of recognition and surprise crossed his face, which I knew meant that what I had said was new but beginning to make sense. I responded to that recognition and surprise, and continued a part of my explanation that I believed also important: "It seemed like my last idea made sense to you and sparked a new thought. I also want to add that I have great faith in the counseling process and strong confidence in *your* struggling through and making *your* decisions."

He responded that he really didn't want my suggestions, that it was just how difficult the dilemma was for him, and that he really did want to decide for himself. We worked together a few sessions more. He decided to openly oppose his father's control and family expectations. He quit college to take time to decide what he would like to do before returning. To do this, he had to give up financial support from his family.

If I had given into my temptation to give him advice when he asked, I would have probably led him to pick a major that he liked more and to talk to his father about this. However, his decision was that a more abrupt, clean break was necessary for him. Once he made that decision, it became obvious to me that it was best for him. I came to see that it gave him the best chance of keeping his resolve now and then reconciling with his father later, having built a strong sense of self-respect. My advice, based on my worries of how he would suffer without his father's support, might only have prolonged his agony. Fortunately, I disciplined myself to trust him and the counseling process, to meet him with empathy and unconditional positive regard—the most powerful and useful tools that any counselor can have. This ability to trust was supported by my carefully thought-through conceptualization of him, concluding his general competence, clear-headed approach to life, reasonable awareness—developed in our work, insight, and reasonable self-confidence, with the exception of his presenting problem. Oh, his health problems had also dissipated before our work together ended.

A Client Who Insists on a Quick Solution—Frequently Helpful Explanations

Another example of a client who asked for guidance, but who seemed entrenched in insisting on using counseling *only* for guidance, occurred from a client who was served by an intern of Jeff's. The young man was referred from a health service that saw his symptoms as depression (e.g., sleeping excessive amounts, continually feeling tired and disinterested in activities). He had begun with one counselor, insisting that he must have immediate relief. When that counselor responded by trying to convince him that he should consider medications, he was angered and asked for another counselor. He had tried medications in the past for depression, and his father took medications for depression but seemed only to have ongoing problems.

When he was switched to his second counselor, an intern in Jeff's class, he began by explaining that he was willing to admit he was depressed but was adamant against considering medication. Rather, he wanted to know what he could do to make the bad feelings go away besides using medication. He seemed almost panicked for a quick solution. It may have been that while he was not feeling hopeless yet, he feared that if he did not find a solution soon or if medications did not help, it would mean there was something uniquely wrong with him and he would then be hopeless. He seemed quite resistant to exploring himself and his emotions. He seemed determined to focus on searching for a quick solution.

In class, we helped his counselor prepare to provide him with information on self-care for managing emotions (i.e., managing sleep, diet, exercise and use of enjoyable activities such as hobbies—such information can be found in a large variety of sources, such as Bourne, 2011). However, we knew that while he was asking for such skills, they alone would be much less powerful than the work he could do with a therapeutic relationship in counseling. So, our supervision group generated a variety of explanations of his possible use of counseling. In this way his counselor could offer one or two from among them when the time was right in his meetings. We include several of them here for you to consider the variety of helpful forms such explanations can take.

The Profoundly Different Counseling Relationship

One intern noted that the client's work with his current counselor would be very different from what he had experienced before in that there would be no judgment or criticism of his decisions from his counselor. Some clients need to hear that a counseling relationship (therapeutic relationship) really is quite different from most relationships and that this very difference brings new opportunities, such as the following.

A Process of Realistic Self-Evaluation

The client's counselor noted to our supervision group that he had repeatedly said "how dumb" his thoughts were. We offered the explanation that in counseling, without judgment or criticism, he could come to see his ideas and himself for who he really is, not who he or others think he should be. In that way, he can get to know parts of himself that he really likes and prizes, and get to know some parts that he would choose to change. Then, as he comes closer to being a person that he generally likes and prizes, by emphasizing the parts he already likes and changing others, he may find that his painful feelings lessen.

Embracing rather than Avoiding Painful Emotions

Another intern suggested that it might be important to add that in his (the client's) process of gaining greater self-understanding through helping his counselor understand him, he may have to face emotions that are quite hurtful and hard to express. We thought this addition both a true expectation and helpful as it would let him see his work as significant.

Facing Painful Emotions with Counselor as "Confident Companion"

Another intern suggested reflecting the client's urge to make his painful emotions go away, then adding a thought from his counselor's perspective that an opposite way of being and an option in counseling is to accept and acknowledge emotions. We added the important thought that, in this case, while his counselor would not be solving his emotional pain for him, he also would not be facing it alone but would have his counselor right there with him as a "confident companion" (Rogers, 1980, p. 142).

Why Attend to Painful Emotions

It occurred to us that the explanation above might understandably lead the client to ask why he would want to accept and acknowledge emotions that hurt and that he wants to be rid of. To answer such a question, we decided that his counselor could explain that emotions are useful. Like physical pain, there is something to be learned from them. For example, if a toddler touches a hot burner, the toddler learns that it hurts and to avoid that action again. While physical and emotional pain is rarely that simple, there is something important to learn from it. Therefore, emotional pain is not something to make go away but is an important tool for finding needed guidance.

The Difficult Knot Analogy

We also thought that the client seemed to be working hard to solve his painful emotions, and we thought of offering the metaphor of trying to untie a difficult knot. Sometimes, the more a person works at it, the tighter it becomes. Then, if the person relaxes with the knot and explores it without trying to untie it, either parts of solutions simply come or you find that the knot has somehow already loosened in your hands. By this, we mean that if he uses counseling to explore his whole self, without trying to make his painful emotions go away, his solutions to his painful feelings may become obvious, or the feelings may begin to dissipate without clear solutions ever being found.

Discovering One's Own Inner Guide

We also noted that he seemed to have had a couple of recent experiences of going to experts for help, then disagreeing with or being hurt by their suggestions. Thus, he could use counseling in which he explored himself, his feelings, and his ideas as a way to renew valuing himself. In this way his new counselor could help him discover his own inner guide vs. the guidance of supposed experts, which might not fit for him.

The client opened his next session with a renewed request for guidance on how to make his painful emotions go away. His counselor first reflected that guidance for managing emotions was what he saw that he most needed and then offered ideas, informed by her knowledge of counseling and change, on ways to manage difficult emotions (e.g., thought change strategies from REBT (Ellis & Dryden, 2007) or relaxation techniques. The young man seemed disappointed and expressed his doubt and frustration that these changes sounded very difficult and didn't sound like they would be strong enough to help him feel all that much better. His counselor carefully reflected his emotions and conclusion within this statement, paused, then added that she also wanted him to consider using counseling very differently than he had so far. She gave one or two of the explanations of counseling for this client that we had offered in class. The young man seemed to like the empowerment he felt with this way of looking at his use of counseling. He continued to struggle, of course, as neither his life nor his use of counseling was simple (we don't believe anyone's is). However, he did make a strong use of counseling and found strength and self-confidence through facing his fears. Through this process, he came to feel less depressed and his symptoms of depression decreased. He chose and made changes in his life that were satisfying to him.

A Client Who has Great Discomfort with Silence

There are silent moments in counseling. As discussed in Chapter 2, this is not necessarily a problem and may be a good thing. Sometimes you will reflect, and your client will pause not knowing what to say next and feel awkward in that silence. Jeff once served a young woman for which this was dramatically true. The customized explanation that helped her may serve as a useful example to consider in customizing explanations for others.

Self-Discovery by Working through Difficulties

Some background may help in understanding the customized explanation that follows. In our (the client's and my) first couple of sessions together, she had discovered and let me know that she very much feared being alone, so much so that she would sleep with men to avoid being alone. She had come to know that these men didn't care for her as a person and would usually not be there for her after sex. After one awkward silence in a growing pattern of such moments, I reflected, "You seemed to come to a moment when you had nothing to say and feel awkward with that." She responded, "Yeah, it feels really weird." She looked at me with an expression that seemed pained and meek. I reflected what I felt from her, "I gather that even beyond weird, the awkwardness seems to hurt and you want it to go away, maybe for me to do something about it." She continued with moist eyes, "Yeah, I can't stand it. Is this the way counseling is supposed to be?" I reflected and explained,

"Sometimes it seems you just can't stand it. [I paused, then continued.] Yes, there are sometimes very awkward silences in counseling. While I know they are very difficult for you, I think you may help yourself greatly by working through them, by finding the thoughts and feelings that come in those silences."

Parallels to Life Difficulties Worked through in Counseling—Alone, but not Alone

This explanation seemed enough for her for a while. Later, when a silence had left her feeling particularly awkward, she again looked at me with a pained expression, near tears, and exclaimed in a low voice that seemed to also convey that she felt defeated, "I can't stand this. I'm not getting anywhere." I reflected and then explained, "It seems it's starting to seem too much for you." I paused and saw the agreement in her eyes, then added, "I think that even as hard as it is, it may be that some of the same thoughts and feelings that you know will hurt so much when you are alone may come up in these silent moments. So, I think for you, counseling may be an opportunity to face those thoughts and feelings, as if alone but not alone, in the safety of our counseling time."

In response to this, she seemed to gird herself up to continue. She moved on to tell me of a time that she had tried being alone over the past few days, some of the critical thoughts of herself, her family, her future, and the pain that had come with those thoughts.

A Client Who Attends Sporadically

While we accept clients choosing to end their work in counseling, either permanently or just for a while, we also know the value of attending counseling consistently. Jeff's work with the young woman of the previous section and his structuring explanation regarding her sporadic attendance may serve as a useful example.

Apparent Consequences of Negative (or Inefficient) Use of Counseling

She fell into a pattern of attending sessions for a few weeks in a row, then missing from one to a few weeks. When she was in counseling, she would seem to make progress. When she would come back after missing, she would return with renewed hurt from her behavior and the actions of others. At the beginning of one returning session, I offered a process reflection of her behavior and my reaction, which also served to help her understand how she was using counseling and its effects, saying, "I'm glad to see you again. I worry that you come to counseling for a while, begin to face some very hard thoughts and feelings, then leave and stay away for a time." I paused to see her shrug what seemed like tentative agreement. I continued, "Then, when you come back, it seems that you have gotten hurt more in the time you were away." She tearfully agreed this was true and told me of her most recent and devastating emotional hurt. She continued more consistently over a longer period after this interchange.

A Client Who Just Does Not Know Where to Start

Saying the First Things that Come to Mind

Some clients simply do not know where to start or what to say in counseling. This can be because the client was talked into counseling by someone else (e.g., parent, romantic partner, roommate, employer, teacher, physician). In this case, your client may come to counseling perfectly willing to use counseling but still have great difficulty getting started. We have noticed that often this is based on the client thinking she has to be a good client, which she has interpreted as consistently talking about a problem and something that seems deep. Our work with children in child-centered play therapy (Cochran, Nordling, & Cochran, 2010) has helped us know that actions, or in this case words, that seem like nonsense can spiral into great existential questions (i.e., Who am I? Who do I want to be? What is my value? Can I measure it— if so, how?) within the process of a therapeutic relationship. Therefore, we have sometimes used explanations like the following:

CLIENT: [Pauses after a reflection, looking at her counselor with questioning gestures.]

COUNSELOR: You seem to have run out of things to say and are looking to me to help you out.

CLIENT: Yeah, I'm sorry. I want to work on this, but I just don't have anything [hesitating pause] that was all I could think of.

COUNSELOR: So, you're working to think of something to say but coming up with nothing.

CLIENT: [Laughs a little.] Well, I think of things to say, of course, but just stupid stuff, not for counseling.

COUNSELOR: Oh, so it sounds like ideas cross your mind, but you rule them out for counseling. I'd like you to know first that a pause in our conversations may not be a bad thing. Sometimes out of awkward pauses, the most useful things occur. Also, you don't need to worry whether the things that occur to you to say are worthy of counseling. You can say the first things that come to mind and the process of our interactions will take us to the topics that are important for you.

There are countless more varieties of customized explanations of individuals' use of counseling. For just one more example, Jeff has often helped clients who want to become more personally expressive or self-reliant see counseling as *a safe place to experiment with being different*. In summary, the following are the keys to helping clients who seem to need explanation to understand how they can use counseling:

- Meet each client with empathy and UPR, as much as possible, of course.
- Don't take a client's struggle with counseling as an indictment of you or your counseling.
- Come to an initial understanding of who each client is, what his situation is, and what he seems to want. Then offer an explanation, based on that understanding, of how he may use his therapeutic relationship with you to help himself.

Process Reflections to Help Clients Understand Use of Counseling

Higher-level reflections, in this case reflecting your clients' process or pattern of behaviors in counseling, can help your clients become aware of how they are using counseling and often make unnecessary more extensive explanations of how they can best use counseling. The added awareness of how they are using counseling gained from your process reflection helps your clients make optimal choices for their use of counseling.

Example 1—Delaying Emotional Topics

If you have a client who consistently waits until near the end of her sessions to get to what it seemed she wanted to say—the topics that have the most emotional content and seem important to her—you can reflect this to her, "I notice that in many of our meetings you seem to start by telling me about your week and get to topics that are emotional for you shortly before our time is up." It is important that your tone in making such a process reflection remains accepting. The rationale for acceptance, as always, is to empower your client's self-responsibility and healthy decision process. However, in this situation, acceptance has a situation-specific importance as well. Consider that the client in this example may greatly fear getting to the things that she came to communicate. She may be building to communicate still more. If so, it is important for you to honor the pace at which she is ready to self-disclose. Pushing her to go faster than she is ready will damage trust and inhibit progress. Reflecting how you see her using her time helps her make fully informed decisions of pace.

Most clients simply acknowledge such a process reflection and continue their communication while adjusting their process based on their new awareness. Some clients also question or comment on your process comment.

For example, clients might respond to the aforementioned process reflection in a variety of ways. They might ask, "Why, is that not OK?" to which you would reflect and explain, "You're not sure if it's OK, and you want it to be. It can be OK. I want you to work at the pace you are ready and with the topics you see as most important. But I also know that the sooner you get to what you most want to say, the better."

Another client in this same scenario might also tell you, "I know I'm slow. It's just so hard for me to say emotional things." To which you may reflect, "You see yourself as slow and want me to know that that's because it's very hard for you to tell me things that are emotional for you." You might add reassurance of the structure, "I am OK with your pace. I noted it to help you make the most informed decisions of your use of counseling and of what you are ready for."

Still another client in a situation like this told her counselor, "Yeah, I try to give you all the background you need to understand, then it seems like we're almost out of time." In this case, her counselor reflected and explained, "Oh, so you're thinking that I need the background to understand the important part. I'm thinking that may not be necessary. You could try just starting with the important part and I may be able to understand without as much background."

Example 2—Approaching, then Moving Away from Emotional Topics

Another example of a situation for which a process reflection can also help clients be aware of how they are using counseling is a client who tends to express emotions and communicate regarding a topic that seems clearly important to him, then quickly changes the subject to talk about something less emotional and seemingly less important to him. In this case, your process reflection could be, "I notice that you tend to begin to tell me about situations and feelings that seem very important to you and to feel strong emotions, then quickly change the subject to something less emotional."

Again, many clients will simply acknowledge the reflection and continue their communication while adjusting their process based on their new awareness. And some clients will comment on or question such a process reflection. We have known clients to say, "Yeah, that's what I do. I try not to think about hurtful things too much" (sounding light and satisfied in tone). To which you can respond, "So you know that's a pattern for you and you seem satisfied with it." Hearing the acceptance in your reflection, he might say, "Well, not satisfied—it's just the best I can do. It seems to work for me ... but the painful emotions just seem to come back—" In this case, your reflection has allowed him to question his pattern with the full awareness prompted by your attention and empathy and within the safety of your acceptance.

To that same process comment, another client might respond, "Yes, this is very hard and I can only deal with so much at a time." To which you might respond, "So this is hard and you see that you are working at the pace that you are ready and able." Again, accepting this client's judgment and communication is the quickest way to allow her to continue to trust you and to intensify her pace. Also, it respects her decision to maintain her slower pace if she continues to decide that that pace is optimal for her in that it is not overwhelming or so painful that she would quit trying.

Explaining the Use of Counseling to Significant Persons in Clients' Lives

It is often helpful to explain counseling to significant others in clients' lives. Versions of the same explanations you might give clients are helpful here, too. We give examples of elements of explanations of counseling for parents here, then address other aspects of consultation with significant others in clients' lives in Chapter 15.

If a parent refers or brings her child to counseling, we often think that the parent has a right to know what kinds of things will go on in her child's counseling or at least may need to know what kinds of things go on in order to be supportive. Elements of explanations that we find helpful in such situations follow:

- "Your son may use counseling to come to better understand himself, then use that new understanding for new and improved decisions about how he really wants to be and act in life."
- "Counseling can be quite difficult and painful. For any person to fully understand himself, he may have to face parts of himself over which he is critical or ashamed. This can be true whether or not he actually has a rational reason for self-criticism or shame. So, your son may not always be eager to come."
- "If your son has acted out, the misbehaviors may have been an attempt to hide these parts of himself. If your son has acted in self-destructive ways, it may well be for the same reasons."
- "As your son comes to see himself clearly, he will come to act differently based on accepting who he is or changing parts of himself in order to become the person that he really wants to be."
- "I ask for your support in being ready to listen with an open mind and heart when he chooses to talk with you about himself or his counseling."
- "I also ask you to support him in not asking for information about his work in counseling, until he chooses to offer it."

Just as explanations of counseling to clients should be customized to their unique situation, so should explanations of counseling to significant others in clients' lives. For a full discussion of parent and teacher consultation around children's use of counseling, in which parent and teacher consultation is much more common, see Cochran, Nordling, & Cochran (2010).

Problems for Beginning Counselors in Explaining Clients' Use of Counseling

Our interns have told us that they know the kinds of explanations of counseling that we suggest are true. They know this from their experience as clients in their own counseling. Still, during their first sessions as counselors, sometimes the explanations do not come to them. Usually, once their early experiences of success lead them to be more relaxed and calm as counselors, this problem goes away.

Sometimes, not thinking of helpful explanations that you know are true comes from getting too caught up in your client's drive to find an immediate solution to feelings that hurt or in your client's despair over not knowing what to say, perhaps not trusting her own judgment in self-direction. It helps in such situations to take a step back and try to see the whole person in context, rather than just her immediate demand or plea for a solution, or perhaps her immediate frustration with counseling. For example, consider again the young man who was so much wanting help with his depressed feelings but was also working hard to make his depressed feelings go away. His counselor was having difficulty thinking of how to help him understand how he could successfully use counseling, because all she could hear was his drive to make the painful emotions go away. When his counselor was able to take a step back, she saw that the young man was not only demanding to make the painful emotions go away but was doing and communicating other things as well. He was working to avoid feeling, he was discounting his own views and asking for those of others, and in working so hard to untie his knot, he was actually pulling it tighter. The overall metaphor of this paragraph is the old expression, "Can't see the forest for the trees." In this case, the counselor was staring so closely at a single distressed tree—the young man's demand to tell him how to make the painful emotions go away quickly—that she was unaware of other facets of her client's communication that would be helpful to reflect.

Activities and Resources for Further Study

- In a 15-minute practice session(s) in which your client (a classmate or peer) communicates to you on a topic that has emotional content for her or him, add the skills of time structuring to your growing repertoire of counseling skills. When in the role of client, give your counselor feedback of what her or his way of time structuring left you feeling and thinking as client.
- Imagine difficult clients for yourself, both some who are similar to examples in the chapter and others who may be different. Have

partner(s) role-play those clients while you work helpful explanations of counseling into their sessions. These practice sessions may need to be 20 minutes long in order to give the opportunities for explanations time to come up and to be reacted to.

- Imagine scenarios where you explain counseling to significant others in your clients' lives. Have partner(s) role-play significant others in practice meetings in which you work in explanations of counseling.
- Journal about these activities. What was difficult for you? What came easily? What do you expect will be difficult for you with clients and significant others in their lives? What will you do to work through these difficulties? What do you expect will be your strengths in such situations? How will you capitalize on your strengths?
- Discuss again or rewrite your response to the focus activity. Notice how your thoughts, feelings, and statements on the topic have changed and/or stayed the same.
- Review writings by authors such as Cochran, Nordling and Cochran (2010), Louise Guerney (1976, 1983, 1995, 2013), Virginia Axline (1947) and Gary Landreth (2012), for counselor behaviors they describe in child-centered play therapy and other works with children that may be considered structuring. Consider how children come to understand, use, and take control of the structures they are provided through play therapy. Then, consider how this may help you think differently about structuring when counseling adolescents and adults.
- Revisit the Primary Skill Objectives for this chapter. If you have not yet mastered them to your satisfaction, please reread, engage in additional practice, and seek additional readings and study opportunities until you have mastered them to your satisfaction.

References

Axline, V.M. (1947). *Play therapy: The inner dynamics of childhood*. Cambridge, MA: The Riverside Press.

Bourne, E.J. (2011). *The anxiety and phobia workbook*. Oakland, CA: New Harbinger Publications.

Cochran, N.H., Nordling, W., & Cochran, J.L. (2010). *Child-centered play therapy: A practical guide to developing therapeutic relationships with children*. Hoboken, NJ: Wiley.

Ellis, A., & Dryden, W. (2007). *The practice of rational emotive therapy* (2nd ed.). New York: Springer.

Guerney, L.F. (1976). Filial therapy program. In H.L. Benson (Ed.), *Treating relationships* (pp. 67–91). Lake Mills, IA: Graphic Publishing.

Guerney, L.F. (1983). Client-centered (nondirective) play therapy. In C.E. Schaefer & K.J. O'Connor (Eds.), *Handbook of play therapy* (pp. 21–64). New York: Wiley.

Guerney, L.F. (1995). *Parenting: A skills training manual* (5th ed.). Bethesda, MD: Institute for the Development of Emotional and Life Skills.

Guerney, L.F. (2013). *Group filial therapy: The complete guide to teaching parents to play therapeutically with their children*. New York: Jessica Kingsley.

Landreth, G.L. (2012). *Play therapy: The art of the relationship*. Hoboken, NJ: Wiley.

Rogers, C.R. (1980). *A way of being*. Boston, MA: Houghton Mifflin.

Pre-Chapter Quote

Ming-Dao, D. (1992). *Daily meditations*. New York: HarperCollins (p. 128).

9 WHEN CLIENTS NEED HELP GETTING STARTED

It is easier to resist at the beginning than at the end.

Leonardo Da Vinci

Primary Skill Objectives

- Understand and be able to explain several reasons why some clients may struggle in starting.
- Understand and be ready to avoid mistakes that a counselor might make that can inhibit a client's beginning use of counseling.
- Understand and be able to implement counselor actions that can help clients struggling in starting.
- Be able to explain the roles of empathy and UPR in helping clients begin to fully utilize therapeutic relationships.
- Understand how and what types of questions or topic suggestions might help clients who are struggling and what types would not. Be ready to implement this understanding.
- Understand and be able to differentiate and explain the parts of your clients' struggles in starting that are within your influence, the parts that are not and how you may best respond to each.

Focus Activities

Activity 1

Think of a variety of clients with situations in which they may struggle to begin to make use of their therapeutic relationship. Strive to understand the reasons why some clients might struggle in starting. Examples might include persons who are generally shy and rarely talk about themselves, persons who feel very anxious but have not realized that they are anxious, persons who usually spend their time helping and focused on others, or persons who were urged into counseling by others and do perhaps feel badly but have no idea why or how to start. Most clients do not need help getting started, but for those who do, there are an infinite variety of reasons why. Try to put yourself in the situations of each person that you imagine need help getting started. What might each person be thinking and feeling?

Contemplate how you might naturally feel, think, act, and be with clients who are struggling in starting. Then, imagine things you might do or say, as their counselor, or ways you might be with each person that you expect would be most helpful in their struggle. Journal and discuss your contemplations on these matters with your peers.

Activity 2

Imagine times in your life when it would have been difficult for you to get started in the counseling processes described in previous chapters. Why might it have been difficult for you? What parts of your self or situation might have gotten in the way? What might you have felt and thought, and how might you have been and acted? What might a counselor have done to help you through that time, if anything? Journal and discuss with peers your thoughts, feelings, and answers to these questions regarding such a time in your life.

Introduction

In this chapter, we focus on ways you can help clients who struggle to begin to make use of their therapeutic relationship with you. We find that when we and other counselors follow the skills of the core conditions as we have described them through the preceding chapters, most clients readily and rapidly begin their work. Yet, some struggle in starting for a variety of reasons. Some may be inhibited by negative preconceptions of counseling. Some may have internalized a perception, stated or implied by family, friends or society, that using counseling means there is something terribly wrong with them or that they are weak and not self-reliant. Or they may have internalized the perception that counseling is disempowering, that the counselor will break them down with analysis, expose their weaknesses and assume a long-term need for ongoing therapy. Others may fear that they have something to hide and that their counselor will see and critically judge this part of their self. Some may be shy and not at all used to relating closely to another person. Some may have anxieties that nag at them and that have driven them to counseling but that they avoid feeling fully and facing at any length. We humans are naturally taught to avoid anxiety because it is, at the very least, uncomfortable. Yet, in counseling, it will be hard to avoid facing painful anxiety. Some clients may have often been judged, have felt hurt by this, and greatly fear critical judgment from you. The reasons that some clients may struggle in starting seem infinite. We would like you to consider that while it is a minority of clients who struggle getting started, their struggle can be quite understandable.

When such slow-to-start situations occur, first review your ways of being for common mistakes that may be inhibiting your clients' progress. Then, after considering the possible effects of your ways of being, consider explanations that may help struggling clients understand how they can use counseling, and finally, consider use of questions that may help struggling clients get a stronger start.

Mistakes that Inhibit Clients' Beginning Use of Counseling

Trying Too Hard or Worrying about Motivating Clients to Make Rapid Use of Counseling

Jeff's grandfather once added to the old expression "You can lead a horse to water, but you can't make him drink" the additional phrase, "but a goat will eat anything." You see, with goats, the problem is not getting them to eat or drink but containing them and limiting them to eating and drinking the things that are healthy for them. Part of what he meant was that some people focus too much on the problems of motivating others and come to see those they wish to motivate as a horse that simply will not drink. Papaw was a good motivator of people, and one of his ways of doing this was to recognize when he could see them as goats, not horses; when he could and should give them good, but limited direction, then get out of their way, having provided an environment that is fertile and safe for their work. A therapeutic relationship is an optimally fertile and safe environment for your clients' growth. So, while there are things you can do to help clients who struggle in starting, the first and most essential thing you must do to help your clients who are slow to start is to *accept their pace as it is* and *trust the process* of providing a therapeutic relationship.

Not Recognizing that Your Client Began to Use His or Her Therapeutic Relationship with You As Soon As You Began to Provide It

If your client is nervous beginning counseling, does not talk as much as you might expect, and has uncomfortable pauses in her early work with you, then rather than indicating that she is not using her therapeutic relationship with you, it means that working through those uncomfortable pauses is an important part of how she *is* using her therapeutic relationship with you. You might offer such a client help getting started in the form of explaining how counseling may work for her or even offering questions to suggest topics. However, this guidance may not even be necessary when you provide empathy and acceptance for how your client *is* starting.

A Quiet Client

Imagine that your client seems quite uncomfortable with repeated pauses, and you feel just how hard and scary getting started is for him. In that case you might reflect your client's process by saying something like, "You seem unsure of what to say and this leaves you very uncomfortable, apprehensive, maybe even afraid of how this will go." Because his experience is happening within the healing environment you are providing, working through this discomfort and fear in getting started is how he has already started and may be a very important part of his use of the therapeutic relationship. Working through to closeness may be a central part of his work in counseling. Your empathy can help him learn from his anxiety and your acceptance can help him be OK with experiencing it long enough to learn from it. This work can then build his confidence to face other challenges, and can help him see the things he fears of himself in a more realistic perspective.

A Talkative Client

Another client who seems slow to start may begin, not by talking less but by talking more, while seeming to express little that is important to her. Some clients who are anxious about starting counseling may try to fill the time with words that seem to express anything but heartfelt experience. Persons in this situation might talk about others in their life, their to-do list, or the weather. Again, this is not really a problem. If it is coming to be how you see a client, after reflecting her content with warm acceptance, you might tentatively offer a process reflection like, "I get the idea that there are things you'd thought you might say or do here, but you seem to talk of anything but those things." If necessary, you could even add a structuring explanation for her use of counseling, such as "While I want you to use this time to discuss any of the things on your mind and heart, I think it may be most efficient if you consider what thoughts and feelings are most important to you and say those. While I don't want you to focus on editing what you say, I also want to help you get to the core things that will be most helpful for you to say." In most cases, nothing needs to be done to help such clients, except to focus yourself in therapeutic listening, especially emphasizing empathy, which will lead to the heart of the matter, and accept this as her start. Just the process reflection and following with therapeutic listening, deep empathy, and genuine UPR will usually suffice. Example dialog of how this might go, following the same process reflection from before, may clarify our guidance for such situations.

COUNSELOR: I get the idea that there are things you thought you might say or do here, but you seem to talk of anything but that.
CLIENT: [Responds with a slight giddiness that seems to be nervousness, and with an apologetic tone.] Oh gosh, I didn't mean to waste your time, it's just, I thought I was supposed to say anything.
COUNSELOR: Oh, you seem to have taken my statement like I was fussing at you. Yes, absolutely, you may say anything. [Counselor combined a quick reflection with a structuring explanation that seemed important to avoid misunderstanding.]

CLIENT: [Sounding slightly exasperated and picking up pace again.] It's just, I'm so busy and have so much on my mind that I wouldn't want to waste time here. I'm sorry.

COUNSELOR: Oh, so you were talking quickly through subjects in order not to waste a minute. I also get the idea that you worry slightly that I am critical of you. I see that you are working hard. [Counselor combined three brief, related reflections that each seemed important.]

CLIENT: [Sounding more emphatic.] I am working hard and no one seems to appreciate it. I am sick of it! [This was her strongest statement yet.]

COUNSELOR: [Responding with same emphatic tone.] You see that lots of people, maybe even me, are seeing you that way; and you've about had enough of people not valuing your hard work!

The conversation may then go to a trend in wanting appreciation and seeming to get criticism, or perhaps to lists and explanations of hard works, but our purpose in offering this example is to show how staying with such seemingly slow-to-start clients can lead to strong starts and beginning expressions that are close to your client's heart. In this example, the client did not respond to the parts of the counselor's reflections that were about their relating in that moment. So, we would assume that those parts were too soon or just not the most pressing things on her mind, and so were not keys to her immediate experience. In fact, it may never be necessary for her to have direct conversations about her relationship with her counselor in order to make good use of that therapeutic relationship.

Lack of Acceptance

Sometimes counselors can care so much for their clients that their way of being communicates, "I will accept you when you show me that you are using our therapeutic relationship." The behaviors of that mistaken way of being often include having a single picture in mind of what it will look like when clients are making efficient use of their counseling, then responding enthusiastically to client behaviors that fit this picture and responding with anxiety and disappointment to client behaviors that do not fit that picture. This beginner counselor error is sometimes exacerbated by counselors' insecurity and belief that their clients must be making clear progress or it means that they are bad counselors, or by counselors seeing their clients as fragile and thus not acceptable as they presently are.

Pedantic Reflections

Another reason your clients may start slowly is that you probably have not yet become artful at therapeutic listening and therapeutic relationships. This is a set of tasks that sounds so simple but that we and many of our friends and peers expect to devote lifetimes to perfecting.

For example, in the previous short dialogue example, the counselor some-times forgoes reflecting content, which can be overly pedantic and repetitive, to reflect what the counselor thinks he sees the client doing. The counselor also mixes in a brief structuring statement, maintains strong empathy, and seems to know what is important to emphasize. Developing such a skill level will take devoted practice and experience. Yet, everyone must start somewhere. Every doctor has her first patients and every counselor her first clients. While it may be easier said than done, we suggest you accept yourself as the counselor you are now. If that means that your work is not as efficient as it soon will be and that some of your clients get off to a slower start, we are still confident that you and your clients will progress more quickly if you accept and work where you are, instead of overly criticizing your work and trying to rush ahead to be the counselor that you are not yet.

Reflections that Sound Like "Aha" Conclusions

Slipping into trying to be a more artful counselor than you are so far can lead to giving too much weight and exuberance to your reflections when you think you have figured something out. For example, you might say, "So you feel disappointed when you *think* you're unappreciated because you *believe* you deserved it." Now, there is nothing wrong with such a response from a counselor, and a lot right about it, but if it comes out sounding like you just thought of the key word that will help you complete the cross-word puzzle or like you are *naming* what your client is going through, rather than *experiencing* it with him, your client will be stopped in his tracks from expressing. This mistake usually comes from trying to rush ahead to get to something important (as if every action and expression in counseling were not already important) or "from coming on big when you're feeling small," trying to be the expert you think you must due to internal pressures to do something.

Slipping into Questions

Along the same lines, if you feel anxious with a client who seems slow to start, which is probably normal, you may slip into asking questions that give your client the impression that you mean to lead her through an investigation of herself or her problem that leads to you spitting out sage wisdom for her. You may have begun to use questions with this client, just to help her get started, but with both of you feeling anxious, it got out of hand. When you make this mistake, your client will probably stop expressing freely and wait for your next question or sage advice. This client is putty in your hands and thus dependent on you for molding. Unfortunately, putty rarely gets to live an active, autonomous life.

When in Doubt, Review

Whenever you wonder if there is something you are doing that may be slowing your clients' starts, please review Chapters 1–8 for other aspects of skills that you may enhance in order to better facilitate your clients' starts. We have organized them to make them ready references for you.

Counselor Actions that Help Clients Struggling in Starting

We developed the following suggestions with a class of interns who had just succeeded with an unusually high percentage of clients who seemed slow to start in counseling. Many of the clients were willing to be in counseling and had things to work on like all of us humans but came to counseling at the urging of others, instead of with a clear internal motivation. A few may have been hostile to making use of counseling, due to defensiveness or inhibition. Each of these suggestions was a solution in helping unique clients work through struggles in starting. We offer them for you to consider, as you carefully develop your own solutions for the unique situations you face with clients. Also, we don't want to imply that the purpose of any of these suggestions was to ameliorate the struggles of clients. The purpose is to strike a balance between allowing each client to gain as much as possible from his struggle in starting, while helping him with his struggles so that he is able to tolerate counseling long enough to work through and learn from his struggles.

Start Where Your Client Is

Acceptance is always key. One client was willing to try counseling for personal growth but may have been unsure where to start. At times, she tended to talk about topics that her counselor understandably saw as superficial. Her counselor explained in supervision that he was at first put off by this, but then realized that as he trusted the counseling process and especially accepted his client where she was, the seemingly superficial issues grew to more personal and personally meaningful topics. For example, a client may begin discussing being devastated by a broken fingernail, then that topic may grow into discovering that the broken nail was a small event but one that prompted her built-up stress and emotion to overflow, and she may discover the value she places on appearance, or a tendency toward perfectionism, or a low tolerance for unexpected happenings.

It is important to add to this suggestion that this counselor could not accept his client's description of her devastation over a broken nail in order to have her move on to topics that might be seen as deeper. This would not really be acceptance or starting where she is. Rather, accepting any client with her feelings at a given time or over a given event is valuable and effective in and of itself. *The healing aspect of acceptance is acceptance.* The point is not to help your clients move to topics that you see as valuable but to experience and accept your clients' values and feelings in that moment. Through your acceptance of their feelings and thoughts in that moment, your clients come to better accept themselves and their values, change if change is needed, and grow in the directions that they choose in the light of their full consideration, brought by your genuine empathy and acceptance of them just as they are. Your acceptance and your clients' self-acceptance over broken fingernails or any other event that might be seen as small may very well be the key to self-improvement.

Respond to the Level of Emotion Each Client Brings

Beginning counselors often think of clients as having started when they express clear or strong emotions, but small expressions of emotions are sometimes missed. So, it is helpful for the counselor to respond to even low levels of affect present in clients' communication. Some emotions are always present in human communications. For example, writing this section is mostly a thought process, yet we also feel *hopeful* that you will find it helpful and feel a *mild concern* for you as you face challenges such as clients who struggle in starting.

Reflections of small emotions may help you see what we mean. If a client is telling you about a housemate's dirty dishes but really doesn't seem troubled by the situation, you may respond with something like, "So while it's on your mind, you're really OK with that." To a client who is talking about his sister more than himself (when you might wish him to focus on himself), you may respond in a tone that conveys both the acceptance and your empathy for the mild emotion he is expressing, worded something like, "As you tell me about her, I get the idea that you have a mild worry and dislike for how she is doing those things." To a client who is discussing future plans but only expressing mild emotion regarding them, you might respond, "So, you have some concern and some excitement regarding these possibilities." In each of these situations, the client would probably not have overtly stated the emotions, but the emotions would have become evident to you through the way the communications were made and through the emotions you feel in empathy. This, of course, once again brings up our suggestion that you continue to uncover and redevelop your natural abilities for empathy. Small emotions lead to bigger ones, if bigger emotions need to be expressed. Then, focusing on your clients' emotions helps them to express the core of what they wish to express and to express the core of themselves to you.

Remember the Uniqueness of Each Client's Pace

There is no parallel path that all clients must take in counseling. One client may seem to start slowly and another to start very quickly. But then, the client who seemed slow in getting to "important" topics may more quickly apply what she is learning from counseling. Some clients seem to gain insight into themselves from counseling, then readily apply what they have learned. Some clients seem to quickly gain insight and then struggle to apply what they have learned. For some clients, it seems to take a long time to start becoming self-aware, but once the self-awareness starts, it grows like a snowball rolling downhill. Other clients never seem to have any profound insight or at least never state it in a way their counselor recognizes yet quickly make behavioral or emotional changes outside of counseling. For efficiency, your goal should not be to help them change but to meet them with the therapeutic relationships you provide.

One beginning counselor explained in supervision that he realized in the moment he was telling a client that he had no expectations for what she might say that he really did have expectations for her. That client came to struggle less in starting as her counselor faced his expectations and came to accept her unique pace.

Remember that It's Natural to Feel Uncomfortable in the Beginning

Uncomfortable feelings, often anxiety, are common in the beginning for both counselors and clients. New counselors may be doing the work for the first time and understandably may feel at least some concern over whether they will do well and be seen as doing well. New clients may very understandably fear being judged, criticized, analyzed, or taken to emotional places they do not want to go. Both are meeting a new person and, especially for the client, are in a new setting, and both are starting a new relationship full of unknowns. So our advice, which is simpler to say than to do, is if this discomfort or anxiety is present, accept it. The more you struggle against it, for yourself or for your client, the more it will grow and the longer it will last. The sooner you accept it, the sooner you may reap its benefits and move on to other challenges.

Give Room

We like that one beginning counselor phrased it as giving clients who struggle in the starting room to figure out what they need and how to use counseling. By this, she meant a similar thing as starting where your client is but also implied toning down her own excited anticipation of profound change. We would add that in counseling focused on providing therapeutic listening, genuine empathy, and UPR, there is nothing else to do but self-discover and change in ever-maturing directions. So stay tuned in, but sit back and give your clients and the process room to work.

Respect Your Client's Pace

Along with giving your clients room and starting where each client is, it is important not to push and to respect each client's pace. It may be an irony that the more you push, the slower your clients move. At one time, Jeff worked with quite a few women clients who had been raped or sexually abused by men: I realized that I was being particularly careful to respect their pace in counseling and their decisions. I was thinking that they had already been very hurtfully disempowered by men, and I wanted to be particularly careful that each of these clients felt safe with me as their counselor and a man. Later, when I realized their rapid use of counseling, the lesson to me was that there was no reason not to respect their pace, and there were many empowering reasons to maintain this same respect with all my clients.

See the Big Picture in Your Client's Communication

When your client seems to go from one topic to another and does not seem to communicate any one with depth, it can be most helpful if you look for the big picture in her communication and reflect themes you see within her communication, such as commonalities between topics (e.g., irritations with others, a concern over how others see her, a focus on the future or past) or the emotions with which the topics are mentioned (e.g., "These seem to be all things you are OK with," "I notice you seem to feel worry over a variety of situations," "You seem to carry hurts from the past and to be cautiously excited about the future," "These thoughts of the future begin with excitement, then seem to carry an edge of apprehension"). In seeing the big picture, you may also reflect your clients' process (e.g., "I notice you tend to begin to talk about one subject or another, then stop," "I have the thought, when you change topics, that there is something you are not saying or that you think to say but don't want to right now," "I notice that when you seem to begin to feel uncomfortable emotion, you end with 'but that's OK' and change the subject"). In seeing the big picture, you may notice incongruencies in your clients' presentations or mismatches in things they tell you (e.g., "I remember you had said that you prefer not to dwell on old hurtful situations, but I see that they also stay on your mind," "I know you told me you had some hard decisions to make, and I notice you haven't talked about those much," "I'm not sure, but I get the idea that you are hurting over some things, and it seems these may be things you haven't told me yet").

It is very important when reflecting the big picture you think you see in your clients' ways of being with you that you say what you see in an accepting way. Otherwise, such statements come across as sounding like a criticism (i.e., perhaps to a client who is already sensitive to criticism) or like an analysis (to a client who expects or hopes for you to analyze him). Your purpose is to let your clients see what you see in them, through your lens of empathy and UPR, and then to make choices informed by that view of them. Such reflections may prompt questions from your clients regarding how they are supposed to use counseling. You would, of course, first reflect what your client has communicated to you with her question, then answer how you see her and what you might suggest for her use of counseling (see Chapter 8 for examples of explaining clients' potential use of counseling).

Dispel Expectations of a Need for a Problem or a Profundity

Some clients try too hard to be good clients. So, part of an explanation you may offer is that their use of counseling does not necessarily mean there is something wrong with them or some big problem that they need to work on. Also, if they seem to be struggling to find something profound or worthy of your and their counseling time, it may be helpful to let them know that they may start with the first things that come to mind, that they need not edit what they might say in order to find something worthy or obviously important, that speaking their mind and heart without editing can be the most efficient and helpful way they can use their time, and that when they communicate without editing, the counseling process will take them where they most need to go.

Sharing Experience in Letting Go

One beginning counselor decided to tell her client who struggled in starting that she had recently made use of counseling for herself and found it an "experience in letting go." This seemed to help her client in a number of ways. It allowed the two of them to share a possibly similar struggle. It normalized her client's struggle. And it introduced the concepts of letting go of control, editing, and forethought in her use of counseling.

While this worked quite well for this client, we caution you to use self-disclosure sparingly, if at all. We find it can turn the topic to the counselor, away from the client, and it assumes a sameness of experience that is unlikely given the uniqueness of each person and situation.

And Finally, Hang in There

One beginning counselor explained that she had worked to accept her client as she was and to start where she was, had prompted with questions and possible topics, and had explained her client's possible use of counseling different ways. But this slow start seemed to last forever. Then, in the third session, her client "just started" and seemed to work rapidly. Then thinking back, this counselor realized her client had started from the moment they first interacted, but it was in the third session that their discomfort dropped and it became clear that her client was working.

Meet Clients "Half Way"

If a client is painfully silent in starting (and you have reviewed for inhibiting actions that you might inadvertently be making), be willing to meet him half way. While being careful not to do it in an overly controlling way, you might suggest topics that you think will be helpful. If it fits, acknowledge your client's difficulty in starting, for example, "It is very difficult for you to talk about yourself." Provide explanations that might help him understand what the use of counseling might look like and why, based on what you understand about him so far. Feel free to attempt other creative solutions that you see as in keeping with therapeutic relationship. If you try something to help a client who is painfully struggling to start, and it takes your work a little off course, you can correct later. Not trying could miss the opportunity for psychological contact (Rogers, 1957)—the opportunity to help connect to you, and miss the opportunity for therapeutic alliance (Horvath, Del Re, Flückiger, & Symonds, 2011)—to have a sense of shared purpose or goal agreement.

If you realize that your client longs for guidance or skill-teaching from you, and you think the guidance or skill-teaching that he desires can be reasonable from your counselor role (i.e., supportive of your therapeutic relationship vs. limiting of your therapeutic relationship), (1) address his longing with empathy and (2) in the spirit of UPR, consider if you can meet his preference and help with skills or guidance. See our guidance in Chapters 13 and 14 for integrative work.

Ask Questions or Suggest Topics that Clients May Find Helpful

Normally, we prefer not to use questions or suggest topics. This allows clients their most self-directed use of counseling and avoids creating misunderstandings of the therapeutic relationship in counseling (e.g., that it is a relationship in which the counselor keeps the power and responsibility by choosing the topics and asking the questions that eventually lead to a counselor-driven solution or suggestions). Yet, we are willing to compromise with this preference in order for adolescent and adult clients (we do not find this necessary with children) to work through their struggle in starting and not to quit counseling. So, we provide guidance here on offering questions or suggesting topics to help clients who struggle in starting.

In some situations, after reflecting a client's great struggle in starting, we will offer to suggest topics in order to make getting started bearable to a client. It goes something like this:

COUNSELOR: [First reflects.] You seem to be struggling to find something to say and you seem to feel really uncomfortable.

CLIENT: [Shrugs with helpless, pained look.]

COUNSELOR: [Reflecting again.] It seems this struggle is downright painful for you.

CLIENT: [Nods acknowledgment and shrugs again with helpless, pained look.]

COUNSELOR: Look, while I want you to work through this struggle, I also don't want the struggle to be so hard that you just hate coming to counseling.

CLIENT: [Gives another smaller nod of acknowledgment and that helpless, pained shrug again, as counselor speaks.]

COUNSELOR: [Continuing.] So, to help you get started, to find the things you might like to talk about, I can try asking you some questions or suggesting topics.

CLIENT: [Relieved, but still struggling.] Oh, OK. Thanks.

COUNSELOR: So, you would like that. [Then offers a question or topic suggestion.]

In thinking of questions, consider the areas of our initial session report; consider which areas the client seems to have said little about or which you are most curious about related to her situation.

Stating Why a Client Was Referred or Why You Offer Counseling

Sometimes an obvious topic to suggest for clients struggling in starting counseling is the reason why they were referred or why you offer counseling. So picking up at the end of the previous vignette, you might offer, "I know that Ms. Smith is concerned for you, and so she suggested that I invite you to talk. I believe she cares for you and has thought you seemed troubled lately." Or in another situation, you might offer, "Your mom has the idea that her divorce from your dad, or something about their situation, has been hurtful to you." After either of these example statements, you would wait to see how your client responds and reflect that before making any more specific suggestions.

Jeff remembers a situation with a boy, "Mike," in which it seemed dramatically obvious that he needed to just tell the boy why he was hoping to spend time and offering himself to listen: I knew that the father of this boy had killed himself. When Mike and I sat down, we both were silent for a moment, then I told him, "Mike, I know your father died." (Actually the details of the death were not clear to me, although suicide seemed certain. So, I stuck with saying only what I knew.) I didn't state any assumptions of what Mike might need or feel. I just stated the little information that I knew and stopped to wait. He then spoke of how he found his father's body, and he became understandably emotional. I was later glad that I had not offered any assumptions of how he felt, as I learned that, of course, his relationship with his father had been quite complex, and he felt a confusion of emotions, even more than the usual, powerful emotions of grief.

Suggesting Common Areas of Importance

There are topic areas over which most humans feel strong emotions and have a complexity of things we might say. These topic areas may include: school/work, family or family of origin, romantic relationships, friendships, current stressors, and future plans. You should only bring up one of these at a time. Select the topic area you think might be most useful to your client. Then, phrase your suggestion with only limited explanations and assumptions. Following from the vignette offered near the beginning of this section, the counselor might say, "Well, as I know you are a student, it seems you might tell me some of your thoughts and feelings related to school." Or the counselor might suggest, "I know that romantic relationships are sometimes important to persons about your age [knowing that the adolescent or young adult is single], I wonder if there are any thoughts and feelings related to that, that you might find useful to talk about?"

Basing Suggestions on Information that You Already Have

If working in an agency or counseling center, you will probably have written information about your client before you start, such as a checklist of concerns that people bring to counseling. In such situations, we have taken this written information as if it were our clients' first communications to us and so reflected the parts that seemed most important to our clients to help them begin face-to-face communication, when necessary.

In schools, you will also usually have some information about your clients before starting counseling (e.g., from teacher, parent or service team that referred to you). So, for example, you may be able to offer a topic like, "I know that your grades have dropped this year. I wonder what thoughts and feelings you have related to that?" Or "I am aware that you have changed schools a number of times. I imagine that has meant making new friends and adjusting to new people a number of times. I wonder what it has been like for you?" Or if I knew that a client had used counseling before and had already given me this information in writing or a statement, I might be curious and ask, "I know that you did meet with a counselor before. I'd be interested to hear about that."

Open Questions

If you use occasional questions, keep them as open as possible. By this we mean that the possible answers are as varied as possible. If we ask, "Was meeting with a counselor a useful experience for you before?" this is a very closed question, as it suggests a yes or no answer. An in-between example would be, "I know that your grades have dropped. I wonder what it is that might be troubling you?" This question carries an assumption that will likely shape the client's answer—that something is troubling him and this causes lower grades. Another modification of a closed question is multiple-choice: "I wonder if your grades may have dropped because something is troubling you, or do you find your subjects harder this year, or do you just like them less?" We find this type question as hard to follow as multiple-choice tests. Closed questions limit clients' communication. These last two closed question examples also suggest that you are moving into a problem-solving mode, which will also limit your clients' taking responsibility in their communication to you. Examples of more open questions include, "Tell me what your previous counseling was like. What did or didn't you like of meeting with your counselor before?" or "I know that your grades have dropped. Can you help me understand why?"

Concluding Thoughts on Helping Clients Struggling in Starting

Guidance for You as Counselor

- If anxiety is there for you, your client, or both, accept it and experience it. It is an important part of your therapeutic relationship in that moment.
- Know that while you may make compromises and help a client who struggles in starting, your responsibility is not to *get* your client started but to be with your client as she struggles and as struggling *is* her way of starting.
- Whenever possible, maintain a safe place and time in supervision or consultation to give yourself an opportunity to voice your frustrations and search your ways of being for elements that inhibit your clients' use of counseling. It has been very helpful to us and other counselors we know to be able to acknowledge or admit when we are having trouble accepting a client. Realizing our lack of acceptance through safe, confidential supervisory or peer relationships has been a great help in growing our acceptance.

Reminders of Your Intent

Another group of Jeff's interns, who represented a range of settings as well as a range of primary counseling theory interests, discussed at the end of their internships what it had been that brought their clients back. Their thoughts included:

- Some clients don't have anywhere else to be listened to.
- Clients appreciate, value and are drawn to a relationship free from judgment and expectations.
- Clients appreciate being understood. (It helped for their clients to be able to think thoughts like, "Yeah, my counselor gets that this situation sucks.")
- Clients are drawn to support (i.e., being met with unconditional positive regard).

We like these reminders to keep these rare qualities in life your intent with each new client.

Activities and Resources for Further Study

- Revisit your answers to the focus activities and consider how you might change or add to your answers at this time.
- Role-play scenarios in which clients struggle to start. When in the role of counselor, pay particular attention to how you feel, what you do to

work through your feelings, and what you do to help your clients with their struggle in the moments that you find it necessary to compromise their responsibility and intervene in their struggle. When in client roles, pay attention to how the situation feels for you, how you are affected when your counselor seems to experience your struggle with you but does not offer assistance, and how you are affected when your counselor does offer assistance. (Note that negative client feelings do not indicate poor counselor responses any more than positive ones. Remember that sometimes clients need to struggle in order to take responsibility.) When observing, carefully consider the effects of the counselors' actions. After each role play, discuss the decisions the counselor seemed to make at various points and the likely long-term outcomes of those decisions.

- Consider the common counselor mistakes that inhibit clients from beginning to use counseling. Which do you think will most likely occur for you and why?
- Consider what might be your greatest difficulty in serving clients who struggle in beginning their therapeutic relationship with you.
- Consider what might most prompt anxiety in you around clients struggling in starting, and discern how you will work through your anxiety.
- Design a set of advice for yourself for such situations. Word it in ways most meaningful to you and focused on the skills you anticipate needing in those situations.
- Work with partners or small groups to design client-specific closed and open questions. You might use clients outlined in Chapters 7 or 8 or imagine others who might need your help with questions.
- Review the Primary Skill Objectives for this chapter. If you have not yet mastered them to your satisfaction at this time, engage in additional practice and seek additional readings to master them to your satisfaction.

References

Horvath, A.O., Del Re, A.C., Flückiger, C., & Symonds, D. (2011). Alliance in individual psychotherapy. In J.D. Norcross (Ed.), *Psychotherapy relationships that work: Evidence-based responsiveness* (2nd ed.) (pp. 25–69). New York: Oxford University Press.

Rogers, C.R. (1957). The necessary and sufficient conditions of therapeutic personality change. *Journal of Consulting Psychology, 21,* 95–103.

Pre-Chapter Quote

Leonardo Da Vinci quoted in E.M. Beck (Ed.), J. Bartlett (compiler) (1980). *Familiar quotations* (15th ed.). Boston, MA: Little, Brown & Co. (p. 152).

10 MANAGING CLIENT CRISES WITH THERAPEUTIC RELATIONSHIP SKILLS

In the middle of the journey of our life I came to myself within a dark wood where the straight way was lost.

Dante Alighieri

What did I know ... What did I know of love's austere and lonely offices?

Robert Hayden

Primary Skill Objectives

- Understand and be able to explain how therapeutic relationships create power to help clients manage crises.
- Be able to explain the roles of empathy, UPR and genuineness in helping clients manage situations of imminent danger.
- Be able to explain the meaning and importance of each principle for managing client crises with therapeutic relationship skills.
- Understand the assessment factors in determining level of risk for a client who seems to have thoughts of suicide.
- Understand non-self-harm agreements, including what they are, what they are based on, how and why they can work, and how they are influenced and enhanced by therapeutic relationships.
- Understand assessment factors and aspects of your therapeutic relationships that can be used to help clients determine their level of risk in situations in which the danger is domestic or dating violence.
- Understand the common difficulties for beginning counselors in helping clients manage situations that may be of imminent danger.
- Develop reasonable confidence for helping clients manage situations of imminent danger with your therapeutic relationship skills, through reading, discussion, contemplation and practice activities.

Focus Activity

Part 1

Try to remember a time in your life when you were at some risk of intentionally (intentional at any level of awareness) hurting yourself or others, and/or a time when you were at some ongoing risk of being hurt by others, at whatever age these situations may have occurred for you. It is not unusual for persons to have had thoughts of suicide at some time in life. If you have had such thoughts at a time in your life, remember what it was like for you at that time. While it may be rarer than serious thoughts of suicide, many people have at least had strong thoughts of hurting others cross their minds. If you have had such thoughts, remember what it was like for you at that time. Often through dating, domestic or family violence, or potentially violent situations, many persons have experienced being in at least some danger of being seriously physically hurt by others in their lives. If you have experienced such risks, try to recall what this experience was like for you.

Remember what your thoughts were at these times of risk in your own life, not just the thoughts that one might understand as potentially dangerous, but the other thoughts that you remember crossing your mind near the time too. Recall what you felt at the time, both physically and emotionally. Recall how you acted, including your actions that did or did not seem related to the risk but that you now see as possibly related. Recall how you were, meaning your qualities of being, such as going blankly or numbly through the motions of daily tasks; keeping over-busy and perhaps avoiding thinking and feeling; seeming weighted, like moving through molasses; or perhaps seeming highly sensitized and hyper-alert.

List and explain the things that you think a counselor or caring other did or might have done to help you. What do you believe such persons tried or might have tried that were not or would not have been helpful? In order to undertand your experience more fully and to begin to further your understanding of what such situations might be like for others, journal, then if possible, discuss and share your experiences with others. Take some time to let others know what it was like for you and to hear what it was like for them. It makes sense to us that you or your peers might feel inhibited or fear each other's judgments what you share. So, please participate in these discussions as much as you possibly can while also maintaining the privacy that you want or need at this time.

Part 2

Whether or not you can remember such risk-filled times in your life, consider what you imagine such times may be like for others. What do you expect different persons might think and feel, and how do you expect different persons might act and be at times when they have thoughts of hurting themselves? What about at times when they have thoughts of hurting others? What about at times when they are at risk of being hurt by others? Imagine what it might be like for you in such situations. Journal and discuss these thoughts.

Part 3

Having considered what it was or might have been like for you and what it may be like for others in such situations, consider what it may be like for you as a counselor trying to help clients in such situations. What thoughts might run through your mind? What do you think you are likely to feel? How might you be and what might you do? Journal and discuss your thoughts and feelings related to these questions.

Introduction: Therapeutic Relationships as a Source of Power and Influence to Help Clients Manage Crises

While we have counseled many clients in situations of imminent danger, we continue to find such situations among the most worrisome. This is partly because imminent danger usually means the possibility of death or other permanent damage. Wrong decisions can have serious results and be final. Our worry is also because, while counselors have ethical and legal responsibilities to prevent harm if possible, the influence that we have as counselors often feels quite limited in such situations.

Considering this, we have worked to figure out what is the most influence that we and other counselors can have in such situations and how to maximize that influence. Perhaps as you have studied *The Heart of Counseling* so far, you will not be surprised that we find that counselors' primary source of influence to keep clients safe through situations of imminent danger is the therapeutic relationship they form with each client. Even if you wanted to prescribe exact actions for clients in imminent danger to stay safe, you would probably have no workable way to enforce your directions. In some cases, you might be able to threaten involuntary hospitalization, but in most situations the case for hospitalization may not be clear and so this would be an empty threat. Besides, your goal should not be just to keep your client safe through an immediately dangerous situation but to keep your client safe so that she can continue to make progress with you in counseling through and beyond the imminent danger. Becoming threatening and controlling around situations of imminent danger would be trading the ongoing healing of your therapeutic relationship for safety through one dangerous situation, while your client may face many more dangerous situations without successful long-term intervention.

We have often made non-self-harm agreements (i.e., an agreement and specific plan for clients to keep their self safe until their next meeting with their counselor) with clients who have strong thoughts of hurting themselves but do not need immediate hospitalization. This is a common practice among counselors. But what would such agreements be based on? Our clients owe us nothing. They do not *have to* do as we ask. We cannot go with them in life to make sure they keep themselves safe. These agreements are based on relationship. The strength of these agreements is the connections made between you and each client.

Principles of Managing Client Crises with Therapeutic Relationship Skills

Self-Responsibility, Dignity, Integrity and Least-Restrictive Interventions

You will need to balance your responsibility to do all that you reasonably can to keep your client safe with respect for your client's self-responsibility, dignity and integrity. It may be tempting to just take over and substitute your judgment for your client's. Don't do this unless it is clear that you have no other more reasonable choice. In our experience, we have yet to come across a situation in which a client could not remain somewhat empowered. So, for example, regarding the risk of suicide, there can be various levels of intervention, with the most restrictive being involuntary hospitalization and less restrictive levels including your client agreeing to get rid of the means to hurt self, letting a friend know how bad she is feeling and how strong the thoughts of hurting herself are, and asking that friend to be available to talk to on short notice if the feelings and thoughts escalate.

Acceptance

Remain focused on the person of your client, as well as the crisis of her current situation. It can be tempting to forget the person you are working with and see only her dilemma and your decisions. Further, if your client has let you know that she is in danger of hurting herself or others—or of being hurt by others—your client may have given you information that was very hard for her to share. It may be information over which she feels shame or embarrassment, or fear that you will then judge her critically or think her stupid, foolish, mean or manipulative. We have heard mental health professionals say of clients who express strong thoughts of suicide, "Oh, she's only saying that for attention." We see such a non-accepting counselor attitude as a serious error and probably a symptom of burnout and a sign of the mental health professional also needing care. Realization of imminent danger is a highly sensitive moment, a moment in which it is most important that the counselor see and connect with the person who is his client in a dangerous situation. In such situations, you may need to remind yourself to accept the person, regardless of her situation and the decisions she has made that led to her current danger.

Empathy

This is also a moment in which it is crucial to continue the flow of your empathy and redouble your care in expressing it. Your feeling with your client will maintain and deepen your therapeutic relationship with your client in the moment when you need it most. It will also help you understand your client more in that crucial moment and thus make better decisions about how to help your client manage her crisis and enhance your assessment of her level of danger. Your empathy will also help you hear any implied doubts that your client has regarding keeping herself safe or any reluctance to a safety plan that you may be making with this person.

Tell Your Client What's Going On with You

Explain Your Assessment and Decision Process

Jeff has realized that he has no choice but to tell clients, who he thinks may be telling him of imminent danger in their lives, what is going on with him: I don't think I have a "poker face." For a counselor, this is not a problem and may be an asset. So, I think that if I am distracted in listening because I am also beginning to assess for potential danger, this distraction would be apparent. I would much rather tell my client what my distraction is than have my client sense that it's there but not know what it is. If my client tried to guess why I seemed distracted, he might very well assume critical thoughts, boredom, and so on. So, once I realize that I am distracted, I find a moment to say so. I usually say something like, "I realize as I'm listening that I'm also distracted. When you told me how tired of it all you were and that you thought you just couldn't go on, I took this to mean you are thinking of suicide. Now I find myself trying to figure out if you are safe, while I also try to listen to the rest of your experience."

Following a statement like that to an adult or adolescent client (the need for genuineness with children is also quite true, but we would not confuse a child client with our adult decision process), we find that clients usually help us or other counselors with our struggle and begin to tell how they assess their safety. If not, we may ask for what we want or need to know. Additionally, we might further explain, saying something like, "Right now, I'm worried for you. I very much want you to be safe and I have a responsibility for your safety." Look for examples of such interactions in the case examples we provide later in this chapter.

Carefully State Your feelings

Because it is always true, it is easy for us to tell clients in dangerous situations that we care for them, that we want them to live and be safe and well. We may also tell them what we feel in response to their situation, such as worry, concern or fear. (Note: This is *our* feeling, not empathy.) While we do sometimes use this statement of our feelings to partially justify our request for them to help us with our assessment or to plan with us, we try to make this statement of what we feel in response to their situation flatly, meaning that we are not implying that they caused our feelings or are obligated to do anything about it, but that we do want them to know how we are affected by their situation.

We are also always aware of hope for clients and often say so. We might make a statement like the following: "While everyone's situation is unique, I know that persons with situations that seem similar to yours have come to get better through counseling. So, I am hopeful for you. I believe you can work through this, especially with your hard work in counseling."

Remember to Reflect

Throughout the process of your assessing and helping plan for safety, you should not stop therapeutic listening and frequent reflection. This remains the core method for you to understand and connect with your client and for your client to know that you are sensitively caring for and connecting with her. You are layering your skills in assessing and planning for safety over your skills in therapeutic listening, genuine empathy, and UPR, rather than substituting assessment and planning for these skills.

So, for example, if one of us has told a client that we have begun listening *and* assessing, that client might respond, "Oh, I'm fine. Don't worry." We would reflect the content or emotion that we heard in this statement, rather than switching immediately to assessment. If we felt some irritation communicated with our client's statement, we might respond, "You want me to know you're fine and you feel a little irritated that I asked." Or, if we felt surprise with our client's statement, we might respond, "You're surprised that that was what I thought. Seems like it must not have been what you meant."

Or if, for another example, after stating a feeling of worry or concern in response to our client's situation, our client responds, "Oh, I didn't want you to worry," and we hear they're upset over this, we might respond, "I see you hadn't wanted to trouble me." We would make these reflections before or instead of continuing assessment or planning. However, if we still see a need for assessment or planning for safety, we would also continue that process.

Help Your Clients Make *Their* Plan

When you help your clients plan for safety, a key to remember is that you are helping your clients plan for *their* safety, meaning you are helping your clients make plans that they will own and implement—the plans will not be yours. It may be tempting, especially if your time is limited—which it probably always will be—to take over and make *your* plan for your client's safety. However, this may produce a plan that your client does not have personal ownership or investment in, one that your client has not thought through in terms of how implementing this plan may work and feel in her life, and thus a plan that your client is unlikely to actually implement.

Plan Specifically

Help your client anticipate any reasonably likely pitfalls. Make the plan as specific as possible and suggest any reasonable difficulties that occur to you around each action within the plan. For example, if your client is planning to call and let someone know when he has strong thoughts of hurting himself, he will need to decide specifically who to contact and may need a backup resource or two in case the first contact person is not there. Then, if it occurs to you that he has had great difficulty paying his bills and that his utilities have been shut off at times, you may need to ask if he is sure to have his phone working or access to a phone at times that the two of you know are high risk.

Err on the Side of Caution

Always err on the side of caution in such situations. For example, in our work we have sometimes felt concern that our intent on specificity and anticipating possible pitfalls may seem condescending. Actually, it seems to have been perceived as caring, but even if it were perceived as condescending, we would rather take that risk and be more sure of our client's safety. We can address any apparent perception of condescension within our therapeutic relationship, through therapeutic listening, and careful, deep empathy and UPR.

Additionally, if you think your client is implying a dangerous situation to you but you are not sure, tentatively reflect or ask this. You won't plant the idea in your client's mind. More likely you will deepen your therapeutic relationship through your expression of your honest concern. If you misunderstood and had it really wrong, accept and acknowledge that correction. However, if your nagging doubt seems really to be what your empathy is communicating to you, then you may need to reassert your concern. It may be that in empathy you are picking up an attitude that your client is as yet denying (perhaps in awareness or not). Be patient in allowing your clients to come to their realizations of concern. More experienced counselors have had practice with clients revealing themselves over time and have discovered that rushing to an insight is not productive. Yet, if you continue to see serious reasons for concern and your client does not, respectfully assert your concerns.

Say the Words

If you think that what you and your client are talking about is potential suicide, go ahead and use the word *suicide*, or phrases like "killing yourself," or, at least, "seriously hurting yourself," whichever is most true of what is actually being talking about. This is not meant to shock but to be specific and clear about what you are talking about, without undue hesitation. You will, of course, say the words with sensitivity and caring.

Respond to the Possible Communication of Danger As Soon As Possible

If you think your client has stated or implied a potentially dangerous situation in her communication to you, don't wait until late in your time together to respond to it. For example, if your client has begun to cry and have great difficulty explaining a difficult situation to you and you have heard her say, at least once, maybe twice, something that sounded to you like giving up on life, you may respond to the strong emotions first but get back to what sounded to you like giving up on life as soon as you can while also attending to her emotions. While beginning to cry, a client with a serious illness might say, "I'm just so tired of being sick. I just can't stand it." Then a little later, she might say, "I just don't know how much more of this I can take." So you might tenderly, empathically respond, "Wow. I'm beginning to get at least an idea of how hard this is for you. I also want you to know that as you spoke, I began to get the idea that you have thoughts of seriously hurting yourself, of ending this suffering that way." In such a situation, if your client does not then elaborate on thoughts of hurting herself, ask about this directly. In such a situation, your question could be phrased, "Shondra, in all this pain, are you thinking of hurting yourself?" (We inserted a name in this example because we couldn't imagine not using our client's name in such a personal moment.)

A point that we want to be sure is clear to you from this subsection is that you should not wait until you are sure from your clients' statements that they are in imminent danger. Instead, it is better to respond when you only have suspicion. In that way, you may open that part of your counseling session while you still have time to listen, maintain your empathic connection, *and* assess for danger and plan for safety. However, it may well happen that your client first gives you reason to suspect imminent danger near the end of a meeting. If that happens, we see this as one of the few legitimate reasons for extending the time of a session and even being late for another.

Local Policy

If your school or agency has a particular protocol around imminent danger (e.g., report of particular interview questions, a written non-self-harm contract) incorporate the principles and qualities that we review while meeting your setting requirements. Working with quite a few schools and agencies, we have yet to encounter local policies that did not allow for common principles and caring therapeutic relationships.

Consideration of Assessment Factors

We offer a case illustration of principles of managing client crises with therapeutic relationships skills. But before the case illustration, it will help you to review the factors we normally consider in assessing such risks and our thoughts on non-self-harm agreements.

A Plan

The factor we often consider first is whether or not a client who seems to have thoughts of suicide has a plan to hurt himself. A client may have only vague thoughts of killing himself, like wishing for the pain to be over, wondering what it's like to be dead, or imagining that others in his life will miss him or feel guilty, but has never thought of *how* he might suicide. In that case, depending on other factors, we may decide that this person is only a minimal risk of hurting himself and mostly needs his counselor to listen carefully to his thoughts and feelings; to ask about these thoughts, any plan, and his determination of risk; and then watch for any change or worsening. On the other hand, if a client has a specific plan of how he would kill himself, this would concern us much more. It may indicate both how much he has thought about it and how close he is to suicide.

When we are following up on what sounded to us like thoughts of suicide, after reflecting that we thought our client may have been talking about suicide and listening to her response to this reflection, we might phrase a question something like, "So, when you think about death and the release that it might bring, I wonder, do you ever have specific thoughts of hurting yourself?" Or, if a client already tried to assure us that while she does think about it, she would never actually attempt suicide, but we're still worried, we might reflect and ask something like, "I hear you assuring me that you'd never actually hurt yourself, but I still worry. So, would you tell me, when the thoughts cross your mind, do you ever think of actual ways that you might hurt yourself?" It is important to ask such questions respectfully and to seek specific, definite answers. It is also important to ask with a true level of concern but also with acceptance and without panic. In such situations, it makes perfect sense for you to be concerned, but panic can leave a client thinking you don't trust or respect her, and that can shut down her communication to you.

Lethality of the Plan

Secondary to having a plan, we would want to know if the plan seems lethal or likely to do serious damage. However, most plans seem serious or at least potentially lethal to us. For example, if a person has a plan in mind to crash her car into a tree, it might not be lethal, but there is a chance that it would do serious harm, so we would still take further action to become more sure of her safety.

A common plan for suicide would be overdosing on medication. Because we would usually not know what danger an overdose with a specific medication may pose, we assume it is serious or lethal.

A Means

If a client has a plan that might be serious or lethal, then we would want to know if the client has the means to implement the plan. If a client says, "Yeah, that's how bad it is. I've thought a lot about it. I've even thought that if I ever did it, I'd use a gun. I'd want no chance that I was injured but not dead." To which we might respond, "You're hurting badly enough to think of using a gun. You'd want to be sure to actually die." Then, assessing the availability of the means, "Look, I see your point about the certainty of using a gun, and I'm trying to figure out if you're safe right now. Do you have a gun or access to one?" Then, if a client has access to a gun or other lethal means, we would see him as being in a high-risk environment and take every reasonable action to provide for his safety. If the client tells us instead that he does not have a gun, know anybody who does, or have any plans to get one, we would still take his situation seriously but would have a possible indication that he does not yet intend suicide.

Preventive Factors

Whether or not a client has a plan and a means, we may also want to know what has kept that person from suicide before. For example, if a client tells us that she would not kill herself because she knows it is a sin, and we know too that she has been troubled by her church and has been greatly questioning her spiritual beliefs, we may see the precarious nature of this preventive factor. If, on the other hand, a client tells us that he would not do it because he just could not hurt his mother that way, and we know how much he cares for and values the strength of his relationship with his mother, we may have confidence in this preventive factor, even while we still see the seriousness of his situation.

Future Orientation

Whether or not a client seems oriented toward her future may help us to be more or less certain of an assessment of her safety and of potential plans to keep her safe. For example, if a client whose safety you are concerned about seems to genuinely want to leave her session on time in order not to be late for class, which would affect her grade, then that might be an understanding of her and her situation that could help you see that she is future oriented and perhaps not in immediate risk. If, on the other hand, that same client did not seem concerned with making it to work or class, that might be more reason to worry, and to assess and help plan for her safety even more carefully. Our general thinking here is that if a person seems to have stopped planning to live, then we might assume that that person has knowingly or unknowingly already decided on suicide.

A Sudden Change or Switch

If a client has had a sudden change in his way of being, this may cause us greater concern. For example, if a client, who did care very much about his work, school, or children, suddenly is much less concerned, we might worry that this means he has given up on life. If a client has always been very driven and inspired in his actions but this changes to a suddenly easy-going demeanor, if we were already concerned with his thoughts of suicide or feelings of depression, we may become more concerned. Even if a client has usually been easily irritated and suddenly no longer seems to care about the same irritations and we were already concerned with his thoughts of suicide, we may become more concerned. You might reflect that possible change, with something like, "Look, John, I know how down you've felt and that you've even had thoughts of suicide. So this sudden change has me worrying that maybe you've given up on life."

Previous Attempts

We would often want to know if a client who we are concerned about committing suicide has attempted suicide before. If we know that a client has attempted suicide before, she may help us and help herself assess her current risk by considering how her current situation is different from the previous time. For example, does she feel as bad as before, does she have a better support system now, does she have different things in her life that may keep her from attempting it?

Lowered Inhibitions and Impulse Control

If we do not already know, we would also want to know if a client we are concerned about committing suicide is engaging in behaviors that seem to lower inhibitions or impulse control. Unless that client is a very new client, chances are we already know about any significant alcohol or drug use, as this is information that our clients have commonly shared with us. If we don't know but we are concerned, we would ask. For example, we might say, "I don't remember your ever having mentioned your using drugs or alcohol, but I want to ask you about this because I know that alcohol and most drugs tend to lower people's inhibitions and impulse control. If this client hasn't already guessed where this was going and interrupted with the information, we might add, "Is alcohol or drug use a part of your life, something you ever do?" Then, if this client's answer is not already specific, we would ask him to help us specifically understand his alcohol or drug use.

Ability to Guarantee Safety

Especially when planning for safety, if a client can convincingly guarantee her safety, we would worry less about her safety but continue to take it seriously, of course. By guaranteeing safety, we mean things like agreeing to give up the means to complete a suicide thought or plan, or agreeing to call a specific person in case of strong thoughts of suicide. Especially in determining this factor, as well as in others such as future orientation, thoughts of a plan, and preventive factors, your therapeutic relationship is the key. If a client is just telling you that she agrees to a plan for her safety to satisfy your worries and you are attending to your client with careful empathy, you will notice her expression of reluctance or reticence. In such a situation, you might reflect something like, "So you're telling me that you will call the crisis line if you have strong thoughts of hurting yourself, but you seem to be only reluctantly agreeing to do this."

And Finally . . .

Remember, while we have listed factors that we would likely want to know about in assessing for safety, we advise you not to switch into assessment, question–answer mode. When you are assisting a client who may be in imminent danger, it is no time to abandon your therapeutic relationship skills. Don't establish a pattern of peppering questions. Remember to reflect.

Non-Self-Harm Agreement/Safety Plan

For a client about whom you are concerned over his thoughts of suicide, consider the previous assessment factors in making a safety plan. Then, make the plan as specific and concrete as possible while remaining focused on the person of your client, his feelings, thoughts, actions and way of being, and your therapeutic relationship with him.

A Good Safety Plan is Time Specific

Such plans are usually time specific. To ask a client who is really hurting to promise to take actions to keep herself safe forever, or for a time that seems like forever to her in light of her pain, is too much to ask. So, we usually just plan with such clients for between the time we are making the plan and the next time we meet. If waiting for a traditional weekly appointment seems too long, we would plan, if able, to meet with her sooner.

Relate Safety Plan to Avoiding Elements within Client's Suicide Plan or Thoughts

If your client has a plan or specific thoughts of how he would suicide, it is important for him to avoid the elements of that plan or those thoughts. So, for example, if your client has thoughts of getting a gun and shooting himself but does not have ready access to a gun, then a part of your plan with your client may be for him to take no action toward getting a gun between that time and the next time that you meet. Or, if your client had always thought that he would go to his family's cabin alone and take an overdose but has not acquired any medications for overdose, he should plan to avoid having time alone at his family's cabin in order not to be so tempted and agree not to acquire any medications for potential overdose.

Remove the Means

If your client has a means to implement a suicide plan, see if she is willing to get rid of that means. (If your client is unwilling to get rid of that means, it may mean she is not really committed to making and implementing a safety plan.) Examples of getting rid of the means might be disposing unneeded and potentially dangerous medications, or disabling a gun. If the client needs the medication or is unwilling or unable to disable the gun, an alternative might be to have a trusted loved one take possession of the medication (to give back in small amounts at a time, as needed) or take possession of the gun.

Avoid Lowered Inhibitions and Impulse Control

If you think of anything your client might do that would lower her inhibitions from suicide or lower her control from impulsive suicide, then plan with her to avoid these actions. Often in such situations, we would be concerned with a client's alcohol or drug use because alcohol and drugs are commonly known to lower inhibitions and impulse control. This can be difficult to plan for, because if your client is seriously addicted, she may not be able to immediately give up drug use. If it seems impossible for your client to give up drug use, a more restrictive plan may be required. For example, your client may need to be hospitalized for safety or to contact a loved one to watch over her during the crisis time.

There are a few ways we have found to make safety plans in which our clients remained more fully self-responsible (i.e., not hospitalized or given over to the care of a loved one), even when possibly addicted to alcohol or drug use. For example, with some clients we have planned for only half a week at a time. To some clients who drank or used drugs frequently and found it difficult to stop, it became much more reasonable to plan for staying away from alcohol and drugs for just a few days. Other clients who knew they would have great social pressure to go out and drink or use drugs have decided to tell some of their friends who they thought might pressure them, either that they have been so down that they have actually considered suicide, so they are going to stay away from alcohol and drugs for at least a few days, or, short of mentioning suicide, have told them that they just felt so down lately that they were going to stay away from alcohol or drugs for a few days. Other clients have decided that they would be all right if they just drank in moderation and so have asked a friend who they knew was able to drink in moderation or not at all to watch over them and help them keep to moderation. As these requests require telling friends of thoughts of suicide, or at least of how down they have felt, they seem to speak to the clients' sincerity in planning for safety.

Prevent Harm by Contacting Someone Immediately

Almost every safety plan we have made that did not require hospitalization or giving one's self over to the care of a loved one included a specific plan of who the client would contact when he had strong thoughts of hurting himself. This can include a friend or loved one that you and your client decide will be available and respond reasonably. This often includes a suicide hotline or a night emergency number of your setting, or another agency that is able to respond around the clock. This usually includes more than one option (e.g., first-choice friend to contact, second-choice friend or family member to contact, then, if neither of these are available, the community's crisis hotline). The key here is to get in contact with someone who can help before the thoughts get so strong that they are hard to stop and your client acts to hurt himself on impulse. So, you may help your client understand that this is not for just passing thoughts but means that he will call for help just as soon as he notices that his thoughts of self-harm seem to be persisting.

Don't Complete Assessment and Plan Alone

Serious thoughts of suicide are a reason to break confidentiality. If you work in a setting with other counselors, it seems reasonable for you to discuss it with your client first, then invite in a coworker to review your and your client's decisions before your client leaves. If you work at a school or other setting where you are the only counselor, you may want to bring in another professional, such as your principal.

Work Slowly and Carefully

Especially if you cannot find another professional to consult with before your client leaves, work slowly and carefully. Even when you are well-practiced at these skills, it will be difficult to remember everything at once. So, pause to think when you need to, refer to notes if it is helpful, and remember that you are planning *with* your client, not *for* your client. Remember to have your client share in the process and to consider her self-assessment and her thoughts and feelings regarding the quality of the safety plan and all its pieces.

And Finally . . .

Remember, the strength of your client's safety plan is the strength of the therapeutic relationship that you establish and maintain. Don't get caught up in planning and forget to attend to your client as a person, to listen therapeutically and respond with genuine, heartfelt empathy and UPR.

A Case Example of a Client with Mild Suicidal Ideation

It will likely be helpful for you to read an example of a counselor using, developing, and maintaining a therapeutic relationship while also helping to assess and plan for the safety of a client who may be in imminent danger of suicide. While no two situations are alike, the following example is a realistic, reasonably typical example of such a situation in which the client can leave the session most fully self-responsible (i.e., not hospitalized or turned over to the care of a loved one). This example also employs most of the assessment factors and elements of a safety plan and, most importantly, our principles of managing client crises with therapeutic relationship skills as they apply to this client's situation. While reading, look for evidence of the counselor using, building, and maintaining a therapeutic relationship while helping her client manage this situation of imminent danger.

Picking up midway through the third session:

CLIENT: [In exasperated tone.] I'm just so tired of it. I wish I could sleep forever. I've got so much on my mind, so much hanging over me.

COUNSELOR: [Matching tone.] You just feel overwhelmed.

CLIENT: Yeah, overwhelmed and tired of it.

COUNSELOR: [Reflecting her immediate statement and going back to one that she saw as important to her client earlier.] Tired of it, too. A minute ago, I noticed you said you wished to just sleep forever. I took that as a big statement of just how hard this is for you. I took it to mean you wish to die.

CLIENT: [A little shocked to hear this said outright.] Well . . . [stretches this word out, then pauses and looks down to think, then responds more definitely] no, I wouldn't do that [pauses and looks down again, briefly]. No, I wouldn't do that.

COUNSELOR: [Accepting her definitive statements *and* the uncertainty she expressed in making them. Also having some difficulty getting the harsh words out.] So, you know that you wouldn't hurt yourself, well, kill yourself. You know that, but it seems you have thought about it and feel some doubt.

CLIENT: [Pauses before speaking. Her way of speaking changes from sounding definite at first, to halting, to sounding overwhelmed and afraid again, and worried by the end of her statement.] Yeah, I just couldn't do it [pause], but I do think about it [pause], well, really, I think a lot about it. The worse this gets, the more it's on my mind.

COUNSELOR: [Continuing in her client's tone and beginning to realize that her client is concerned for and assessing her own safety.] Oh, and it's on your mind enough that this is troubling you; these thoughts of suicide are worrying you.

CLIENT: Oh, it's silly. I'd never have the nerve to do it. I hate pain.

COUNSELOR: [Starting too quickly, beginning to think of assessing.] So, that's one of the things that—[stops somewhat abruptly, realizing that she was about to be only going through the motions of therapeutic listening]. Gina, I realize that I'm concerned for your safety. While I'm still wanting to understand your experience, I also find my mind trying to think through just how safe you are in this very difficult time. I know you said that one thing that keeps you from it is the pain. I also heard you dismiss it, saying it was silly for you to even think about it.

CLIENT: Yeah, I'm just a big baby. I don't even deserve this. I'm just feeling sorry for myself.

COUNSELOR: [Reflecting what she sees, with empathy in her tone.] You have no patience for yourself with these thoughts.

CLIENT: [Rising frustration in tone.] Yes, it's wrong. It's a sin. God, I'm so weak!

COUNSELOR: You see it as an absolute wrong and yourself as weak for even thinking of suicide.

CLIENT: [Pauses for a long-seeming half minute, then shrugs at counselor, as if to say, "I give up, I have nothing more to say, what now?"]

COUNSELOR: [Reflecting with tender empathy, pausing, then questioning.] You're so tired of this [pauses as client looks down]. Gina, as I think about your safety from suicide, I notice that one thing that keeps you from it is the pain; another might be that you know that it's a sin [client nods at both, tearing a little]. If you will allow me to ask [she looks up, indicating consent], I wonder if, even while you'd not likely ever even to attempt suicide, when it's been on your mind, you'd thought of how?

CLIENT: [Disliking the situation but not the question.] Oh god, how did I get to this place? [Short pause.] Well, you know I have a lot of pain pills around. Last weekend I lay there one night alone, lonely, feeling sorry for myself, of course [this last part said with at least mild self-disgust], and I thought, "You know, I could use a little wine anyway to help me sleep." You know I almost never drink anymore. It just puts me to sleep. I've had the same bottle in the fridge for weeks. Anyway, I thought of it then. And I thought, "I've got half-bottles left of a couple of different kinds of pain pills. If I took them all with the wine, it just might kill me. Then this would all be over and my sorry excuse for a family would really be sorry then." But you know, I chickened out. God, I can't even do that!

COUNSELOR: [Genuinely moved.] Ungh. You are really hurting with this. You're down from your situation, down on yourself for thinking of suicide, and down on yourself for not going through with it.

CLIENT: [Crying, trying to stop crying. Whispers.] I'm so sorry.

COUNSELOR: [Whispering a reflection in matching tone, then shifting to assessment for another moment.] So sorry. [Pause. Speaks tenderly, clearly and carefully.] Gina, I want us to plan for your safety. Will you work with me on that? [Gina nods her assent.] I want to ask some questions and suggest ways to keep you safe. [Gina looks up and straightens, indicating her readiness. Counselor realizes the time.] Oh, I realize we would normally have only 5 minutes left. I think this is a very important and unusual situation for you. It's important to me to be sure you are safe. I'm going to call our secretary to ask her to ask my next appointment to wait. Can you stay another half-hour? [Gina agrees and the counselor calls to arrange the additional time.]

CLIENT: [Having waited through this short phone call, Gina smiles when her counselor's attention returns to her.] Thank you. I'm sorry to be so much trouble.

COUNSELOR: You see yourself as trouble. I want to do this. [Counselor states this tenderly but without undue emotion, as it is the truth of her reaction to her client. Counselor takes a short pause to think.] Besides the pills, have you ever thought of other ways of hurting yourself, of suicide?

CLIENT: No, really I won't do it. Gee, what if it didn't work? How embarrassing!

COUNSELOR: Oh, so you know you won't and there's another strong reason not to attempt suicide—you'd feel terribly embarrassed for others to know. [Gina shrugs.] I'm wondering if you need all the pain pills?

CLIENT: Well, maybe not. The one bottle is nearly empty. I take stronger ones now. And the other I don't take any more, 'cause when I started them, they made me sicker. I could just dispose of those bottles.

COUNSELOR: So, you'd be willing to get rid of them completely?

CLIENT: Then, with the ones I use, I can just have the prescription filled in bottles with fewer of them, 10 at a time. Smaller bottles are usual, anyway. They just made up larger bottles for me.

COUNSELOR: You seem OK with this idea. [Gina nods her agreement.] I'm relieved to hear this is possible.

CLIENT: Yeah, I'll be OK, then.

COUNSELOR: You say that with much less hesitation. You're becoming more sure now.

CLIENT: Yes, I do appreciate your concern.

COUNSELOR: So that has been helpful to you. [Gina nods and smiles.] If I may, I want to ask a couple more things. First, I know that alcohol can lower inhibitions and impulse control, but I also remember that you never really drank to excess, right? [Gina clearly affirms this in her gestures.] Even so, I worry that you might get even a little tipsy and increase your risk.

CLIENT: No, half a glass just helps me sleep some nights. When I have that half a glass, then I just get to sleep right away. [Gina says this with clear confidence.]

COUNSELOR: OK, my other thought is that normally with a person suffering so much as you seem to be, I might ask that you call someone, perhaps the suicide/crisis hotline when you have strong thoughts of hurting yourself.

CLIENT: I think I can do that. I've thought of telling my minister, 'cause I wondered if, you know, for spiritual reasons, what it would mean, but

I just didn't want her to know. But this crisis line, it's private, right? No one has to know it's me, 'cause I feel silly enough already?

COUNSELOR: Yes, it can be completely private. You seem quite sure of these steps we are planning.

CLIENT: Yes, I'm glad to have a plan.

COUNSELOR: OK. Well, I'm afraid I'll seem a little condescending, but if you'll let me, I'd like to review to make sure we have a plan for your safety until the next time we meet. [Gina says OK and looks up, paying attention.] So, you'll get rid of the pain pills that you don't need and keep only small amounts of the ones you do use. [Gina nods to say, "OK, got it."] And you will dispose of the useless ones as soon as you get home. [Gina smiles a little at the quizzing and says yes.] Then, if you have strong thoughts of hurting yourself—by strong I mean that they continue for more than a passing thought and you begin to get that anxious feeling [Gina nods, meaning both that she agrees and that she remembers that anxious feeling that her counselor refers to. She has described it before]—you will call the crisis hotline and talk to the person there about what you are feeling until the thoughts have passed and you can go on. [She nods her agreement again.] And you can keep this plan until we meet next week.

CLIENT: Yes, really I'm fine, well, better now. I'm glad for your help and for having helped me think this through.

COUNSELOR: [Smiling.] OK, thanks for indulging my need to be sure. You are important to me. I'll get you a pamphlet about the crisis hotline on the way out and we'll schedule for next week.

The Issue of Hospitalization

Situations where clients had to be hospitalized, as in the case example following this section, have been vastly rarer than situations in which we have been able to successfully plan for clients' safety in our work. This has also been true of our students' and friends' works. But it remains critical for you to think through and develop your readiness to handle such life-or-death situations with your therapeutic relationship skills.

Know Your Local Laws, Guidelines and Procedures

Every community has laws and procedures that guide the behavior of mental health professionals regarding hospitalizing persons for their own safety. Make yourself familiar with the laws and procedures of your community, and the rules or guidelines and procedures of your work setting.

When to Seek Hospitalization

Usually, a client would be helped into the hospital when he is unable to guarantee his safety in a way that satisfies his counselor. Generally, this means that a client will not agree to a non-self-harm plan with confidence. For example, if a client has a plan for how he would suicide and has a means but will not agree to give up the means and/or avoid other risky behaviors, then his counselor would have strong reason to doubt any guarantee of safety and would urge or insist on hospitalization in order to insure his immediate safety.

Maintaining Maximal Client Self-Responsibility

We used the words "urge or insist on hospitalization" because, even in cases requiring hospitalization, we believe in keeping clients maximally empowered and in charge of their self and decisions. While with help a counselor probably could force a client into the hospital for her own safety, so far in our works this has not been necessary. However, we have helped many persons decide on hospitalization for their own safety.

Responding with Empathy to Clarify Intent

We also used the phrase "unable to guarantee their safety in a way that *satisfies* his counselor" intentionally. An example of what we mean by "satisfies" could be a situation in which a client is stating his or her agreement with an aspect of a non-self-harm plan but seems to be communicating something more at the same time. If one of us had a client who agreed to a non-self-harm plan while sounding annoyed and saying, "OK, OK, I'll do it," the one of us who is counselor to that person would likely respond with something like, "So you're telling me that you will, but you sound annoyed, like I've just nagged you into this, but you don't really agree." To which a client might respond (calming and becoming less argumentative in response to our UPR inherent in the tone of our response), "Oh, it's not that, really. I just hate going to all that trouble. But I guess that's where I'm at right now." Then, we might proceed with greater confidence to conclude a non-self-harm agreement.

If, on the other hand, a different client started from that same annoyed statement, "OK, OK, I'll do it," and the same accepting response, to then say, "Well, hey, I know the game. I know what you gotta hear so I can go home," then that response would have confirmed our doubts, and we would seek to have this person choose hospitalization in order to stay safe in the immediate future.

Counselor Responsibility

However, we wish to reiterate carefully that while we think in terms of "urging and insisting" and clients "choosing hospitalization," counselors and other mental health professionals do bear an ethical and legal responsibility for their clients' safety. So, care for clients in such situations is a balance between maintaining maximal client empowerment and self-responsibility, and the responsibility that mental health professionals have to protect clients' immediate safety. We illustrate this balance in the case example that follows shortly.

The Issue of Paying for Hospitalization

One more thought before presenting the following case example. In helping clients choose and plan for hospitalization to maintain their immediate safety, we usually also discuss with them how they will pay for it. We think of this as only being considerate during a difficult time; we don't want them to be surprised with the issue at the hospital. So, as much as possible, we help them think through whether or not their insurance will pay. Often times we have been able to call the hospital we were considering and have their receptionist direct us to help with this. Through similar actions, we have also been able to help the client start planning for payment arrangements when she does not have insurance. And finally, for young adults who will need their parents or parents' insurance to pay, we have been able to make this initial parent contact for or with them.

Example with a Client Experiencing Strong Suicidal Ideation

Note: We have changed this case example so that it is similar to the situations of numerous clients we have served but unlike any particular person. However, we tell it in the first person, as if straight from memory, in order to make telling it less cumbersome.

A teacher brought Wanda to counseling. Wanda had completed a short story assignment in which she depicted herself sitting in her garage with a concoction of dangerous chemicals mixed in a jug and intending to gulp them down. The teacher was obviously and naturally worried that the story was true. She explained this to me, in my office with Wanda, and then left us to talk privately.

I had worked with Wanda the year before. I knew her to be a bright and driven student, hoping to specialize in chemistry and study medicine. While she had not yet articulated it clearly to me, I knew that she felt a great pressure to succeed academically for her family and doubted her abilities. When we worked together before, Wanda had been referred by a different teacher for apparent test anxiety. Wanda had not wanted to engage in personal counseling but only wanted to learn skills that she could use to manage her test anxiety. So, I had helped her learn cognitive-behavioral emotional management skills (Beck & Beck, 2011; Ellis & Dryden, 2007) and encouraged her to continue in counseling to explore herself through her feelings and in that way make changes that would complement and enhance the skills she had requested. I respected her decision, and while I had known she felt worrisome pressure, I had not been concerned for her safety at that time. Now that she was brought back to counseling, I was glad that she had apparently used her short story to let her teacher know of her danger.

The following dialog picks up early in our session, after the teacher had left:

COUNSELOR: So the scene in your short story is real. [I reflected this calmly, as a fact, even though I was also immediately concerned for her safety.]

CLIENT: [Looking me straight in the eye, with a thoroughly serious, determined look.] Yes, some night soon, I will do it.

COUNSELOR: And you are absolute about that. No "might," only "will."

CLIENT: [States no response but looks sometimes into my eyes and sometimes down, seeming determined to hold her ground on her intent to kill herself.]

COUNSELOR: Wanda, I'm deeply concerned for you. I want you to live. I want you to give us a chance to work together to discover changes that will help you want to live again.

CLIENT: [Continues to stare or look down with a determined look on her face.]

COUNSELOR: Wanda, you seem so determined to kill yourself. I imagine you must be deeply hurting over something in your life.

CLIENT: [Speaking in measured tones but with apparent irritation.] I just want to die. It's my decision and I want to do it.

COUNSELOR: Ughmph! [A genuine sound that bubbled out of me, seeming to indicate that I'd been hit hard by what she'd just said. Continuing after a pause of a second or two.] While I want to respect your wishes, I also want you to live, and I have a responsibility for your safety. While I'd like to hear any concerns you might wish to express, I hear clearly that you are not safe, that you wish to die, and that you have a ready means to kill yourself.

CLIENT: [Simply nods, then waits for me to continue after a short pause.]

COUNSELOR: Still, I'd like to ask a couple more questions to see if there is a way that we can keep you safe.

CLIENT: [Shrugs, as if to say, "Go ahead."]

COUNSELOR: May I ask that you get rid of the chemicals that you would use to kill yourself?

CLIENT: Yes, but I can always get more. And besides, it's all stuff we need around the house, you know.

COUNSELOR: OK, so you don't see that idea as useful. [Short pause.] I notice that something has kept you from killing yourself so far, that at least you've paused to think about it.

CLIENT: Oh, I only need time to get up my nerve. I'm afraid, but I'll build up my nerve soon.

COUNSELOR: Yes, you have me convinced. [After a long pause to collect my thoughts.] Wanda, you seem absolutely unsafe on your own right now. [The look on her face continues to confirm this.] So, I want to find a way that others can be involved in keeping you safe in the immediate future. Two ideas occur to me. We might be able to contact your parents and see how they can help, or we may have you admitted to the hospital in order for the professionals there to keep you safe and evaluate your ongoing safety.

CLIENT: [Starts to get up, seemingly shocked, outraged, raising her voice.] There ain't no way you're putting me in the hospital!

COUNSELOR: [Interrupting quietly but firmly, remaining seated.] Wanda, please stay. [Wanda sits back down.] I want to find a way to keep you safe.

CLIENT: Call my parents then, but no hospital.

COUNSELOR: So that's the idea that seems better to you. You'd be OK with that. You seem to think that might work.

CLIENT: [Shrugs, apparently still angry.]

COUNSELOR: You seem so angry. [Wanda gives no further response.] I assume then that you trust them to help you stay safe?

CLIENT: I guess.

COUNSELOR: Wanda, I'll call them, but you're not exactly inspiring my confidence.

At this point, I asked for and Wanda gave me her stepfather's phone number and her consent to call her parents. Before calling, I checked if there were things that she specifically did and did not want me to say. She didn't stipulate anything. Fortunately, I was able to get him on the phone right away. I spoke to him briefly from my office phone. He called Wanda's mother (his wife), and then called us back at a speaker phone so that all three could take part in the conversation.

He concurred that he wanted Wanda to come home instead of going to the hospital. He said that he and her mother had decided that she gets too stressed over school and so should stay home a few days. Picking up in the middle, my conversation with them went something like the following:

COUNSELOR: [Regarding Wanda staying at home for a few days.] So, I guess you or your wife would be there with her to watch to see that she is safe?

CLIENT'S FATHER: Well, no. We'll have to go back to work. [He begins to tell of their jobs and the demands on their time.]

COUNSELOR: I'm not sure you understand my concern. Wanda means to kill herself. She has a means to do this and she intends to do it.

CLIENT'S FATHER: Is this true, Wanda?

CLIENT: [After a pause.] Yes. I don't know. [Another pause.] Yes.

CLIENT'S FATHER: [To Wanda.] Why would you do this? You know we'd do anything for you.

CLIENT: [Interrupting.] Do anything? You're never there!

[*They argue for a short time and then I interrupt.*]

COUNSELOR: Mr. Jones, I want to admit Wanda to ___ hospital, where the professional staff can keep her safe while they evaluate and help plan for her ongoing safety and wellness.

CLIENT'S FATHER: Yes, but that's not necessary. Please, we'll just come get her. I'll be there in an hour.

COUNSELOR: I see that that's what you want, how you would help, but right now, I am also responsible for her safety. I worry that it may take time for you or your wife to clear your time, and I worry that there is some discord between you that may make it hard for you to help right away and there may not be time.

CLIENT'S FATHER: Wanda? [She doesn't answer.] Are you there?

CLIENT: Yes, I'm here.

CLIENT'S FATHER: Is it true, baby, 'cause you just can't do this. You know we got a lot going on right now. [Wanda sighs, slumps, and covers her face.]

COUNSELOR: [Speaking calmly, carefully, and respectfully.] Mr. Jones, there are a couple of choices to make. If you want her admitted to ___, rather than ___ hospital, you will need insurance or a way to guarantee payment. Can you do that?

CLIENT'S FATHER: Well, yes, if you can't just let us handle this at home.

COUNSELOR: So, that's still what you want, but I hear that you're willing to go along with my concerns and request that she be admitted to the hospital. [After a pause, in case he wanted to say more.] If the police drive her to the hospital, they will have to take her in handcuffs. Would you rather drive her?

CLIENT'S FATHER: Well, yes, if you really think all this is necessary.

CLIENT: OK, look, I won't do it. [Rolling her eyes a little as she speaks.] I'll get rid of the chemicals. I won't do anything to hurt myself.

COUNSELOR: You're telling me that, but I gather it's just to ease the difficulty for your family and yourself right now.

CLIENT: No, I mean it.

COUNSELOR: So, you really mean it. I know that you want to get us out of this dilemma, but my worry is that as sure as you were of your decision to kill yourself just a little while ago, you might change your mind again. [She says nothing to this but looks at me in anger.] You seem furious with me now.

CLIENT'S FATHER: [After a pause.] Mr. Cochran, I agree with you. I'm leaving work in just a few minutes and I'll be there to drive her to the hospital.

He did come. While we waited, Wanda and I called the hospital and spoke with an intake counselor, who concurred with my rationale for the hospitalization and was able to prepare for her arrival. Later, as he had agreed to do, her father called and left me a message that she had arrived at the hospital and had been admitted without any difficulty.

Afterthoughts: Hospitalization did not end Wanda's and her family's troubles. In the short run it may have intensified them. The point had been to provide for her immediate safety, which was accomplished. After her short hospital stay, I saw her on a weekly basis. I think she continued to resent being hospitalized, but I think it helped set the context and tone for our ongoing work that I explained my genuine reactions and decisions; listened with empathy; continued to accept her, if not her intent to kill herself; and left her as much self-responsibility as possible.

An Example of a Client Who is At Risk of Harming Others

In this next case example, we want you to see how the counselor assesses and helps the client plan to avoid the risk of harm from the client to another person, while maintaining critically important therapeutic relationship skills, in hopes of both understanding the truth of the current danger and laying the foundations for ongoing work, and with the therapeutic relationship enhancing the work of assessments and safety planning. The following story is again told in the first person, even though we have changed the situation from that of any one client to be like that of quite a few clients. Telling it in the first person allows us to write it with the emotions and thoughts that we have experienced in such situations.

John came to counseling at the insistence of his girlfriend, Denise. He explained that she had insisted he come because they had both been drunk at a recent party and he expressed strong anger toward her. He was verbally abusive, yelling and calling her very harsh names. He also threatened her physically, and she had been understandably scared that he would hurt her. She insisted that he get help in order to avoid such behavior in the future. At first, as he explained these things, he seemed to work hard to maintain a casual air about his dilemma. Picking up early in our conversation, our dialog went something like the following:

COUNSELOR: So, you seem to be saying two things at once. You remain casual when you tell me how you acted, as if it was no big deal, but you also seem shocked by your actions.

CLIENT: Well, yeah. I sure didn't mean to be that way, I was shocked. And I know it was a big deal. Everyone stared. Denise might not see me any more. I was totally stupid, but it was also the alcohol. [Takes a momentarily dismissive tone, when mentioning the alcohol.]

COUNSELOR: So you go back and forth. You know from Denise and others' reactions that it was a big deal, you know it was stupid, but then again, you know it was partly the alcohol.

CLIENT: Yeah, alcohol makes people crazy sometimes.

COUNSELOR: So, you figure it made you crazy that night.

CLIENT: Yeah, well, like I said, not just that. [After a momentary pause.] See, three times she was talking to her old boyfriend. He's always boastin' how he could have her back anytime. I just got so jealous. She should know not to do that.

COUNSELOR: So, your jealous feelings were intense.

CLIENT: Yeah. I mean that's no excuse. God, I can't lose her. But I can't stand that bastard. I could just kill him.

COUNSELOR: Such a mix of feelings. You know that you could hardly stand to lose her.

CLIENT: She's the best thing that ever happened to me. She's beautiful, so sexy. And I'm, well I'm all right, but I'm lucky to have her. Any guy would want her.

COUNSELOR: Seems she's so great that while you know you're all right, you see it's almost a dream for you to be with her.

CLIENT: Yeah, like it's not real. Now, it might not be. She told me that if I *ever* do anything like that again, she'll break up with me; she'll never speak to me again. She told me I humiliated her, and she can hardly face her friends now.

COUNSELOR: [I notice about this time that he has dropped the casual way with which he had told of his actions early on.] And now you're afraid of losing her. You feel guilty for what she feels.

CLIENT: I feel awful. Man, she's sweet. She's been so patient with me. And the things I called her.

COUNSELOR: So you're really feeling great remorse, telling me and yourself that she didn't deserve the abuse.

CLIENT: Yeah, she didn't deserve it. I'll do better.

COUNSELOR: Again, I get the idea that you have a mix of thoughts. Now you seem to take it all on yourself, but if I remember right, a few minutes ago, you were thinking that she should have known.

CLIENT: I'm not making any excuses. I know I was wrong and that's that.

COUNSELOR: So, you do accept full responsibility but still there's some lingering something.

CLIENT: Well, come on. She was drinking too, and I don't know what she might do when she's drunk.

COUNSELOR: I gather you mean she might have some sort of affair, cheat on you.

CLIENT: Oh, no. I know that's not true. But all the girls love that bastard Jason. God, I hate him. He thinks he can just have anyone any time.

At a point a little later in our session, after taking as much time as possible to know him but leaving enough time to assess and plan for safety, I interrupted and changed the subject in order to let him know my concern and began to assess and plan. Picking up again just before that point:

COUNSELOR: So, you've let me know how guilty you feel, how you mean to take absolute responsibility for your actions, and how, even before last weekend, you've had some uncertainties about your relationship.

CLIENT: Well, she really kinda out rates me, but now I can't live without her.

COUNSELOR: While I very much want us to continue your work in discussing these things, I also want to raise a couple of my concerns of immediate safety with you. [John nods his consent.] I have some concern that you might take action to hurt Jason.

CLIENT: Oh, I'd love to, but I know I won't. Even if we got in a fight, people would break it up. Besides, he wouldn't fight anyway. Why should he? He's gets everything he wants, or almost everything anyway.

COUNSELOR: So you don't actually even have any specific thoughts of hurting him.

CLIENT: No, he'd never fight me by himself anyway. He's always got his friends with him.

COUNSELOR: My other concern is that, even as guilty as you feel, you might hurt Denise. [John looks taken aback.] Well, what I mean is that I notice the passion you feel towards her, how much you want her, and I worry that could quickly turn to jealousy and anger again. [After a pause.] You seem OK that I'm saying these things.

CLIENT: Look, I've just gotta not screw this up. I'll do anything not to screw it up.

COUNSELOR: So clearly you want to make sure. [John nods yes.] Will you let me ask some questions that occur to me to think about toward making sure you don't do something else abusive toward Denise?

CLIENT: Yeah, OK. Ask away.

COUNSELOR: I know that alcohol reduces a person's impulse control. As you said, it makes people crazy. I want to know if you can stay away from drinking, at least until we meet again in a week.

CLIENT: Well, I won't drink around Denise, but I already have plans with the guys.

COUNSELOR: I gather those plans would be hard for you to change. [He nods his agreement.] My concern there is that you or she might find each other, after the time with the guys, when you've been drinking. Do you agree that's possible or likely?

CLIENT: Yeah, OK.

COUNSELOR: Now, I imagine that that part might be hard, to cancel or change your plans with the guys this week.

CLIENT: [Speaking almost inaudibly.] I already look like an idiot.

COUNSELOR: [Responding softly.] That part is hard for you. It feels lousy.

CLIENT: [Lifting his tone, with determination.] Yeah, but it's worth it for Denise. She is *so cool.*

COUNSELOR: That part keeps you going, gives you strength for this work. [John smiles his agreement.]

CLIENT: My best friend Jarred will understand. I'm gonna tell him the whole truth. He saw it anyway. But then I think I'll have him and me tell everybody else that I'm just staying in—a "getting serious about school" phase.

COUNSELOR: You sound definite about this plan. I have a couple more questions I'd like you to think through. [John nods his readiness.] Has anything like this ever happened before? Have there been times when you've lost your temper and become physically threatening, abusive, with Denise or anyone else?

CLIENT: No, never. [Pauses] Well, I've wanted to. I can't stand the thought of her with anybody else.

COUNSELOR: So, you've not gotten so mad or acted that way, but you've hurt enough just thinking of her with anyone else that it was kinda close.

CLIENT: Yeah, but I didn't do anything.

COUNSELOR: So, you've never acted that way before with Denise. What about with others in your life?

CLIENT: Well, I've never really had a girlfriend before. [After a fairly long pause, several seconds, in which it seemed he was going to say something more.] But me and my mom used to really fight.

COUNSELOR: That was hard for you to say. And it seemed important to you.

CLIENT: [Pausing first and speaking softly.] Well, I guess I'm ashamed of that.

COUNSELOR: That's very hard for you to tell me about. I'm guessing that maybe your behavior was similar then, since it came to mind when I asked.

CLIENT: I never threatened her. I just screamed and felt that mad.

COUNSELOR: [Knowing this from John's way of telling this part.] And it still feels lousy to you. John, in the long run you can change the things that give you impulses to act in ways that leave you feeling so lousy. To help in the short run, think of what you feel like just before you get so mad.

CLIENT: [After a long and thoughtful pause.] I feel small, like a little kid.

COUNSELOR: You seemed to be able to recall that exact feeling. [John nods and shrugs as if to say, "I sure do."] So, if you get that feeling around Denise, your mom, or anyone else you may have very strong feelings toward this week, then I want you to either remove yourself from the situation, if possible, or at least stop to think and realize that you are moving into a dangerous moment, that you might lose your temper and act in hurtful ways.

CLIENT: OK.

COUNSELOR: Now I worry that it may sound condescending, but I hope you'll let me review what we've planned. [John nods that this is OK.] Until we meet next week, you won't drink. You'll tell Jarred what's really going on, then he and you will tell the guys that it's school. Then, if you get that feeling of feeling small, like a little kid, you'll know that might signal upcoming rage, and you'll either remove yourself from the situation or stop and think, be aware and watch that you stay under control.

CLIENT: I can do this. I can't lose Denise. Thanks.

There are several things we would like you to note from this example. From what we have told, it would be hard to know what would happen next: I believed his sincerity and noticed that he seemed to get dramatically more serious and real as our session continued and therapeutic relationship developed. I also thought his plan was specific, workable and voluntary. He left that meeting with a plan to stay away from a trigger for violence (alcohol), and an idea of what it feels like just before he becomes enraged, so that he has a better chance to avoid the rage. I accepted as truth that this really was the first incident close to violence.

Planning for safety with John will be ongoing. In counseling, he seemed ready to begin to realize some of his self-criticisms, shames, thoughts, and feelings behind his anger. Well beyond keeping him safe with Denise, the personal development springing from that work can help him be much more than safe in the future. It can help him become a partner able to love from a position of knowing his self-worth, having faced his shames and achieved a real self-acceptance. The potential imminent danger situation may have brought him to counseling, but the counseling focused in a therapeutic relationship may bring him a much richer and fuller life.

Also, it may be helpful for you to know that it was tempting to argue with him early on when he attached blame to things outside of himself. It was also tempting to argue and try to prove how serious the situation was, when he initially seemed to speak of it casually. However, as soon as I realized these impulses, I reminded myself to focus on him as a person and his experiences in that moment. That got me back to responding to him with genuine, deep empathy and UPR. Responding to him in that way helped him break through his understandable defenses and helped tap into his motivation that was there all along to develop to his fullest potential.

Finally, while this chapter has provided three examples of potential imminent danger, there are many, many more possibilities, and we know of no checklists that encompass every possibility. So, your judgment is necessary. Try not to handle such situations alone but to consult with peers. If alone, do your best with the plan to think through the dangerous situation, what makes it dangerous, and how the danger might be avoided. Then consult. If in consultation or review, you think you missed something important, bring it up at the next meeting or on rare occasions where the thing you decide you missed seems too important, contact your client before the meeting. Ultimately, it is not possible to do such work perfectly. We believe that your moral, legal, and ethical obligation is to do your best and to take the actions that any other reasonable counselor would. But especially when this responsibility is so grave, we want you to see from the examples we have offered that you must never lose sight of the therapeutic relationships you are developing with your clients, that your therapeutic relationships not only help you work through the current crisis but well beyond.

Assessment Factors and Safety Plans in Domestic Violence Situations

In case it is helpful for you to think through the factors we often consider in assessing for safety in domestic violence situations (which also apply to dating violence, as in the last case example), we offer brief thoughts on factors here.

Physical Violence

While domestic violence situations seem always serious and potentially dangerous, such situations may or may not equal imminent danger. Some may be chronically unhappy, dysfunctional relationships, needing the help that can come from counseling but not immediately threatening. In order to help a client discern which might be more true of her relationship, we would want to know if there has already been physical violence. Threats or perceived threats or intimidation are serious, but once actual physical violence has occurred, it has crossed a threshold to greater danger. Even if the initial violence was minor, we worry that past violence may make future physical violence more acceptable and more likely. However, we would also want to consider how the couple has reacted to the violence. For example, perhaps the couple reacted to the violence by realizing that their relationship is in great danger and have decided to make consistent and ongoing efforts to change. Or, perhaps they have told each other that it would never happen again, without instituting any real change.

The Extent of Violence and Potential Pattern

We would also want to know the extent of the physical violence. Actual hitting and previous injuries from violence leave us much more worried for escalating violence than grabbing or pushing. However, it is very difficult to discern this difference and there are no absolutes rules. Through listening with deep empathy and UPR, you can discern how fearful your client is (assuming your client is the one more in danger), even through her potential bravado or attempts to make herself and her spouse sound not so bad. Then this understanding of your client's fear can assist you in helping your client assess her safety.

As for the pattern, we would want to know if there seems to be any pattern in the physical violence that might help client and counselor discern the level of danger. For example, is the violence escalating? Is it recent? Is it becoming more frequent? To discern the meaning of such information, we again rely heavily on our therapeutic listening, careful empathy and UPR to help our client discern the meaning of the information. We find that often our clients know their level of danger but only know it deep within their being. So, our therapeutic relationship skills help clients realize and fully admit what they already know and then act on this knowledge, sometimes spurred by having discovered a level of self-worth that makes self-care seem worthwhile.

Triggers and High-Risk Behaviors

Along with discerning patterns, we find it helpful to identify what seems to trigger violence or dangerous situations. This is helpful to know in planning with a client for avoiding dangerous situations in her relationship. For example, there may be increased violence in the relationship when one or both are drinking or using drugs. If your client seems to be more the victim and your client wants to try to stay and work through relationship problems, then she may need to plan to stay sober and plan for a clear means of exit if her potentially violent partner might not stay sober.

Children

We also work carefully to help clients who seem to be in violent relationships understand that if they have children, their children *are harmed and affected*. At whatever age, whether the children appear to understand what is going on or not, they do know that something bad and dangerous is going on. Children *sense what is going on*, even when parents are trying not to show feelings such as strong anger or sadness outwardly. Again, we find that often once we have brought up the effects on the children, while also listening with deep and genuine empathy and UPR, our clients who seemed to be victims of domestic violence realized that at some level they already knew this truth.

Planning for Safety

Such plans may vary greatly, depending on whether a client sees the need to at least temporarily remove herself from the relationship. Any plan for safety must, of course, include the children. Generally, we find that if a client who we see as in potential but not imminent danger decides that she sees herself as safe enough to stay with her partner, and we see no clear reason to disagree, the safety plan should include anticipating the danger in order to leave before a violent situation has escalated to the point where it is greatly difficult to leave, and knowing ahead of time where to go for safety and how to get there. As with any safety plan we develop with a client, we would work to help our client be specific and think through potential difficulties with the plan.

Common Difficulties for Beginning Counselors Helping Clients Manage Imminent Danger

Situations of imminent danger are among the most difficult for our students who are beginning counselors, just as they are for us. Suicide or suicidal ideation is painfully common and the problem cuts across all of society (Bongar & Sullivan, 2013; Centers for Disease Control and Prevention, 2012; World Health Organization, 2014). Our experience in our own clinical work and in supervision, plus research, suggests that client suicide may be the most common fear among clinicians (Joiner, Van Orden, Witte, & Rudd, 2009), who are affected by discomfort and lack of confidence in managing the client's suicidal ideation (Rudd, Cukrowicz, & Bryan, 2008).

In order to help you do your very best through such situations, we share some of our understanding of what has been most difficult for our students when they were beginning counselors and our thoughts related to these difficulties. While the work of helping clients manage situations of imminent danger gets less difficult with experience, the gravity of such situations should never let the work get easy.

The Seriousness of the Situation and the Weight of Decisions

Of course, it is the very seriousness of imminent danger situations that leaves many beginning and advanced counselors feeling stressed and worried. The fact that a situation may involve imminent danger means that death or serious injury is possible. This naturally is a source of fear and worry to us as counselors because we know a person's bringing about his own or another's death is one of the few irreversible decisions a person can make.

A simple-sounding thought reminder has helped our supervisees and us through the difficult decisions involved in assisting persons facing imminent danger. It has helped us through the difficult second-guessing that can occur once the client potentially in danger has left the counseling session in any way short of the near-absolute, temporary safety of hospitalization. This thought reminder is that when any counselor has maintained deep empathy, UPR and genuineness throughout the time of helping manage the crisis, that counselor has used the most powerful and effective tools available to any counselor. The tools of therapeutic relationships are the primary tools we have. The case management tools of assessing and planning for safety are certainly important but secondary. Fortunately, the tools of therapeutic relationships are powerful and effective.

"What if I Panic and Know What to Do, but Forget?"

We find this an understandable and common fear of beginning counselors. Fortunately, we have never found it to be true of competent persons. We find that our beginning counselors surprise themselves by rising to the occasion.

The most helpful advice we know for this fear is to work to see that you are well grounded in the core conditions for therapeutic relationships. Developing these ways of being in yourself will not only serve well as tools for you and your clients in times of crisis but developing them in yourself will also develop your personal strength, focus and clarity of mind.

Developing them in yourself can help you develop the dual qualities of being both solid as a person and fluid enough to meet each client where he is in the moment.

A further piece of advice to ready you to avoid panic is to *practice and then practice some more.* Pair up with peers to practice the skills of therapeutic relationships and helping clients manage situations of imminent danger through role plays as often as possible. Seek as many and difficult clients as possible early in your work, while you have maximum supervision and support.

The Pressure of Never Being 100 Percent Sure

In helping clients plan for safety, you will almost never be 100 percent sure. As one beginning counselor put it, referring to a client who had completed a non-self-harm agreement with her, "All I have is whether I believe or not." What she meant was that all she had after the session was that she believed that her client intended to keep the safety plan.

But her statement is not quite true. It is very difficult to mislead, intentionally or otherwise, a counselor who is deeply focused in empathy and UPR. If, through her deep empathy and UPR, she had heard some reservation, something in her client's way of agreeing had left her with nagging doubts, she would have reflected this. So, as she contemplated her work in that session, she realized that while all she had was that she believed her client, her belief was strong, solid and supported by powerful skills for reaching the truth.

Additionally, while she had thought slowly and carefully in evaluating her client's safety and in evaluating their non-self-harm agreement, she had also empowered her client through these evaluations. She had been open in sharing her thoughts and feelings in evaluating and invited her client into partnership in the evaluations. Her client had participated in rectifying pitfalls in their plans, from the perspective of her expertise in her life and situation.

Discerning the Difference between Your Feelings and Empathy

Differentiating between client and self can be challenging in crisis situations, when client concerns strike emotion in you. If you are worried over your client's situation, you may mistakenly assume your client is worried. It is useful to state your concern so that your client knows the level of seriousness in which you see the situation, can respond with her own judgment of the situation, *and* because of saying it aloud and owning it as your feeling, can help you separate it from your perception of her experience. This distinction is important. In some cases, realizing that your client is not worried and why can help you realize that you need not worry so much. In other cases, realizing that your client is not worried can help you see that she is not taking the situation seriously and thus may be putting herself at greater risk.

Errors in Empathy

We have seen two opposite errors in empathy among counselors assisting in situations of grave danger. Some beginning counselors seem to keep themselves blocked from fully realizing client despair, taking action beneath awareness to avoid experiencing client despair. Other beginning counselors fail to see cracks in clients' despair. For example, a client may worry that her boss will be mad *and* also have serious thoughts of suicide. While that bit of possible future orientation may not make her situation much less dangerous, it is important to respond to it. We think of such hints of hopefulness as cracks of light in a dark room. They do not make vision clear or the room bright, but they do make the room contoured and detailed versus solid and dark. We remind you to maintain your empathy with depth and nuance as much as you can through each crisis.

Preoccupation with Liability

A typical preoccupation of some counselors is expressed in the common lingo "CYB" (cover your b___). This mindset perpetuates counselors' focus on their own liabilities rather than on the persons of their clients. We urge you to be aware of your liability but to maintain your primary focus on the person of each client. Keeping that balance will be both safest and maximally therapeutic through the short and long term of your work with clients.

Having to Let Go and Let Clients Be Responsible—Trusting that Each Client Will Actually Do the Plan

Beginning counselors have communicated to us their realization of their ultimate need to trust their clients. By this they meant that once they have trusted their client's intention for safety and believe that they, their client, and, whenever possible, a more experienced colleague have developed the reasonably best safety plan, they cannot personally watch over their client's safety between counseling sessions. So, short of taking societal measures that override client self-responsibility (e.g., hospitalization, mental health arrest, warning potential victims), counselors must ultimately trust their clients to be self-responsible. Once that decision to trust the clients' intention for safety is established, the ultimate decision is out of the counselors' hands.

Each client's commitment to keep safety plans is based on the strength of the personal connection, the therapeutic relationship established. Fortunately, as a strong personal connection, a strong therapeutic relationship equals a strong client commitment that can see them through a safety plan from one counseling session to the next.

Self-Confidence to Make Such Decisions

Many beginning counselors struggle with having the self-confidence or self-perception of competence to make decisions for client safety. Fortunately, counselors are rarely charged with making such decisions. Rather, your primary responsibility is to help your clients make them.

However, even beyond that, review the evidence of whether or not you have such competence. For example, is there evidence that your other counseling skills are adequate or beyond? Is there evidence that you are otherwise a competent decision-maker? If not, you can work to achieve such competences through your own counseling, through your studies and practice. If you find you do not have the evidence to reasonably conclude, then seek the feedback you need. One way to seek this feedback is extensive practice under observation, and another is initial work under very close and careful supervision. Use your advisers, mentors, loved ones, and your carefully considered intuition to guide your decision of your readiness and your path to proceed.

Coordination with Other Professionals—Fearing to Ask for Help

Some beginning counselors have let us know that they were hesitant to consult with other professionals (peers or workplace supervisors) due to concern over breaking a client's personal trust in privacy with them. The thought behind this hesitancy is flawed. Each of your clients should be able to trust confidentiality with you, but this is not the same thing as privacy. Suspected imminent danger is a reason to break confidentiality. Plus, frequently and ideally, the person invited in to consult on the plan for this client's safety would be another counselor or a supervisor from the same setting, and regular consultation for the improvement of your work is an additional limit to confidentiality identified when beginning with clients in many settings.

There can be an added nuance to fearing a breach of privacy. We and other counselors, both novice and veteran, have experienced workplace situations in which we did not entirely trust the way the peers or supervisors in whom we would be consulting may influence the situation. If such a lack of full trust exists in the long run, it behooves each counselor to try to work through it. Discussing differences and getting to know the peer or supervisor in question better can be one way to work through that lack of trust. Discerning which peers and supervisors are best to seek in which types of situations can also be important. Then, if this lack of trust can't be worked through, seek to make changes in the workplace such that you can have a more comfortable situation for consultation. However, in the short run, you cannot let such a lack of trust allow you to isolate yourself. Regardless of whether you fully trust your peer or supervisor, it is best not to finalize decisions for safety over which you are not already quite certain, alone.

Coordination with Client Loved Ones or Significant Others

Many safety plans require coordination with client loved ones or significant others in clients' lives. In some plans, you and your clients may decide for you to contact persons who will be involved in their plan. Some clients may prefer for you to initiate a contact and request for help due to their own inhibitions for making these contacts. When we have felt nervous and hesitant to do this, perhaps worrying over whether we were ready to add that additional skill set, it helped us to remind ourselves that it is surely easier for us than our client to make the contact in that situation. It has also helped us to remind ourselves that our skills in consultation are more developed than our clients, owing to our training in genuine and empathic therapeutic communication. It has also helped us to remember to use our skills of therapeutic listening, empathy, UPR and genuineness in the consultations. These skills go far in establishing alliances in consultation relationships just as they do in counseling sessions. And finally, it has helped us to jump in and make the contact, without too much overthinking, in the situations where our making the contact seems best.

The Infinite New Situations for which There is No Script

A fear that many beginning counselors share is that they cannot be prepared for every possible scenario of imminent danger. With numerous practices, beginning counselors can prepare for a great many scenarios, but we agree that counselors cannot possibly think through in advance all possible imminent danger situations. Fortunately, the principles of helping in each new situation are quite similar. Therefore, it is our belief that it is very helpful to practice for the unexpected but not necessary to have practiced or thought through every possible scenario. In situations that strike you as quite new, it will be helpful to stop and think of what you know to be universal principles for helping manage situations of imminent danger. You *can* and *should* give yourself moments to stop and think.

Shifting into Crisis Management Panic Mode

This could be understandable as it is difficult to do two sets of things at once. Certainly making such a shift would greatly diminish your effectiveness and heighten the danger for your client. But fortunately, as you practice, your genuineness, empathy and UPR can become like breathing—something you just always do. As you develop strong therapeutic relationship skills, the error of forgetting these skills will be rare and only momentary at most.

Activities and Resources for Further Study

- Deeply consider and discuss each of the common difficulties for beginning counselors helping clients manage situations of imminent danger that we discussed. Which may apply to you and why? Create explanations of other difficulties that you expect might affect you and other beginning counselors. Discuss and explain how you may address each of those difficulties.

- Practice making (thinking through and writing out) non-self-harm plans for a wide range of client situations with suicidal thoughts or plans by exchanging possible scenarios with peers.

- Practice making (thinking through and writing out) safety plans for a wide range of client situations that put clients at risk for harming or being harmed by others, including dating or domestic violence situations.

- Journal or essay regarding the need for the core conditions in helping clients manage situations of imminent danger. Imagine numerous realistic scenarios in various settings in which counselors may help clients manage situations of imminent danger. Illustrate the need for the core conditions in each scenario of managing imminent danger that you have imagined. Broaden your views and answers through discussions with peers.

- Practice using your therapeutic relationship skills in helping clients manage wide varieties of potential imminent danger situations (including mild and severe suicide risk, danger to others, and domestic or dating violence) in role plays with peers. Practice handling these situations without the assistance of a consulting peer. Then, when you have a third partner participating as observer, have that partner play the role of consulting colleague, who comes to consult when you and your client believe you have worked through the situation as far as possible and are ready to consult. Plan with your partners to have role-play practices with clients experiencing mild suicide risk (such that you may practice implementing non-self-harm agreements), experiencing much stronger risk and need for hospitalization, experiencing other types of imminent danger situations, and clients bringing unknown situations.

- Try assessing and planning for safety with a role-play client *without* using your therapeutic relationship skills in order for you and your partner to feel how this would be different. Discuss thoughts and feelings of the difference.

- Research factors described by other authors for assessing the risk of imminent danger due to suicidal thoughts and other modes of imminent danger. Compare and contrast these factors with ours.

- Research aspects of non-self-harm agreements and safety plans described by other authors. Compare and contrast these aspects with the aspects that we describe.

- Discuss the issue of hospitalization for mental health reasons; what you expect it may mean to your clients in imminent danger and to you in assisting them.

- Revisit your answers to the Focus Activity for this chapter and explain how they have changed based on your studies and practices through this chapter.
- Review the Primary Skill Objectives of this chapter, checking that you have mastered each to your satisfaction at this time. Seek supplemental readings and repeat practice activities until you have mastered each to your satisfaction.

References

Beck, J.S., & Beck, A.T. (2011). *Cognitive behavior therapy: Basics and beyond* (2nd ed.). New York: Guilford.

Bongar, B., & Sullivan, G. (2013). *The suicidal patient* (3rd ed.). Washington, DC: American Psychological Association.

Centers for Disease Control and Prevention. (2012). Suicide: Facts at a glance. Retrieved from: www.cdc.gov/violenceprevention/pdf/Suicide-DataSheet-a.pdf

Ellis, A., & Dryden, W. (2007). *The practice of rational emotive therapy* (2nd ed.). New York: Springer.

Joiner, T.E., Van Orden, K.A., Witte, T.K., & Rudd, M.D. (2009). *The interpersonal theory of suicide.* Washington, DC: American Psychological Association.

Rudd, M.D., Cukrowicz, K.C., & Bryan, C.J. (2008). Core competencies in suicide risk assessment and management: Implications for supervision. *Training and Education in Professional Psychology, 2,* 219–228.

World Health Organization. (2014). Health topics: Suicide. Retrieved from: www. who.int/topics/suicide/en/

Pre-Chapter Quotes

Alighieri, Dante (1265–1321) *The Divine Comedy,* Inferno, canto 1, line 1, translated by J.D. Sinclair. Oxford: Oxford University Press (p. 23).

Hayden, R. (1996) Those winter Sundays. In A. Poulin Jr. & M. Waters (Eds.), *Contemporary American Poetry.* New York: Houghton Mifflin (p. 216).

11 ENDING THERAPEUTIC RELATIONSHIPS

Parting is inherent in all meeting. Transience is what gives life poignancy. Every person is responsible for himself or herself. There is no road to walk but your own.

Taoist meditation

Primary Skill Objectives

- Understand the principle of independence and be able to explain how it is woven throughout the skills of therapeutic relationships.
- Understand and be ready to apply the skills of planful endings through natural and arbitrary endings.
- Be ready to implement the skills of reviewing for client progress, satisfaction and decisions toward ending within your core therapeutic relationship skills.
- Be ready to recognize and reflect in review varied forms of progress for clients.
- Understand the problems that arbitrary endings can bring and how to empower your clients through arbitrary endings.
- Understand common difficulties for beginning counselors around endings.
- Be able to describe commonalities of the great majority of endings of therapeutic relationships.

Focus Activity

If you have been a client in counseling that involved a deeply therapeutic relationship, contemplate what it was like for you to end. If you have not yet had such an experience, imagine what you expect this ending would be like for you. What did you or might you feel related to the ending (a mix of feelings is likely, of course), and why? What was or might be primary and secondary among your thoughts, and why? What are some of the ways that you did or might act, in and out of counseling, around this ending?

Also consider what your reactions have been to ending other close, personal relationships life. What did you think, feel and do related to the ending? How do you expect these reactions may be similar and different from ending therapeutic relationships in counseling?

Now generate and contemplate a wide variety of reactions (feelings, thoughts and actions) that you expect clients may have related to endings of therapeutic relationships. Then, generate and contemplate the wide variety of reactions that you think you and other counselors may have to ending therapeutic relationships. Journal and/or discuss answers to the questions with peers.

Introduction

We sometimes think of ending therapeutic relationships as difficult and as including painful emotions. But really, that's not usually true. In fact, we just like saying hello much more than goodbye. And we dread the goodbyes, at least a little, even when we know they are best and the time is right.

When a therapeutic relationship has been well built, often the client knows that it is time to end, and doing so can be more joyous and satisfying than difficult. Oftentimes, other uses for the meeting time simply become more motivating to the client than time with you. While in the beginning a client's seeming reluctance to attend a session may mean avoidance of hard work, near the end, it can be a positive sign. A client's readiness to end can be like a season changing, like winter to spring, summer to fall. We may miss the season that is ending but still know it is time.

It can be like the end of an era in a child's life. While a part of us may want a child to stay innocent and young, autonomy and adulthood remain our goals for the child. The coming of autonomy and adulthood are the ideal of life's development, so it is best to plan for and enjoy the changes along the way.

When a therapeutic relationship has been well built, ending is not a complex, new skill set. Rather, it can be simply letting the therapeutic relationship run its natural course. That relationship is always meant as a temporary assistance, helping each client find his footing and continue on his unique path.

The endings of therapeutic relationships in counseling come about in different ways. In some situations, after ending individual counseling, you and your clients will have ongoing relationships. Perhaps some of your clients may continue their work and contact with you in group counseling. It is normal for school counselors to have ongoing relationships with clients after ending intensive individual counseling. As a school counselor, you would usually continue to see former individual clients in the school community and continue to have a role as one of the guiding adults in your clients' lives. In most settings, clients have the option of restarting counseling at a later time, if needed.

Some endings may be arbitrary, based on the end of an academic year, the client or counselor leaving the setting, the end of available services, or other artificial interruptions. While this is not ideal, it can be planned for, and progress in the therapeutic relationship can be consolidated and continued beyond the work in counseling.

Your clients may work through some of the grief of ending their therapeutic relationship with you while still with you. Even when this is not openly discussed, it is often a part of the ending, and you may watch for and address it. Above all, of course, we wish for you to maintain your therapeutic relationship with each client through to the last moment. We offer guidance in the coming pages on how to do this, as well as how to add helpful skills for ending.

The Principle of Independence

Work for the end from the beginning. Your goal with each client is independence. While powerful and important, you are only a temporary part of your clients' lives. This overarching principle of independence, of having your clients end their time with you in counseling maximally self-reliant, is why you do not give advice or take control of clients. It is why you work through the process of developing therapeutic relationships, which may well be harder work than attempting to exert control over clients, harder than attempting to do for or live for your clients. It is like watching a child struggle to master a task that you know you could just take from her and do for her, quickly ending her struggle with the task. In doing so, the task would get quickly done, but the child would have still not learned to do the task for herself and would likely have received a message of your seeing her as incompetent. Doing for clients would leave your clients always in need of you. Working through the process of therapeutic relationship helps your clients to continually develop self-responsibility, to end in a state of independence from you and interrelated autonomy with key others in their lives.

While you may love your clients, feel great warmth and caring for them, it should be a non-possessive love. You should love them every bit as much when they are moving on from you as you did when they seemed to need you greatly. Again, you are only a temporary part of each client's life.

Planfulness

One of your tasks from nearly the beginning in each therapeutic relationship is to determine when the end may be. When external factors will control the ending, such as a limited number of sessions allowed or the end of an academic term, you should make this limitation clear to your client(s) near the beginning of your relationship and take it into account as you structure or explain each client's use of time in relationship with you.

If the ending will not be arbitrary and the therapeutic relationship can reach its natural conclusion (which will not necessarily take a long time—some therapeutic relationships reach their natural conclusion quickly, even after just one meeting), discern when your client expects that ending to be. You can usually do this when you are explaining how she might use counseling. Whether a part of this explanation or not, at some point early in your time with each client, discern what you think each client's time expectations are and reflect what you think you see.

For example, if a client has met with you and vented or explained his frustration with a romantic partner, parent, teacher or others, and you have listened therapeutically and found it easy to meet him with genuine empathy and UPR, and he seems quite satisfied before the end of the meeting, you might reflect and make structuring statements something like, "John, I have the impression that you've gotten what you'd hoped for in our time together, that you wanted this confidential setting to tell your concerns, to sound them out and learn from them. I would want you to tell me if it is not the case, and we could plan to continue, but I'm assuming from your seeming to be satisfied and sure of your next steps that this is the only time you're expecting us to meet, at least right now." That statement is long. So, of course, you would allow for and attend to interruptions of reactions that your client may have to any parts of it.

Committing to Review for Client Readiness to End throughout Ongoing Work

For an example in which we might expect the relationship to be ongoing, imagine that your client seems quite troubled and dissatisfied by the things she has come to communicate. Within your first meeting, you might reflect and begin to structure the ending, saying something like, "Jennifer, I get the idea that this situation has been troubling you for some time, that it hurts a lot right now. I would be glad for us to continue beyond today and I have the impression that you would, too." Assuming she affirms this, you might then suggest, "Let's plan ongoing weekly meetings and plan to periodically review your progress, if you are getting what you hope for from our time, and your decision of whether and how long we might continue."

Please note that this explanation assumes that, with your input, it can be your client's decision on whether and how long to continue. If that is not the case for some setting-based reason, such as a limit on the number of sessions or the coming of the end of the school year, then include those limitations within your structuring statements. For example, you might amend the statement to say, "Let's plan ongoing weekly meetings, for as long as the seven weeks until the end of school or 'for as long as the seven meetings that we may have' and periodically review your progress, whether you are getting what you hope for from our time, and your decision on whether and how long we might continue within those seven weeks." Again, as with any such long statement, allow interruptions and attend to client reactions to any part of it.

For another example, perhaps the things your client has come to communicate are not yet clear to either of you. Such situations are fairly common. In that case, your statement that reflects and begins to structure the ending might sound something like, "Sara, I get the idea that you are very ready to use counseling, that there are lots of things on your mind, and that we are only just getting started. I'd like us to continue, and, correct me if I'm wrong, but it seems like you also want us to continue. So, I'll suggest we plan ongoing weekly meetings and to periodically review your progress, whether you are getting what you want from our work, and your decision on how long we will work together."

Reviewing for Client Progress, Satisfaction and Decisions toward Ending

Now that we have committed to periodic reviews, you might wonder just how these reviews happen. Explanations and examples follow.

While we may find that we review progress, satisfaction and expectations for ending with our adult and adolescent clients about every three meetings (with children, we see this as an adult decision, with the child's way of being/ behavior providing input), we don't believe a definite amount of time must be prescribed for this. Rather, such reviews can be made in reflection when they occur in the flow of communication. If you have it in mind to look for opportunities to make such reviews, then when your client communicates things that indicate progress or that indicate his reaction in review, you can see them and respond.

Reviewing for Progress

For example, if your client tells you of taking actions outside of counseling that you know to be within a direction of change that she had hoped for, you can empathize and reflect progress (with a smile and relieved tone that matches the client's in that moment), "I remember that you'd feared and hoped to reach out to others and now that you've taken steps to this, you seem pleased with yourself." (Consider, with this statement, that first steps may not mean it's time to end. Normally, paths to progress include new steps, missteps and falters.) Alternatively, you also may empathize and reflect lack of progress: "You still feel depressed and you are aggravated with it, frustrated that it's ongoing!"

Reviewing for Satisfaction

Review regarding whether your client is getting what she hoped for can come as you notice your client's process in her use of counseling: "Sara, I get the idea that you've been working hard, risking looking at parts of yourself that seemed scary to you, and while this is hard, you are motivated to do it." Alternatively, you might reflect a lack of meeting her hopes: "Sara, I see that you are frustrated with our work. You had hoped I could give you answers that would work quickly, and you are finding that's not the case." Note that empathy with either encouraged and discouraged feelings can be examples of counseling that is working. The encouraged or discouraged feelings are a part of the client's work. Clients need to hear their frustration expressed aloud to fully realize it. A client may also need to understand her frustration and her counselor's inability to provide quick, easy answers to motivate her for the hard work of finding the answers that are unique to her and that she truly owns.

Reviewing for Client Intentions toward Ending

Regarding reviewing client expectations for or readiness to end, an example of a reflection and structuring statement that reviews this is, "I notice that you seem to have gotten a lot of what you hoped from our time and that it's getting harder for you to schedule the time, as other things are becoming more important. I'm going to suggest that we begin to end our work together." Then, after listening to your client's response, you may suggest a time-frame based on your perception of his intentions and readiness. Your client may have responded to your reflection and time suggestion by saying (with a brief, sheepish expression) "Yeah, our time has been very important to me. I, I'm going to miss it. But, yeah, these other things are kinda more important to me now. I just don't quite want to stop our time yet." So, you might respond, "We seem not quite at an ending time, but very close, so I suggest we plan for three more weekly meetings." Or, if the events that seem to be becoming more important than counseling sessions and your client's attitude suggest it, you might offer something like, "I have the idea that you value and enjoy our time, that you seem to see yourself as ready but not wanting to end. So, I'd like to suggest that we plan to meet three more times but that we meet every other week."

With clients who are not near ready to end, reviewing intentions toward ending usually takes the form of saying nothing at all and assuming the client's intention to continue from her way of being. The review may take the form of your structuring by stating your intention or desire to continue. An example that combines a process reflection, a statement of the counselor's view of counseling for that client, and an understanding of that client's intentions toward continuing is, "Sara, I see that this work is hard for you, and that it hasn't yet produced what you want. But I remain confident that you will get there and I want us to continue working."

Setting a Tentative Plan for Counseling, Reviewing Progress, Satisfaction, and Decisions about Whether and How Long to Continue with an Initially Reluctant Client

You may also serve clients in whom you or others in their life see the need for them to work in counseling, even when that person does not. For example, there may be situations in which a spouse, parent or teacher wants a person to use counseling with you, but the person who is to be the client has misgivings. In such situations, it is of course imperative to listen therapeutically and meet your client with genuine empathy and UPR, but in addition we find it useful to make structuring statements similar to those above in order to set a time-frame for counseling. An example of beginning to plan for the ending might flow as follows. The example begins in the reflecting process and continues with an example explanation of how counseling might apply to a reluctant client. Picking up in the last minutes of the initial session:

COUNSELOR: So, while it wasn't fully your choice to come and meet with me, you seem like you might be interested to know just what possible benefits our work could be.

CLIENT: Yeah, no offense, but I just don't see the point. Yeah, I get mad sometimes, but this is just so unfair. I am really tired of it. I've just about had enough!

COUNSELOR: You're aggravated and mad about it now!

CLIENT: Yeah, so enough already. Tell me, what's the point in continuing? I'm busy and I could just go be mad somewhere else.

COUNSELOR: Well, at this point, I have a few thoughts, but I don't know for certain. You find yourself in situations that make you mad but that you don't see any way of changing. A short-term use for counseling might be for you to express some of your anger to keep from blowing up, like letting some pressure off before too much builds up.

CLIENT: Yeah, maybe.

COUNSELOR: But I'd like to work beyond that. For many people, anger is an emotion that is on top of other things. As we shine a light on what you think and feel in our work together, you may come to see more clearly the meaning of the situations of your life to you and begin to see more possibilities for yourself.

CLIENT: Yeah well, I see that you believe that, but I'm not sure what the heck that even means.

COUNSELOR: Right now, it sounds pretty strange to you and you're not sure if you're interested.

CLIENT: Nah, it's interesting. You're a trip, but I'm busy.

COUNSELOR: Then I'll suggest this: Let's plan to meet weekly for the next three weeks. That can give you enough time to get an idea of what I'm talking about. Before the end of that three weeks, we'll consider whether you're any more or less interested, and see what you are thinking at that time about whether to continue and maybe for how long. [Slight pause.] As I was talking, I thought your facial expressions were both interested and reluctant.

CLIENT: Well, yeah. I can do the three meetings, but then, we'll see.

Considering this client's openly stated reluctance in response to his counselor's expressions of empathy, opportunities to review his progress, satisfaction, and decisions toward ending may very naturally occur. With such a client who is initially reluctant, we would, of course, remember to meet him with empathy and accept his decision, whether that decision is to continue beyond the three sessions or not. For such a client, it would also be important to remember that while it is within each counselor's role to help most clients understand their potential use of counseling, it is not within any counselor's role to convince a client to use a therapeutic relationship in counseling. Trying too hard to convince a client would shift the counselor away from providing the core conditions and lead to the temptation to hold out false promises.

Recognizing the Many Forms of Progress

The *American Heritage Dictionary* (1982) includes these phrases in defining *change:* "to be different" and "a transition from one state, condition, or phase to another: *the change of seasons*" (p. 258). *Webster's Dictionary* (Grove, 1976) includes these: "to give a different position, status, course or direction to . . . a shift from some mode of personal action or disposition or matter of concern to a different one" (pp. 373–374). The *American Heritage Dictionary* includes these phrases in the definition of *progress:* "movement toward a goal," "development; unfolding," "steady improvement," and "to advance to a more desirable form" (p. 990).

So, your clients' change can take many forms. It might be changes in behavior; it might be changes in your clients' ways of being; it might be a reawakening of maturation processes; it might be different ways of seeing concerns or self; it might be changes to different sets of concerns; it might be goal directed, or the steady unfolding or blossoming of your clients' persons. Change in counseling can be both initially inconspicuous and life altering.

Examples of the Many Forms of Progress

Consider the examples of forms of client progress that we offer here. You may be able to recognize progress as an attitude change. For example, as your client comes to trust you and others more, she may look more directly at you when speaking and express emotions more fully and openly to you. A client who had been in frequent fights might let you see his initial progress by expressing his true remorse over having hurt others. Changes may appear more outside of sessions. A client who had been quite fearful may begin to take reasonable risks. A client who had been frequently angry may begin to exhibit a more calm, accepting way both in and out of sessions. Fuller examples of progress follow:

- One client began counseling, realizing she felt a great anxiety and a desire to conquer it. Early change for her came in reframing how she saw her anxiety. As she talked about her anxiety and experienced her counselor's understanding and acceptance, she realized that she saw her anxiety as a huge entity. She realized that she believed that others had tools that she did not have for battling anxiety. The more she discussed her thoughts and feelings related to her anxiety, in light of her counselor's acceptance, empathy and warmth, the smaller her anxiety came to seem. Soon, her counselor noticed that she developed a way of acknowledging her anxiety when she felt it, then waiting to allow it to pass. As she came to accept her anxiety, she came to accept herself. Her progress became measurable in behavioral terms but was first seen by her counselor as a change in perception and accompanying way of being.

- Another client came to his counselor having ended abruptly with two previous counselors. Initially, he seemed to ask and long for a name for what was wrong with him and a quick solution. When his counselor met him with empathy and UPR, as well as suggested how counseling might work for him and her hope that he would engage in a self-exploration process, he was initially taken aback. So, initial progress for him was becoming able to accept this notion of help that was very different from what he had expected. A later measure of progress was his realizing and explaining that while he had asked previous counselors to name and solve his problem, he resented the labels and resisted the suggested fixes that seemed out of his control, such as recommending that he consider medications aimed at changing his emotions and behaviors. Well before he articulated these new understandings, his behavioral improvement was under way.

- One client came to realize the extent and hurtfulness of his actions in anger and his dissatisfaction with this, plus the parallel of his anger to his father's anger. He developed a greater awareness of his pain that resulted from his father's actions in anger, its relationship to his anger, his fear of passing this pain onto his children, and his great remorse over that possibility. He realized that his anger seemed to cover up more core emotions that he had not realized but still had feared greatly. From these realizations, he began to dare to express his more scary feelings in sessions. When angry, he began to stop to question what he was doing and feeling and then decide what to express and how so. He found the motivation to begin his path toward becoming the person that he really wanted to be.

- Another client, who let his counselor know that he had been repeatedly sexually molested as a child by a family member, was experiencing difficulty functioning in school and in family relationships, and was suffering from insomnia or nightmares. Through his therapeutic relationship with his counselor, these measurable trouble areas outside of counseling improved. But even before clear changes outside of counseling, there were more subtle changes in his ways of being. In his first sessions, there were long silences (almost half the session time), in which his counselor would accept and feel with him in silence, and occasionally express her empathy or understanding of what he seemed to be feeling or seemed to gesture. He also spoke very quietly and softly during these first sessions. Soon, he built trust and came to talk more directly to her. He came to spend more time on subjects that his counselor saw as hard (his current alcohol use, his molestation) vs. easier subjects (school). His stories became increasingly more intimate and were told with annunciation, animation, and direct eye contact. He came to have a full understanding of what he felt and why (i.e., "I flinch when he tries to hug me," "I feel afraid," "I'm still deciding who I can trust and working to let go, when I know that I really can trust a loved one"). His counselor was able to review these changes in reflection (i.e., "I notice your growing confidence in speaking to me," "You understand what goes on with you in such moments and how you want to change"). These reviews helped him track his progress and feel encouraged to continue.
- Another client began her sessions seeming depressed and with her communication emotionally flat, even while telling things that seemed quite hurtful to her. She soon realized and explained that she was dissatisfied that she did not stick up for herself and came to realize that she put undue value in what others thought of her. She came to realize she didn't trust herself or others, even while she was heavily weighing the critical views she assumed from others. She spent much of her early time in counseling telling her experiences of others hurting her. Soon she began to trust her counselor and so expressed more of herself. Her counselor could see her self-trust in the fact that she expressed more of herself, but also in the way she expressed herself. When she spoke, even of troubling, hurtful things, she came to seem full of herself, as if she had been physically insubstantial but then became solid. She began to make direct eye contact when communicating with her counselor. Her speech became full with a range of emotions, rather than flat. She began to take responsibility for her decisions, to act and move in the directions of her goals, even when she suspected that others might not approve of them. Instead of using her time in counseling to tell of the ways others had hurt her, she gravitated to using her time in counseling to tell more purely of her experiences and discussing her choices and decisions.

- Another client was quite nervous getting started. As her counselor accepted and expressed her empathy of this nervousness with her, and helped her understand counseling and how it might work for her, the first progress he saw was her becoming comfortable with using counseling; becoming able to speak more smoothly, rather than fearfully; knowing more what she wanted to say or being willing to improvise freely instead of worrying so much over whether what she said was right or OK. As she progressed, she came to see herself as holding back too much from expressing herself, in and out of counseling. Her change began through experimentation with expressing herself in counseling, learning just what she felt and thought about her new level of expression, then carefully moving to express herself more fully out of counseling as well.

- For a client who began counseling expressing belligerence toward counseling and disgruntlement in being there, his counselor was able to observe his first progress as settling into his work in counseling and seeming to accept his situation of that moment. Little by little, then all at once, he seemed to come to embrace his work in counseling, to look forward to his meetings with his counselor, and to want to get the most out of every meeting. As this initial progress was taking hold, he began to discuss parts of himself that seemed to bring troubling emotions for him and to change those parts, even without taking the step of describing any parts of himself as flawed, as some might have assumed necessary.

Further Considerations of Reflecting Progress

We do not mean to say that all clients' progress, across all settings and situations, will look like the examples above. Rather, we offered those examples to help you think broadly and specifically for opportunities to see client progress. It is important to note that with those examples, the realization parts were never analytically interpreted for clients and were not always stated by clients. Although it might be nice, it is not necessary for a person to say such things aloud or even to have the ability to articulate such thoughts. Clients can experience the internal change and act on it, and counselors can see the internal change, even before outward behavior change is clear, as long as the counselors are listening therapeutically, attuned with careful, genuine empathy and UPR.

Also in those examples, counselors tended to reflect aspects of progress in terms of noticing clients' changes in ways of being, as much or more often than reflecting specific behaviors. For example, reflecting a change in eye contact can leave some persons feeling overly self-conscious of their physical self. An alternative is to reflect the different feeling that you feel with your client in connection with the change in eye contact (e.g., "You seem to have become much more confident in speaking over our last couple of meetings").

In a final note, the counselors above also used their connections with their clients to help them to know when to reflect in review of progress and when not. Of course, when a client is in the midst of feeling and expressing strong emotion, that is usually a time to respond to that emotion, not to the progress that emotion may also represent.

Consideration of Alternative Modes of Planful Endings

Standard Blocks of Time

Some counselors frequently plan for a set number of sessions, such as six. The thinking behind this method may be that clients will have a greater awareness of the finite and be more motivated to work quickly. While counseling based in a therapeutic relationship is efficient and can be very short term, planning for specific short segments of time can leave a client expecting quick solutions and feeling wary of letting his counselor know his real self, for fear that they would just get started, then would have to end. On the other hand, if a client began to work in earnest, letting his counselor know his real self, a lot can be accomplished in just six sessions.

Having Clients Decide to Continue Each Week

When working with adolescents or adults in settings that facilitate working this way, we like having clients schedule for the following week at each session. This seems to have an effect of making clients recommit to their work upon ending each meeting. In such situations, we tend to end each session by addressing the issue of continuing. For example, unless it is just incredibly obvious and therefore redundant, we frequently end sessions with a reflection and structuring statements like, "I would like us to continue and this seems your intention, too. Come and let's schedule for next week." If we thought a client's intention to continue was less clear, we would modify the statement and allow more time for her reply, saying, "I'd like us to continue, but I have the feeling you are ambivalent about it."

A problem with bringing up such a decision near the end of the session is that it can take more than a moment or two to decide, and taking more than that moment or two could either interfere with your client's full session and ability to work under his own direction up to the end, or possibly make you late for your next meeting. Therefore, while we like the practice of rescheduling each week, we also like the practicality of scheduling weeks in advance, and reviewing progress, satisfaction, and client decisions related to ending as these topics come up during sessions.

Counting Down to Ending

Once you have discerned when the ending will be, you have given yourself the opportunity to count down to it. By this, we mean that when there are about five meetings left for you and a particular client, you may begin a session by saying, "After today, we have about four more meetings." Then, in the next session, "After today, we have about three more meetings," and so on. You should make your countdown statements with a tone that indicates that the time and relationship are important to you but that is also neutral. By neutral, we mean you are not indicating with your tone that five sessions is either a very long or a very short time. Some clients will react to hearing that their remaining time with you can be given a finite number and begin to speed up, learning and communicating as much as possible in the time they have. However, your purpose in counting down the time is not to hurry your clients but to have your clients be aware of the time, make whatever meaning of it they will, and then have the opportunity to plan and own full use of their remaining time.

For some clients, this countdown to ending and awareness of remaining time allows them to grieve the loss of their time with you while they are still with you. However, most often, especially with naturally occurring endings, clients simply hear and acknowledge your countdown reminder, and then move on with communicating experiences of the moment.

Letting Your Clients Know They May Return

If it is possible for your clients to resume counseling with you after initially ending, then of course, let them know that. For example, when discussing ending or counting down, you might add a statement like, "Of course, if you decide there is more work you want to do in counseling or you want to meet for some other reason, then please make an appointment and I'll be glad to see you."

Telling Your Clients How You See Them

Some counselors think of telling clients how they see them and feel toward them in final sessions, kind of like telling a friend how much they mean to you in parting. However, in order for each client to own her use of time in counseling up to the end, it is important that your actions in the last session be quite similar to your actions up to that point. So, there would be nothing wrong with your telling a client how you see and feel in response to her, if you have done that throughout.

Of course, we hope that you have done that throughout counseling, as such statements can be high-level reflections. Helping a client see himself better through your view of him is one of the core mechanisms producing client change in therapeutic relationships. Telling a client how you feel in reaction to him can also be a reflection and a tool for that client to learn more about himself through your reaction. This is a subtle skill. A delicate aspect of this skill is discerning if what you feel is more due to your cognitive constructs, belief systems and transferences, or if what you feel is more purely a response to your client. For example, do you have negative feelings toward certain actions of your client because you believe that all persons should act in certain ways? Do you feel affection for your client because his respect for you helps you see yourself as effective?

Also, the following question may help you think through sharing your feelings in reaction to clients. If you would tell clients of whom you have very warm regard those feelings in response to them, would you also tell clients for whom you are experiencing more negative-seeming feelings in response to them? Of course, it is easier to express the warm feelings, but if you would only express the warm feelings, you must consider whether you are using your expression of your feelings to help your client understand herself or to push some other, less therapeutic purpose, such as trying to convince her of her worthiness or that she should cheer up. Due to the delicate and subtle nature of the high-level reflections needed for this skill, we have included multiple activities for self-development and understanding that relate just to this section with the activities at the end of this chapter.

Arbitrary Endings

Arbitrary endings are common. By arbitrary, we mean something unrelated to your client's decisions about ending and unrelated to your client's progress or readiness to end, such as the end of a school year, an agency or insurance limit on numbers of sessions, or the relocation of client or counselor. Arbitrary endings require special planning and consideration on the part of the counselor and client, but they certainly do not mean that significant progress has not been made or is negated by the ending.

Years ago, we were at a presentation by a counselor who worked with highly behaviorally and emotionally troubled children (unfortunately, we don't remember the person's name in order to give credit), and the presenter was asked to address the problem of the children he served frequently moving and thus having counseling services disrupted. He first addressed efforts to contact counselors in each child's new community in hopes of more smoothly continuing services. He then went on to offer a metaphor that has long stuck with us. The metaphor asks that you imagine that you are traveling in the desert and you cross paths with a person who is thirsting to death. While you may not be able to give this person enough water to supply the rest of his journey, the water you can give will still have strengthened him for his challenges of the desert, and we do not know what other resources it may help him reach.

Additionally, even a small experience with a therapeutic relationship can have powerful, lasting, catalytic effects. For example, consider the mindset we see as common to children whose behavior may be described as conduct disordered. We have seen that such children often believe that they cannot be loved, liked and accepted, and that everyone will reject them. Yet, if you meet such a child with deep, genuine empathy and UPR, especially while allowing that child to let you know who he really is, to let you know real feelings, whether those feelings are easy for you to experience with him or not, then his absolute belief system must begin to allow for exceptions and so it may begin to crumble. Once one significant exception to an absolute belief is experienced, the absolute is in great danger of faltering. We have also seen that behind that belief system, another set of beliefs implies that he is inept for and undeserving of human connection. Yet, as you invite and anticipate such a connection with your skills, that second absolute belief system must also begin to crumble.

Take for another example a client who feels great anxiety. Imagine that a young woman has seen others for help with this anxiety before. Each time, she asked for suggestions of what to do to make her anxiety go away. Then, the suggestions she tried only worked a little, if at all. It seems likely that she is acting from a belief system saying that there must be an external solution to her distress and that *she* is not competent to master. It may well be that this belief in her incompetence is an important part of what drives her anxiety. Then she meets with you, and you meet her with your confidence in the process of building therapeutic relationships, including your confidence in her self-actualizing tendency and the power of her self-discovery to reinvigorate her self-actualizing tendency. In order for her to understand what you offer, you would, of course, explain such things to her in terms that would seem to make sense to her and that are applied to what you know of her. But instead of offering more advice, you offer your trust of her use of counseling focused in self-expression and self-discovery. Then, even if the unlikely worst-case scenario happens (unusual in our experience) and she leaves an initial meeting with you thinking you a little odd, she is forced to reconcile her experience of you with her belief system. Moreover, if you only have one or two meetings with her, due to some arbitrary limiting factor, while you may inform her of resources for her continued work, the most powerful and lasting thing you can do is to have met her with your confidence in the self-responsible work that she could do in a therapeutic relationship.

From even a brief interaction with you, if you have made your time worthwhile in therapeutic relationship, persons can be forced to reexamine sets of beliefs about others and self that may have driven much of their misbehavior or exacerbated much of their pain. From a brief encounter, there is no guarantee of change, but you can know that it will be difficult for the client to maintain troubling absolute beliefs, and the behaviors and emotions driven by those beliefs.

While the results may be more subtle with less extreme examples, the same principle is true for all clients: a brief encounter with you in a therapeutic relationship can be quite powerful in producing ongoing effects. So, while arbitrary endings require additional thought and planning, we, of course, encourage you to engage fully to make the most of the time you have.

Help Clients Plan for the Premature Ending

If you think of your time with a client as limited to less than what you expect she might need or want, make your client aware of the time you have with her. Then, as with any structuring comment, be ready to respond to her reaction to the information with empathy. Then explain further if necessary. An example follows. Picking up early in an initial session:

COUNSELOR: Nina, before we get too well started, I want to be sure you realize that there are three weeks left in the semester and that I won't be here next semester. So, we can have about three weekly meetings to work together.

CLIENT: [Seeming hesitant, taken aback, speaking haltingly.] Oh, well, OK, I guess.

COUNSELOR: [Not yet sure whether the client is bothered by this information or just doesn't know what the point is.] You had some reaction to what I said. You didn't seem to know how to respond.

CLIENT: [Still hesitant and speaking haltingly.] Well, no. I don't know what you mean by that. Is that too little time to work? I, I don't know. Maybe I should have started earlier.

COUNSELOR: You're worried that I mean it's not enough time to be useful. No, while I wish we had unlimited time, we can get a lot done in the time we have. I just don't want the end to sneak up on you. So, I'm letting you know now.

Whatever the situation of the limit, you should keep your tone caring but neutral when informing your client of the limit. Your purpose is not to convey a message to hurry up. Rather, your purpose is to make her aware so that she can make an informed decision of how to proceed. If you have a sense that a client is stalling or hesitating to communicate something that she seems to want to communicate, then that is a different matter and may more honestly and effectively be handled with a process reflection (i.e., "I get the idea that there is something that you came here to say, but for some reason you are putting it off.").

Counting Down

When the end is coming soon and quite possibly in the middle of a client's work, you should be especially careful to count down sessions toward arbitrary endings. This is to keep clients mindful of the time remaining so that the end is not abrupt.

Discussing/Suggesting Continued Work and Progress

With naturally occurring endings, it is usually unnecessary to initiate a discussion of ongoing self-development. If needed, the discussion occurs naturally and is client driven. However, with arbitrary endings, we think it can be helpful to offer your thoughts on ongoing work. For example, you might suggest that a client consider continuing with a counselor that you recommend, explaining how and why so. Or, if you think a client has begun a particularly useful area of self-discovery, you could suggest that she continue that work in counseling, journaling, or contemplation. Example counselor statements of such thoughts follow:

COUNSELOR: Nina, I see you as having gotten a big start on work that is quite important to you. I also have the impression that you've come to value our work. So, I'd like you to consider continuing counseling with my colleague Susan next semester. While it would be something like starting over for you, you'd be starting at a very different place than when we first met. Also, I know Susan pretty well and believe you can expect working with her to be much like working with me.

COUNSELOR: Nina, I have the impression that the work you've started with me is quite important to you. You seem particularly excited to have begun learning some of the thoughts that seem to drive the anxiety you feel, and you seem to have begun evaluating and even changing some of those thoughts. Perhaps you already know this, but if not, I'd like you to consider that you might be able to continue this work outside of counseling as well. I'm suggesting that you consider journaling your feelings, thoughts that seem related to those feelings, and your thoughts about those thoughts and feelings. [Further explanation of how she can continue work on her own may need to follow her reaction to your statement.]

These counselor statements are long. You would need to attend to client reactions when those reactions are conveyed, whether through a statement, facial expression, a body contortion, or other modes of expression.

Also, it may be important to note to you that we do not make referrals to counselors whom we do not know. If we are only making a general suggestion that a client continue in counseling, we might say something like, "As you seem to be considering continuing in counseling, I hope you can find a counselor who you respect and can value working with in ___ [city where the client is moving to]." Then, it might even be reasonable to help your client know how he might recognize a good counselor for him: "As you seem concerned about whether it can work the same way for you with a new counselor, consider in your first meeting with that counselor whether you believe you are respected, listened to, and understood. If not, I encourage you to say so and then consider the counselor's response to your comment."

Finally, we want to reiterate that you may make such suggestions, meaning you do not have to. We only make such suggestions for ongoing work when the situation seems right and the suggestion quite helpful or necessary.

Special Problems that Occur with Arbitrary Endings

Special problems that are much less common during naturally occurring endings can arise during arbitrary endings. As long as you keep yourself focused in a therapeutic relationship with each client, one which prompts and honors client self-responsibility, then most problems with arbitrary endings are not really problems, but instead situations for you to consider that will help you further the planfulness of your work. Examples follow.

Some Clients May Adjust their Pace Following Awareness of the Upcoming Ending

Some clients may speed up their work and others may slow down with the awareness that their time with you is nearing an end. By speeding up, we mean that when nearing a planned for, arbitrary ending, some clients seem to realize that they have much that they want to do in the time they have and so increase their rate of disclosures. Other clients may have the opposite reaction to realizing that their time with you is nearing an end and seem to pull back or begin to detach, appearing to prepare to separate from and to be without their work with you in counseling. Still other clients, and perhaps the majority, may remain mostly steady in their work with you, right up to the planned for, arbitrary ending.

It is important to realize that none of these client reactions to an impending ending are wrong, better, or worse. Each person's reaction to the ending of her therapeutic relationship with you is simply that person's reaction, her actions based on the thoughts and feelings that she experiences. While we may like it if our clients speed up their rate of disclosures and self-discovery near the end, this could potentially leave a client feeling open and exposed when the ending does come. But we respect this as each client's decision that she has a right and responsibility to make. While we may be disappointed to see another client pull back, that person may realize that he needs to detach and reimplement psychological self-defenses in order to weather the arbitrary end of his work in counseling.

You should accept each client's reactions to ending, just as you have accepted each client's decisions throughout counseling. You should strive to understand each client's reactions to ending through deep empathy. You should say what it is you see through this empathy so that your clients can be fully aware of their choices around ending and grow from this, as they have from seeing themselves in other moments in counseling. As it is not clear that there is a best way for a client to utilize such an ending, we would not usually explain our views on how a client could best use the time to ending. For example, with a client who speeds up, you might reflect, "I notice that the closer we get to the end of our time, the harder and faster you seem to work. Seems like you've decided to get the very most from all of the moments we have left."

An interchange with a client who is pulling back might go like this:

COUNSELOR: [Noticing that her client seems to have become less talkative and that there are more long pauses in which she seems to be thinking of things to say and discarding them.] I have the thought that you've begun to pull back from letting me know you. I get the idea when you pause for a moment that you are thinking of things to say, then deciding not to.

CLIENT: [Another pause.] Yes, well, I just don't know what to say.

COUNSELOR: So, while you don't know what to say, there seems more to it than that. You seemed to also acknowledge my idea that you are considering things you have an urge to say and discarding them.

CLIENT: Well, I just have these little ideas [momentary pause] but none of them seems quite right. [Longer pause.] I guess I have some thoughts that just seem so, well, new, or big, or personal. [Longer pause] I have some thoughts. Then I think, well, I'd better not go there. I mean, really, that's too big for the time we have left.

COUNSELOR: So, there are things you'd like to say, but you see that we'd only get in the middle of them and then have to end.

CLIENT: [Long pause] Well, isn't that true? [Sounding a little frustrated or exasperated.] What am I supposed to do? We only have so much time!

COUNSELOR: [Responding in tone to the pain she feels from her client.] I don't know how much we have time for, as I don't know what you might say or where it might lead. However, I do hear your frustration with our shortness of time. Also, I do know that the time we have left today and our remaining meeting next week can both be a short time and a long time. You might have time to say and experience much of what you need, but I do also assume we are going to end unfinished.

CLIENT: [Sounding both somewhat frustrated and pained.] So, if it's unfinished, then what's the point? [Taken aback by her own words, beginning to speak more slowly.] I'm sorry I do appreciate your listening to me and caring. I'm just not sure where to go from here.

COUNSELOR: I get that while you want me to know how much you appreciate our time, you are quite distressed over our ending. I gather that you wanted to be at a certain point before we ended. You see that you're not there, and it's scary.

CLIENT: [Very long pause.] Yes, it is scary. Sometimes, I think my life is a terrible mess. Sometimes, I think I am a terrible mess. Other times, I think it's not so bad. I see myself as strong. I've been through a lot. OK. I can handle it. I can handle anything.

COUNSELOR: So, it's a real mix, worry if you're going to be OK, and knowing that you are OK.

Note that the counselor stuck with her client and her client's processing of her own thoughts and feelings toward ending, toward her use of the time, and toward her self-evaluation of readiness. The counselor did not offer false reassurances, though she did offer her limited views on ending. Most importantly, the counselor remained focused in deep empathy and UPR for her client, as she had throughout their time together. The counselor may also choose to talk with this client about where to go from here with her work and development, especially since she seems to be ending in a difficult place, feeling vulnerable.

The Potential for Feeling Raw in Ending Mid-work

Jeff remembers a time when he was making use of a therapeutic relationship in counseling: I remember that I had been letting my counselor know of some old hurts that were still there and of my actions that I felt ashamed of. I remember feeling raw from this work, even outside of counseling sessions. An image came to me, when I was walking one day, that it was as if I had opened a wound that would remain open until I had finished more of my work in counseling at that time. It seemed to me that my rawness with this open wound was even evident to others, although I knew that it really wasn't.

As other clients may experience their own rawness in the middle of their work, we worry a bit that arbitrary endings might leave clients in such a raw state. But we have learned that the combination of planfulness around ending (i.e., making your client aware of when the end will be and counting down) and highly attentive therapeutic listening and deep empathy keep this from happening. If your clients fully understand when the end will be, if you are attending carefully to all that they are communicating to you (e.g., what is not said and what is implied), and if you are feeling deeply with them, then your clients will take the opportunity to realize if they are feeling raw or otherwise unready to end, and take the opportunity to discuss that with you and to bring themselves to a readiness to end. They may decide to hurry to finish their work before the end or decide to close down and consolidate the work completed so far.

Ending with a "No-Show"

In settings where clients have full control over showing up for appointments or not, we have had adult or adolescent clients end counseling by just not showing up for the last possible appointment or two. A memory from Jeff's work may help illustrate this: I had worked with this young man for a couple of months. Before individual counseling, he had attended a workshop, then a small psycho-educational group regarding career decision-making. In our time together, he and I had learned that his indecision was highly personal, as he felt strongly that he knew the career direction he really wanted and believed right for him, but was just as sure that his loved ones would withdraw support—moral, emotional, and financial—if he took such a potentially impractical direction. He was also becoming aware that such indecision was influencing his other life decisions. As our ending had been planful, he was aware of our final two meetings and chose not to show up. He called and cancelled the second-to-last session, giving some plausible reason, then simply did not show up or call to cancel the last possible meeting. I felt close to him and personally, emotionally invested in his decisions. After the no-show, I was standing in the break room feeling sad. When I told a coworker, who also knew him, what had happened and told her that I'd wanted a chance to say goodbye, my coworker responded, with caring in her tone, "I guess that is how he said goodbye."

Now, looking back, I wonder if the no-show had been his way of deciding to close his metaphoric wounds over any of the healing that he had completed so far and that he had left to do. Maybe at some level he reasoned that in those last meetings he might not be able to stop from opening himself further, exposing areas that he could not close in time to leave the safety of our therapeutic relationship.

We tell this story in order for you to be aware of such events. We also want you to know that while you may not know your client's reasons for such an ending, you can know that as long as you have been planful and provided a strong therapeutic relationship, there are reasons, and if you knew them, you could accept them.

The Possibility of Ending with a Bang

In Chapter 8 we told of Jeff's work with a client who ended by disclosing, as he walked out the door, new information that was personally big and painful to him. We revisit that story in this context.

From the way it happened, it was quite clear he meant to end our time together with that disclosure. Of course, our ending had been planful and our relationship deeply therapeutic. So, this was his choice of how to end. Perhaps he decided to lance a wound that had been so far only healed over, to let out some of the infection left behind but to close it immediately back up, before it was too far open to close it back quickly. While it was shocking to me and I was momentarily confused as to how to respond or to think about this ending, I now see that his way of ending seems to have been a wise choice of how to do the most work in the time that we had. But still, I never would have guessed or suggested such an ending.

Seeking Feedback in Final Meetings

Especially early in your work, you may want to seek feedback in final meetings. You will, of course, have received feedback throughout as you have reviewed for client progress, satisfaction, and decisions/intentions toward ending. But in the end, your clients may be able to give you feedback with a greater perspective, especially when your work together has come to a natural conclusion. A client-led discussion of your work in counseling, including what it has meant to them, how so, and why, will usually occur naturally when ending with adults and adolescents. If that discussion does not naturally ensue, you can initiate it. We suggest you start by stating your desire for the feedback. For example, "Shelly, I want to know more of how you have experienced your work with me so that I can understand better what it has been like for you and I can continue to improve for my work with others." Then, if your client does not start to offer such feedback, you could foster the discussion with a reflection of what you think it has been like for her: "I have the idea that this work has been hard for you, that there were times when you were aggravated and wanted more from me. But now you are at a point where you see how far you've come. You seem to appreciate your progress, your hard work." Offering such a reflection gives your client some solid notion from which to let her thoughts and reactions grow, an initial statement to which she may agree, disagree, add to or subtract from. On the other hand, if you ask it as an open question: "Tell me your thoughts on your experience of work with me and counseling at this time. What has it meant for you? How has it worked or not and why?," you may overwhelm your client with the broadness of the question. Since your client will have done deep, subtle, abstract and meaningful work in her time with you, such an open question is likely to prompt an answer that underrates this work and reduces it to an answer like, "It was good" (with a shrug).

If you know that you are going to want such a discussion in the final meeting and know that it will take up some of your client's time in the final meeting, let your client know this as you count down. Casually clarify this for your client in your last couple of countdown statements, "We have one more meeting after today, and in our last meeting, I will want to take a small amount of time to hear from you what your work has been like with me."

Common Difficulties for Beginning Counselors Around Ending

Not Wanting to Let Go

Of course you will miss many of your clients. We miss clients from years past. Some of our clients have ended their time with us in counseling but continued to live in what we knew to be dangerous or difficult situations. So, we would expect that it is natural for us and for you to worry over such clients. Fortunately, our worry is not too strong. Our experiences of clients' lives have taught us just how resilient humans are. Especially once the light of self-awareness is turned on, the drive to self-actualize becomes much more difficult to disrupt. This enhanced drive helps persons survive and thrive through dangerous or difficult situations.

However, if your anticipation of missing clients or worrying over ending with them seems excessive and drags you down, especially if it causes you to hold yourself back from relationships, examine carefully (in self-reflection, contemplation, consultation and in your own counseling) whether or not your warmth toward clients is non-possessive. If your warmth is possessive—for example, if you have thoughts that some of your clients *must* have contact, help or control from you—then the resulting way of being in you will not only be hurtful to you in ending but to the usefulness of the counseling you offer.

The Frequent Happy/Sad Endings

Most endings with clients are a mix of happiness and sadness. We are happy to see each client go beyond us on their path. We are happy to have the time open again, and then again also sad to see each go. As our connection with each client was real and personal, we feel a void for a while after the client is gone. We miss our clients. That feeling often makes Jeff think of the wistful sadness of fall. He enjoys fall, loves it, but somehow it brings a greater awareness of the passage of time and of missing loved ones who are gone. It's something like the feeling of clients moving on. It's a good feeling, but sad—a good sadness.

Seeming to Want Too Much to End

In case you sometimes find yourself longing to end with some clients and perhaps feeling guilty or thinking yourself a bad counselor for it, we would like you to know that this has sometimes been true of us and of many fine counselors that we know. Some clients can be hard to connect with, and so your connecting with those persons can be hard work. The difficulties that some clients experience can be quite painful, and so those emotions are painful to feel with them. Also, sometimes when clients end, it represents a little break from some workplace responsibility.

However, we find that with clients who have been able to continue counseling to a natural ending, we usually have that happy/sad feeling around ending, and while we know it is time to end, we really don't want to end. Those persons who were hard to connect with as clients have usually become much easier to connect with. Those persons whose pain was hard to feel have usually come to experience a fuller range of emotions, even if many of the difficulties of their lives continue. As they have come to accept aspects of their difficulties that they cannot change, so have we.

So if you think you may be overly longing to end with clients too often, take time to contemplate problems that may be in your way of working. You may wish to consult with a trusted colleague or receive your own counseling. You may need to reconnect with some of the concepts of Chapter 1 that underlie counseling and review our core skill chapters that follow. We offer a few additional questions for you to consider in such situations: Have you gotten burned out? Are you trying to take undue responsibility for clients? Do you need to find a way to renew your trust in your clients and the self-actualizing forces inherent in life? Do you look to your clients for personal affirmation? Are you trying to do too much?

Client Reluctance to End

In natural endings, clients are not usually reluctant to end. Most often we find that clients feel the same happy/sad feeling around ending, plus confidence in readiness to end. Sometimes clients may want to continue, sometimes not, as it has been hard work. But even if a client does want to continue, there is a difference between wanting and needing. Some days we might want to stay home all day, but we also enjoy the sense of accomplishment that work brings, so we move on.

If you do find that one of your clients is highly reluctant to end, search your work for errors you may have made in planning to end and providing a therapeutic relationship. Perhaps you have misunderstood this person in some significant way. If you have provided a strong therapeutic relationship, for however short a time, and planned to end well, extreme reluctance to end will be very rare, whether the ending is arbitrary or natural.

If extreme reluctance does occur, feel that reluctance fully with your client and connect with him at that level. If it is possible to extend your time together, let him know that you see his reluctance and suggest adding time for additional meetings. Even if you cannot add additional time for more meetings, it will still be best to fully empathize, accept and connect with his reluctance. This reluctance must be necessary for him in his unique situation. So connect and help him to learn from it, just as you would have at any time throughout his counseling.

Surprise That a Client Seems More OK with Ending than You Do

Sometimes we or other counselors are surprised that a client seems more OK with ending than we are. It may simply be that a client is a less sentimental person than his counselor. It may be that he has connected deeply and used counseling well, but to him when it's time to move on, it is simply time to move on. It could also be that in ending, he just does not want to get into his emotions over not wanting to end or missing you. If so, respect this preference, just as you have respected his decisions for what to express and when throughout his time in counseling.

Unknown Reasons for Clients Ending and the Temptation to Speculate

This would be more common in agency-like settings, where the adult has more control over keeping appointments or not. We have often found that when clients choose not to continue, beginning counselors find some reason to blame themselves for their client's choice. Some of this introspection could be useful, as there is always room to improve. Also, some beginner counselor errors in therapeutic relationships can discourage client engagement. For example, if a counselor is going through the motions of reflecting but not really feeling with and prizing his client, that client might understandably feel judged, misunderstood or patronized by the counselor in ways that she may not articulate. However, we know of numerous cases where the counselor's self-blame was generated solely from not knowing why the client chose to end, often after only a small number of sessions. Following, we offer a few of the many possible happy endings from counseling that often remain unknown to the counselor.

- We know of one client who worked briefly with her counselor, crying hard through her first couple of sessions. She had begun counseling because she was having great difficulty in stopping her crying outside of sessions. After three sessions in which she cried a great deal and in which her counselor felt deeply with her and accepted her tears, she called to cancel two sessions in a row, and it was assumed she had ended counseling. The agency followed up with her, partly because her counselor was worried about her and was riddled with self-blame over the assumed failed ending. In follow-up, the client was able to tell the agency that she felt very well, that she had mostly stopped crying, or at least she only cried what she considered a reasonable amount (she did, of course, have some understandable ongoing difficulties). With this information, the counselor was able to theorize that her accepting her client's pain and tears, while feeling the pain fully with her, helped this client also accept her pain and tears. Then, as this client stopped fearing and fighting her pain and tears so much, she found that they lessened and weren't so strong. So, there was a happy ending for the client, but until knowing this, the counselor had blamed herself and assumed an unhappy ending. Remember this in the many situations in which you will not know for sure the outcome of your work with clients you serve.
- We know of numerous clients who came for only one meeting with their counselor and found that one session with the opportunity to freely self-express, to be heard, felt with and understood, was enough to sustain them and recharge their movement along their path of self-actualization.
- We know of many clients who have made a solid start in counseling in a small number of sessions, then decided to end for a while, and returned to work in counseling later when they felt ready to move into their next phase of work. We know of some clients who have made such decisions quite openly, actually telling their counselors something like, "There really is more that I have to say [implying that it's big], but I just can't go there yet." Because of Jeff's work overseeing counseling interns in settings over a period of years, he has had the opportunity to see clients who had ended with their original counselor return to pick up their work later with their next counselor.

There are countless other endings in which there is no clear knowledge of why the client chose to end when she did. In too many cases the counselor's tendency was to assume the worst and blame herself for failing. An excellent remedy for not knowing is well-planned, systematic, but simple research into client satisfaction and counselor effectiveness (such as client satisfaction surveys, pre- and post-measures, and comparisons with similar groups who do not use counseling). Such research cannot determine a counselor's effectiveness with every single client, but it can provide evidence of a counselor's general effectiveness and give insight into how the counselor might improve.

Great Satisfaction and Joy in Endings

Great satisfaction and joy in endings is the norm, rather than the exception. As you build and maintain your therapeutic relationships with clients, you can experience great satisfaction and joy in your clients' progress with them. As you build and maintain therapeutic relationships, you help your clients build a process of ongoing, self-aware self-actualization and self-aware decision-making. This is a process that easily snowballs to become a way of living for each person. It can be growing strongly long after meetings with you have ended.

Activities and Resources for Further Study

- Journal and/or discuss your explanation of how the principle of independence is woven throughout the skills of therapeutic relationships.
- Working with a peer study group, create a variety of counseling scenarios (different types of people, different kinds of concerns for those persons, different life situations, natural and various arbitrary endings). Plan together how you might structure a planful ending for each different situation, why you would structure it that way, and how you think it might play out, including both the most likely scenarios and possible problematic situations bringing up difficulties in ending. Role-play aspects of these scenarios, such as final sessions. Practice some problematic situations, but don't over-emphasize them. Remember that the strength of the therapeutic relationships you provide prevents most problems in endings.
- In consideration of our section "Recognizing the Many Forms of Progress" (page 243), discuss with peers and/or contemplate alone the many more forms that progress can take that we have described so far. Think in terms of internal changes in clients and then new behaviors that would likely be natural and durable outgrowths of those internal changes. Consider clients that might use a variety of different counseling settings and clients that bring a variety of initial concerns in order

to generate an understanding of as many different forms of progress as reasonably possible.

- As it relates to being able to tell a client how you see her in a final meeting and throughout her therapeutic relationship with you, explore the issue of feedback with a peer group. How is giving feedback that you expect will be positively received different for you and others than feedback that you expect will be negatively received? Contemplate and discuss your thoughts on that question as well as how to tell clients the ways you see them that may be received positively and those that may be received negatively.

- In a safe atmosphere, such as in group counseling, practice giving your impressions of others that you think may be important to them, both those impressions that may be received positively and those that may be received negatively. Also, seek such feedback for yourself. Contemplate, journal, and discuss your immediate, then longer term reactions to giving and receiving such feedback.

- With a group of your peers, generate counseling scenarios, some of final sessions, some of earlier sessions, where you role-play telling clients how you see them. Include perceptions that you expect will be received positively and those you expect to be received negatively. Remember that when you are telling clients how you see them in final sessions, what you say should not be news but review.

- Carefully consider difficulties and strengths you may have in letting go of clients whose struggles you know will continue after their time with you in counseling. Carefully consider difficulties and strengths you may have in letting your warmth for clients be non-possessive. What strengthens you in these endeavors? What makes your work more difficult in these endeavors? Can you find beliefs (spiritual or otherwise—i.e., about yourself and your relationship to your world) that strengthen or weaken you in these endeavors? Contemplate, journal, discuss, and essay your findings on these questions.

- Consider the case of a counselor who longs too much to end with clients. Whether you imagine that this person might be you or a colleague, review the concepts of this book in seeking to discern the possible problems in a counselor's ways of working that produce this over-longing. Discern the possible difficulties these problems might be causing in this counselor's therapeutic relationships. Then consider ways that this counselor may be able to work through some of the most likely problem areas. As with so many of our activity suggestions, you can contemplate alone—take the time to think and journal in a disciplined way. However, it will be even more productive to further develop your ideas and learn from those of others through discussion and ongoing contemplation.

- Following the same guidelines suggested for the preceding activity, explore the potential meanings for a counselor's work if he frequently finds that his clients are often highly reluctant to end. Also explore the possibilities of events in clients' lives that might be prompting their reluctance to end.

- Identify examples of research that seem simple and provide evidence of counselor effectiveness. Share your examples with your peers. Plan how you may employ research in your work settings in order to help settle your mind over the effectiveness of your work and help you discern areas to improve. Periodically implement such research in your practice in order to confirm your success, build your confidence, and shed light on areas in which you can improve.

- For the first clients to whom you provide significant therapeutic relationships, essay, then discuss with peers (within limits of confidentiality) how those clients have changed and what aspects of your relationship with them seem to have affected that change. Make clear the qualities or behaviors that have changed for each client or how his/her life has improved and/or is improving. Explain what it was about your therapeutic relationship that helped your clients change or that benefited them. Be as specific as possible in describing the mechanisms or aspects of your therapeutic relationships that brought change or benefit to each client. In individual cases, you cannot prove what it was that helped clients change, but your task here is to articulate what you think it was about your therapeutic relationship that helped your clients change and to consider evidence that leads you to your beliefs of what helped your clients change. Repeat this exercise periodically throughout your career.

- Revisit the focus activity for this chapter and consider how your thoughts and answers have changed or been reconfirmed.

- Review the Primary Skill Objectives for this chapter. If you have not yet mastered them to your satisfaction at this time, engage in additional practice and seek additional readings and study opportunities until you have mastered them to your satisfaction.

References

American heritage dictionary (2nd ed.) (1982). Boston, MA: Houghton Mifflin.

Grove, P.B. (Ed.) (1976). *Webster's third new international dictionary*. Springfield, MA: G. & C. Merriam.

Pre-Chapter Quote

Ming-Dao, D. (1992). *Daily meditations*. New York: Harper (p. 98).

12 THERAPEUTIC RELATIONSHIPS ACROSS CULTURES

If we are to achieve a richer culture, rich in contrasting values, we must recognize the whole gamut of human potentialities and so weave a less arbitrary social fabric, one in which each diverse human gift will find a fitting place.

Margaret Mead

Primary Skill Objectives

- Be able to explain why counselors must reach out in order to serve persons that are or seem to be culturally different from them.
- Be able to offer several ways that counselors can reach out and make the counseling services they wish to provide seem useful and valuable to persons who may have understandable reluctance to seek counseling from a person or who appears to be culturally different.
- Be able to explain the importance of the conditions in reaching across cultural differences once counseling has begun.
- Understand how meeting clients with humility is beneficial, especially when the counselor and client are culturally different from each other.
- Be able to explain what it can mean to "think broadly" regarding cultural differences and add examples of your own.

Focus Activity

Imagine that you have decided to use the counseling services available at your college, school, or community. This imagined scenario may take place at the age you are now or at a time in the past. Try to create a clear mental picture of why you are seeking help. Whatever your reasons for counseling, know that your reasons likely involve some emotional distress or pain, as without distress or pain, most persons will not seek counseling. Imagine that you made the appointment to begin counseling without actually meeting the counselor you will work with. You are given an appointment time, but that is all the information you have. Now imagine that between the time of making the appointment and beginning counseling, you start to form a mental picture of what counseling may be like and what your counselor will be like. In your mental picture, do you see that your counselor has had similar experiences, will easily understand you, has had a life much like yours, and is on a parallel course, just a few stages ahead of you? Or have you begun to think that nobody's experiences are like yours and that there is no way that this counselor will be able to understand you? As you create this scenario, create the mental picture that is most like what *you imagine* your expectations would be.

Now put yourself in the position of arriving for your first appointment. When you arrive, you see that apparently your counselor is quite unlike you. The counselor is not dressed as you expected or as you would dress. The counselor is not the age you expected, appearing to be much older or younger than you. The counselor is a different gender and seems to be of different background in ethnicity and/or sexual orientation from you. Imagine meeting a counselor that upon first introduction is apparently very much unlike you.

Now take a moment to picture and put yourself as fully as possible in this scene. Fill in details in your imagination of what the place looks like; what the counselor looks like; how you feel physically; how you feel emotionally; what you are thinking about counseling, the counselor, and yourself; what feeling seems to be "in the air" (i.e., tension, anxiety, calm); and how you are and/or imagine you would be responding to all of this.

Write or discuss with partner(s) your answers to the following questions, then keep your answers in mind throughout this chapter:

- What is your visceral reaction to the situation—that is, what do you feel physically (e.g., suddenly at ease, tense stomach, sweaty palms, energized, fidgety, hot, achy)?
- What emotions do you feel?
- What thoughts do you have of or toward your counselor?
- What do you now imagine counseling will be like, and to what degree do you expect it to succeed or fail?
- What may help you come to be most ready to work with your counselor? What qualities in this counselor would you need to feel comfortable in relating?
- What would not help? What qualities in this counselor would make you feel more uncomfortable in relating?

If you have not already experienced this personally, imagine how difficult it might be to seek counseling with a person who is or seems culturally different. You might naturally expect, at least beneath full awareness, to be prejudged and misunderstood. You might assume communicating what you mean to say will feel and be awkward, and it may be.

All Counseling is Cross-Cultural—But You Have To Reach Out

We lived on Guam for a couple of years, where we were among a small minority of foreigners. Even though we intentionally chose to live and work in a more rural area of the island among persons local to the area, we would periodically realize that we had unknowingly separated ourselves and that we spent much of our time with other persons from the United States—persons who, like us, were from various states on the US mainland and who had come to Guam as teachers, counselors, or other professionals but who had not grown up on or were not local to the island. Each time we realized what we had done, we would increase our efforts to more fully integrate with the local cultures and traditions.

This experience continues to serve as a lesson and reminder for us of just how hard it can be to comfortably connect with persons who are culturally different. For us, at the time, it was just easier and more relaxing to be with other people from the US—we understood the same jokes, used similar expressions, and we didn't have to *deal with the discomfort* of being culturally different or "on display" as foreigners when we were together. Though we attended church, worked in schools, and took part in many wonderful traditional activities with cultural groups local to the island, we were always aware that we were not part of the main cultural background of Guam. We were not local to the island. We were in the minority. Though we were often made to feel included, we were also at times reminded that we were "outsiders" and unwelcome. It was a good, sometimes painful, and often humbling experience for both of us.

Interestingly, it was during our work hours there—as a school counselor and a school psychologist—that we were best able to reach out, relate and build relationships with people local to Guam. During our work hours, we spoke with, joked with, cared for, ate with, listened to, played with, laughed with, cried with, fought with, and fought for a diverse group of clients and coworkers of various ethnicities, ages, lifestyles and backgrounds. We interacted with grandparents and parents, children and teenagers, teachers, school staff and administrators. During these work hours, we rarely felt in the minority, and we often felt the common bond of the human struggle and the healing power of human relatedness.

Indeed, it became apparent to us that the *nature* of our work as counselors was what allowed us to become more "the same" and feel more at home with the people of Guam. In the striving for our own best work as a school counselor and a school psychologist, we were both able to reach out—to share ourselves as unique and caring human beings who were willing to connect in a genuine manner with respect for other unique human beings.

We found this connectedness of shared experience and human relatedness to be most apparent and powerful in the language of play and art shared by children in counseling sessions. It is in our counseling of children and providing child-centered play therapy (Axline, 1947; Cochran, Nordling, & Cochran, 2010; Landreth, 2012) that we have most often been reminded of the importance of the providing the core conditions, allowing each client to set the pace and use the language most natural for self-exploration and self-expression. When a child is given the opportunity to experience his true essence and communicate freely without fear of reproach, punishment, or judgment, it becomes possible to glimpse the real and wonderful potential of diversity. We have found no better way to affirm our faith that *each one of us is unique*—each human being an unrepeatable miracle—than to facilitate such self-exploration and self-expression in therapeutic relationships.

To us, all counseling is cross-cultural if focused in the core conditions and skills of therapeutic relationships. The whole point of counseling with the core conditions and deep therapeutic relationships is to experience with another person, to enter the other person's world and allow that person to learn from her experience with you and your expression of your experience with her. Revisiting the meaning of just one core condition, empathy, remember that it has been described as walking a mile in another's shoes. Also, Rogers (1980) explained, "[Empathy] means temporarily living in the other's life, moving about in it delicately without making judgments" and "[t]o be with another in this way [empathically] means that for the time being, you lay aside your own views and values in order to enter another's world without prejudice" (p. 142–143).

However, just as you might provide a comfortable, safe space for a dear friend, you will want to explore your ability to create a safe, comfortable space for a diversity of clients. This is indeed part of showing respect, empathy, and warmth. For example, you have to make your practice accessible to persons who may be culturally different from you in order to have the opportunity to reach across cultural differences with the core conditions and your skills in forming therapeutic relationships. You have to become a person in a place that those who sense themselves as culturally different from you can feel reasonably comfortable and accepted.

There are many ways to reach out and be more approachable. Some counselors have surveyed schools or communities regarding services that might be needed. This has the effect of suggesting services that are possible and letting the school/community know that you are there and interested. Presentations on the services you offer and mental health-related topics can be an effective way to reach out. Often it is helpful for the people you wish to reach to see you humble yourself and even be a little nervous in presenting to them, to see that you are not so unusual or intimidating—but just a caring person who really wants to be of service. At times, if you can make one professional friend with knowledge of a community you wish to serve, that person may be able to point you to key individuals in that community who may help you broaden your contacts.

Reaching across Cultural Differences with Your Skills and Your Self

Once your client has come in for a first appointment, your real reaching out is with the core conditions that you have developed in yourself and all your skills in forming therapeutic relationships. It is impossible to match techniques to persons or populations, so it is best to focus on *ways of being* in counseling that reach across cultural differences. To us, that way is through using the skills of therapeutic relationships. Empathy means you are trying to come as close to understanding that individual as possible, which includes his unique set of cultural experiences. UPR necessitates that you accept and prize him, meaning also the person that his cultural experiences have developed. UPR leaves *no room* to prejudge cultural groups or values.

Genuineness means both that your empathy and acceptance of the individual are real, and also that you know what you know. You bring yourself into the counseling relationship—meaning that you are not an amoeba of various counseling techniques, ready to change and/or use a technique depending on the culture or age or socioeconomic background or gender of your client. Genuineness with empathy for and acceptance of each individual client allows you to use what you know about counseling and connecting with people to reach a diverse group of clients.

Humility

Instead of merely studying or reading about issues of diversity, make it your job and way of life to learn about and experience persons who may have differing sets of experiences from you. Realize what you don't know and that it will be impossible ever to know it all, but strive for that goal just the same. Perhaps more importantly, strive to meet each client with the humility of knowing that you don't know what her life and cultural experience is like for her, even if you think you know what cultural group she belongs to.

Be Wary of Cultural Assumptions

Jeff had an experience in counseling that has helped him remember not to assume he knows another person's cultural experience: In reference to a current situation and other life struggles, a client happened to say, with mild disdain, something like, "You know what it's like to grow up Baptist in these mountains." I think he actually meant, "Everybody knows what it's like to grow up Baptist in these mountains," using the stereotype for a shorthand explanation of his experience. But his statement struck me because from my background, I probably do know a lot about what it's like to grow up Baptist in the mountains that he was referring to; at least I know a lot from family experience, and I still feel emotions related to some of my early experiences there. So, my first impulse was to respond something like, "Yeah, I sure do," or "I guess I do" (implying understatement). However, this client was just beginning to let me know something about him and his life, so my second impulse was to realize that I really did not know what it was like *for him* and may have been making dangerous assumptions from my experience. The reflection I stumbled into came out something like, "I might. I'm not sure. There seems something of your experience that's important for me to understand." He then took the time to tell me what it was that I (and perhaps he) needed to understand about that part of his experience. As it turned out, I think his experience was very different from mine. That moment in my work helped me to remember not to assume I understand another person's cultural background. We appeared to be of the same ethnicity, gender, regional and religious background, and even somewhat the same age. But that didn't make our unique, individual experiences the same. Sometimes we think it is easier to meet a client with humility when the client and counselor appear to be very different. We find it important to meet each client with that same humility whether that person appears quite similar or quite different.

Know Yourself through Immersing Yourself

Part of being genuine is knowing the values and prejudices that you bring to each relationship. No one is completely open, a blank slate. If you were, you would not be an effective counselor, as you would not be a real person. So, you must work to know yourself. Contemplate what you have learned from your own culture, from your family, your communities, your religion or spirituality. Consider *how* you have learned this. Read and study other cultures, but be careful not to take the scientist/observer approach, like looking at bugs under a microscope. Travel and immerse yourself in other cultures. Don't visit them like Disneyland, where you only view representations of other cultures—truly immerse yourself. The purpose in such a major life endeavor is not only to help you understand the other cultures you immerse yourself in but also to help you understand your own by experiencing cultures that are different. By removing yourself from the culture you identify most closely with, you are then better able to understand those clients who seem most culturally different from yourself. By immersing yourself in another culture for a time, you will be able to view your own cultural expectations and attitudes in a way you have not previously. Stepping away and getting a new perspective may be the best way to have a clearer view of your own cultural background. Finding yourself in unfamiliar territory and taking notice of your own fears and defenses may be the best way to develop empathy for all your clients.

Think Broadly

Don't narrow your expectations for persons whose cultural differences may be significantly different from your own to include only persons who seem to be of different gender, ethnicity, and geography. The concept of human diversity is informed, complicated and at times oversimplified by the many attempts to define it. Jeff finds himself quite different from some of his relatives, even though they share the same heritage and can be considered to represent some of the same cultural categories. Indeed, many of us have grown up to have very different values, interests, behavioral norms, and worldviews than our relatives or main culture of origin. We remember a coworker, who is African American, who seemed to feel great irritation when it was assumed that she would naturally understand the experience of students who were African American and from the city, when she was from a small town in a rural area. The irritation she felt was in part due to the assumption based solely on her skin color that she would be the best counselor for African American clients.

Nancy remembers working with two young boys—both had lost their fathers in the war in Chechnya and were visiting the US in a program for orphans of war. Because the boys had this common experience and were in a foreign country and community, they were connected by this experience. But, at the same time, they were two unique and very different boys. During a counseling session, one of the boys grew frustrated and angry that others assumed he was in any way "like" the other boy, and he exclaimed, "He [the other boy] is nothing the same . . . he lives in another place . . . far . . . far . . . many miles . . . from me in Chechnya . . . he is not like me and my family!" It was apparent that this boy was in special need of holding onto his individual heritage while in a foreign country and community. Though he had some things in common with the other boy, he did not want to be confused with him or to lose his sense of individuality.

By thinking broadly, as counselors and helpers we can hopefully relate to those individuals who may feel misunderstood and restricted by stereotypical viewpoints, assumptions, and prejudice. When we were foster parents, we remember persons who felt no hesitation in making remarks or giving us advice about our African American foster daughter. Because we are Caucasian, we always stood out whenever we went out as a family with our foster daughter. As is many times the case when talking about children, remarks were often made in front of our foster daughter with little respect for her feelings. One of the most memorable remarks was made on several different occasions by persons of both races. It always seemed that those who said it meant the remark as a compliment. "There will be a special place in heaven for you," they would say in reference to the "reward due" us for having taken our foster daughter into our home. Though we are both Caucasian, we both grew up in rural southern areas and attended rural southern public schools. Both Jeff and our foster daughter grew up attending southern Baptist churches. We shared with our foster daughter an understanding of the rural, southern, sometimes very painful, and lasting attitudes about social class, race, and poverty in the South. All three of us understood that in some ways this thoughtless remark was simply "southern." All three of us also understood, each time it was said, that it carried a hidden message that was hurtful to us all but mainly to our foster daughter—an implication that she was "trouble" to us and that we were due a reward for the sacrifice we were making.

We came to mostly feel more connected to each other through these uncomfortable moments. Most of the time we were all just trying to enjoy the moment eating our pizza or sitting on the beach. When people would intrude with such remarks, it seemed that the three of us began to share an awareness that some people sometimes say too much. Knowing this, and somehow coming to expect it, seemed to help us feel more "familiar" and bonded to one another. Thankfully, we were also able to talk with our foster daughter openly, and listen to and accept her feelings about instances when she felt uncomfortable, sad, angry, or ashamed about being with us. We were able to laugh and talk, pray and eat, sing and cry, dance and play together. We seemed to have a lot in common as human beings. Her 9-year-old thoughts and remarks on the issues of race, poverty, family, and life in general were always refreshingly honest, wise, and to the point. She certainly helped us to think broadly!

The Fairly Foreign World of Children

Most adults don't engage in pure fantasy play. If we were seen doing this, we might be thought insane. For adults in our society, role-plays, day-dreams and spinning stories with words are seen as acceptable, creating art is seen as acceptable, acting in a play is seen as acceptable, but just pure, spontaneous fantasy play is not. The vast majority of our adult communication is with words, but as Axline (1947) explained: "Play is the child's natural medium of self-expression" (p. 9). Even when adults go to a gym, which in childhood may have been an indoor place to play, we "work out;" count pounds, miles, minutes, or calories; or tend to play goal-oriented, competitive games.

Children, when freed from the requirements to meet expectations or perform for adults, play naturally and from the pure core of their being. They use this play for emotive release during stress, for resolution of problems, and for mastery of life situations. Nancy has often explained to students that it is in working with children that she finds it possible to see the real potential and beauty of human diversity. It is in working with children that both of us have built our faith in human beings and have truly seen that each individual child has her own unique voice, language and style of communicating. It has been possible to extend this faith in human beings and in the unique individual when working with older clients. We remind ourselves that "words get in the way" sometimes, and that our older clients are often restricted, feeling guilty and afraid to fully self-express. We remind ourselves of the power of the therapeutic relationship—of being a safe and freeing place where both children and our older clients will experience the warmth and acceptance necessary to be and express who they truly are.

A child does not have the words, or at least does not have the cognitive-emotional integration *to use* words to work on such existential concepts as seeking self-identity and acceptance of it, discerning what he believes his relational potential with others is, and what he would want it to be. But children need to and do work on these concepts. In fact, such concepts may be set by the end of childhood and the beginning of abstract thought, even *before* a child has the *ability* to examine core beliefs in the ways that adults would. Core beliefs are, in effect, established, confirmed, and set in darkness. If those core beliefs are errant and troubling, they are much harder to change than they would have been before becoming solidified. So, when events or a child's perception of events have damaged or are blocking his path to self-actualization, that child can benefit greatly from counseling focused in a therapeutic relationship. This requires, however, that the adult find a way to reach across the formidable divide from adult thought and expression to the child's innocent and pure expressions in actions and play. This is indeed a "foreign world," a world where the skills and the core conditions for building therapeutic relationships are the necessary bridge between these two worlds— the worlds of adult and child (for more on reaching and helping children through therapeutic relationship and play, you may like to read Cochran, Nordling, & Cochran, 2010; as well as other authors, including, of course, Virginia Axline, 1947, 1964; Clark Moustakas, 1953, 1959; Garry Landreth, 2012; Dee Ray, 2011; and others).

Working with children requires an understanding of and respect for children as a diverse population—diverse as unique individuals but also as a whole population that is different from the adult population.

Clients and Others Who May Not See the Value of Counseling

Among counselors and mental health professionals, we form a culture that holds similar sets of beliefs about the importance of self-awareness, self-responsibility, communication, human connections and other counseling-related concepts. These concepts can come to seem self-evident within our culture. Yet, such concepts may not be self-evident to larger cultures. Jeff remembers a momentary debate about "just what Jeff does for a living" among his elders at a family reunion. Some of my aunts and uncles were discussing just what I did for a living, and there seemed to be some confusion. One of my great uncles joked, "You ought to be one of those doctors where people just come to tell you their problems and you just tell them what to do." One of my cousins, who has a pretty good understanding of counseling and what I do for a living, quietly answered, "I think he is." I realized from her look of sympathy in that moment, and from my own common sense, that I had no real chance to explain what I do for a living to my elders in that moment, even though they love me and might be interested in understanding. I had no real chance to explain that counseling is *so much more* than just telling people what to do. But the explanation would take too long and also put a damper on the fun of the day, so I let my great-uncle's teasing explanation of what I do for a living stand. I realized the gulf of differences in our experiences and background knowledge. While we love and respect each other, our backgrounds of experiences, in this case for understanding counseling, have been hugely different. That moment also stands as a reminder to me to continually redouble my and my students' efforts and abilities to explain to clients, loved ones, teachers, administrators, or third-party payers just what counseling is and how it helps our clients and our society.

Another cultural gulf for counselors and other mental health providers is presented by the predominant medical model mindset of our society. In our travels we have realized that we Americans have a well-deserved reputation for impatience. We tend to hope for "quick fixes" and "magic pills." Truly, medical doctors are able to do amazing things, helping many live longer and better. Because medical care has provided so much, our society may have come to rely too heavily on and to have unreasonable expectations for its power. For example, the onslaught of advertisements for medical drugs inundates us with a sometimes subtle and sometimes not-so-subtle implication that if one finds the right pill, all will be well. We have realized from the implications of these ads that apparently there are pills to fix all our moods and troubling thoughts. The ads that we have seen don't seem to mention that a person experiencing depression might also need to make life- and self-changes to feel well. Apparently there are pills to improve men's sex life or penis size that would then cause them to be more confident and competent and to be seen as different—suddenly changed for the better by all those who they meet, suddenly happy in relationships. Apparently, there are pills, easy diets, or medical treatments that can make all women more beautiful and cause them to automatically feel better about themselves and their lives.

As a result, explaining counseling can be difficult. Self-development through self-discovery, change that may take time, great effort and may be emotionally painful, is a tough sell in a society that advertises "quick fixes." Almost any thinking human would doubt the assertions of the advertisements that we mentioned having seen when the assertions are stated outright, as we have done. But the assertions aren't stated outright; rather they are an ever-present, emotionally manipulative undercurrent in our society. They assert commercial interests by relentlessly feeding voice and imagery into an undercurrent that appeals to our hope for simple solutions and a tendency toward linear, straight-line thinking. It can be easy to assume that the quickest route from point A to point B is a straight line (anyone who has lived in mountainous areas may tell you this is often not true). When linear thinking is related to the work of counselors, one could easily think that if behavior is the problem, the solution must be behavioral. We find that this is at most a partly true assumption. If behavior is the problem, a behavioral solution may help but would be greatly enhanced if the emotions and thoughts that drive the behavior or the complexities of the behavior itself were more fully understood, explored, and expressed by the persons for whom the behavior in question is a part of her experience.

It is important for members of the culture of counselors to remember that while counseling solutions seem natural to counselors, members of the culture of teachers more naturally gravitate to and much more readily grasp thoughts of teaching applications for the very same problem. Likewise, administrators more naturally gravitate to administrative solutions to the same problem. Quite possibly, some combination of the approaches may be most helpful. But now that we are considering combinations of approaches, life is getting complex again. And working to implement complex combination solutions in a society that wants quick, easy fixes will tax the explaining skills as well as patience, listening, empathy, and UPR of the counselor who wants to make it work.

Because concepts that become second nature to counselors and mental health professionals are usually not second nature to persons outside of our culture, each counselor and mental health professional must be ever vigilant for how the assumptions of our culture about human nature, problem solving, counseling, and related concepts affect our thoughts, actions, and communications. Those from our culture must be ever vigilant to translate our culture's beliefs and actions into terms acceptable and understandable to the larger cultures. For example, when you advocate for funding and support for an expansion of counseling services, put your request in terms of the goals of the community, with a practical, understandable explanation of how counseling will help achieve those goals.

The same goes for explaining counseling to a client. Generic explanations and platitudes may be only minimally helpful, but explaining the potential of a client's use of counseling, related directly to her life and what she has told you about herself and her situation, will help.

Common Problems of Beginning Counselors in Counseling across Cultures

Opportunity to Experience a Diversity of Clients

It is a natural inclination to stay within one's "comfort zone" to avoid anxiety-producing contexts. We encourage you to take your opportunities to serve in settings with maximum client differences for you early in your work, especially while you still have maximum supervision to help in this work.

Difference as Advantage to the Counselor

Counseling persons who seem quite different from you can be an advantage in keeping you from the habit of assumptions about clients' experiences. We have known beginning counselors to struggle not to assume that their client's experience is quite similar to their own when serving clients who seemed very much like themselves. So, again, seek experience with clients who seem to be different from you and remember not to assume that your experience is your client's experience, because considering the diversity of our individual human experiences, odds are your two sets of experiences actually have a great many differences.

Missing the Feelings for the Cultural Context

Some beginning counselors have explained that in trying too hard to understand the cultural context and differences of clients who appeared quite culturally different to them, they missed connecting through feeling with those persons. If counselors first connect with client's feelings, which are core to our humanness, then it becomes easier to understand that person's cultural context.

Missing the Content for the Context

Likewise, some beginning counselors working with clients who appeared quite culturally different have missed getting the gist of what their client was telling them by getting caught up in the intellectual task of understanding the client's very different-seeming world. This was especially true when they weren't native to the same language or they spoke with very different accents. There again, it is most helpful to connect on a feeling level. You can know a person's feelings even without words. Then, if you connect with the person through feelings, more of the words will become obvious, and understanding every word will become unnecessary.

Significant Value Differences

Beginning counselors who we know, and we ourselves, have experienced the greatest difficulties connecting with clients who have significant value differences. For example, one counselor, who was on her own from an early age and is a largely self-made success story, had great difficulty understanding a client who seemed overly attached or enmeshed with her family and struggled to separate or individuate. We and other counselors we have known have struggled to understand clients who have abused children, spouses, or other weaker persons in their lives.

Realize that such difficulties in understanding and connecting may be difficulties in accepting and empathizing. We remind ourselves that it is, after all, acceptance and empathy that may help the person who has values that are significantly different from our own, and that we may view as harmful or immoral, move on to be more mature or optimally self-actualized. For example, for a client who negates her individuality and growth potential by remaining enmeshed with her family, the experiencing of her counselor's acceptance and empathy will help her more fully feel what she feels, come to see her situation clearly, and move to change. For a client who seems less than genuinely repentant for abusive actions and may be working hard to keep the effects of his actions out of his full awareness, the experience of his counselor's empathy and acceptance (which does not mean agreement) will help him accept the truth, and thus move to change.

The Experience of Connecting

We would like you to know that overall our students do not experience great difficulties connecting with clients who are culturally different. Rather, we and our students have found great joy and excitement in connecting with clients across cultures, and experiencing the commonality of our human beingness.

Sensing a Need for Information and Context Education

As we have worked with groups of beginning counselors, we have often had the experience of one member of the group letting the rest of the group know that she feels uncomfortable with her lack of knowledge of the cultural context of a client who seems very different from herself. We admire the counselor's self-awareness and humility in realizing and saying this aloud. From this disclosure, often a group discussion follows that first focuses on how she feels with her client, then gravitates to a discussion of how she sees her client as different. This, of course, requires her to discuss her own cultural background, values, and biases, as they relate to her client. So, it is not only a discussion of the client's context but yet another opportunity for the counselor to learn more of herself. Usually, after those initial areas of discussion, comes a sharing of perspectives, information, and understanding of the two cultures in question (the counselor's and the client's), including relevant professional literature that members of the peer group suggest.

Reaching Out and Becoming Accessible

A problem that we see for some beginning and experienced counselors is reaching out and becoming accessible to persons who are or sense themselves as culturally different. It is the task of every counselor to reach out to the communities she serves. If the community doesn't know you are there, see you as approachable and useful, and think that the counseling you offer might be helpful, then why would persons in the community seek counseling? Many persons who gravitate to the counseling profession can be introverted and might prefer to shy away from reaching out to the communities they serve. If you combine that understandable shyness with looking or feeling different from those communities, then there is a danger that you might not reach out.

It may help to remember not to worry if you look nervous and fumbling in your attempts to reach out. This may serve to make you come across as real and gutsy for being nervous and trying anyway. Jeff is often shy in these tasks. Public presentation has not always been his strength, and making small talk at social gatherings certainly is not. However, he has found that when he finds ways to join with others in community projects, he doesn't think so much about presenting himself, and others usually come to like and respect him. We would also like to offer a story of Jeff's experience with reaching out as a new elementary school counselor, while also suddenly immersed in a different culture: I got my job as an elementary school counselor by accident. I had never meant to work with children. They seemed foreign to me. But when we were moving overseas, the contract I was mistakenly sent was at an elementary school. I told Nancy, "I don't know much about children." I had always been an "ideas and behavior" guy, great with troubled youth but made for adolescents or adults. But we were too poor to afford the overseas phone calls to have my contract changed (this was way before cell phones, showing our age). So, while quickly learning to adapt my skills for children, I also had to learn how to reach out to them. They didn't get my jokes or understand some of my words.

I found that the most effective way for me to reach out to kids was through play and following their lead on the playground and in other free play moments. I decided not to try to talk or present myself (although I did classroom presentations that were reasonably competent but not great). Whenever I could make a free moment, I immersed myself in play with the children of my school. I focused on one child or one small group at a time and joined them in play in their ways and at their level.

I probably looked silly to some adults (no one else joined in free play this way), but soon I became like "Elvis" to the under-10-year-olds in my village. Walking on the playground, I would be surrounded by throngs of adoring "fans." It was as if word spread among the children, "He gives undivided attention! [Rather than just instruction, like other adults]. He likes us as we are! [And didn't come to judge us or teach us to be better, like so many adults.] He thinks we're cool." Now don't get me wrong, I remained an adult. I knew when it was time to play and when it wasn't. But when it was time to play, I played.

My play therapy became highly sought and prized. My free play, combined with my presentations to children and school adults about what counseling was really about, quickly began a flow of eager referrals. As the community of adults saw the effectiveness of my work, they came to respect and value me. Our point is that there is always a way to reach out and begin a connection, even for shy people. So, we encourage you to let yourself go and free yourself to find a way that works both for you and for the clients and communities you wish to serve.

Activities and Resources for Further Study

- Revisit the Focus Activity for this chapter and consider how your thoughts, feelings and answers related to the situation(s) you imagined have changed.
- We recommend you read and consider Glauser and Bozarth's (2001) "Person-Centered Counseling: The Culture Within." We find it offers a helpful perspective on counseling across cultures.
- Journal and discuss with peers ideas for reaching out across cultural differences to make counseling known to be useful and valuable for all persons and cultures. Imagine as many cultural differences and situations/contexts as possible. Generate as many methods for reaching out as possible.
- In order to deepen your understanding, journal and discuss as many scenarios as possible of ways in which counselors work with clients who have significant cultural differences. Remember to think broadly. For each scenario, imagine how the core conditions may help the persons establish a working and healing connection.
- Engage in ongoing study of other cultures, perhaps through fiction as well as factual study. It is often only minimally helpful to attempt to research a culture from which you appear to have a client(s). However, if you make cultures other than your own a consistent part of your interests, you may continually open your mind to the infinite range of possibilities for humans and gain a perspective that helps you better understand the culture that you bring to each relationship.
- Study of the cultures that you see yourself growing from. Consider the meanings and influences of those cultures in the relationships you form.
- Contemplate the differences between the worlds of children and the worlds of adults. How do you see your skills in therapeutic relationship working to bridge the divide?
- Revisit the Primary Skill Objectives for this chapter and see if you have mastered them to your satisfaction at this time. If not, seek additional readings, practices and discussions in order to master them to your satisfaction.
- Travel. Experience what it is like to be a stranger in a strange land.

References

Axline, V.M. (1947). *Play therapy: The inner dynamics of childhood.* Cambridge, MA: The Riverside Press.

Axline, V.M. (1964). *Dibs: In search of self.* Boston, MA: Houghton Mifflin.

Cochran, N.H., Nordling, W.J., & Cochran, J.L. (2010). *Child-centered play therapy: A practical guide to developing therapeutic relationships with children.* Hoboken, NJ: Wiley.

Glauser, A.S., & Bozarth, J.D. (2001). Person-centered counseling: The culture within. *Journal of Counseling and Development, 79,* 142–147.

Landreth, G.L. (2012). *Play therapy: The art of the relationship* (3rd ed.). New York: Routledge.

Moustakas, C. (1953). *Children in play therapy: A key to understanding normal and disturbed emotions.* New York: McGraw-Hill.

Moustakas, C. (1959). *Psychotherapy with children: The living relationship.* New York: Harper.

Ray, D. (2011). *Advanced play therapy: Essential conditions, knowledge and skills for clinical practice.* New York: Routledge.

Rogers, C.R. (1980). *A way of being.* Boston, MA: Houghton Mifflin.

Pre-Chapter Quote

Mead, Margaret quoted in E.M. Beck (Ed.), J. Bartlett (compiler) (1980). *Familiar quotations* (15th ed.). Boston, MA: Little, Brown & Co. (p. 853).

13 CONNECTING HEART TO HAND

Doing More, Going Beyond, Staying True

In the authentic relationship, there is a facing up to the feelings and issues, an exercise of wills, without the will of either side being negated, impaired, or broken. The will ignites the fires of determination and enables one to face the old patterns of criticism, adversity, and rejection; enables one to live with the negative feelings and thoughts while creating new images and meanings in the process.

Clark Moustakas

Primary Skill Objectives

- Explain how action approach tasks are naturally accomplished within therapeutic relationships.
- Explain the principles for when to go beyond therapeutic relationships in individual counseling and when not to do so.
- Develop your guide for when and why you may work beyond a focus on therapeutic relationships and when to remain mostly focused in therapeutic relationships in individual counseling.

Focus Activity

Think back to the quote given to begin *The Heart of Counseling*. The quote, attributed to Muhammad, reads:

> There is an organ in the body that, if it is righteous, ensures that the whole system will be righteous . . . This organ is the heart.

As you know, the therapeutic relationships you form can be seen as the heart of your work, as the core and passion that makes all the rest of your work righteous, so long as it is righteous. So now think of the full range of your work as a counselor. Think of all the major areas that you can anticipate being a part of your work as counselor: skill-teaching, assessment, sharing your views, diagnosing, saying the things aloud that may be hard for a client to hear, providing information for self-care or career exploration, guiding a client through test results, providing guidance, leading groups, serving families and more. First journal, then discuss with peers:

1. The ways that you see your therapeutic relationship skills connecting with and strengthening each of the important areas of your work that seem beyond your core, one-to-one therapeutic relationships.
2. Areas of your work as counselor that you think are or will be completely beyond, unconnected from your therapeutic relationship skills, and why.

Expanding Out from Your Core

You may be anticipating your workplace and thinking, "How can my therapeutic relationship with clients be enough for all that I do?" This is a good question. To answer we refer you back to the quote presented in the introductory chapter of *The Heart of Counseling* and repeated above. With the quote and the Introduction to this book, we give the assurance that a healthy heart or emotional core makes all of the body work well. The heart or emotional core extends to our minds (thought and language), our hands (written language and assessment) and even our feet! There are times in which you as counselor must genuinely speak your mind, as well as respond from your heart; and there are times that your feet will carry your counseling skills through applications of therapeutic relationships well beyond your counseling setting.

In this chapter and the few that follow, we strive to have you see your skills of therapeutic relationships in all that you do as counselor and person. We guide you to consider connections of your heart skills in assessment, in career counseling, school hallway moments, skill-teaching, guidance, leading groups and more. We guide you to explore connections with major counseling theories. We explore counselor thought processes and actions for effective integration of comprehensive counselor tasks into your relational core.

Action and Cognitive Approach Tasks Accomplished Naturally within Therapeutic Relationships

We often have students who are looking to integrate cognitive or behavior skills into their work, to consider first if the skills they hope to teach or integrate are already naturally occurring within their therapeutic relationships. Tursi and Cochran (2006) explored examples in tapes of Rogers's work in which clients worked through the ABCs of REBT (Ellis & Dryden, 2007), without their having instruction in the concepts/techniques and without Rogers doing anything beyond therapeutic relationship to make this happen. Modern examples of this natural occurrence follow.

Questioning an Absolute (and Irrational) Belief

Derik left class and arrived angry at your office (he knows this is allowed twice per week, as part of his behavior management plan, to prevent his previously frequent angry outbursts in class). Once safely with you, he begins to rant.

DERIK: [Talking loud, tensely, angrily.] I just hate this s**t. It ain't fair. I'm sick of being treated this way. And I'm just about to blow out of this place.

COUNSELOR: [You respond to his emotion, knowing you can come back to the loose implication of threat, or the probable errors in thinking that seem connected to his emotions. You speak filled with empathy, nearly matching his emotional level.] You are really *mad* about this! You're just enraged, so much that you can't even sit down.

The comment on his standing was *not* criticism. You have no problem with his standing. Rather, it was just what came to your attention as you strove to communicate what you saw and felt of his communicating just how mad he is.

DERIK: [Realizes his position—standing while you are sitting, sits down, but stays tense, barely on the edge of the chair.] You're d*** right I'm mad. He treats me like s**t. It's not fair and I've had enough!

COUNSELOR: [Attending to some of the implications of his communication.] Sounds like something happened in class that has you knowing you are treated as the lowest nothing there could be. [While the counselor could use the s**t word, as the client did, we usually avoid "cursing," to avoid gaining a reputation as "the counselor who curses."]

DERIK: Yeah! Everybody treats me that way—like I'm the lowest there could be!

COUNSELOR: [You already hear a faint uncertainty in his voice as he speaks the absolute, but you stick with reflecting the main emotional impact of his thought.] You are knowing that it's everybody. Everybody treats you that way!

It is important that this last empathic reflection is not a question, challenge or correction. A question or challenge at this point would take him out of his emotional experience and at least temporarily damage your therapeutic relationship by stopping his processing and putting you in "teacher role."

DERIK: [Upon hearing in empathy his absolute claim and beginning to calm.] Yeah, well, not everybody. But it feels like that.

COUNSELOR: [Still keeping with the main communication, because it continues to be more important to accept Derik through his emotional experience than to jump into teaching; plus you can already see Derik adjusting the absolutes.] It does, it feels like everybody.

DERIK: It feels that way, but I know it isn't really everybody. [He's much calmer now, becoming reflective.]

COUNSELOR: OK, so not everybody, but still it feels that way! [Again, it is important that this is said to attend to his experience, not to correct his thinking.]

DERIK: Well, there's [slight pause as he looks toward you, but can't quite name you as one of the exceptions, which is too personal at this point], there's Mr. Smith, and of course my guys.

COUNSELOR: So Mr. Smith doesn't treat you as the lowest and also not your guys.

DERIK: No Mr. Smith just tells me straight [Mr. Smith has a disciplinary role at the school, but he and Derik have connected a bit] and, of course, my guys always know I'm right.

COUNSELOR: You're knowing there's a difference in how you see yourself treated by Mr. Smith, your guys, and Mr. Wade [you use the language of *perception* here, being well-versed in the importance of and imperfection of perceptions, as well as other concepts from cognitive therapy (Beck & Beck, 2011)].

DERIK: Yeah. Wade is always riding me for no reason—like I'm his d*** donkey.

COUNSELOR: It hurts as you see that he's . . . that's the way it feels to you. That he is riding you for no reason.

DERIK: [Grinning a bit, in spite of himself.] Well, maybe not for no reason. It could be, I also give him a pretty hard time sometimes.

COUNSELOR: So two thoughts, it feels like he rides you for no reason, and you also know that you give him a pretty hard time, sometimes.

Derik: [Pausing, in responding with a frustrated sigh.] Yeah, I do some stuff, but that don't make what he does OK.

COUNSELOR: [You are tempted to go into the REBT explanations of one person's behavior not directly causing another's response, but resist to stay with his communication, both for time and because the teaching doesn't seem needed—the learning is occurring naturally. Derik has processed a good bit, and with efficiency, and he should get back to class soon.] So you're knowing you do some stuff and also knowing that what you do can't justify the mistakes you see in Mr. Wade.

DERIK: Definitely not. But I guess I can cut him some slack.

COUNSELOR: So, you're thinking maybe you can cut him some slack. [Then structuring the ending.] You seem calm now and it seems that you are seeing the situation somewhat differently now. And also I need to watch the time and you need to head back to class, if you also see that you are ready.

DERIK: [Standing to leave and commenting with a positive and little bit teasing tone.] Yeah. I can cut the old guy some slack, and I need them credits—Can't get the credits, if I'm not in class.

COUNSELOR: You're ready, especially knowing you need to be in class to earn credit.

DERIK: OK. Yeah. See you tomorrow at our session.

There were many temptations in the exchange above to stop and address the errors in Derik's thinking. But Derik didn't come to learn new skills. *He came to be heard.* So, ironically, he began to change his thinking through being heard. The counselor's skills in therapeutic listening, the process of self-discovery and self-reflection of therapeutic listening, helped him learn new skills. It doesn't always work this simply or this quickly, but it often does, as long as your skills are developing and your head and heart are in the right place for therapeutic relationship.

We should note that there was a faint implication of threat in Derik's first statement, "I'm just about to blow out of this place." It seemed pretty clear that Derik was thinking of leaving in anger vs. "blow up this place." But either way, depending on what else you know about Derik, you might need to go back and address that (leaving school without permission could also be imminently dangerous, depending on the context). The counselor in the situation above had thought to go back and address it, but in the end, Derik seemed quite calm and resolved to reinter class. There seemed no longer to be any threat implied. If you, as his counselor, viewed the situation otherwise, you could check before ending, with a question somewhat like the following to Derik's last statement:

COUNSELOR: Derik, before you go. I remember that one of the first things you said when you came in had to do with "blowing out of here." I want to ask what you meant to make sure you are not thinking of something unsafe.

DERIK: [Seeming to try to recall what the counselor is referring to.] Oh, I think I just meant to storm out of the school. Really, that was what I first thought to do when I left class. But I also remembered our agreement, the part that I can come here before I do something really bad, and if you aren't with someone else, we can talk.

COUNSELOR: So that was what you meant, but seems like that was then and it's not really even on your mind now. [Heading out the door together.] Come, and I'll walk back to class with you. I'm going that way.

Testing New Behaviors, Taking Action toward a New Goal

Janet came to counseling at a community outreach clinic because she was feeling depressed and couldn't seem to shake feeling down. As she spoke with her counselor regarding her feelings and thoughts, and the context of her life, she continued to return to the topic of not feeling as if she was valued by her husband. It became apparent to her and her counselor within a couple sessions that this was the core of what had been bothering her.

Hers was a second marriage. Her husband had an adult daughter with very significant addiction problems. As Janet saw it, his daughter's addictions caused her (daughter) to misuse her husband and herself, requiring a huge commitment of time and energy, and draining their finances, at times even stealing from them.

When she tried to talk with her husband about new ways of parenting, including getting help at the clinic as a family or as a couple, she saw that he didn't listen, didn't seem to care, and only saw her as uncaring, even mean. She and he were drifting further and further apart. She either asserted and was ignored or rebuffed, or chose not to assert and distanced herself.

By a couple sessions after narrowing down her issue to her relationship with her husband and his daughter, she seemed stuck. Janet saw only two dichotomous options: leave things the same, which to her meant living in misery, or leave the relationship.

Janet's counselor was in a quandary over what to do. He had reflected to Janet more than once that she only saw the two options with no other alternatives and no middle ground. But Janet responded by explaining, perhaps politely arguing that there really were no other options. He suggested a couples counseling option that would help the couple learn to listen empathically to each other and talk to each other more openly (what he had in mind is relationship enhancement therapy; Ginsberg, 1997; Scuka, 2005). Janet explained again that she didn't think her husband would be open to that.

Janet's counselor decided that he had no choice but to trust the therapeutic relationship process. Instead of trying to help Janet get unstuck, he redoubled his effort to be with her empathically in her "stuckness." During this clear, focused work, Janet began to gather input from legal counsel and acquaintances regarding what the impact of divorce would be, and whether she could afford it. Then, seemingly out of the blue, Janet described a recent painful scene of her husband arguing, pleading with his daughter over a particular incident of self-destructive behavior. Janet described realizing her urge to tell him how he was mishandling the situation and how to handle it better. But as she thought of it, she realized this would not work, she decided to be with him as he struggled for what to do, without trying to tell him what to do. She explained to her counselor that the more she listened, the more he made decisions toward the kinds of actions that she would have suggested. He even asked her opinion, but by then he was already moving toward the kinds of actions she thought would help most—and so she told him so. But most of all, Janet was so pleased with the new closeness that she felt with her husband, as she explained, "It's like we have a new marriage."

As she continued in counseling, it was not exactly a "happily ever after story." She and her husband still had great difficulty caring for his daughter, but Janet was OK with that, as she made listening her usual way to closeness with her husband. Even though listening didn't solve their very difficult problems, it kept them close and helped her see that she was loved and valued.

And she reported that it seemed to be contagious—the more she listened to her husband, the more he listened to her.

In providing this example, we are not saying that it always works this way—that all that the counselor needs to do is trust the process—later and in the following chapters we focus on the more you can do to support the work your clients are doing in therapeutic relationship with you. But we find in situations in which we or a supervisee thinks, "Oh this client is stuck. I must do something to help her become unstuck!" often the client begins to test new behaviors and take action toward goals just after the moment when we wanted to give up and start in another direction. Sometimes it seems to us that our own feelings of stagnation and possibly of impatience with our client seemingly "being stuck" coincides with the client's feelings of also being fed up with feeling stagnant and not changing. Empathy helps the client realize the level of her misery and tips the scale to change. In the following sections, we discuss decision processes for when and how to integrate techniques from action-oriented counseling approaches with your core therapeutic relationship.

Decision Guides for When to Do More and When to Do Less

Client Desire for Information, Guidance or Skills—Stated or Implied

The simplest decision guide for when to add techniques from particular counseling theories, often skill-teaching, into your therapeutic relationship, is whether or not your client is asking for some particular kind of help. For example, Jacob came to see his high-school counselor. She had only known him as a quiet, good student. He explained that he had seen her display about the effects of depression and anxiety, and the benefits of asking for help. They spent about 20 minutes talking about how he felt, how he was being affected, and the context of his life—family, friends and romantic relationships. Jacob described everything being well, but having "always" felt terribly anxious. He now knows he is moving on past high school and is not sure how he is going to handle it. In those minutes, the counselor was aiming to gather basic information to have an understanding of his situation and context, while also striving to listen well and connect to Jacob empathically.

Shortly after the first 20 minutes or so he makes his desire for immediate help clear:

JACOB: [Speaking fast, tense.] Yeah, yeah, I don't know. I gotta tell you this is just about driving me crazy!

COUNSELOR: [Responding at his emotional level.] It is. It's that bad. It's just about driving you crazy.

JACOB: Yeah. I appreciate being able to tell you about it. But I was hoping you could tell me what to do about it. [He sounds a bit pleading here, as he is becoming more aware of and uncomfortable with his difficulties.]

COUNSELOR: I think I can help you with that. And it sounds like you are also saying that that was your view of how counseling would work—that you would tell me what you were going through and I would tell you how to make it better.

JACOB: Isn't that how counseling works?

COUNSELOR: It can be. I can help you with information and skills to help manage your anxiety. But I also want you to think about another way that counseling can help. If you come with the idea of talking about yourself in order to learn about yourself as I listen and share what I understand with you, you can learn and grow in ways that help you be much happier and reduce your anxiety.

JACOB: [Hesitant, starting to feel more anxious.] Oh, well, OK.

COUNSELOR: You are willing to consider that, but even just thinking about it has your anxiety going back up.

JACOB: [A bit bemused.] Yeah.

COUNSELOR: OK. And I can also help you with information and skills to help begin to reduce your anxiety.

JACOB: Great thanks [relieved].

COUNSELOR: That's a relief to you. First let's think about how you take care of yourself.

From this point, the counselor talks with him about key areas of self-care, including nutrition, exercise, habits around sleep, and engaging in recreational tasks that might help him reduce his anxiety. Her goals are to review basic concepts in self-care in these areas, to see how he is taking care of himself now and to find one or two areas in which he might begin to change. She will be clear that no few changes will change everything for him, but that even small changes can help him begin to take control of how he feels and to stem the tide of his anxiety.

In the next meetings she taught Jacob several skills that helped to put him in charge of his emotional reactions. She taught Jacob to evaluate his core thought patterns and to replace irrational and troubling thought patterns with rational, helpful ways of thinking. This process is associated with cognitive-behavioral therapies (CBT; Beck & Beck, 2011; Ellis & Dryden, 2007). She carefully helped Jacob understand that it involves changing long-term thought patterns and this can be powerful, but not a quick or easy fix.

Along with strategies for thought change, she taught Jacob to be his own behavior analyst, investigating the antecedents of his particularly anxious reactions and evaluating what behaviors or reactions he prompts within himself, rewards, or strives to ignore. These are concepts from behaviorism (Skinner, 1976) or behavior analysis (Pierce & Cheney, 2008).

Notice that when Jacob seemed to be asking for skills, his counselor first continued to respond empathically, then addressed his expectations for counseling, before switching to information providing/skill-teaching mode.

She let Jacob know right away that she could help with his request, maintained empathy as her primary mode of response to client communication, helped him think through his options of how to use counseling, and then addressed his request directly.

There were and always are many applications of empathy to grow self-awareness within the CBT and BT skill-teaching that Jacob's counselor provided. For a person to explore his deepest, mostly unconscious thoughts can be an emotional and scary experience, which requires a guide strong in empathy and unconditional positive regard. To begin to see what one does to stimulate his own mistaken behaviors, and how the mistaken behaviors are rewarded in his context can tap into the longing *not* to change, or fear of change, which, if not addressed in empathy and unconditional positive regard, can jeopardize a person like Jacob even continuing to the next session.

Counselor Judgment of Client Desire for Informational Guidance or Skill-Teaching, or that Basic Care Guidance is Needed

Some clients will not be as direct as Jacob. Latisha's first session at the community clinic was taken up with an extensive and required intake interview (an extensive set of questions required by the agency to inform treatment team decisions). As her counselor listened to Latisha in her second session, he sensed Latisha's frustration and discouragement. He understood that Latisha felt quite depressed and that she rarely asked for what she wanted in life and often drifted away from relationships as they got difficult. Their interchange deciding to take an integrative approach in her counseling follows.

LATISHA: [Speaking with little energy, sounding discouraged.] That's how it is. I get up every morning and get to work, but I hate it. It's so hard, like walking through a pool of molasses.

COUNSELOR: So you get yourself to work, but you have to force yourself through molasses.

LATISHA: Always, I hate it.

COUNSELOR: You hate it. Latisha, especially knowing how bad it is for you, how discouraged you feel, I want to talk some about what we can do in counseling.

LATISHA: [A bit surprised, brightening up a bit to listen.] OK.

COUNSELOR: First, in regard to our working together, knowing how you already see that you find it hard to assert your views with others, I want you to know that if you don't like the way we are working together in any way, I want you to let me know. Your work in counseling will likely be difficult at times, but if you were ever to feel so discouraged with it such that you might think of not continuing, I want you to let me know. In most cases, I can adjust how we are working together.

LATISHA: [Surprised, but pleased, at least tentatively.] OK. I thought there was probably just only one way and if it didn't work for me, then it just meant I have a really bad problem.

COUNSELOR: I'm getting the idea that that has been your way. If a relationship doesn't work out, you just assume it was your fault and move on.

LATISHA: Yeah, that's maybe true. So how long is this gonna take, our working together?

COUNSELOR: That's an important thing for us to talk about. I'm glad you asked. [Short pause to think.] Well, I don't know an exact amount of time. But one thought is that you have been feeling depressed for quite some time. It seems like your depressed feelings have been building over time. So, I have short-term, long-term and longer-term ideas.

LATISHA: OK, but I told you I don't want medicine. My mom has been on every medicine and it only got her addicted.

COUNSELOR: That's important to you—no medicine. I am not recommending that you meet with a physician to consider medications. I would rather you work through your difficulties in counseling.

LATISHA: OK. I'll try it.

COUNSELOR: You are willing to try it. [Pausing, with a bit of a grin to carefully tease Latisha a bit.] You are conceding to try my suggestions, but I haven't made them yet.

LATISHA: Good point. I guess that's what you were saying that I do.

COUNSELOR: That's what I'm thinking, so far. But before we run out of time today, I want to explain more of what I have in mind. Short-term I want to talk you through general advice for persons feeling great depression or anxiety regarding how to take care of yourself, mostly physically, that affects how you feel emotionally. Then I can also teach you skills designed to help you take greater control of your emotions, especially through uncovering and gradually changing deep-down thought patterns that have probably been affecting how you feel since before you were old enough to think about what you are thinking. But while doing these other parts of our work, I want you to keep in mind to come to each meeting ready to share the thoughts, feelings, experiences and events that are on your mind. As you do, my first and most important job is to listen, strive to understand what you are telling me of you and your context, then to share with you what I think I understand.

LATISHA: Wow, OK, that all sounds good. And I really mean that. [That last part was said in teasing her counselor back a little.]

COUNSELOR: You seem encouraged hearing what I have in mind. I'm glad. And also, I never answered the question that came up of how long to use counseling. I'm not sure, but I would suggest you think of 6 to 12 meetings, with us checking at least each third meeting on your satisfaction with our work.

LATISHA: OK.

The counselor reviewed very similar self-care information as with Jacob and pursued very similar skills. In our work, we have relied heavily on such information and skills from cognitive therapy and behaviorism with adults and adolescents who seemed to need information and skill-teaching within their counseling sessions.

We would also note of their interchange that even when suggesting integrating guidance and skill-teaching into their work, Latisha's counselor continued to respond empathically, addressing a theme of Latisha's ways of being that related to their work in counseling (agreeing, when she didn't know if she agreed), addressing what was going on between them in their working relationship. Plus he explained a structure for their work, a guide for a reasonably comprehensive use of counseling for her situation.

Time-Sensitive Imperatives, Crisis or Significant Client Impairment

There can be pressure to integrate direct intervention techniques into your therapeutic relationship from real or perceived time sensitivity, crisis or impending impairment. Pressure may come from your own desire to hurry the help to a person who is suffering. The pressure can come from a suffering client who wants to "make the problems go away—now!" The pressure may come from having a waiting list for services. We encourage you to stick with your work in therapeutic relationship as purely as possible, think through your decision to vary from your focus in relationship carefully, and resist making adjustments based on perceptions of pressure. Remember that your therapeutic relationship is often the most powerful tool that you and your client have for *efficient* work in counseling, including managing crises. Remember that "haste makes waste" and that therapy cannot be hurried.

A Time "Imperative" Example

Jeff can remember a time early in his work, serving as a middle-school counselor, he had a client who appeared to be choosing to fail, to stay back in middle school another year. In beginning work with Jenny, Jeff bought into the belief that he must convince her to work to get her grades up, pass the eighth grade and move on to high school. This brought Jeff and Jenny to cross-purposes: Jeff's goal was to get Jenny motivated and prepared for high school, but, as he learned, this was not her goal. After a few meetings at cross-purposes, Jenny explained, "Look, I'm small for my age, my friends are in the grade under me—why would I want to go on to high school this year?" But Jeff was a pressured (feeling pressured) young counselor. Jenny's point was counter to Jeff's value system (e.g., time is important, we should always be moving forward with most efficient pace).

At least with time, Jeff did accept Jenny's point of view, if for no other reason, Jeff came to see that they would get nothing done while he caused the two of them to work at cross-purposes. Dropping his agenda and focusing in what he came to think of as therapeutic relationship, Jenny ended up exploring with Jeff issues of friendship and feeling herself small and young compared to others—small beyond physical stature; her love of music—she and her best friend (a grade younger) hoped to form a band; her relationship with her parents—good but strained regarding her impending repeat of eighth grade, her own second thoughts regarding her decision.

They touched on these things only as their time together ran out. The irony is that out of pressure to help Jenny to a time-pressured solution, Jeff wasted valuable time. Had Jeff begun with a consistent focus on therapeutic relationship, which would have been the greatest benefit to Jenny's decision—who knows what valuable topics might have been addressed? But most importantly, they would have used their time together to better address Jenny's core sense of self and confidence issues. And while this work should be valued in and of itself, Jeff has since learned many times over that work on the core sense of self and confidence issues through therapeutic relationship consistently leads to the best client decisions.

Client Impairment

If clients are slipping into deep disorder, the counselor should carefully and quickly consider guiding the client through interventions to stabilize decline. For example, disorders within clinical depression or anxiety (i.e., significantly more than normally occurring down feelings or more than situational anxiety and normally occurring nervousness) can be self-perpetuating. Persons slipping into great depression or anxiety often have disrupted sleep, diet, exercise and life enjoyment activities.

It doesn't matter whether these areas of functioning are a cause or effect of disorder—either way, making changes has positive effects and can help begin to stem the tide of growing disorder. Beyond better health, it often helps persons who are becoming clinically depressed to decide and begin at least some small positive steps. Doing so can become self-rewarding and the feeling of accomplishment grows. Similarly, beyond better health, we have found that taking action in self-care often helps persons who are slipping into clinical levels of anxiety begin to take back control.

Especially with depression, generally our goal in such an interchange is to reach agreement on one or two positive steps to take in self-care before our next session. If a client were to persistently resist any positive steps, we would first attend empathically to her negative reactions, gaining an enhanced understanding of her. If she absolutely would not agree to any positive steps, we would worry about suicidality and follow procedures of managing client crises with therapeutic relationship skills (Chapter 10).

However, with that said, we remind our clients when prompting better self-care that each step in self-care is an important step, but no step alone is *the solution*. And we remind our clients, and ourselves, that the most important work is the client's self-expressive work in counseling—the therapeutic relationship.

Key Questions to Consider in Deciding When to Do More and When to Remain More Exclusively Focused on Your Core Therapeutic Relationship

1.   Would doing more help your client perceive unconditional positive regard and empathy?

- Not providing information or skills that your client is asking for or strongly implying desire for would seem unaccepting, if it is reasonably clear that she wants such help.
- If the additional information or skills would shut down client communication, i.e., the two of you solving a "surface area" problem vs. following a self-expressive counseling process to critical core personal issues, then it would seem more helpful to help your client continue work focused primarily in therapeutic relationship, which of course often means helping him understand how this self-expressive work can be helpful to *him* (remember this should usually be an individualized explanation—see Chapter 8). You would need to address his stated or implied desire/expectation, then explain options and what you recommend for him and why.
- In either case, remember to explain counseling options in such a way to make your client an equal partner in making an informed decision for her use of counseling.

2.   What is going on with you related to your inclination to begin work beyond the focus of your core therapeutic relationship skills?

- Do you feel a strong drive to "do for," or take care of your client, as if she is a fragile being? This relates back to question 1 above. If a significant part of you sees her as incapable, then you are not maintaining the unconditional positive regard that would have you seeing her as capable; your negative view of her, perhaps beneath awareness, may be confirming her view that she is incapable of caring for herself.
- Might you be avoiding connecting, choosing to work more on the problem-solving surface, perhaps because something about him is hard to like? Perhaps something about him pushes a button of being too much like you? And thus you think he should do what you do? Or you find him hard to like as if you are looking at your own faults? Perhaps you find him hard to like as he crosses against strongly held values?
- Or might you feel the urge to problem-solve because you perhaps find her too easy to like? Maybe you feel yourself just wanting to do what

she wants, whether you know it to be best or not? Maybe you see that she could learn from self-expression regarding her suffering, but you feel you can barely stand to watch her hurting? Remember: the shortest line from where she is now to where she needs to be is rarely straight and obvious—if it was, wouldn't she already see that path? Wouldn't she already be on it?

3.   What does your client want and why? In discerning what your client wants, go beyond what is being asked or not asked for. Go to the level of client conceptualization. What does her whole self (words, actions, thoughts, inner thoughts, surface feelings, deeper feelings, way of being and context) tell you that she really wants? Remember that at least early in your work, you may understand her and her wants better than she does herself. Through your sensitive empathy, she will come to know herself more.

Consider these questions and reminders, especially as you read the next couple of subsections.

Client Who Asks for New Skills, but Does Not Apply Them

There are exceptions to every guideline. We have known of many times in which clients seemed to be asking and ready for informational guidance and new skills, but then seemed not to apply the new skills, or to apply them with so little heart that any effect was minuscule. An interchange that exemplifies such an exception follows.

Ramon was clear from the beginning that he didn't want all that touchy-feely counseling stuff and he didn't want to talk about himself or his family. Rather, he wanted help making his low motivation and difficult feelings go away, so that he could do his best on the upcoming standardized tests at his school. His counselor, Ms. McFerrin, had agreed to his request. She talked him through self-care and emotional regulation skills for his strongly negative feelings, which could be considered an anxious depression, and which seemed to be crushing his motivation. Because his request seemed reasonable, and also because their work time up to the exam was limited, Ms. McFerrin decided that it made sense to work with Ramon to solve the problem of his anxious depression, low motivation and discouraged feelings. So in each of their first meetings, she worked to discern his areas of difficulty, then introduced new skills, which she planned for him to practice between meetings. In their second meeting, she found that Ramon had not practiced his skills, but he may have had understandable reasons not to—other things that got in the way—and Ms. McFerrin also reasoned that maybe the first skill set she provided Ramon did not happen to be the best fit. However, in their third meeting it became apparent that again Ramon had not applied the guidance or skills, or only half-heartily applied them.

COUNSELOR: [Reflecting.] So you didn't really have time for that this week, or at least not much. And you've still felt really bad. You so much wish for things to be different.

RAMON: Yeah. I do. But I guess nothing will help.

COUNSELOR: [Reflecting.] You are thinking maybe nothing will help. [Then, offering her view and opening the door to restructuring their work.] Ramon, I'm not willing to accept that. I know that you hadn't wanted to do "touchy-feely" work or to talk about yourself much, but sometimes when we are experiencing negative feelings, it is wrong to just make them go away. Sometimes there is something of ourselves that we really need to learn and change. Especially hearing you say that even though you are hurting, nothing can be done, I just have to tell you I disagree. Rather than there being nothing that can be done, we might just be trying to do the wrong thing.

RAMON: [Grinning a bit.] I knew you were going to go there. You counselors are all alike. [Becomes serious over a pause.] Look, here's the thing. There are some parts I just can't tell you, just can't talk about. Can you be OK with that?

COUNSELOR: There is something, some parts of your experience that you cannot tell me. Yes. I can be OK with that. If the privacy of what you say is what holds you back, then you should understand that what you say to me is confidential, with only a few limits. [She explained confidentiality and its limits to Ramon at this point.]

RAMON: Well yeah, there might be some stuff that's illegal, but also there's just some stuff that . . . [Pause] I don't know.

COUNSELOR: You are not sure about something. It seems like you are thinking you are more open to talking about yourself in counseling, but also you have some hesitation.

RAMON: [Perplexed, not knowing what to say.] Yeah, I guess so.

COUNSELOR: So what I have in mind is that I can still suggest new skills or activities for you from time to time, but mostly I think you should focus on letting me know who you are—and learning about yourself in that process.

RAMON: [Quizzical look.]

COUNSELOR: Most of us think we know ourselves pretty well. But when we focus on ourselves in counseling, with a counselor seeing us from the outside, but as we see ourselves, we learn all kinds of new stuff. And in this process, you might learn what you need to from these painful feelings—you might learn why you have them; not so much why as in, "What's wrong," but why as in, "What's next in your development."

Clients for Whom Requests for New Skills Seems to Be Avoidance

Clients who seem to be avoiding talking about something important present another reason to maintain your focus in therapeutic relationship, rather than guidance and skill-teaching. For example, one can easily understand how persons grieving the death of a loved one, or persons who had been abused or even recently raped might just want the bad feelings to go away. We have known many clients suffering in these ways to come to counseling because their suffering was affecting their functioning or their painful feelings felt overwhelming, with the expectation that in counseling they would learn to make the bad feelings go away, not to talk more about their loss or traumatic abuse.

In each case, we have responded that we can help with guidance and new skills to reduce bad feelings, but also explained that it may not be possible or helpful to make the bad feelings completely go away. With persons grieving a death, we have suggested that while difficult, talking about his loss and his relationship with the loved one who died might open the door to what his grief means to him, and what it means that might come next in his development in order to move on. With persons recovering from traumatic abuse, we have explained how we can understand that she would not want to talk more about the abuse, "If talking about it makes you feel worse, it makes sense that you would not want to come to counseling to talk about it. But it may be that not talking about it is resulting in the symptoms you are having. Talking about it may help you work through the harm and hurt of what he did to you, instead of staying trapped in it."

Often in such situations, we need to explain to our client how talking about the loss or trauma would be different in counseling. For example, our client might need to hear and consider that the notion of talking "all the way through" an issue in counseling is different from saying the same things over with friends or family. Or he might need to consider how the counseling process is quite different than constant, if brief and upsetting, bouts of thinking about the trauma, which one might describe as fixated on the trauma, without thinking it through. Or he might need to hear and consider how the reflecting process in counseling can serve to uncover hidden thoughts, feelings, and connections between thoughts, feelings and actions that he is not likely to uncover without hearing how you see him as you get to know him, from your sensitive and objective view. These explanations or phenomena are addressed in earlier chapters, including Chapters 2–4 and 8.

Often in agency settings counselors have information of each client's presenting problem as well as history and context related to the problem. In school settings, counselors normally begin counseling without extensive information about the client's presenting problem, history and context. And in both settings, counselors often work with clients without knowing that the client is holding something inside that she really needs to say, but is avoiding saying. Empathy is the answer to that dilemma. If attending with sensitivity to your client's communication, striving to feel what she feels, listening to what she does not say, to her pauses, to how she says what she says as much as what she says, you will be able to reflect that there seems to be something she needs to say, but is holding back from. An example of such an interchange follows.

COUNSELOR: Reena, what you are telling me about your work and your plans sounds important to you. And I notice that when you pause or come to the end of what you can think to say, you become anxious.

REENA: Well, yes. It's weird to sit silently looking at a person without talking.

COUNSELOR: Yes. Those silent moments that can happen in counseling are not like usual conversation and I think they can make a lot of people feel at least a little nervous in counseling. But to make the best use of counseling, you may have to sit with that discomfort a bit, see what comes to mind and say that. Often I find that when people have something that deep down they think they maybe should say in counseling, but are not sure if they want to, it gets hard to think of anything else to say.

REENA: [After what felt like a long pause, she starts tentatively.] Well, OK, but I really just want to feel better. I mean it's not just my relationship at work, but I have a boyfriend, too—well, sort of. [Another long pause, becoming anxious, then shifting the subject.] But can't you just help me feel better?

COUNSELOR: I might be able to help you with information and skills just to feel better. We can try that and it may help. But it also seems, like just now, like there is something you were thinking to say, but then stopped.

REENA: Well [another pause]. See, my relationship with my boyfriend is good, but there's some stuff that's gone on that . . . [She pauses about to speak, then seems to give up on how to say it.] Well, it's just hard to say.

COUNSELOR: So, there is something about your relationship with your boyfriend and it's hard to say. It seems it is really big to you. I encourage you to just tell me at the pace that you are ready.

REENA: [Beginning to cry.] Well, I really wanted a relationship with him. I thought he was the best. Every girl wanted him. My mother loves him. But . . . then. [Stops talking and just cries. After a moment, she looks up at her counselor, as if to say, "What do we do next?"]

COUNSELOR: There is something about him that is very hard to say. I notice you said you *wanted* [emphasizing the past tense of Reena's statement] a relationship with him.

REENA: Yes. I don't know how to feel about him now.

From this point, Reena continues to gradually tell of having been raped by him. She blames herself. She is confused. If the counselor had pushed ahead with her request to just learn how to make the feelings go away, the positive effects of new guidance would have been overwhelmed by Reena's inner turmoil and confusion. She may have concluded from a failed and misguided counseling attempt that she was broken, that she could not be fixed by the counselor, and thus is "unfixable." She would not have gotten the chance to tell the safe, caring person of her counselor what had happened. She would not have had the opportunity to sort through what the trauma meant to her, how it changed her views of herself and others. She would not even have gained access to help with information on what her options are in programs and resources meant for persons who have been similarly traumatized.

Go Slow with "Teachable Moments"

There is the expression among educators who work with youth of the "teachable moment." It refers to a moment in which, outside of a planned curriculum, an opportunity presents itself to help a youth develop further with a particular skill or concept. For example, in a time when Nancy and Jeff ran camps for children in therapy following founded cases of abuse, Jeff helped a child out of the water and stumbled into a teachable moment. Sheree had panicked in the water—it was a river-based activity in which the girls were quite safe, but in which the water still seemed dangerous to a child—each child needed only to ask and an adult could immediately help them out. When helping Sheree out, she was making it clear what she wanted, and Jeff was with her and moving her to the shore, but she was staying upset and Jeff wanted her to learn more to calm herself and be direct in saying what he wanted rather than letting her emotional upset speak for her. So, while supporting her and beginning to move to shore, Jeff asked Sheree, "Tell me in words. Use your words to tell me what you want." And in the second it took her to say, "I want out," they both were standing on the shallow shore.

In the van heading home that day, Sheree told the story to one of the camp adults. She related it to what she was also learning about using her words to let a safe adult know, about situations that feel wrong, unsafe or leading to abuse. But this was a mentoring relationship. Along with all the context of such a camp, a mentoring relationship can be powerful. But in a counseling relationship, a therapeutic relationship, Sheree has more and different opportunities to develop than in the mentoring relationship. Sheree did her individual counseling work through the year in child-centered play therapy with Nancy. In that work, she worked on her evaluation of who she is and who she wants to be. She developed a realistic view of herself, including her many competencies. She came to accept and trust herself, to tap into her internal resources as a guide much more than to doubt herself. If Nancy had tried for similar such teachable moments in her individual counseling, it would have undermined vs. bolstered her growing assertiveness. It would have gotten in the way of her self-reflective process: To try for teachable moments in her individual counseling risks, trading short-term gain for the much greater long-term benefit of a therapeutic relationship.

Common Problems

We think of therapeutic relationship skills and counselor guidance on a continuum. Different contexts require more of one than the other, setting up two directions of errors.

Too Conservative in the Balance—Not Bringing Your Whole Self

The caricature of a counselor's work focused in therapeutic relationship is the counselor driving the client crazy by repeating back what she says. When beginning counselors err in this direction, we usually find that the counselor is inhibited in bringing herself into the relationship, afraid that if she does she will make terrible mistakes. Ironically, in failing to integrate herself into her therapeutic relationships, she is failing to form therapeutic relationships. So our advice in this situation is for the counselor to aim for the core principles of therapeutic relationships while also freeing up to be herself, mistakes and all. It is easier to correct mistakes made with the intention to connect than to correct the lack of therapeutic connection born of inhibited and stilted counselor responses.

Too Liberal in the Balance—Too Much Information!

"Too much information!" (TMI) has become an icon of communication meaning that the speaker has given far too much personal information. We find that TMI could be extended to the work of counselors. Counselor-TMI usually happens from beginning counselors trying too hard to help vs. trusting the counseling process. It seems that the counselor is doubting the counseling process, perhaps believing that his client is unable to help herself, unable to cope with life without the new skills that he would teach or guidance that he would provide.

With counselor-TMI, we find it helpful to help the beginning counselor explore or reexplore his view of human nature, emphasizing where this doubt may come from, and reviewing the predominant views of human nature that underlie most counseling approaches, with which we began *The Heart of Counseling*. As in many counseling sessions, once awareness of the error and its meaning to the individual are experienced, the individual is far along on his path toward change. At that point we would encourage the counselor to go into his next session ready with his customized self-talk that reminds him to trust the counseling process and his client's capacities. In this way, he can continue to be open to providing skill-teaching and guidance, but without his thinking that he "has to" teach or guide.

Activities and Resources for Further Learning

- Reconsider and reanswer the questions of the focus activity for this chapter. How have your answers shifted through your study of this chapter?
- Review: Tursi and Cochran (2006). Then consider the major counseling theories with which you are familiar. Speculate possibilities, on your own or with a small group of peers, how all or some of the tasks of each theory may naturally be accomplished through therapeutic

relationships. For example, can you describe, write out, a scenario in which the client's narrative of her life naturally changes through therapeutic relationship (i.e., narrative therapy—White & Epston, 1990), or in which a client begins to accomplish some of the tasks associated with mindfulness (Brown, Marquis, & Guiffrida, 2013; Greason & Cashwell, 2009)?

- Think of as many examples as you can of scenarios in which a client may prefer an informational guidance or skill-teaching approach to counseling, but in which it may be better to maintain a focus in client self-expression and therapeutic relationship, so long as the client may be willing. Share your scenarios with peers. Discuss and/or role-play how you might talk with each client about her/his directions for use of counseling.

- Imagine on your own or brainstorm with a group issues or situations in which you might feel pulled to shift to an informational guidance or skill teaching approach to counseling. Explain what your motivation would likely be in each case. Decide which of the situations you would make the shift and which not. Then decide which of the situations in which you would not make the shift that the client is likely to need explanation from you of what you are doing in his counseling and why (e.g., how counseling may work for him and why). Write out or practice your wording with a partner.

- In the section "Clients for Whom Requests for New Skills Seems to Be Avoidance" (page 294), three situations are briefly noted in which, while difficult, it might be best for a client to focus in the self-expressive work of therapeutic relationship. Create scenarios for each situation. Role-play or write out the wording that you may use in communicating how and why the client might best use counseling.

- Whether you consider your work person-centered or not, we encourage you to consider some of the recent great works of the person-centered approach. In our view, such works provide thoughtful analysis of the extent and power of a therapeutic relationship as well as an integrative therapeutic relationship. We find reading such thoughtful essays and chapters helpful, even when we do not fully agree. Suggestions to get you started in this study include: Cooper, Watson and Holldampf (2013), Cornelius-White, Motschnig-Pitric, and Lux (2013), Ladd (2012), Mearns, Thorne, and McLeod (2013), and Wilkins (2009).

References

Beck, J.S., & Beck, A.T. (2011). *Cognitive behavior therapy: Basics and beyond* (2nd ed.). New York: Guilford.

Brown, A.P., Marquis, A., & Guiffrida, D.A. (2013). Mindfulness-based interventions in counseling. *Journal of Counseling & Development, 91*, 96–104.

Cooper, M., Watson, J.C., & Holldampf, D. (2013). *Person-centered and experiential therapies work*. Ross-on-Wye: PCCS Books.

Cornelius-White, J.H.D., Motschnig-Pitric, R., & Lux, M. (2013). *Interdisciplinary handbook of the person-centered approach: Research and theory*. New York: Springer.

Ellis, A., & Dryden, W. (2007). *The practice of rational emotive therapy* (2nd ed.). New York: Springer.

Ginsberg, B.G. (1997). *Relationship enhancement family therapy*. Hoboken, NJ: Wiley.

Greason, P.B., & Cashwell, C.S. (2009). Mindfulness and counseling self-efficacy: The mediating role of attention and empathy. *Counselor Education and Supervision, 49*, 2–19.

Guerney, B.G., Jr. (1977). *Relationship enhancement: Skill-training programs for therapy, problem prevention, and enrichment*. Hoboken, NJ: Jossey-Bass.

Ladd, P.D. (2012). *Person-centered diagnosis and treatment planning in mental health: A model for empowering clients*. Philadelphia, PA: Kingsley.

Mearns, D., Thorne, B., & McLeod, J. (2013). *Person-centred counselling in action*. Thousand Oaks, CA: Sage.

Pierce, W.D., & Cheney, C.D. (2008). *Behavior analysis and learning* (4th ed.). New York: Psychology Press.

Scuka, R.F. (2005). *Relationship enhancement therapy: Healing through deep empathy and intimate dialogue*. New York: Routledge.

Skinner, B.F. (1976). *About behaviorism*. New York: Knopf-Doubleday.

Tursi, M.M., & Cochran, J.L. (2006). Cognitive-behavioral tasks accomplished in a person-centered relational framework. *Journal of Counseling and Development, 84*, 387–397.

White, M., & Epston, D. (1990). *Narrative means to therapeutic ends*. New York: Norton.

Wilkins, P. (2009). *Person-centered therapy: 100 key points*. New York: Wiley.

Pre-Chapter Quote

Moustakas, C. (1995). *Being-in, being-for, being-with*. Northvale, NJ: Aronson (p. 70).

14 HEART AND MIND
Major Counseling Theories and Therapeutic Relationships

Knowledge is coterminous with caring and not in opposition to it. If you care about someone or something, you wish to use all your talents, including the intellectual, to arrive at contact with an understanding of the situation. Knowledge can be an important ingredient of compassion; a reflection, in part, of how much you care.

David Brandon

Primary Skill Objectives

- Explain and give examples of how your expertise in an array of counseling theories may enhance your work in therapeutic relationships.
- Generate possibilities for an integrative approach to counseling that maintains your focus in therapeutic relationships, while also going beyond with tasks and activities from action-oriented counseling theories.
- Explain common problems or challenges in such integrative approaches.

Focus Activity

If your experience is like ours, you might be appreciating what you are learning of counseling skills, but also studying counseling theories and falling in love with each new, so different, and often mind-blowing way of thinking of human nature and change. You are fascinated with each new line of thought and love learning each, but you wonder: How can each be true, when they are so different? Can they work together, when they would work so differently? How could you integrate each of these amazing and different ways of thinking into your work as counselor and still focus on the therapeutic relationship that you are learning is so powerful and so essential?

Take time to contemplate these questions, journal and discuss. In this chapter, we show examples of how major counseling theories can support, enhance, and work within your therapeutic relationships.

Examples of Major Counseling/Psychotherapy Theories Affecting or Informing the Work of Therapeutic Relationships

Existential Therapy

We have long been influenced by the great concepts of existentialism that we see as underlying much of modern counseling. Yet they are concepts that were not always the accepted points of view that they are today: That persons can change, and that change comes through new experiences and meaning made of new experiences. Every passing moment of life offers opportunities. This influence in our thought comes from having studied existential therapy (Yalom & Josselson, 2011), as well as having studied just a bit of philosophy, as well as having experienced the loss of loved ones at critical ages, thus learning albeit sometimes the hard way, the beauty and value of existence, and feeling the strong drive, within an existence that we know is finite, to make the most that we possibly can of our time.

So in a counseling session, we are attuned to notice when a client seems to feel he has "all the time in the world." Consider a young teenager who has developed some interest in a new career idea for after graduation, but yet feels that graduation is far away. As we strive to see him as he is, we also see him through the filter of our world view, and thus we might reflect with a view of the meaning he makes of his experience and his perception of the finite, "You like that idea. It feels right and exciting! [Shifting naturally from excitement to something more like complacency as we realize his shift.] And it seems that a year to commit to action is a relaxing distance. [Now focusing on the shift, as realizing it] At first you felt a strong urge to move forward, then settled back."

Consider a client who seems to be experiencing her feelings as unchanging. From our world view influenced by the concepts of existential therapy, we might reflect "And how you feel right now feels like how you will always feel." But if our point of view is too far from and thus unacceptable to her, she may correct us: "But this is how I have felt for a very long time." Knowing it as her right and responsibility to correct for her true self-expression in the therapeutic relationship we are forming, of course we accept correction: "That is how it is for you, maybe not for always, but for a long time you have felt this way and so you expect that to continue for a long time." Thus, we have accepted her correction, but also her point of view seems to be already opening from interacting with our world view within therapeutic relationship. Our views shaped by existential thought help us to both value and accept her experience as she sees it, and maintain a constant knowing that she can and will change.

To another client we might reflect: "Especially with what you've gone through, you feel compelled to make the most of each moment." With this and other example reflections of this section, we would not hold the intention of shaping clients toward particular philosophical points of view. Rather, the philosophical points of view have shaped how we see others. The philosophical points of view have shaped who we are in therapeutic relationships with others. Our intent is to respond purely to each client's true experience, but our responses are shaped by our world view, influenced by all our studies.

Psychoanalytic Concepts

And there are notions of Sigmund Freud's that have shaped our views of clients' communications. For example, when working with a client who seems not to see an important part of his experience, we might think of the concept of denial (Luborsky, O'Reilly-Landry, & Arlow, 2011) and reflect, "I notice you talk about everything except that series of grades and what they mean for your choices. I'm guessing it's hard for you to face what that might mean." Or with another client who we knew was often mad at herself for a particular kind of mistake, then is very angry with an acquaintance for the same thing, knowing the concept of projection (Luborsky et al. 2011) might help us to see and reflect "that you don't like when you are that way, and it irks you terribly when she does that."

Jungian Concepts

The Jungian concept of the push–pull or dark sidelight side of personalities, of trait opposites within the person (Douglas, 2011), might have us reflect, "So there's a part of you that feels compelled to ask her, and another part that screams 'wait!'"

Cognitive Therapies

Jeff has significant background in cognitive therapies. Concepts of these therapies have greatly influenced our world views and thus our therapeutic relationships with clients. From Jeff's studies of common irrational thoughts identified in REBT (Ellis & Dryden, 2007), it has become automatic for Jeff to hear the thought driving a client's strong emotions when striving for empathy. Meaning to reflect the emotion, Jeff's words are the thought, while his tone captures the emotional experience of the moment: "What hurts so much is your knowing it isn't fair, while you have such a strong thought that it really should be fair! You're seeing that it is wrong for him to carry on like that, wrong because it isn't fair and so your urge is to do just about anything to make it stop!"

Or knowing common patterns in thought errors from cognitive therapy (Beck & Beck, 2011), Jeff might naturally see the error in a client's logic and reflect, "So, when your mom reacted that way, it really hurt. So, now when anyone's reaction looks even a little like that, your guard goes up. It's like in the back of your mind you're thinking, 'This will hurt terribly and I won't be able to stand it. So, I must stop it now!'." Or to another client, "So, it's really only Jeanna and your teacher last year who called you that, but that *feels* like *everybody*."

Narrative Therapy

From the core concept of narrative therapy (White & Epston, 1990) we are reminded that "everyone's stories about others are always about themselves." In other words, no matter what your client is telling you about, he cannot help but be telling you about his experience. And so it is just a step further to begin to listen for core beliefs about self and others implied through the perceived story of one's life, the narrative, that has come to stand in place of meaning. And from this view of narrative coming to stand for meaning, it is not hard to see that the narrative has already and is apt to continue to change over time. From this mind-set, we might reflect, "You're knowing that you have been wronged in this situation. [Seeing that the client heartily agrees] I'm starting to see that that is what you see the pattern of your life as being: you put yourself out there for others, then they wrong you, then you turn your back on them."

Of course, with any such lengthy, analytic reflection, we are especially ready to accept correction or to respond empathically to a client's reaction. For example, if to the above, the client says, "Well I don't turn my back on them for a long time. Almost never. I try not to." Then we might respond, "Something about the way I said that, the way I misunderstood you hurt. It seems the part that I did not get right is to understand the lengths that you will go to for others. It's not just that you put yourself out there once, but that you try and try and only give up, only turn your back after you conclude that you just could not possibly have an alternative."

Reality Therapy and/or Adlerian Therapy

From Adlerian therapy (e.g., Mosak & Maniacci, 2011) we internalized the concept that all behavior, including mistaken behavior, is goal driven. From reality therapy (Wubbolding, 2010), the notion that there is sometimes a mismatch between goals and actions is reinforced. These concepts influence our perception of clients, such that we might reflect, "I know that a big part of what you want is to be free of all that pressure. And I see that you continue to put yourself in high pressure situations." Further, from Glasser's notion of basic needs (1999), we regularly see the choices between areas of needs in clients' experience, shaping such reflections as, "One of the things you find yourself wanting is power and control, but in achieving that, you find that you give up the freedom and fun that you also value" or "You see yourself as working to survive right now, telling yourself that you will work to fit in or have a sense of belonging with others later."

Family Systems

And of course when we first studied family therapies (e.g., Goldenberg, Goldenberg, & Pelavin, 2011), it opened our minds to seeing the world as systems of interactions. These also often inhabit our reflections, as in, "It seems that the two of you are in a pattern or a system of interactions: You want him in your life and let him know that, but then the more he pushes forward, the more you pull back, and the more you pull back, the more he pushes forward." Helping your client see the patterns of interactions as patterns that she is describing even without meaning to can help her make better, more conscious choices for herself within the system of interaction.

The Person-Centered Approach

And of course, last but certainly not least for us, our view of our clients and the world are significantly influenced by the person-centered approach (PCA; e.g., Raskin, Rogers, & Witty, 2011). Through our emersion in the PCA, we developed a greater reverence and a much more subtle understanding of the core conditions. But the PCA can be much more than the core conditions and therapeutic relationship. From the PCA we have learned a deep respect for each client's potential and the power of the self-expressive therapeutic process. And we have been led far through our own development, including openness to the world of many theories and infinite ideas. This continues, and for this we are grateful.

Integrative Case Scenarios

Therapeutic Relationship Qualities Maintained Throughout Cognitive-Behavioral Work with a Student Struggling with Test Anxiety

Assume you are the counselor in the following scenario. You gave a workshop for the teachers at your school about test anxiety. You presented anxiety as a possible explanation for students whose work in daily assignments and class participation suggests they are quite bright and learning well, but perform very poorly on tests, especially high stakes tests. And you present test anxiety as an emotional condition that can be treated in counseling. You explain how beliefs of self and others are felt, affect the student and her performance, even when they are felt beneath a conscious level.

A few days later, Mr. McCrae comes to see you about Jamila. The two of you discuss that she seems to fit the description you presented of a student struggling with test anxiety. You agree to follow up with her and schedule meeting times. In your first meeting, Jamila explains that she doesn't really want counseling, but is willing to try this as Mr. McCrae sees it as important for her. You spend some time hoping to get to know her, to connect through the therapeutic listening process, but Jamila seems closed to that. She begins to talk about her hopes of the future as you reflect her longing to perform well on tests. In that moment, your dialog went something like the following.

COUNSELOR: [Expressing empathy of her process.] You were starting to explain what you hope for with college and how much you want it, but then you seemed to just stop.

JAMILA: Yes. It is what I want. And I *really* wish it could come true, but I'm not doing it. So I don't know. And I really don't want to talk about all that. I just want to know what to do.

COUNSELOR: This is quite hard for you, both your difficulties in succeeding toward your dreams, and your work in counseling.

JAMILA: [Exasperated.] Yes. Maybe there's just no help; no point.

COUNSELOR: [Responding with empathy first, but feeling the intensity of Jamila's upset and so shifting to skill-teaching, but after empathically noting one more important seeming way of being for Jamila.] It hurts so much that it feels that way to you right now. As I think you know from Mr. McCrae, I have a set of skills that I want you to learn that can help you improve your performance on tests. If I could make one more comment before we start, I get that your frustration, your struggle and hurt is intense, very upsetting; but I also notice that you keep yourself well composed on the outside, while bottling up *turmoil* on the inside.

JAMILA: [Becoming the most openly emotional yet.] Yes, and all this talking about it makes it harder to hold it in. So, please, if you have suggestions?

COUNSELOR: Yes. OK. What I want you to learn is how your thinking affects how you do on tests. [You see that Jamila looks interested and is calming with the beginning of skill-teaching.] The thoughts that matter would not be so much the kind of everyday, on-the-surface thinking, but some of the deep-down beliefs about yourself and others, and what is possible in relationships. For most of us, these beliefs began in childhood, long before we could evaluate them logically. [Pauses to check in with Jamila.] You seem interested, intrigued about that, but also maybe a little skeptical.

JAMILA: Oh, I don't mean that. Sorry. But how can it be that we have beliefs before we can think?

COUNSELOR: I know you meant no disrespect. You strike me as *always* respectful, but this doesn't make any sense yet.

At this point you share a version of the "Baby A and Baby B" story from Chapter 1 (page 12) and the explanation of self-talk that analogizes beliefs from early childhood to background music at a gym, also from Chapter 1 (pages 14–15). From these explanations, Jamila seems to be intrigued and getting it. You reflect this change: "I think you get what I am saying. Now you seem mostly just intrigued." Jamila nods. So you continue to explain Ellis' ABC model from REBT (Ellis & Dryden, 2007). You explain how most of us think that activating events cause consequences (e.g., "Tests make me nervous;" or "[to a loved one in an argument] you make me so mad!"); but in fact, events interact with those background thoughts, and the interaction can produce consequences like the test performance that does not represent what you know.

JAMILA: But I'm not nervous in tests. I don't feel anything.
COUNSELOR: [Knowing it's almost always best to reflect doubt, even if it can't yet be explained away.] So you're intrigued with these ideas, but there is that catch that makes you not sure it applies to you. [Knowing the time and that the concepts can be true, even when not initially obvious.] I want you to hang in with me. I've oversimplified in explaining. I think I have to ask you to try this, to work with me, before it quite makes sense.
JAMILA: [Nods her "OK."]
COUNSELOR: So let me ask you, between now and our next meeting, to stop 1–2 times per day; think back to times that day that you felt some sort of stress, at least a moderate level of emotion.

You continue to draw out an outline for journaling, with a line or two to describe the event, a line or two to try to write in single words for emotions, then the rest of the page to write free rambling thoughts. Midway through this explanation you gave the 5-minute warning to ending.

JAMILA: [Is saying OK, but seems apprehensive.] OK. I think I can do that.
COUNSELOR: You do, but you are not quite sure, a bit apprehensive.
JAMILA: [Nods and exhales relief at having this accepted.]
COUNSELOR: OK. So three things I want you to remember from now to the next time we meet: (1) This work is not easy or simple, but I have a good feeling that it will work for you [the therapeutic connection that you and Jamila have built, through empathy and unconditional positive regard combined with action based on understanding her, gives you the right to make such a statement and the likelihood that she will accept it]. (2) Write down any thoughts, whether they seem related and logical or not. The silly or "crazy" seeming ones may be helpful. [Checking to see that she is still listening and engaged.] (3) What I am asking you to do is not easy. If you don't get as much of it done as I ask and you hope, we will continue next week either way.

When she returns, she explains that she has not written it down, but she has thought about it. But when you ask what she thought, she responds with doubts of it making sense for her instead of thoughts from stressful times through the week.

JAMILA: I just know that I feel fine with tests. I just don't know what happens.

COUNSELOR: [So you go with that, accepting her apparent reluctance.] More than journaling, you mostly wondered if this can make sense for you. Well, let's try doing this together. As you feel fine during tests, but you do feel stressed about school and your future, can you think of another time that you feel that stress?

JAMILA: Well, I know right when I'm about to get my grade, I'm feeling, "Oh my God, Oh my God; this is gonna be terrible. I can't look!"

Continuing to increase her self-awareness through reflection, while searching her expression for thoughts of self and others, you uncover the question in her mind, "What will others think?" To which you reflect, "A part of that strong emotion before your grade is a worry about what others will think." You question for the thought behind the thought, "And when you think that 'others,' who comes to mind first?" Jamila describes picturing her parents, but explains:

JAMILA: Well my parents, but I know they know I'm trying.

COUNSELOR: So you parent can represent this "other" who may think critically. You know they know you are trying, but still you have some worry of what they will think of you.

JAMILA: Well, they always say they will love me no matter what.

COUNSELOR: They say that. And I get the idea that a part of you knows they will and a part of you doubts [seeing Jamila's reaction you soften the statement] doubts, at least a little.

You continue this way with Jamila across a few sessions, balancing accepting her as she is, attending to her emotional experience, with also questioning for the thought behind the thought, one step at a time. In this process of attending to her as a person and to the experience she expresses while teaching the skill of discovering and evaluating troubling thoughts, you uncover her fear that she will make her parents feel depressed. You stop to review the ABC model, making the point that the activating event (her low grade) cannot cause consequences in her parents (their feeling depressed); rather, the event interacts with their thoughts of what must be and that it would be the interaction that produces their depressed feelings.

Jamila half accepts this, which is normal in CBT work—old beliefs do not change without great practice. You accept and reflect her sort of agreement and her difficulty in letting go of long-standing ways of thinking. From there you discover the tragedy of her brother's experience and her parents' hurting for him. From there you discover her drive to be perfect for them, as if an anecdote for their hurt over her brother. And from there her thought and fear that she may not be loved if she cannot perform for them, to succeed to her potential in school, college and life.

Each step along the way is slow—as meaningful, important change always seems to be. Within each step you respond with empathy—the things she is discovering are not easy and she needs connection with you to keep going. The things she is discovering hurt and press fears at her core. So, you attend in order for Jamila to feel cared for, accepted, and to hear her experience back. You know, and at times reflect, her tendency to look cool, while keeping the turmoil stuffed inside. You don't push to any next thought before seeing that she is ready.

Throughout this process, which felt excruciatingly slow at times but was actually about seven meetings of 30–45 minutes, depending on her school schedule, across two months, Jamila begins to change and report increasingly better focus on tests (along the way, she discovered her anxious feelings during tests that she had previously stuffed deeply away). And her test grades began to bear results.

With your help, she has pushed herself through a gauntlet of fears to face, then evaluate succeeding fear after deeper fear. And she changed her thinking. The old thoughts didn't go away, but were brought into awareness, where she could evaluate them, see the error and the logical alternative, but also to accept herself enough to think the logical now thought, while still nagged by the old belief. And she had gained a skill with which to continue to work on the nagging old beliefs, as well as to discover more.

You ended after several sessions as your schedule is tight and she didn't want to miss class time. Months later you came across her taking tickets at a school charity event that her club was sponsoring. She pulled you from the line to explain that she was doing better in school, but more than that the work had changed her life. Jamila explained that she applies the new way of seeing herself and others in all areas of her life. She gave you a tiny hug and moved you through the line to attend to the next customers.

We would like to note that work like the counselor's above requires expertise at both therapeutic relationship focused counseling—empathy and unconditional positive regard, and at least limited expertise in CBT/REBT— a combination well within range of beginning counselors with expertise developed through focused use of class assignments, extra readings, thoughtful practicum and internship supervision.

Reality Therapy or Solution-Focused Goal Setting in Therapeutic Relationship for Depression

In his first session, John had explored the depths of his depression. I got how profound it was for him. I got that feeling of pervasive dark, like grungy, just can't get clean, can't feel fresh. I had listened for and we had established his reasonable safety from imminent danger, but still he felt just so stuck in a rut. He longed to move from it, yet couldn't seem to get himself to move.

John seemed to feel more down in response to my empathy and acceptance. He seemed to shift from disliking his level of misery to loathing it. I explained how I saw his feelings and his depressive actions and lack of self-care from those feelings as a very difficult cycle to break. I asked and he agreed to hear as I reviewed self-care information around healthy eating, sleep, and activity. John seemed to feel connected when I talked about the cycle being very difficult to break—he was certainly tired of others telling him to just feel better or just start acting right. But then he just politely listened as I explained about healthy eating, sleep, and activity. And so I reflected:

COUNSELOR: You like the idea of making at least some of those changes, but I get the idea you don't think you will.

JOHN: No. I want to. You have to know I do. But I just don't. [He trails off.]

COUNSELOR: I know you want to, and I also think I get a good idea of how impossible it feels. I have an idea that might help. It will not be easy or quick, but it sometimes helps to focus on the times in life when you had the most ease in pushing forward and possibly discovering what was different about that time? Maybe then you can find an acceptable plan to take any step forward, no matter how small and no matter what else? Would you like me to try and explain how that could work?

JOHN: I guess so. Yes, I would. But I've been like this a long time.

COUNSELOR: You have. It's been a long time. But still you are open to trying it.

JOHN: Well, yes, I want anything to feel better; to do better.

COUNSELOR: You said that part of what drives you is feeling guilty, like you're thinking you've not been *doing* right. [I checked in with John with his eyes and shifted to planning.] In planning to do something different, the first thing that I would notice and want you to consider is that you do not have zero motivation now. You are feeling bad enough, and a little guilty, so much that you really want to be open to trying. It seems that even if it is through great hardship, you do feel some motivation now.

JOHN: Well, maybe that's part of what they mean by hitting rock bottom.

COUNSELOR: So it feels like this might be you hitting rock bottom, such that you may be able to start back up. [I shifted again to search for solution.] Think of some times when things were quite different for you. What were things like then? How were things different?

JOHN: Well, I've kind of been down this bad before. The last time I was I met Rachel, but she's gone now.

COUNSELOR: OK, but what if we planned for you to do just a thing or two of the things that you started to do differently at the time you met Rachel.

JOHN: Well, this sounds dumb, but I remember wanting to be clean for her. Thinking back to what was different, I remember wanting to feel clean.

COUNSELOR: So you have that idea. And it seems you feel a little excited about it. [Remembering his "dumb" comment.] And it doesn't seem dumb to me. I think I get that feeling of new love, which feels fresh, and wanting to be fresh for the new person. [Shifting to planning again.] One possibility is to simulate some of that. What did you do to "clean up" for Rachel?

JOHN: Well, mostly I'd get up every morning, shower, shave, and put on fairly nice clothes; you know, just clean jeans and a fairly nice shirt.

COUNSELOR: Sounds like you remember that time well. You sound a little bit like your longing for it, but I also hear a bit of hesitancy.

JOHN: Yeah, well, I do want to do those things again. But I don't have Rachel. I'm not in love.

COUNSELOR: So you both want to, but it feels out of place right now.

JOHN: Yes, out of place; I guess that's it. Like it just doesn't make sense.

COUNSELOR: Part of what's hard, part of what holds you back is it's doing something out of place.

JOHN: Well, I guess it will be weird, cleaning up for nothing.

COUNSELOR: It seems like it's for nothing. I know what you mean—that it's not for love or for a new love, at least not right now. But what I have in mind, the skill set that I hope to suggest is to think of the exceptional times, times when it wasn't so dark, to think of what you did then, to bring in a little light, to do some of the actions of feeling better, as if you had a reason to feel better—to begin to feel better, a little, maybe to create a reason.

JOHN: [Interjecting.] Well, I guess I'm not going to meet someone at home feeling grungy.

COUNSELOR: You're joking around it a bit, but I think you also meant that. It seems to make sense to you.

JOHN: Yeah, I will do it. At least I'll try it tomorrow, but I think I need somewhere to go, something to do.

COUNSELOR: I notice you are working hard at this planning now. You'll do it, but you're thinking to pull it off right you need somewhere to go, something to do.

JOHN: Yes, but I hate eating out alone. I know people do it at the coffee shop, but I also can't afford that, at least not much.

COUNSELOR: So, you're knowing that you need that something to do, but your first thoughts of that don't seem to work too well for you. For the skills we are working on, you might notice that I kind of looked at your first ideas as your first ideas, but knowing how bad you have felt lately, I suspect they felt to you like the only ideas. [It was tempting to offer a suggestion here—it can feel satisfying to "solve the problem," but John's process was most important; so I held back, waiting.]

JOHN: Well, OK. I'm getting what you're doing. How about this—this is a little crazy for me: To dress nice more than one day, I'll have a ton of laundry to catch up. So, I've got one nice shirt clean. I got it for Christmas. It's still in the package. I might just have to put on sweat pants with it. But I'll shower, shave, and put it on. Then I'll start on that laundry. I can watch TV and eat during the loads, then the folding will be a little active—I need that. As soon as my better jeans are out, I'll wear them, too, maybe start to cook something a little nice for dinner. I have soup in the freezer that my sister made me.

COUNSELOR: [I realized that if I had suggested my idea (coffee shop just one day), it would have been far less innovative and ambitious than where John went with it, because I waited for his response.] Wow. You've got a string of ideas running. It seems you're feeling encouraged.

JOHN: I am.

COUNSELOR: Much as I hate to cut you off now, I do have to watch the time. We have about 5 minutes left today.

JOHN: No, I'm OK. I'm thinking I can do this.

COUNSELOR: You are. It feels doable now. I'm glad. [After continuing to process with empathy and my genuine reaction, my hunch is it is better to risk "stepping-on" John's positive feeling while together, as I think he is at high risk of doing that himself, when alone.] There are a couple of thoughts that I want to add. First, I'm so glad for the momentum you have found. And I know how down you've been. So, what I want to make sure to say, before we end today, is that if our plan goes great, I want you to come back. And if our plan does not go great, I also want you to come back. The skill set I have tried to begin to share is thinking of the positive exception, and making a workable plan from things you were doing in the exceptional time. But there could have been lots of other plans vs. the one we made today. And also there are lots of other ways to focus our work together in counseling. If this first try doesn't work— work to begin to change this very difficult cycle, it doesn't mean nothing will work. It just means we have more work to do.

JOHN: OK. This feels good. Thank you. I think I can do this.

COUNSELOR: It does. Even after my warnings, it still feels good. Come and I'll walk out with you to schedule our next meeting.

JOHN: [Standing and preparing to walk out, extending his hand to shake.] I appreciate your working with me. It feels good, like partners. I need this.

COUNSELOR: [Standing, shaking hands and beginning their walk out as John spoke.] Working with you is meaningful to me, too. I'm glad to.

John did come back the next week. He had done the plan, sort of. It was difficult. He had made effort, and he had "back-slidden." I accepted that.

We continued our work together. Sometimes I initiated planning. Sometimes John did. But more than anything else, we continued to explore his experience. While working directly for future orientation was helpful to him, he also needed to continue to feel what he felt, fully, and to share that with me. He had guilt, remorse, self-loathing to face. He needed our therapeutic relationship not to face it alone. His empathy enhanced emotional experience, within our close personal connection, fueled his motivation. And he was not near ready to stop learning from what the severely painful bad feelings meant to him in those early sessions. He had work to do in discovering what they meant for what his life had been and the person he came to choose to become.

So, our work was mostly therapeutic relationship. But the therapeutic relationship had also facilitated our planning steps to change and my teaching the concepts behind the steps. And our planning steps, although far too small to conquer his depression alone, also facilitated our therapeutic relationship. It helped cement a feeling of a partnership between us, which helped him feel immediately less alone, in order to be encouraged enough to do the hard work of learning from and making meaning of his experience through depression and beyond.

Common Problems

Consider areas of common problems for beginning counselors stemming from the integrative approaches we have suggested through examples.

Doing Too Much Too Fast

Especially with clients who are suffering with great depression or anxiety and who seem "stuck in it," there is the temptation to try too hard and fast to move to "action steps," neglecting your therapeutic relationship. For this we return to the metaphor of trying to hold a flow of water back with your hands—even if you are able to succeed with a small flow for a few moments, it won't last. While we encourage you to combine your therapeutic relationship skills with what you learn from the great theories of counseling and change, therapeutic relationships should remain the core of your work. Therapeutic relationships are the opportunity to change the whole situation— the person's context in thoughts, feelings and actions vs. simply redirecting small parts of the flow within their context. Plus, therapeutic relationships are needed to facilitate action steps, and action steps can further empower the personal connection of and for effective therapeutic relationships.

Trying to Do Too Many Things

In preparing to integrate from specific counseling theories with your therapeutic relationships, we recommend that you learn the gist of 10–12, but develop expertise in only a couple. Each major counseling theory presents a view of human nature that drives what counselors would do and why. Some are at times presented in ways that make them sound simple, but they are not simple. Each can be enough for a life of study and learning through application. We find that almost any set of counseling theories can be integrated, but doing so requires careful thought, as at first blush many would be mutually exclusive of each other. So counselors must consider how the different theories fit together and how to handle the contradictions.

Getting Lost in Guidance

It is easy for a beginner working to integrate from a selected theory to get caught up in the theory and lose contact with the person of your client and her experience. Each of the major theories are complex and provide you with a lot to think about—so many choices and decisions to make. Whenever you feel lost, remember that the most important thing is to connect with your client. When you feel lost, ask yourself, "What is she feeling now?" Reflect that with sensitive empathy and warm acceptance, your therapeutic relationship will be engaged anew.

Wanting to Solve the Puzzle for Your Own Reasons

One of the things that can lead counselors to get lost in guidance is one's wanting too much to solve the problem for the client. Most people who go into the counseling field, which is usually learned in graduate school, are quite bright. We have often been rewarded or valued in life for our problem-solving skills. And we joined the counseling field because we want to help. But at times, such strengths and good intentions can lead us astray, causing us to solve problems for clients, with brilliant techniques from the great thinkers in the counseling field, while leaving the person of our client far behind.

Activities and Resources for Further Study

- For the examples of integrative counseling with John and Jamila, work to pick out the parts of the counselors' work that would seem to have been based on CBT, reality therapy (RT) or solution-focused therapy (SFT) and the parts of the counselors' work that were mostly focused in therapeutic relationship. Discuss the lists you create with peers, comparing notes. Then consider, list and discuss how the counselors' work in the therapeutic relationship may have benefited the work categorized as CBT, RT or SFT. And consider and discuss how the counselors' work categorized as CBT, RT or SFT may have benefited the work in therapeutic relationship.
- Go through the many examples of reflections influenced by various counseling theories within the first half of this chapter. Imagine on paper or act out with a peer a few different directions in which any of the sessions might have gone from the reflection offered. Notice that some would lead to more conversation fitting within the mindset of the counseling theory that influenced the reflection, while others might not.
- Consider the two or three theories of counseling, human nature and change that resonate most with you, and thus you expect to be the greatest influence on who you are as a counselor and a person. Discuss or journal about why those theories seem to fit for you, perhaps fitting with your existing world view (explain how and why), or perhaps opening a new and exciting world view for you (explain how it is new, how it differs from your existing world view). From this, create examples of how these theories may influence how you see your clients

and thus how you reflect your client's experience. Generate examples of reflections that might be shaped by your awareness of these theories, while remaining true to and accepting of your client's experience. Act out scenarios for your examples, if possible.

- Revisit your answers to the questions within the focus activity of this chapter. How have your answers changed or grown and how have your answers been confirmed?
- Review your level of accomplishment with the Primary Skill Objectives. From your review, plan your ongoing study and development.

References

Beck, J.S., & Beck, A.T. (2011). *Cognitive behavior therapy: Basics and beyond* (2nd ed.). New York: Guilford.

Douglas, C. (2011). Analytical psychotherapy. In R.J. Corsini & D. Wedding (Eds.), *Current psychotherapies* (9th ed.) (pp. 310–341). Belmont, CA: Brooks/Cole.

Ellis, A., & Dryden, W. (2007). *The practice of rational emotive therapy* (2nd ed.). New York: Springer.

Glasser, W. (1999). *Choice theory: A new psychology of personal freedom.* New York: Harper Perennial.

Goldenberg, I., Goldenberg, H., & Pelavin, E.G. (2011). Family therapy. In R.J. Corsini & D. Wedding (Eds.), *Current psychotherapies* (9th ed.) (pp. 310–341). Belmont, CA: Brooks/Cole.

Luborsky, E.B., O'Reilly-Landry, M., & Arlow, J.A. (2011). Psychoanalysis. In R.J. Corsini & D. Wedding (Eds.), *Current psychotherapies* (9th ed.) (pp. 310–341). Belmont, CA: Brooks/Cole.

Mosak, H.H., & Maniacci, M. (2011). Adlerian psychotherapy. In R.J. Corsini & D. Wedding (Eds.), *Current psychotherapies* (9th ed.) (pp. 310–341). Belmont, CA: Brooks/Cole.

Raskin, N.J., Rogers, C.R., & Witty, M.C. (2011). Person-centered therapy. In R.J. Corsini & D. Wedding (Eds.), *Current psychotherapies* (9th ed.) (pp. 310–341). Belmont, CA: Brooks/Cole.

White, M., & Epston, D. (1990). *Narrative means to therapeutic ends.* New York: Norton.

Wubbolding, R.E. (2010). *Reality therapy.* Washington, DC: American Psychological Association.

Yalom, I.D., & Josselson, R. (2011). Existential psychotherapy. In R.J. Corsini & D. Wedding (Eds.), *Current psychotherapies* (9th ed.) (pp. 310–341). Belmont, CA: Brooks/Cole.

Pre-Chapter Quote

Brandon, D. (1990). *Zen in the art of helping.* London: Penguin, p. 59.

15 BRINGING HEART TO ALL YOU DO

It is an exciting struggle to honor the love I have for myself,
For my clients, students, and friends.
The simplicity expresses itself, in me, as my wish to speak directly
To myself and those others from that love –
To speak from my heart
In a way that is respectful and noncontrolling.

Armin Klein

Primary Skill Objectives

- Understand and be able to offer examples of how the paradigm of the core conditions can guide you through the complexities of multi-faceted relationships with clients.
- Understand and be able to give examples of the roles in and benefits of therapeutic relationship skills in assessment, career counseling, group work, consultation, family services and beyond.

Focus Activity

In your counselor preparation you will also study such things as assessment, diagnosis, treatment planning and comprehensive counseling programs. Individual counseling will almost always be central to your job, but an array of services is needed for adequate client care. You may think of these related tasks as above and beyond or separate from your work in therapeutic relationships—many beginning counseling students do. But you may guess by now, we disagree. We see your work in therapeutic relationships as carrying over into almost everything you do.

So, please pre-think this issue now. List as many task areas for your job and counselor setting as you can think of. For each, list the ways that skills from therapeutic relationships might apply within the task area and aspects of the task area that seem mostly separate from your work in therapeutic relationships. Share your thoughts with peers.

Our thoughts and examples of how your work in therapeutic relationships inform, enhance and interact with your work in assessment, testing, diagnosis, career-focused counseling, group work, family therapy, guidance and mentoring follow.

Therapeutic Relationships and Assessment

Professional counselors have responsibilities beyond the immediate needs of the counseling relationship. For example, counselors in schools and agency settings often take roles in counseling-related assessment. Your skills for therapeutic relationship should infuse all you do, including assessment tasks. Examples of how that can work follow.

Discussing Depression Questionnaire Results with a High School Student

A depression and anxiety screening table was set up in the corner of a large wellness fair geared for high-school-aged students. Asia's friends brought her over teasing and laughing, but in retrospect it seemed also with serious intent. The table and display were set up for students to be able to quickly take and discuss brief screening instruments for depression and anxiety. Sitting her friend in the chair across from the counselor, Ms. Chambers, one friend says, "Girl, you need to take this test. You are depressed." Another girl, Alexus, who the counselor knows well, asserts, "Ms. Chambers, you gotta talk to this girl. She's messed up."

Ms. Chambers: [Seeing that Asia looks uncomfortable with all this, addressing Alexus first, with their same teasing tone, then the group, then to Asia.] Why thank you for the referral Alexus—referral is the highest form of compliment. Girls this all seems a little public. Would you be willing to let us talk a few minutes, just the two of us? And will you stay a few minutes to talk as your friends suggest? [As others are leaving, with a few parting teases.] I've seen you around, but I don't know your name?

Asia: I'm Asia.

Ms. Chambers: What do you think your friends had in mind, saying you are depressed?

Asia: Oh, they just wanted me to take that test because I'm quiet.

Ms. Chambers: OK. We can do that. [Getting out a screening survey; it's 20 questions addressing suicide ideation, depressed feelings and thoughts.] I notice that you kind of accept your friends' concerns and kind of not.

Asia: Yeah. I feel down a bit, but they exaggerate.

Ms. Chambers: So, you feel a bit down, at times, but you are certain it's not as bad as they say. Your answers on this survey give us a way to put a rough number to how down you feel and then a chance to talk about what some of the particular items mean to you.

ASIA: Yeah. OK. I'll answer, but really, it's nothing. I just get a little down sometimes.

MS. CHAMBERS: OK. So it will only take a minute and while we are here. [Hands Asia a pencil and the questionnaire.]

ASIA: [Answers a few items, then stops on an item about feeling discouraged about her future.] See, like this one here. I do feel discouraged about it, but it's only because I don't know what I'm going to do or how I'm going to afford it.

MS. CHAMBERS: I get the idea you want me not to over-react. And one of your difficulties is being unclear of what will come next or how to afford what you see that you might want.

ASIA: Yeah. I might want college ... but ... we'll see. Let me finish this for you.

ASIA: [A few items later.] See this one, too. I'm not a failure, but I do have a lot more going against me than most folks.

Ms. Chambers begins to wonder what might be difficult for Asia from her peers, who all have a lot going against them. She thinks "having a lot more going against her than most folks" might be an important belief for Asia to evaluate the evidence behind, but in the split second of that thought, she remembers that right now the only thing that matters, before any other work that Asia and she might do later, is to "get" Asia, to understand her, to convey her understanding of who she is—to connect. And so she responds from therapeutic listening:

MS. CHAMBERS: So, that's something I should understand—that you know you are not a failure, but you also have a lot going against you.

ASIA: [Finishes questionnaire quickly, but thoughtfully, with some consternation, but also willingness—she doesn't like feeling investigated, but she is drawn to being heard. Upon finishing, she hands it to Ms. Chambers almost like a little challenge, as if to say, "There it is. Now what you gonna do?"].

MS. CHAMBERS: [Having seen that quite a few of her answers were mid-range and knowing that this suggests at least low-level depression, plus having had a couple minutes to think about what Asia has said and to consider that she definitely wants her to follow-up in counseling, Ms. Chambers spoke to her.] Well, I noticed enough of your answers to know that, while you've made clear that you are OK, still you are going through something. I have to stay here at the table now to talk with others, but let's make a time to at least talk briefly before you leave today.

ASIA: [Big sigh.] I knew it was going to come to this. Alexus has a big mouth.

MS. CHAMBERS: You didn't want me to ask to meet with you, but it sounds like you might be OK with it.

ASIA: Yeah. I guess. But I don't wanta be treated like I'm crazy. And if too many people know about this, it could make problems for me.

Ms. CHAMBERS: OK. I know you are not crazy and I will not treat you that way. And also, students work with me for lots of reasons including planning for after high school, which seems like one of the things that concerns you.

ASIA: Yeah. Sort of.

They schedule a 15-minute meeting that seems to work well enough in their busy schedules. Ms. Chambers notes to herself that Asia had not wanted to miss some class moments that may have heavy future impact, which is a positive sign of future orientation. But also, because Asia's answers did indicate at least some strong signs of depression, she cannot let Asia leave the school day without working with her to assess for imminent danger, which she will do in their 15-minute meeting, continuing beyond the 15 minutes if it seems like immediate planning for safety is required.

We see successful integration of assessment and therapeutic relationship in Ms. Chambers's initial meeting with Asia. Ms. Chambers did not hide behind the assessment, but began to listen and connect to Asia immediately. Listening and connecting immediately prompted Asia to complete the questionnaire, communicating through her answers to the questionnaire as well as commenting while completing the questionnaire. Offering the questionnaire is what brought Asia to Ms. Chambers. Good therapeutic listening is what helped Ms. Chambers connect with Asia and helped Asia communicate more.

From the things Asia has said, Ms. Chambers can already begin to form the view that:

- Asia doesn't like being singled out; definitely does not want to be seen as weak or as a "victim," but she does seem to see life as overwhelming and might be seeing her circumstances as unfair to her.
- She seems both future oriented, but also worried for and discouraged of her future, which are reasons to continue to monitor her safety and imminent danger.
- Ms. Chambers has the thought that the hint of a focus on the unfairness of Asia's circumstances might suggest that Asia should or may want to evaluate her view of herself and circumstances for possible irrational views, thus possibly adding a cognitive therapy (Beck & Beck, 2011; Ellis & Dryden, 2007) to their work. Yet Ms. Chambers is well aware that she has far to go in getting to know Asia, in helping Asia self-express and learn about herself, long before thinking of asserting such a view of Asia or asking Asia to consider such a view of herself.
- Ms. Chambers also has the thought that career informational resources may be a part of helping Asia. Discouragement of her future seems to be part of what troubles Asia, yet it seems that Asia may not yet have a clear view of what she wants, what seems possible, and resources to access what she wants.

A Young Adult, Resistant to Counselor Connection, Prepares to Hear Results of HIV Testing

Joseph came to the clinic to ask about an HIV test. Agency policy required him to meet in the 20 minutes or so needed to develop results and continuing after to process his reactions to results. He made it clear that he was not interested in counseling. He just wanted the test, as his girlfriend insisted.

His counselor, Sarah, explains the policy to sit together while he waits for results. She explains that his test results will be brought to them as soon as they are ready, usually within 20 minutes. She then initiates conversation, asking from his intake questionnaire, "I see that you have been tested before, but didn't put when. Can you remember what year it was?"

JOSEPH: About a year ago.
SARAH: So, fairly recent. What was that experience like?
JOSEPH: [Seeming not to want to be interacting.] I don't know. I guess I passed [said with a shrug].
SARAH: So your results then were negative. I imagine that pretty much anyone would be relieved in that case.
JOSEPH: Yes.

Sarah acknowledged the meaning of his simple "yes" in reflection, noting that he really does not want to talk with her. She also notes in reflection that he didn't answer any of the questions on at-risk behaviors. (He hadn't answered yes or no to any of them on the intake questionnaire.) Joseph explained that he was just here to get his girlfriend off his back.

Joseph had begun to relax only a little by this point, but still seemed "wound tight." He became a little animated in talking about his girlfriend or her demand. Sarah reflected, "While you are annoyed about the testing, I gather she is quite important to you to go through this for her." Being used to the stress that others in Joseph's position go through, Sarah is fairly easily able to see him in a positive light and to reach for UPR. But still he seems to push away any closeness.

SARAH: [Speaking her genuine reaction and reflecting what is going on between them.] Joseph, we seem to be in a pattern of me hoping to encourage you to talk with me more about what led to your testing, or your girlfriend wanting your testing and you not wanting to. I want to be clear that you absolutely do not have to talk with me. It is absolutely OK to just get your results, be aware of our additional services and go. But I gather that there is something that worries you and your girlfriend. I am hoping to know what it is to help you better understand if you are at risk and to learn to avoid risk if you may be.
JOSEPH: [Calming in response to her openness, including her acceptance of his choices.] OK. So I see how this must look. It's nothing. It's just that I did some drugs in the past; long time ago.

SARAH: So that's the reason you are worried that you might be HIV positive—drug use in the past. But I don't get why test again now. I gather maybe you did not trust the results.

JOSEPH: [Interrupts her with an exasperated, "augh!"]

SARAH: I'm sorry. It seems that it got under your skin that I didn't get your explanation. The test is very close to 100 percent accurate beyond three months after exposure.

JOSEPH: [Long pause.] OK. I might have done some things with a man, but I am *not* ["not" said with clenched teeth] gay. I know lots of gay people come here. I'm not one of them! I have a *girlfriend* [said with emphasis for obvious meaning].

SARAH: That is a part that's important to you, that it be clear that you are not gay and are not associated with gay people. You're kind of not seeing how I wouldn't get that.

JOSEPH: [Shrug.]

SARAH: At our clinic, we always want persons to know that HIV does not discriminate. It doesn't make any difference to us or to the HIV test if a person is gay or not.

JOSEPH: [Upset.] I know, I know! [Pause.] Look, I'm scared. I love my girlfriend and I want us to be together. I want to be a man for her. But she has to know, well, I mean she heard rumors about me and so . . . this test. I can't have her doubting what might happen.

Sarah waits a moment, as it seems he is going to say something more. He deflated quite a bit when speaking and more so when she paused.

JOSEPH: [After the pause, quietly.] I'm so confused.

Sarah has many thoughts running through her mind: "So that's it." "Confused about sexual orientation?" But she pulls herself back from investigator mode and remembers, therapeutic relationship—respond with empathy to what you know. What do you know that is going on with him right now?

SARAH: Right now you just feel so confused.

JOSEPH: [Deflated, slumping into his chair.] Yeah.

At this time, Joseph's results arrive. They are negative. He and Sarah are relieved. Sarah asserts, "Joseph, I want to ask if you would continue counseling with me. If our testing office is uncomfortable to you, we can meet at one of our other offices. I can continue to provide you information on what things can put you at risk. We can also talk of other things. You seem to have a mix of feelings about your relationship and some uncertainties that bother you, aside from testing." Joseph agreed and seemed to mean it, "I'm so happy right now I'd agree to almost anything!" Sarah points out that they have about 15 minutes left before she has to get ready for her next appointment, and then adds, "Let's schedule one meeting. Maybe that will be our only meeting. I'll ask you to help me get to know you. Then you can decide from how it is for us to work together and what you are learning about yourself through my efforts to understand, if you might want to continue." Following that, he tells her a bit of how much he loves his girlfriend, and also of another close friendship he has that seems kind of also romantic. Sarah concludes, "So a part of your confusion, and maybe your girlfriend's *insecurity* [she stated this last word tentatively, as she didn't yet know how to think of his girlfriend's response] is because a part of you is greatly and fully committed to a relationship with her and a part of you is not sure. That is a confusion that you can definitely work through in counseling."

Somewhat similar to Asia's story, assessment, or in this case test results, were a way to open the door to interaction, but therapeutic listening and therapeutic relationship were required to help them move through the door together. Joseph's story also helps clear up the misconception that work in therapeutic relationship is non-assertive. Certainly Sarah did assert. Some of her responses might even be considered confrontational. But she was never confronting without warmth. And she was always striving for empathy. In fact, much the opposite of lacking empathy, the confrontation was *powered* by empathy. The confrontation was not *by the counselor*, as in me versus you/ person versus person, but *confrontation by his experience*. As Sarah attended to him as a person, and expressed what she felt and understood of his experience, Joseph's experience was hard for him to hear and "sit with." What he hoped for was "relief and return to normalcy." But through her empathy and UPR, he became more open to his experience and a nagging, gnawing confusion, which when attended to therapeutically, amounted to a confrontation of what he wanted his experience to be vs. what his experience actually was. He left feeling that he could get more than back to normal, that he could have a new normal that would feel more secure than what he was becoming used to.

Discussing Diagnoses within Therapeutic Relationships

Often in clinical mental health settings and sometimes in schools counselors need to assess for, discern, and provide a DSM (APA, 2013) diagnosis. The purposes usually include that each diagnosis may have a role informing the agency or counselors treatment planning for the individual, but as a greater motivating factor, often a diagnosis is required to justify services and obtain reimbursement. This role is sometimes thought of as antithetical to a therapeutic relationship, but that is not necessarily so. The issue of diagnosis can be handled within a therapeutic relationship and can enhance the counselor–client connection.

In most cases, we recommend explaining the structure of what is needed, in similar ways to explaining other aspects of the structure of counseling (see Chapter 8), we recommend use of higher level reflections in explaining your diagnostic thinking of a client, and we recommend empathic attunement as a tool to bring clients into as equal a partnership as possible, similar to the partnership sought with other decisions within counseling (see Chapter 8).

A Scenario of Discussing Diagnosis within a Therapeutic Relationship

Often in clinical settings a diagnosis needs to be entered into the records within the first three sessions. In some clinics, an intake—an initial meeting devoted to information (bio–psycho–social history) gathering—is conducted first by a staff member who may or may not be the counselor who will follow up with the client, once it is determined that individual counseling seems a reasonable match for the client's needs. In those cases, the counselor needs to address the issue of diagnosis by the end of the first counseling session, in order to finalize a diagnosis by the third counseling session. Thus, in that first meeting, the counselor has the responsibilities of hearing, understanding and connecting with the client, along with thinking of the client in diagnostic categories.

The counselor, Ms. Morgan, has been focused on the multiple tasks of therapeutic connection and diagnostic thinking in the first 20 minutes of her first meeting with Aldus. At the point where the example begins below, she realizes she has missed in empathy based on her responsibility to multitask her thoughts. So she uses that as an opportunity to explain the structure and share her thoughts on diagnosis for Aldus.

MS. MORGAN: So, I get the idea that I didn't quite get how upsetting that was to you. Aldus, one reason that I missed part of what this is like for you is that I need to think two ways at once in our meeting. The main thing I want to do is to listen to and understand you, and to share my understanding with you. But I also have to come to understand what you are going through in diagnostic terms. [She sees the surprise and a bit of anxiety cross Aldus's face.] By our third meeting, I have to enter a diagnosis in order for your healthcare to cover part of the cost of your services, as well as to inform the center's services for you. I gather from your reaction that you weren't aware of that.

ALDUS: Yeah. It might have been explained at that meeting with the other woman, with all the questions. But I was pretty tore up then. So, I'm not sure I got it.

MS. MORGAN: So you might have known it, but still it's a surprise.

ALDUS: [Nods, taking it in.]

MS. MORGAN: [Pauses to see if Aldus wants to comment and to collect her thoughts.] Yes. For your insurance to help with the cost, I have to enter a diagnosis. Whenever possible, my way of doing that is to discuss my thoughts with my client.

ALDUS: OK. I guess I'm alright with that. What are you thinking?

Ms. MORGAN: Well from your history—all those questions from the meeting with Ms. Massacoy—I think there are two diagnoses that we can consider.

From this point, Ms. Morgan begins to briefly explain each, noting the parts that she sees as fitting Aldus's history and situation, and those that do not. At one point she notices Aldus's reaction and responds.

Ms. MORGAN: [Stated with a tone conveying openness to his reaction.] You have some reaction to that aspect of the diagnosis related to you.
ALDUS: No, it's not that. It's just that this all seems so cold. I suppose it's true, but I really don't want to think of myself that way.
Ms. MORGAN: So I get the idea that this conversation is forcing us to be quite specific about what the pattern has been for you and what that might mean. And it feels that that is pushing you too much.

Aldus nods assent and slumps in his chair. Ms. Morgan pauses to take in his reaction and think for a second or two. Out of the pause, she explains.

Ms. MORGAN: Aldus, there are a couple of things that I want you to always know about our work together. First, we can almost always go at the pace that feels alright to you. I will take responsibility for moving us forward, if I see that we must. But most of the time, you can be responsible for our pace. If something feels like "too much, too fast," I need you to let me know. And I need you to keep the responsibility for helping me know you, for sharing who you are and how you are at this time. To me, that includes your letting me know when you are bothered by our work, like just now.
ALDUS: [Nods assent, brightens a bit, and looks at Ms. Morgan as if to say, "And so what do we do now?"]
Ms. MORGAN: So, you are wondering what next. Well, I can have one more meeting before entering a diagnosis. And I would like us to agree, because a diagnosis is so personal and can have an impact on your medical records. So, we can go back to that conversation now and I will answer any questions that you have. But we also can set that aside for now. What you were telling me when I realized I was distracted with that line of thought seemed important to you. What you were saying was . . .

Aspects of the interchange above that we want you to see include the following. Even while speaking in diagnostic terms, which can be reductionist of the person, Ms. Morgan did not waiver in her respectfulness toward Aldus. And both fostering and growing from that respect, she never stopped listening and responding empathically. And in this case, the diagnostic work even seemed to prompt them to more open and honest communication, requiring higher level reflections, expressions of how she sees him, requiring precise and perhaps hard to hear descriptions of what his behavior patterns seemed to be, and forcing both to look at the big picture of his past and his present experience.

Concluding Thoughts on Therapeutic Relationship Skills in Assessment

The most poignant examples are often the most dramatic. But there could be plenty of examples of elements of therapeutic relationships in lighter moments of assessment. For example, as a group of well-functioning middle-school students discuss results of an initial career interest inventory, there would be lots of opportunities to reflect the themes of their aspirations or to reflect their reactions to occupations identified by the inventory as possibly related to students interests. Their reactions may range from excitement to perplexed wonder at why a particular occupation might be listed, or even what it is. In such a conversation, the next steps in guiding their career decision readiness may rightfully take a back seat to reflecting such that each is heard and each begins to learn from her reaction to the assessment results. Further thoughts on the role of therapeutic relationships in career-focused counseling follow.

Career Counseling and Therapeutic Relationships—Balancing the Personal and the Informational

Tiffany Brooks is co-author of this section, which has grown in part from her work in career counseling and collaboration with Jeff (author order for this section is Cochran, J.L., Brooks, T.P, & Cochran, N.H.).

Helping an Indecisive Student See What She is Communicating Through Her Actions/Inaction

Sofia wants to go to college. She has clearly explained this goal. Her counselor, Ms. Rodriguez, sees no reason why she should not. Her grades and school success suggest she has the ability. While college is always difficult to afford, Ms. Rodriquez has identified a number of sources of funding that might be available to her. Yet with each step along the way, it feels to Ms. Rodriguez like she has to drag Sofia along.

In one meeting Ms. Rodriguez realizes that Sofia has missed a due date for one of the actions that might have helped with funding. Her most natural reaction is to ask Sofia, "Why!—Why not just do it when it was all there before you, so clear, so ready, such a great opportunity?" But as she feels her frustration build, about to burst forth with a series of pointed questions, she remembers, "I am Sofia's counselor, not just her college prep guide." And so she remembers to respond from her therapeutic relationship skills. She asks herself, "What is going on with Sofia right now? What is she experiencing right now? It seems there is something beneath the surface that I am not attending to. Empathy will get us there . . ."

MS. RODRIGUEZ: [After the pause to center herself.] Sofia, in this moment you look shy, timid.

SOFIA: [Speaking in a small voice.] Well, I was pretty sure you'd be upset. [Speeding her rate of speech.] But really, I was just too busy and couldn't get it all done.

MS. RODRIGUEZ: [Realizing her error: lack of empathy or attention to Sofia's feelings in the background of her plan for college, i.e., *conditional* positive regard—accepting who she will be when well on her way to college vs. who she is now. Ms. Rodriguez decides to become congruent and genuine in openly telling Sofia what has been going on with her, but reflecting first.] So two things: there has just been too much for you to get done lately and you were anticipating that I would be upset with you.

SOFIA: Yes. Please don't be mad. It's just that, you know, with my mother and my little brother, Roberto . . . and Anthony, sometimes I can't get it all done.

MS. RODRIGUEZ: Yes, I hear you. It adds up and so sometimes you can't get it all done, and so your priority of college has to drop. And I also think that I have gotten so caught up in planning for college for you that I have forgotten to pay attention to some of the other very important parts of what you are going through.

SOFIA: Well, yeah, but you were just trying to help.

MS. RODRIGUEZ: I'm glad that you see that in me. And one of the things I see in you is how much you take care of others; like even now you are trying to take care of me, not wanting me to feel bad.

SOFIA: [Paused for a second, not sure what to say to that.] Well, you shouldn't feel bad. You are only trying to help.

MS. RODRIGUEZ: Thank you. [Moving on to a big picture reflection, while striving for a renewed tone and intent of acceptance.] And one of the things I notice about you is that you want to go to college, for you. And you want or feel the need to take care of others, your mom, and your brother. And so sometimes you are pulled in different directions.

SOFIA: Well no, Mom wants me to go! [This first statement was spoken strongly. The next follows more softly.] But if I do, who would take care of her and Roberto?

MS. RODRIGUEZ: So your mother says, "Go! I want you to!" But it is difficult for you to accept that.

In this interchange, Ms. Rodriguez feels the urge to argue with her, to convince her to take care of herself, to move her generation forward. When she feels this, she takes extra care in her wording, remaining careful to attend to Sofia rather than respond from her agenda.

SOFIA: Yes, I couldn't stand it if anything were to happen to them, while I am focused on me.

Ms. RODRIGUEZ: So that's a big part of a pull away from college for you—your worry that something might happen to Mom or Roberto when you are focused on you.

SOFIA: Well, you know it could! You know what they have to go through.

Ms. RODRIGUEZ: Yes, I know it's possible, but I also tend to think, maybe differently from you, that taking care of you, and taking care of them, at least a bit less, would not necessarily interfere with each other. [Ms. Rodriguez realizes this last statement was a little bit argumentative, but at this stage in their work together, she thought it more valuable to openly give her thought than to be overly restrained in her relationship with Sofia.]

SOFIA: [Accepts Ms. Rodriguez's thought and moves on, getting tentative again.] Well, and it's not just Mom and Roberto; Anthony isn't going to college.

Ms. RODRIGUEZ: You said that carefully. Again, I'm guessing you assumed I would not want to hear it.

SOFIA: Well, yeah. You've never said anything about Anthony, but you probably don't approve.

Ms. RODRIGUEZ: Perhaps, but I also know you have strong feelings for him. And so now I am glad you are letting me know how it is for you. On one hand, you want college for you. It fits with your dreams for you. And Mom says "Go." But on the other hand, you feel how much Mom and Roberto need you. You worry what might happen for them without you. And Anthony might not want you to go.

SOFIA: Oh no. He says "Go!"

Ms. RODRIGUEZ: So you have Mom and Anthony saying "Go!" But for some reason, you cannot quite accept what they are telling you.

SOFIA: It's not that I don't accept it . . . Well, OK, maybe it is that I don't accept it.

Ms. RODRIGUEZ: I imagine you're thinking, "That's what they say, but not what they mean."

SOFIA: No, I know it is what they mean. Oh, well, at least in part, I guess. But that's part of what's hard. They want me to stay for them. They want me to go for me. But they also want me to go for them, partly because they couldn't go. That's a lot of pressure. I don't know if I want that.

Ms. RODRIGUEZ: So, with the pressure, you're not sure if *you* want it.

SOFIA: Ugh. This is so hard!

Sofia and Ms. Rodriguez's conversation continues from here for a few pages (what takes moments to say in interactions take pages to report in transcript). In their meeting that day, Sofia decides to move on to the next opportunity. And it seems that she is is deciding much more freely, of her own wants versus those of Ms. Rodriguez or others.

As Sofia becomes more open with Ms. Rodriguez, it is like the floodgates begin to open wide toward her greater openness with herself and with others.

She does not decide to act that day, but begins to consider sharing her back and forth thoughts about her decisions with Anthony and Mom, or at least Mom for now.

Her ambivalence is not over. Such feelings of push and pull from life and relationships are never resolved in a single meeting or single moment. But the most important thing is that Ms. Rodriguez has realigned herself to be Sofia's counselor, her objective (or nearly objective, while still personally engaged) confidant. And she continues to feed her career, college preparation resources, and Sofia knows Ms. Rodriguez preferences for her to go to college and do it for herself and her future. And Sofia knows Ms. Rodriguez accepts her for who she is, ambivalence and all, whether she chooses college or not. Ironically, perhaps, as it feels like pressuring a young person into an action is the best way to get them to act, Ms. Rodriguez's newly invigorated therapeutic relationship is the most powerful tool possible to help Sofia make her most mature decision, the decision that best fits what she wants for herself and her life, being well-informed by self-awareness grown through her therapeutic relationship with Ms. Rodriguez.

Helping a Student See the Impact of Cultural Self-Limitation

For another example of therapeutic relationships within career counseling, imagine what if Sofia, from the story above, or Asia, from one of the stories illustrating therapeutic relationships in assessment, were limiting herself in her aspirations based on input from others regarding what is possible for her or based on the models that she has been exposed to. Our expectations are that this cultural self-limitation will be implied at some point, as the counselor working with Sofia or Asia sensitively attends to her client. And we find that this communication is likely to be implied, not stated. It would require reflecting the implications of the client's communication (i.e., not just what she says, but how she says it, what she does not say, her actions, and the implications of what she has said on other matters). And also, we would note, many such reflections are not pure experience coming from the client. Rather, such reflections result from the client's implication, filtered through the counselor's world view, which includes knowing to look for such problem areas, from her background in education and experience.

What about the Student with Unrealistic Positive Occupational Aspirations?

For another example of therapeutic relationships in career counseling, imagine the dilemma the counselor may be in with a client who has unrealistically high career aspirations. Of course, for young children, there is very little reason to limit aspirations—until closer to direct implementation, we have little ability to know what limitations an individual may or may not encounter. But many counselors helping students or other clients with career decisions have encountered clients who have unrealistically high aspirations in time-frames in which they need to be realistic.

Typically, this is handled through letting the career preparation data provide the feedback (i.e., help the student learn to research requirements for various career choices and ask himself if he is motivated and feels able to meet those requirements). Sensitive empathic attending can at times help bring self-doubt to light. If the self-doubt is unrealistic, it is best for the client to realize this openly in order to let go of the doubt. And if the self-doubt is realistic, empathic attending can also help the client recognize vs. deny it.

And in the rare, worst case scenario in which the client's denial is so strong that he seems unwilling or unable to see it, a reflection built through the counselors' world view (knowing her client, knowing the world of work, and knowing to check carefully for practical limits to career choices) and built through counselor openness to expressing her genuine views and reactions, might sound like, "Isaac, I know how much you want to go to ___. And I see how much excitement and thought time you are putting into it. And it occurs to me that there is a mismatch between the average acceptance requirements of ___ and your success so far. I have the thought that you are looking past the difference."

Isaac might then explain his plan for addressing the difference—perhaps his counselor missed hearing that. But such a direct reflection, delivered with warmth, can help the client see his choices and actions, thoughts and feeling, with clarity.

Therapeutic Relationships in Group Work

We think of groups on a continuum from groups focused almost completely on the group's process (individual members are responsible for bringing the topics of their lives to share with others) to groups that are highly psycho-educational (almost like a "class" but still with at least some opportunities for group members to process (talk about experiences and what they mean with each other). With any group, anywhere along the continuum there are ample opportunities for the counselor to attend to individuals with therapeutic relationship skills. This can help draw members out to say more to the group and can help model the kinds of responses to each other that she would like from group members.

However, there are reasonable limits to this way of individual attending in group counseling. Too much would be an individual session in front of the group. The ultimate goal in process for many groups is to help group members respond to each other with a combination of therapeutic attending, and sharing their own reactions and related experiences. So group leadership brings a need to structure the group, balancing providing information and skills for how to be in group with therapeutic attending. It can be helpful to instruct the group what you are aiming for in their interactions, while also modeling attending.

For a specific application: At times in group counseling there is the issue of what to say if one group member is monopolizing the time. Consider a response to the person who is monopolizing from the perspective of therapeutic relationships:

1. If you as group leaders are perturbed or bothered by the "monopolizer," work to discern what part of your upset is you and what part of it is her behavior.
2. Strive to continue to accept or even prize the person of the "monopolizer," even while choosing to limit the group time that she monopolizes.
3. Prepare to assert the structure needed in the group.
4. Sandwich your assertion of the structure with empathy.
5. Maintain a tone of acceptance, which you have grown to be real in you through steps 1 and 2 above.

So your response may sound like:

COUNSELOR: Jackie, it seems like when we talk of emotional things, you have tons of thoughts. You begin to tell us your thoughts and you get lost in them. It gets hard for you to know where a stopping point is. I want to make sure that we have time to hear from everyone on this. So I am going to ask you to stop here for the moment.
JACKIE: Oh I didn't mean to talk too long. That's what I always do.
COUNSELOR: I know that wasn't your intention and it sounds like you're a little embarrassed as you are thinking it is something of a pattern for you. I want to come back to that. At this time, I'd like to hear how others reacted to . . .

Therapeutic Relationships in the Hallway

School counselors often take on a guidance role in hallway moments that can be instructive across settings. Jeff was often called to intervene in crises, large and small, when working as a school counselor. His typical mode when walking into a behavioral power struggle (i.e., adults extremely upset at a child's behavior, child screaming and yelling, crying, or barricaded under a table), his normal first mode was to stop for just a moment to calm himself before entering the fray, then enter and immediately go and sit near the child. Once seated, he could begin to respond with empathy to the child's upset. If needed, he could respond empathically to the adults who were caught up in the conflict as well.

One individual moment of crisis took place something like the following. Vince was outside the classroom door on the sidewalk. He looked like he had been crying and was still pacing, seeming very mad. Vince had had great behavioral difficulties in years past, but through extensive work in individual counseling, caring teacher relationships and behavior management programs, he had made great progress. But this day, his group was with a teacher who was not their usual teacher. She was a teacher who struggled with classroom discipline. She only knew Vince from his old reputation for bad behavior, and seemed to have engaged him in a power struggle, and then sent him out of the room. This was a kind of thing that used to happen to him a lot, but which had become almost non-existent after his progress the year before. Jeff walked up as Vince was picking tiny rocks or dirt clods to toss toward the window.

JEFF: [Sitting down beside him.] Vince, what's going on? You look pretty upset.
VINCE: [Sits, but stares straight ahead, saying nothing.]
JEFF: [Pauses, feeling the air between them to get in tune with what Vince is feeling. After a pause of a moment or so, Jeff responds.] You are pretty mad about something; something that went on in there [gesturing to the classroom].
VINCE: [Fumes a second, then explains.] It's Ms. Santos. She made me leave.

Jeff was aware of his impulse to try to make this a teachable moment, perhaps making a point about responsibility for our own actions in any interaction, from his background in control theory or reality therapy (Glasser, 1999; Wubbolding, 2010) based programs for troubled youth or the cognitive error of attributing responsibility for one's own internal reactions to the action of another, from his knowledge of cognitive therapies (Beck & Beck, 2011; Ellis & Dryden, 2007). But Jeff knew that Vince needed empathy first to gain calm through this crisis that was huge to him.

JEFF: So, it felt so unfair to you; like you had no choice but to do and say more, until you were sent from class.
VINCE: Yeah. She's the worst teacher in the world. This is crazy.
JEFF: You're seeing that this got badly out of control. And you're thinking it was entirely her fault.
VINCE: [Silence for a moment or two; then a big sigh.]

Jeff felt the shift and knew that Vince had softened and was ready to consider other perspectives beyond the absolute. Jeff also knew that he couldn't stay long and wanted to help Vince back into class before too much more time passed. So he suggested the following.

JEFF: Vince, I'm thinking you are ready to go back. So, can I suggest a way to think about this? First, I might suggest you consider, what is it that you want, maybe especially from Ms. Santos?
VINCE: [After a pause.] Well, mostly I just want her to let me be in there with everybody else. I just want her to leave me alone and let me stay in there.
JEFF: [Continuing to respond with empathy first, even when switching to guidance.] That is what you'd most want. Do you know what you could do now to rejoin your class? Has Ms. Santos let you know that?

VINCE: She said I could come back when I'm calm and ready to go quietly to my seat.

JEFF: OK. You look kind of calm and ready to go to your seat.

VINCE: [With body language showing that he is still mad.] Yeah.

JEFF: OK, but I still hear that part of you that is still very mad. I think that might catch Ms. Santos's attention in a bad way.

VINCE: [Softens himself, hearing the feedback/reflection of that part of his demeanor.]

JEFF: So I think if you go back in now, very quietly to your seat, and stay soft like that, you can end up staying for the rest of the period in Ms. Santos's class.

VINCE: [Almost began with a glum response, then picked himself up, knowing it mattered to his being able to be with his class.] Yeah. Yeah. I can do that.

What we want you to see in this story is the example of the necessity for empathic responding before and during a guidance interchange. The guidance would not be possible without the empathy.

The one other observation we would add in this moment is to point out one of the assets of the counselor's role in a school. Jeff knew Vince very well from their work together in individual counseling. So, this work made Jeff know Vince well enough to know to respond with empathy first—knowing very well Vince's history of resisting guidance from even caring adults without empathy first. And Jeff's previous relationship with Vince gave him a right to shift to guidance earlier in their interchange than might have otherwise been possible. But as we have come to learn, the principle of empathy first that Vince taught Jeff, is a principle that applies efficiently every time.

Therapeutic Relationship Skills in Consultation

We urge you to be creative and take your therapeutic relationship skills, especially the core conditions, with you into all of your professional consultations. We offer a few of examples here.

With Teachers

For counselors who work in schools, teacher consultation is a regular, important part of the job. A most typical example might be one in which a teacher comes to you as counselor worried or complaining about a student's behavior. Your natural reaction might be to offer to see the student in counseling and/or to suggest changes that the teacher might make in order to better manage the student's behavior. However, in doing so, you would have whisked responsibility away from the teacher and onto yourself without being asked.

A better and more time-efficient approach would be to stop and listen first, to listen with empathy that allows the teacher to fully express his experience of the student, to listen with warm acceptance, which might require you to be aware of and set aside the prick of annoyance you feel at being asked to feel pain and sit with yet another person in a difficult situation, after all the students and parents you have served in your day. Such effort has not always been easy for us. But it has paid off.

Listening with empathy, you can help the teacher find that after venting his frustration, he knows more of what to do than he realized. If you are going to participate in helping this student or make suggestions for the teacher, listening well first will help you make your actions more thoughtful and useful. Further, having listened fully and felt with this teacher will make your actions or suggestions more credible and acceptable to the teacher, when or if the time for actions or suggestions comes.

Listening with unconditional positive regard assists and enables your empathy (and vice versa). Listening with UPR also helps you see this teacher as a person struggling with a situation that is difficult for him, rather than as "complaint 1001 for the day" or a teacher who *should* know better and *should* be a perfect teacher for all such problem situations."

Listening with a genuine sense of self helps you be secondarily aware of your experiences while primarily meeting the teacher with empathy and positive regard; lets you listen therapeutically, as long as reasonable and productive; and allows you to assert your point of view when it will be most effective. In consultation, as in counseling, you are not a listening machine. You are a real person. In consultation, there is time to listen with empathy and UPR, and time to assert what you know.

Because we are fine counselors, but probably not great teachers of school children, humility has often come naturally to us in consulting with teachers. Jeff remembers one teacher he knew to be very talented coming to him and expressing his frustration with certain students in his class frequently leading the larger group into conflicts. Jeff listened therapeutically first. In this way he avoided prompting the teacher to disengage and lose his talents for the situation. After listening well, the teacher asked Jeff if he could come and teach some sort of conflict resolution or manners in the classroom to solve the problem. Jeff felt a flash of fear at the request and realized that the base of that fear was that he believed if this great and skilled teacher could not teach the behaviors he wanted in the classroom, then he (Jeff) could not either. Jeff told the teacher this truth. The teacher appreciated and accepted the compliment, but also still hoped for more. Jeff also offered to keep the goal in mind as a theme for future classroom presentations and to provide a small group counseling experience for some from the class, in which the students would have naturally occurring opportunities to resolve conflicts with each other in the group and thus learn skills to augment those they were learning in the classroom. Jeff's interventions certainly were helpful. However, a key to their success was the empowerment that this teacher received in consultation, which served to keep his formidable skills in play.

With Parents and Loved Ones of Clients

We maintain this same humility and sense of self with parents and loved ones of clients as often as possible. In listening with empathy and positive regard, we are often reminded that we do not know their child or loved one better than they do. Rather, we know their child or loved one differently, and both our understandings can benefit each other. The parents or loved ones can help a counselor understand their troubled child or loved one better. And the counselor's unique perspective of the client through her therapeutic relationship can help her educate loved ones in how they may be most helpful. Additionally, a well-educated counselor has significant universal knowledge and wisdom of how persons develop mental health, which can benefit many parents or loved ones in their desire to help.

With Professionals from Related Fields

A friend and former student's work comes to mind on this topic. This young counselor needed to work closely with a psychiatrist who initially tended to try to tell her what to do in counseling, what was possible and what was not. Her approach in talking with him was to listen to his perspective and try to understand it, to listen to the hopes and fears for clients that he seemed to imply in his assertions. She didn't quite reflect what she thought was implied as it was not clear and her intuition told her it might prompt defensive reactions, but she listened to him with empathy and warm, caring acceptance for him as a person.

While this professional counselor was young and just gaining experience, she was confident that she had studied and trained well, and found ways of counseling that were both effective and fit deeply for her. So, *after* listening with deep respect, she asserted for how she worked and why. As she had earned the right to assert through listening deeply, this psychiatrist listened to her in turn. We doubt he agreed with all that was said early on. Yet he seemed to respect this young professional counselor, as she had respected and listened to him and because she seemed to have deeply considered and to strongly believe in what she was saying and doing.

He took the time to see the success of her work. Through her strong therapeutic relationships, she helped clients succeed with whom he had been exasperated. In time, he came to seldom allow psychiatric medications for clients who fell into her areas of service until those clients had tried counseling first. They became a strong mental health team. We see that their work together had a strong start and shifted from likely conflict through her listening first with all the empathy and positive regard she could muster for the situation.

Therapeutic Relationship Skills in Job Task Negotiation

We have learned that therapeutic relationship skills, especially the core conditions, can also be used in job task negotiations. For example, counselors in schools are often asked to take on tasks that are not counseling related. Some of this is only fair, as many people have to pull the weight of some tasks that ought not be their job, yet need to be done. But sometimes the non-counseling tasks requested of counselors go too far. Some tasks, like taking on a rule-enforcement role beyond that of all adults in schools, are antithetical to counseling effectiveness. Some tasks just take too much precious time away from counseling. Again, we find that a sense of self, gained from growing the core conditions in your way of being, asserting your point of view with empathy and warm acceptance of other views and persons can be most effective in negotiating job tasks. A story from Jeff's work may help illustrate this.

In a school where there were many pressing works needed from the counselor (me) early in my first year, my principal told me to begin keeping all students' cumulative files in my office and to oversee and maintain the quality and correctness of the content of the files. This would have been a huge undertaking and one that would have occupied much of my time and energy—probably an inordinate amount as I am admittedly terrible at clerical tasks. I tend to worry over and overwork them.

My first impulse, back then, was to dig in my heels, lock horns, and say, "No way am I taking on that task!" Fortunately, I had enough respect for my principal to think again before responding. I had already felt with him as we worked through some early school-year crises and enjoyed some initial successes. So, instead of initiating a fight, I initiated conversation to further discuss why he made this request. As I listened conversationally but therapeutically, it prompted him to explain his reasons for asking me, such as his concern for confidentiality, his thought that the task needed someone who understood testing, and his fear about the task needing to be done conscientiously and carefully. Listening and really trying to understand his perspective helped me connect with his concerns and respond with alternative suggestions that were more respectful and reduced the need for conflict between us.

Perhaps most importantly, building my approach to the potential conflict on empathy and unconditional positive regard kept me from saying "No, I will not do it!," which would have been insubordinate and would have locked us in conflict. But my approach also kept us in open communication over the task. I never said "No." Rather, I said "I wish you wouldn't ask me that, because . . ." and "Please consider this alternate solution . . ." I continued to listen and strive to really understand his perspective and request, but I also continued to assert for alternatives and compromises. In this case, a compromise was eventually found that I was satisfied with. In other cases, I conceded to his requests and simply took on helpful tasks. (It isn't worth the time and energy to discuss everything that could be debatable.)

Therapeutic Relationship Skills in the Classroom

We find many applications for therapeutic relationship skills in the classroom. We help teachers to see the benefits of a more child-centered approach in the classroom (one where feelings are acknowledged, limits are set consistently with empathy, and a child learns to rely on self and intrinsic control) as opposed to an adult-centered approach to the classroom (one where children repress feelings, conform to the group, blame each other, and rely on adults for rules and controls). We consult with and work with teachers in a proactive and respectful manner—also using the core conditions as a guide in relating to teachers and staff who are under great stress in the job of schooling our children. We offer a couple of examples here.

Empathy Sandwich

We know the concept of the "empathy sandwich" from our work in play therapy with Bill Nordling (Cochran, Nordling, & Cochran, 2010) and it has multiple applications, including in the classroom. Empathy sandwich is Bill's term for a part of the limit-setting procedure in our approach to child-centered play therapy, developed from the work of our mentor, Louise Guerney. In that model, limits set on children's behavior are preceded and followed by expressions of empathy. The empathy is what "holds it all together," like two slices of bread. Limits are much better listened to and accepted when "sandwiched" between two "slices" of empathy. We have shared this concept with some teachers and have known other teachers to naturally set classroom limits this way.

A hypothetical classroom example follows: Let's say that without realizing it is going to upset him in that moment, the teacher asks a troubled student, Johnny, to do a certain task. For unexpected reasons, Johnny finds the task embarrassing and scary. So he responds to his teacher's request by yelling at her, "It's not fair! All you do is pick on me!" If the teacher simply and correctly responds that he is not allowed to speak to her in that tone, she and Johnny will be locked in a time-consuming power struggle that will not be conducive to learning. If she takes just a minute more to notice Johnny as a person in that moment and to feel what he feels, she could respond something like, "Johnny, something about what I asked you to do has hurt your feelings and you see it as completely unfair. Still, one of the things you cannot do is yell at me like that." Because she has acknowledged Johnny as a person and his feelings and thoughts in that moment, this helps him calm down, and he is more likely to do as she asks, be ready to problem solve with her, or at least withdraw from conflict. In some cases, a student in Johnny's situation may continue to show disgruntlement and reluctance but sulk off to do the task. In a child-centered play therapy session, the counselor would also respond to this action and way of being with empathy, but in the classroom, sometimes that step can be skipped, as noting his consent to do the task in front of the group may prompt more embarrassment and reluctance. However, the teacher may decide later, when she has a moment alone with Johnny, to say, "I know it was hard to stay on task today when you were angry. You did it anyway, and I want you to know that I noticed. Thanks."

This would "top the sandwich off," so to speak, and would likely motivate more cooperative behaviors from Johnny in the future. More importantly, however, Johnny would benefit and grow from experiencing a relationship with a teacher who actively shows care and concern but still expects respect and responsibility.

In any example like this, it is essential that the teacher's empathy be real, at least as often as possible. If she is just going through the verbal motions, the same statement can be heard as condescension, rather than caring. If she speaks with real empathy, then he can know that she cares for and accepts him as a person, even though he has reached a line in behavior she will not let him cross. That kind of teacher-to-student interaction can be particularly important and helpful to students who are already working in counseling on issues such as whether they expect to be liked and cared for by others, and therefore how they wish to act toward others. In our view, the reasonably consistent setting of structural limits, such as not allowing Johnny to yell at her in class, is an outgrowth of being a genuine person in the classroom. While the teacher is a caring person, she has her limits and ways that she is not willing to be treated.

Project Special Friend

When Jeff was a counselor serving an elementary school, he worked with a teacher to initiate a project to help an extraordinarily behaviorally and emotionally troubled first-grade boy achieve acceptance, safety, and a learning environment with his classmates. Once again, let's call this boy "Johnny." Johnny's behavior modification programs and counseling services were extensive, but to augment these actions, we asked his classmates to take a role in helping him. Especially because Johnny was at risk for soon being removed from the regular classroom, the approach was taken to allow his classmates to view his behavioral and emotional problems *as a difficulty and problem that they could have a role in helping change*—to talk openly with them about his difficulties and their roles.

With his presence and with his consent in advance, we helped them accept him and develop empathy for him in spite of his aggressive behavior by helping them see that each person struggles with learning and development problems at different times. We explained what our actions would be in response to Johnny's wise (behavioral) choices and poor (behavioral) choices, and what our goals for his development were. We gave them a genuine sense of power in asking them to befriend him when he made wise choices, and ignore him or ask for help if needed when he made poor choices. But perhaps most importantly, the classmates saw his teacher model deep empathy for the pain that was at the core of Johnny's outward aggressive, hurtful behavior. His teacher was able to show acceptance and prizing of Johnny in spite of his misbehavior, and to show the genuineness of being a person who would also enforce reasonably firm and clear limits for his behavior in the classroom.

This helped the whole class grow in their ability to show empathy and acceptance for each other, while also knowing that it is OK to set limits, problem-solve, offer help, or get help when someone is angry or sad and acting out.

"Project Special Friend" has been repeated (with modifications according to situation, age, and grade) to allow success and inclusion for many other students we have worked with. Students who struggle with emotional and behavioral difficulties are too often excluded from the regular classroom without being given a chance to learn how it feels to *genuinely be wanted* as part of a group. Asking for help from the whole class and modeling a safe environment that promotes understanding and care for all students—even those who are struggling emotionally and behaviorally—is possible. One of our schools' greatest natural resources is the natural capacity for empathy that *all children have* and that *will develop* in classrooms where the core conditions are modeled, developed, and experienced.

Teaching Clients and Others to Use the Skills of Therapeutic Relationship in Family Therapy, Conflict Resolution and Beyond

We have also found applications for teaching skills of therapeutic relationships for use in non-counseling relationships. We offer a few examples here.

Many models of family therapy have significant teaching components. Our favorite approaches, relationship enhancement therapy (Ginsberg, 1997; Guerney, 1977; Scuka, 2005) and filial therapy (Guerney, 2013), work to a large degree from teaching family members to engage elements of therapeutic relationships with each other. Relationship enhancement uses a structured model to teach couples to listen to each other with empathy, as well as to express their inner selves to each other. Filial therapy teaches parents to approximate the skills of child-centered play therapy (Cochran, Nordling, & Cochran, 2010; Landreth, 2012) with their children in special playtime.

We adapted the relationship enhancement model to facilitate conflict resolution among children. Our guide to this approach (Cochran, Cochran, & Hatch, 2002) helps elementary school-age children reach naturally occurring solutions to their conflicts through complete communication and deep empathy. Through this approach, the children continue to own their conflict, rather than having it taken away by an adult or other mediator, and learn to have a different relationship with the one they are in conflict with by seeing the world through that person's eyes. We have found it time efficient with long-term effectiveness in schools and camps, and have even adapted it for use in university residence halls. Former students are now applying the approach with middle- and high-school students.

We also find in conflict resolution or family therapy that the individuals need to be attended to with the qualities of therapeutic relationships as well as new skills. A parent who is learning filial therapy may be affected by memories of how she was parented or may need to express her frustration with her child, before becoming fully engaged in the filial therapy that she is learning. In couples work, the counselor often needs to listen sensitively to members' hesitation, hurt or other upset that is in the way of learning new communication skills. A parent, who is to learn new ways of parenting, may need to be heard in expressing her frustration with her child, before she becomes open to trying a new approach. A family member preparing for the return of a hospitalized loved one may need to have the counselor's sensitive empathy bring out the hurt and resentment, or resistance to change, in order to communicate in a genuine way and effectively plan to adjust for the needs of the hospitalized loved one.

Note on Common Problems and Chapter Conclusion

As this chapter is about integrating your therapeutic relationship skills into all that you do, we can't identify common problems as in most other chapters. The applications are broad and the possibilities for integration may be limitless. Certainly, we have not found the limits yet.

With that note, after considering and perhaps implementing the activities and resources for further study below, we hope you will read our last mini-chapter, which is a kind of book-end to the Introduction—Concluding Thoughts. In those pages we offer our thoughts and ask you to consider the possibilities for and from integrating the qualities of therapeutic relationships into not just what you do, but who you are.

Activities and Resources for Further Study

- Work with peers or on your own. Generate as many counselor tasks or areas of tasks as you can. Speculate roles that your therapeutic relationship skills may have in each. Discern the ones that may not have a connection with your therapeutic relationship skills. Explain why. Compare your answers within this activity to your answers to the focus activity questions that began this chapter.
- Imagine and describe in a journal or with peers ways that elements of therapeutic relationships may have been present for you outside counseling in your times of need. Then describe how they have been lacking for you in times of need. Consider the effects of each. Keep in mind the challenging as well as the supportive elements of therapeutic relationships as you generate each list.

References

APA (2013). *Diagnostic statistical manual of mental disorders* (5th ed.) . Washington, DC: American Psychiatric Association.

Beck, J.S., & Beck, A.T. (2011). *Cognitive behavior therapy: Basics and beyond* (2nd ed.). New York: Guilford.

Cochran, J.L., Cochran, N.H., & Hatch, E. (2002). Empathic communication for conflict resolution among children. *The Person-Centered Journal, 9*, 101–112.

Cochran, N.H., Nordling, W.J., & Cochran, J.L. (2010). *Child-centered play therapy: A practical guide to therapeutic relationships with children.* Hoboken, NJ: Wiley.

Ellis, A., & Dryden, W. (2007). *The practice of rational emotive therapy* (2nd ed.). New York: Springer.

Ginsberg, B.G. (1997). *Relationship enhancement family therapy.* Hoboken, NJ: Wiley.

Glasser, W. (1999). *Choice theory: A new psychology of personal freedom.* New York: Harper Perennial.

Goldenberg, I., Goldenberg, H., & Pelavin, E.G. (2011). Family therapy. In R.J. Corsini & D. Wedding (Eds.), *Current psychotherapies* (9th ed.) (pp. 310–341). Belmont, CA: Brooks/Cole.

Guerney, B.G. (1977). *Relationship enhancement: Skill training programs for therapy, problem prevention, and enrichment.* Hoboken, NJ: Jossey-Bass.

Guerney, L. (1980). *Parenting: A skills training manual.* Frankfort, KY: Institute for the Development of Emotional and Life Skills (IDEALS).

Guerney, L. (2013). *Group filial therapy: The complete guide to teaching parents to play therapeutically with their children.* Philadelphia, PA: Kingsley.

Landreth, G.L. (2012). *Play therapy: The art of the relationship* (3rd ed.). Hoboken, NJ: Wiley.

Scuka, R.F. (2005). *Relationship enhancement therapy: Healing through deep empathy and intimate dialogue.* New York: Routledge.

Wubbolding, R.E. (2010). *Reality therapy.* Washington, DC: American Psychological Association.

Pre-Chapter Quote

Klein, A. (2000). *Songs of living.* Self-published (p. 57).

CONCLUDING THOUGHTS
Growing Your Therapeutic Relationship Skills to Become Who You Are

Just be sure when you step, step with care and great tact, and remember that Life's a Great Balancing Act.

Dr. Seuss

Primary Skill Objective

- Begin to consider how developing your therapeutic relationship skills, especially the core conditions, already have and can continue to benefit you personally.

Focus Activity

Journal and/or discuss your answers to the following questions:

- What have you learned in your study of *The Heart of Counseling?* Of course, that is so broad a question, it would take a book to answer. So, start with the first thoughts that come to mind. Then build on those thoughts and develop until you can boil your answers down to the few principles that stand as shorthand for you for the volumes of your learning.
- How have you changed through your study? How do you want to continue to improve yourself, and how can both giving and receiving the core conditions in counseling and other relationships benefit you in these improvements?
- In what other ways and in what non-counseling relationships and situations can you imagine employing and sharing your skills of therapeutic relationships and the core conditions?

Introduction

With these concluding thoughts, we want you to begin to solidify what you have learned and consider where else your journey into developing you with therapeutic relationships, especially Rogers's core conditions (1957, 1961, 1980), may take you. Our work in these areas has taken us a great many places so far.

Developing Yourself through Developing Your Skills in Therapeutic Relationships

We are better persons for having put our hearts into developing our skills of therapeutic relationships. At first we put ourselves into this endeavor in order to be the best counselors we could be. Soon we learned that the work was making us better persons. As we strive to warmly and non-possessively accept and prize each client, we find we are better able to accept each other, ourselves and a great many others in this way. As we strive to connect with our clients on an emotional level, we find our empathy skills continually growing, and in this way, we are also able to connect with ourselves, each other, and a great many others. As we strive to be genuine in our counseling sessions, to be aware of our feelings and underlying thoughts, to understand the meaning of those feelings and thoughts, and to make reasonable (although sometimes so instantaneous as to be intuitive) decisions as to when to express our experiences, we find that we can't "turn off" this awareness and that decisions as to when and how to express ourselves come more and more naturally throughout our relationships. We also find that this *way of being*, as Carl Rogers put it, has helped each of us develop a strong sense of self. We are both better able to assert ourselves in times of conflict and are better able to do so in empathic, warmly accepting, respectful and even loving ways. We find that we are well in many of our relationships, although far from perfect; we are still growing and we are grateful for that.

We find that developing our skills in building therapeutic relationships brings reciprocal warmth and successes in a great many relationships. Earlier in our lives and works, we were much more the fighters, metaphoric "dragon slayers"—we saw ourselves as powerful child and client advocates. We felt that as long as we were "fighting for a good cause," our tactics were also automatically good. Looking back, we now see that we may have sometimes lacked empathy for and warm acceptance of our "dragons." We may have relied more heavily on charisma and the power of persuasion than on respectful listening and the power of communication. Now that we more consistently combine empathy and acceptance with our assertiveness, we find we are able to be even more influential and more content with our works and ourselves. We are more accepting of what we are able to accomplish and what we aren't, but in accepting this we find we are able to accomplish more. We attribute a great deal of this influence, effectiveness and contentment with our work to the skills and the *way of being* we continue to develop for building therapeutic relationships with our clients. Relationships are complex. We use the paradigm of the core conditions to guide us through complexities.

Therapeutic Relationships in Coaching, Volunteers and the Big Picture of Who You Are

Jeff sometimes coached Erzhan's children's teams, when they were in leagues with a low level of competitive expectations. In doing so he sometimes found himself caught up in game preparation or trying to ensure the skills they need, when he would get a feeling of working at cross-purposes with his team or with a player. In those moments, he usually remembered to stop and pay attention to what his players were feeling: "What can I feel that is going on inside with them?" In that context, it he didn't always stop to say what he sensed, but still his therapeutic relationship skills had taught him to stop and listen, to attend to feelings, to feel the incongruence, and to put this attentive way of being ahead of goal orientation—ironically to better reach the goal.

We have often noticed the excellent listening of many of the volunteers who staff our local crisis hotlines or serve as big brother/big sister mentors. Typically, the training for these programs focuses on *heavily* on empathic listening, and almost leaves out any training in guidance. It may be that the guidance part hardly needs to be taught, but the emphasis has to be heavily on listening, as this is not what most volunteers intuitively think is needed. And so sometimes we wonder, why do some of the volunteers we know listen better than some of the professionals we know—one possibility is the pressure the professionals feel to *produce*, possibly at times forgetting that to be with a suffering person in the moment *is* the best avenue to productive progress.

And we have known some students encountering the heavy emphasis on therapeutic listening in a good counselor education program to initially react as if to ask "That's what I came to graduate school for, to learn to listen?" To us, and we hope to you, that answer is "Yes! Therapeutic listening is a professional counselor's most powerful tool, and a professional counselor's most often used tool as well." And the more each of us can build our therapeutic relationship skills into the persons that we are, the more effective we can be in each client interaction.

Activities and Resources for Further Study

- Journal and discuss how developing your therapeutic relationship skills, especially the core conditions, already have and/or may change you for the better.
- Meet with groups of your peers now and in the future to brainstorm new ways to apply the skills of therapeutic relationships. Also brainstorm ways you can participate in each other's favorite projects. Counseling and related works can be hard enough alone, and counselors and related mental health professionals often work alone with clients, so take opportunities to work together and support each other.

- If you have studied this book with a group of peers, you have already begun your peer support and peer supervision groups. Make plans now to follow up later to meet regularly to support and supervise each other into your futures.
- Review journals like the *Journal of Humanistic Counseling* and other American Counseling Association (ACA) journals, the *Person-Centered Journal, the Journal of Person-Centered and Experiential Psychotherapies*, and journals of related professional associations for ongoing and exciting examples of applications of skills of therapeutic relationships and the core conditions in and out of counseling relationships. As you find them, share them with your peers.
- Seek out professional associations of like-minded persons. Our favorites are the Association for Humanistic Counseling (a division of ACA), the Association for the Development of the Person-Centered Approach, the Association for Filial and Relationship Enhancement Methods or the National Institute for Relationship Enhancement, and World Association for Person Centered and Experiential Psychotherapy and Counseling.
- Review and reconsider the concepts presented in Chapter 1 and how you may have changed since first contemplating those concepts. As you continue to develop, revisit those concepts periodically to keep them in mind and to mark the strengthening of your knowing what you know.
- Remember that developing your therapeutic relationship skills may be and probably should be a lifelong journey. Take heart and enjoy the ride.

References

Rogers, C.R. (1957). The necessary and sufficient conditions of therapeutic personality change. *Journal of Consulting Psychology, 21*, 95–103.

Rogers, C.R. (1961). *On becoming a person.* Boston, MA: Houghton Mifflin.

Rogers, C.R. (1980). *A way of being.* Boston, MA: Houghton Mifflin.

Pre-Chapter Quote

Dr. Seuss (1990). *Oh, the places you'll go!* Pop-up version. New York: Random House Children's Books (p. 9).

INDEX